COLLINS

CDT

Craft, Design and Technology

Design and Realisation

Written in association with
Lincolnshire County Council

Authors: C. Chapman
M. Peace
Editor: A. Breckon

Collins Educational
An imprint of HarperCollins*Publishers*

ACKNOWLEDGEMENTS

The publishers are grateful to the following individuals and organisations for the photographs and illustrations in this book:

AA Photo Library, fig 6.37;
J. Allen Cash, fig 4.97;
Allsport UK Ltd, fig 6.39;
Ann Ronan Picture Library, fig 5.2;
APV Baker, fig 7.76;
Argos Distributors Ltd, figs 1.9, 1.20, 1.23, 1.25, 1.26, 1.27, 1.28, 1.29;
Austin Rover, figs 7.60, 8.19;
Avery Denison Ltd, fig 4.46;
Aviation Photos, fig 7.33 (McDonnell Douglas DC10)
Barnaby's Picture Library, figs 3.3, 3.32, 4.1, 4.2, 4.3, 4.35, 4.38, 4.54, 4.72, 4.84, 5.226, 6.34, 6.38, 6.39, 6.47, 8.20;
Benson Verniers Ltd, fig 5.20;
Black and Decker Ltd, figs 5.30, 5.37, 5.227;
Boxford Ltd, figs 5.6, 5.61, 8.25, 8.26, cover (125 TCL lathe);
Britain's Petite Ltd, fig 7.30;
BBC Hulton Picture Library, fig 3.44;
British Market Research Bureau Ltd, fig 8.17;
British Petroleum (BP Oil Ltd), fig 5.146;
British Railways, fig 3.2;
British Telecom plc, figs 1.11, 1.12, 1.13, 1.14, 1.15, 1.16, 1.17, 1.18, 1.19, 4.132;
British Plastics Federation, figs 7.35, 7.36, 7.40, 7.41, 7.42, 7.43;
Cadar Measurement and Control Systems Ltd, fig 5.22 and cover (Moore and Wright Micro 25);
Canon UK Ltd, figs 1.1, 8.11;
Cincinnati Milacron UK Ltd, figs 7.70, 7.75, 7.82, 7.84;
C. Chapman, figs 7.58, 7.69, 5.133 (concrete casting);
C.R. Clarke and Co (UK) Ltd, figs 5.81, 5.91a;
Commotion Ltd, fig 4.150;
CZ Scientific Instruments Ltd, fig 8.8;
The Design Council, fig 3.43, 8.1, 8.3, 8.4, 8.7, 8.10, 8.21, 8.22, 8.24 (transputer and mini aircraft);
Eagle Cars Ltd, fig 4.4;
Educational Services to the Plastics Industry (ESPL) figs 4.130, 4.131, 5.124;
Energy Facilities Management (EFM), figs 5.94, 5.195;

Electricity Council, figs 3.9, 4.11;
Engineering Magazine/Microscribe Computers, fig 7.32;
Eric Albinson Design, cover (paper clock);
Ever Ready Ltd, figs 1.22, 1.24;
Ford Motor Co Ltd, figs 3.21, 4.30, 7.10, 7.27;
Forestry Commission, figs 4.96, 4.98;
Sally and Richard Greenhill, figs 1.8, 1.41, 4.39, 6.33;
John and Penny Habley, fig 4.62
Institute of Civil Engineers, fig 6.40;
JAC Design, fig 4.72 (zinc crystals), 4.73;
Jaguar Cars, fig 3.45;
Mihal Karol, Heights Design, figs 8.27, 8.28;
Kerry Ultrasonic Machines, fig 7.18;
Linear Graphics Ltd, fig 6.14;
Ian Marshall, figs 4.148, 5.1, 5.7, 5.31, 5.35, 5.64, 5.65, 5.79, 5.83, 5.93, 5.104, 5.134, 5.182, 5.206, 5.228, page 137, 7.14, 7.15;
Marconi Electronic Devices, fig 7.55;
McDonalds Hamburgers Ltd, figs 8.14, 8.15;
Mothercare UK Ltd, fig 6.12;
National Trust Photo Library, figs 4.85, 4.86, 6.43;
Parker Pen Company, fig 8.18;
Philips Electronics Ltd, fig 4.5;
Princes Design Works, cover (kamel table);
R.S. Components Ltd, figs 1.21, 7.54;
Record Marples Ltd, figs 5.8, 5.44, 5.48;
Rolls Royce, figs 7.3, 7.16;
Ruston Gas Turbines figs 4.41, 7.8, 7.9, 7.12, 7.13;
Sarah Dallas Knitwear, fig 8.24 (knitwear)
Science Photo Library, figs 4.13, 4.14, 4.22, 4.69, 4.113, 4.115, 7.2, 7.56, 7.57, 7.81;
Simon Engineering (Dudley) Ltd, figs 8.24 (firefighting platform)
Brian and Sal Shuel fig 8.13;
SKF and Dormer Tools Ltd, fig 5.32;
Stanley Tools Ltd, fig 5.49;
Teal Furniture Ltd, fig 8.2;

Cover design by Sands-Straker Studios Limited, London

Artwork by Sam Denley, Peter Harper, Illustrated Arts, Kevin Jones

Typeset by Burns and Smith, Derby

Printed in Great Britain by Caledonian, Glasgow

CONTENTS

ABOUT THIS BOOK

This book seeks to cover the appropriate material for courses based on the National Criteria for CDT under the endorsed title of Design and Realisation. The book is based on the principle that CDT is an activity focused area of the curriculum concerned with designing and making artefacts and/or systems to meet a specific purpose. This book provides the information necessary to tackle a wide range of design problems. It does not seek to solve them, but offers support and guidance in the process of transforming your ideas into reality. An important feature of the book is to place CDT in the context of the world in which we live. Most sections end with a range of questions based on the chapter, arranged so they become progressively more difficult. Finally, the book is intended to stimulate those studying the course to extend their interest in designing and making either by appreciating and/or improving the man-made environment, or by studying the subject further and perhaps pursuing an associated career.

TEACHER'S PREFACE

The material in this book is part of a comprehensive curriculum development programme for CDT in Lincolnshire. This began in 1981 and led to the publication of the CDT Foundation Course and its companion Teacher's Guide in 1986. Initially the material was written by teachers in the form of pupil guide books, which have now been evaluated and completely rewritten by the authors. This Design and Realisation book is a natural progression from the Foundation Course book as well as providing a comprehensive text for the full range of GCSE courses in CDT: Design and Realisation.

Design and Realisation is one of a series of three GCSE textbooks for CDT. They have been written by a team of six teachers. The principal authors of *Design and Realisation* are Colin Chapman, Advisory Teacher for Design and Technology, Lincolnshire County Council, and Melvyn Peace, Head of CDT at De Aston School, Market Rasen. They were ably assisted by Kevin Crampton, Michael Finney, Peter Fowler and Michael Horsley. I am indebted to them for their commitment and professionalism in working so successfully as a team on this venture. I would also like to express my gratitude to the wives and children of these teachers for their patience and understanding throughout the absorbing, but very demanding task of writing this book.

This book was made possible by the encouragement of the former County Education Officer, Mr F G Rickard and the continued support of the Director of Education, Mr D G Esp. Their professional support has been encouraged by enthusiastic members of Lincolnshire County Council, in particular Councillors W J Speechley and P Newton, whose positive approach to the development of CDT have greatly benefited the education of many pupils in Lincolnshire and hopefully, through this book, many others.

Finally, I would like to thank the many pupils and teachers who, through their interest and enthusiasm, have made such a positive contribution to the creation of this book.

A.M. Breckon.
Education Inspector (CDT).
Lincolnshire County Council.
Member of Secondary Examinations Council
GCSE and 18+ CDT Committees.

DESIGN AND DESIGNING

fig 1.1. 1987 camera

fig 1.3. Common logos

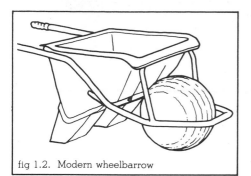
fig 1.2. Modern wheelbarrow

Design plays a very important part in our lives. It controls and affects much of what we do in our everyday lives, and we are all capable of designing.

You might design the pattern of your day, the layout of your bedroom or the way you travel to see a friend. From this you can see that design is always with you, whether it is the shelter you live in, your means of travelling, or the clothes you wear.

This chapter looks at design and designing which are central to the whole subject of Craft, Design and Technology (CDT). It illustrates the different forms of designing related to CDT courses, and offers two frameworks which can help you to solve the design problems central to your course.

The rest of the book provides the necessary information and some helpful ideas for tackling a wide range of design problems.

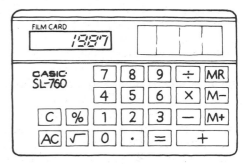

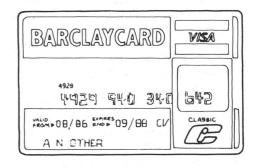
fig 1.4. Calculator and credit card

fig 1.5. Food packaging

fig 1.6. JCB excavator

fig 1.7. Lloyd's building

1

DESIGN AND DESIGNING

WHAT IS DESIGNING?

Designing is an activity which uses a wide range of experiences, knowledge, and skills to find the best solution to a problem, within certain constraints.

Designing involves identifying and clarifying a problem, making a thoughtful response, and then creating and testing your solution. You can then usually start to modify your solution, so that the process of designing begins again.

Designing is a creative activity. You may often use known facts or solutions, but the way you combine these to solve your own particular problem requires creative thinking.

Designing is far more than just problem-solving. It involves the whole process of producing a solution from conception to evaluation. This includes elements such as cost, appearance, styling, fashion, and manufacture.

Designers work in almost every area of life — textile design, product design, graphic design, interior design, engineering design and environmental design. Each area requires a different type of knowledge, but they all involve a similar design activity.

fig 1.8. Modern clothing

WHY DESIGNS CHANGE

There are various reasons why designs change. One is the change in the needs of society. An example of this is the fairly recent change to smaller cars. These were designed in response to the demand for economical, easier-to-park vehicles as our cities became more congested. You might argue, however, that the designer creates the change, and society then reacts to this change (as with fashion for example).

A second reason for change is the development of new technology which can be applied to traditional products. The new designs of computer have only been possible because of the development of 'microchip' technology. This was itself stimulated by people's desire for space flight.

fig 1.9. Cordless kettle

HOW DESIGN AFFECTS OUR LIVES

A world without calculators, televisions, trains, aeroplanes, house insulation, advertising, shopping precincts and microwaves is difficult to imagine. These products have by and large benefitted us. Few people would like to do without all the products designed in the last 20 years. However, designers have responsibilities to society because of the way their designs can affect us.

As well as solving the problem, designers may also work under timing, financial, and political pressures. However they must always place people first.

fig 1.10. Interior design of kitchen

LOOKING AT DESIGN

These first two pages show various designs which illustrate the fashion, style and technology of today. Design is all around us and the next three pages illustrate three different aspects. Page 3 looks at the historical development of the telephone, page 4 looks at how designers have developed differing solutions to the same problem, and page 5 looks at how designers communicate ideas, images and information. There are many other examples which you may also wish to investigate.

DESIGN CHANGES THROUGH TIME

The telephone was invented over 100 years ago. It is a vital part of our lives which we use all the time to communicate.

Its function has remained almost identical over the years, but new technology has allowed changes from metal to wood to plastics, and from mechanical switches to electrical switches.

The flexibility of modern electronics allows the designer to create almost any shape of telephone. This page shows some of the external design changes. At the same time there have been many improvements in the telephone's performance, which cannot be shown here.

fig 1.14. Telephone c. 1929

fig 1.18. Viscount Super 4

fig 1.11. Ericson Magneta table phone c. 1895

fig 1.15. Telephone 1937

fig 1.19. BT Sceptre — memory and clock

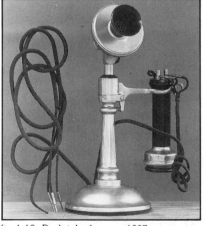
fig 1.12. Desk telephone c. 1907

fig 1.16. Telephone 1968

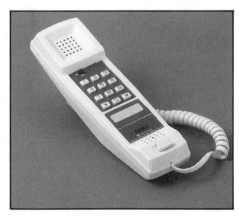
fig 1.20. One piece wall mounted telephone

fig 1.13. Strowger calling dial c. 1905

fig 1.17. British telephone 1960s to 1980s

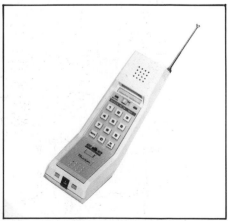
fig 1.21. Remote control telephone

DESIGN SOLUTIONS TO SIMILAR PROBLEMS

This page shows some solutions to the problem of providing a portable source of light. Most have been designed to meet other needs as well, but they are all design solutions to the same basic problem.

When looking at a problem, designers think about how their solution will be used. A torch has two principal uses — to provide light to see, and to act as a warning device. Sometimes both these functions are required at once. For example, you cannot cycle safely along country roads at night without a front light which does both.

When developing a new torch, the designer is likely to be constrained by the size of the batteries and bulbs. Another constraint for a cycle lamp is likely to the means of attaching it to the cycle frame. These things are fixed because the designer is unlikely to be able to demand a specially designed battery or bicycle frame. There may be additional constraints, such as making the torch waterproof. Can you think of other possible constraints?

There are many other torch designs besides those shown here. Can you think of some other design solutions to this problem?

fig 1.25. Ever Ready cycle torch

fig 1.26. Motorist's lantern

fig 1.24.
Ever Ready
small torch

fig 1.22. Ever Ready swivel head torch

fig 1.27. Dual purpose torch

fig 1.28. Pifco waterproof torch

fig 1.23. Durabeam torch

fig 1.29. Ever Ready rechargeable torch

DESIGN IN COMMUNICATION

You are constantly being bombarded by the communications industry creating images — either television, newspapers, magazines, posters, shop displays or exhibitions.

These images are created to communicate — to get a message across. The message may encourage you to buy a product or service, or it may provide entertainment or information.

The designers who create these images must be very sensitive to people's feelings, because they want to catch the eye of the consumer without offending.

The designer will use colour, texture, cartoons, pictures, and printed letters to get the message across. The development of computer graphics has also made the communication of information more effective.

Look carefully at some of the images on this page to see what messages or information they are getting across.

fig 1.31. Communicating through cartoons

fig 1.30. Company trademarks

fig 1.35. International communication symbols

fig 1.32. Communicating weather forecasts

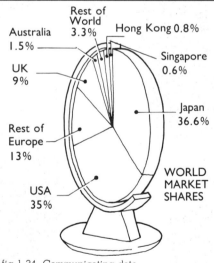

fig 1.34. Communicating data

fig 1.36. Advertising through carrier bags

fig 1.33. Comic strip

FRAMEWORKS FOR DESIGNING

In your CDT course, designing is concerned with the whole process from identifying a problem, through to creating a solution and then testing it. This process requires you to consider many factors, and make a number of decisions.

There are many different methods or routes for doing this, and the one you choose will depend on the nature of the problem. This chapter introduces the idea of a framework which will support you in your design work.

A framework is a series of linked stages which will help you solve your problem. At each stage you will need to refer back to earlier stages. This chapter looks at two frameworks, although it is quite feasible to use others. Equally, these two frameworks can be adapted to suit your own particular problem.

This page looks at the **outline designing framework**. This gives simple guidance on solving straightforward problems, or problems where time is very limited.

The following pages then look at the **integrated designing framework** which gives a lot more detail. This is suitable for more complex problems, and problems for which you have more time.

When designing, points you might consider include:

1. What is the problem I am trying to solve?

2. What is the purpose of my solution?

3. How will my solution be used?

4. How realistic are my suggested solutions?

5. Are the materials available?

6. Is my solution economical?

7. Is there sufficient time to make it?

8. Is this design task a challenge?

NOTE: Specific syllabuses may have a defined design process or framework. You should check this before tackling a design task as the framework may be linked to the assessment scheme.

OUTLINE DESIGNING FRAMEWORK

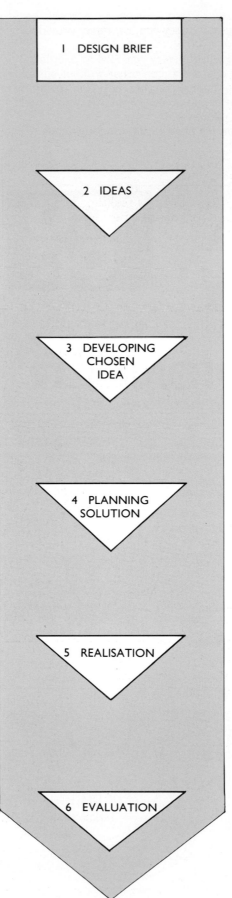

1. **The design brief** is a clear description of the problem you are going to solve. You may have to form the brief from either a situation (such as the layout of your kitchen) or a theme (such as storage). Before finalising the brief you may need to do some investigations.

2. From the design brief you should get some initial **ideas** for your design. You may then need to carry out research before beginning to sketch these ideas. It is wise to sketch a number of realistic ideas so you have some choice about the solution. On completion of the ideas you should decide which one to carry forward, giving your reasons.

3. It is important to **develop the chosen idea** into a practical solution. This may involve further drawing of how it fits together, or modelling to see how it will work. At the end of this stage you should have a sound idea of what you are going to make.

4. The **planning of the solution** involves two stages. First, you need to make some drawings from which your solution can be made. These are often called working drawings. Secondly, you should plan how your solution is to be made and which materials and components are required.

5. **Realisation** means making — either a scale model, a prototype or the final product. It is the realised model or product which will be evaluated, so the quality is very important. The realisation is one of the most exciting stages, but if the work in the previous stage has been poor, you may have difficulties.

6. **Evaluation** means finding out how well your solution works, and comparing it with your initial brief. Your evaluation should also suggest possible improvements.

fig 1.37.

INTEGRATED DESIGNING FRAMEWORK

Stage 1. Brief
Recognition of problem
Identification of needs
Recognition of situation
Formation of design brief

Stage 2. Investigation
Research into topic
Collation of useful information
Analysis of topic
Specification of requirements

Stage 3. Ideas
Generation of realistic ideas to
satisfy design brief

fig 1.39. Thinking and sketching an idea

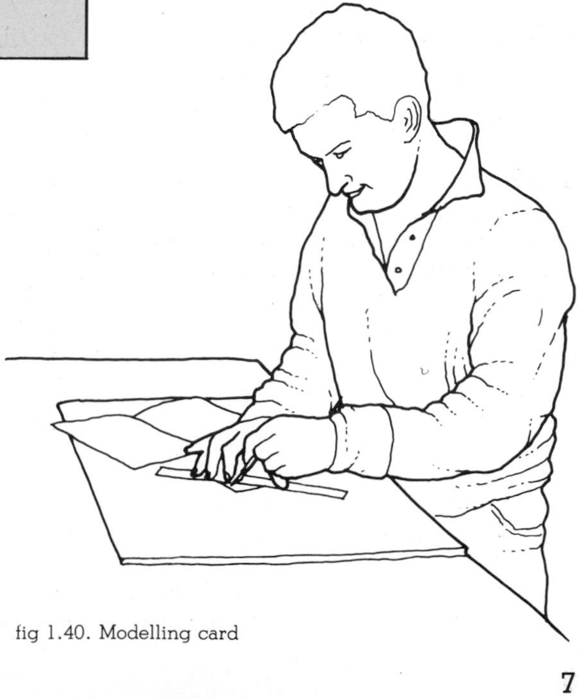

Stage 4. Evaluating
Evaluation of ideas against the
specification
Identification of a proposed solution

Stage 5. Developing
Modelling, developing and refining
the proposed solution

Stage 6. Planning
Drafting drawings from which it can
be realised
Planning and organising proposed
realisation

Stage 7. Realisation
Realisation of solution in the form of
a model, prototype, artefact or
system

Stage 8. Testing
Testing to see if it works and how
well it works

Stage 9. Evaluation
How does it meet the brief?
How can it be improved?
How did I tackle the problem?

fig 1.38. Integrated designing framework

fig 1.40. Modelling card

INTEGRATED DESIGNING FRAMEWORK

Designing becomes a lot easier if you have a framework to follow. The following pages explain how the integrated designing framework can be used. It is important to recognise that this should not be followed laboriously, but should be modified for specific problems. Various design methods and techniques are covered, but they are only suggestions which might be helpful.

STAGE 1: BRIEF

Where do you begin when you write a design brief? In some cases you might begin by recognising a problem, for example, how to get books to stand upright on shelves.

Another starting point might be seeing the need to improve something, like the instructions for fitting a burglar alarm.

A third starting point might be recognising an area where things are not working well because of layout — for example, in the kitchen. In this case you might have to do some research to find the real need.

From these differing starting points you will need to write a design brief. Design briefs range from the simplistic (*Design a seat*) to the more precise (*Design a garden seat which will be used by elderly people who may wish to sit in pairs*). This second brief is more useful because it sets out clear guidelines. The brief could go on to define more clearly details of colour, or describe the environment in which it would be situated.

The amount of detail given in the brief will decide the amount of freedom the designer has to experiment. If for instance, a design brief stated '*Design a birthday card*', the designer would have difficulty, because it could be for an 8-year-old or a 90-year-old. However, '*Design a birthday card for a teenager*' states the target without restricting ideas.

It is important not to give too much detail in a design brief, otherwise the designer can do little creative work. There are therefore four key points to remember about your design brief:

1. Identify a task which you are keen to work on.
2. Make sure the brief has a purpose.
3. Do not begin with such a vague brief that you have no idea where to start.
4. Do not define the brief so precisely that there is no room for innovation.

fig 1.41. Situation with design opportunities

fig 1.42. A need to package these biscuits

STAGE 2: INVESTIGATION

Investigation leads to a clearer understanding of the limits of the design problem. First of all you should read and understand they key words in the brief.

Consider the brief, '*Design a storage unit for kitchen roll, cling film and aluminium foil, which will take up a visible position in the kitchen and will dispense the material easily.* The key points are storage, the three rolls, dispensing ability and appearance. These give a useful starting point for your design. Having analysed the brief you then need to research into the problems. For example:

1. Visit shops or exhibitions to view current products.
2. Draw up a questionnaire to discover further information.
3. Interview people about the problem.
4. Visit libraries and read magazines and books to find further information.
5. Write to and/or visit industry to discover more information.
6. Take a similar existing product or system and analyse it carefully.

Having carefully researched the topic, it is important to sort through the information and decide what is most useful. You should then have a good understanding of the task and can set out the exact limits and constraints for the designer. This is called a **specification,** and helps to focus towards the key aspects of the problem. A simple, systematic way of seeing if you have created a

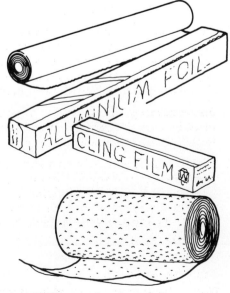
fig 1.43. How can these be stored?

good specification is to check whether key factors are covered. These may not all be appropriate to any one problem, but having checked them, at least you will know the point has been considered. For example:

size	function	appearance	storage
cost	safety	environment	materials
manufacture	ergonomics	shape	reliability
maintenance	finish		

The order and priority will change according to the design problem. For example, the design of a 'pop-up' brochure would place low priority on safety, whereas a child's toy would give high priority to safety.

The design factors will often result in a series of conflicting points being raised. However, balancing these points is the essence of good design and it is now that you move into the third stage of creating ideas.

STAGE 3: IDEAS

Generating ideas which solve the problem is the most creative area of the whole designing activity. The quality of these ideas is one of the key elements in CDT work. Ideas can be generated through thinking and sketching. At this stage you might want to draw complete artefacts very precisely. This is a mistake, as it tends to create rigid, isolated ideas. It is far better to make quick sketches of outlines and rough forms which you can easily modify.

Different problems will lead to differing approaches. For example, if you are designing a car jack, the functional operations will be a key part of the design. However, if you are designing a piece of jewellery, the starting position may be looking at shapes and forms. The sketches should be a means of thinking on paper, using notes where appropriate, and ensuring your rich ideas are recorded. Many syllabuses expect to see between three and five realistic ideas as minimum. With complex problems, ideas may be created for parts of the problem rather than the whole solution.

It should be recognised that ideas do not automatically appear when you wish. Ideas may come at any time, and you must sketch or note them when they occur, because they can easily be mounted in your folder at a later stage. However, solutions to design problems cannot wait for ideas to just arrive, they must be worked at to determine solutions. There are several ways of working at the generation of ideas and different methods can be used, depending on the problem. The following may be helpful.

1. **Observation and adaptation.** Look at existing solutions to similar problems, and then from these you can usually develop ideas. Look at nature to see how it solved the problem and then consider how this can be adapted. Remember that design is about solving problems in the best form, rather than always creating original ideas.

2. **Ideas from drawings.** The creation of ideas for drawing is particularly useful for work in creating the shape and form of a product. This method may begin from shapes such as lines, circles, cubes, prisms or pyramids, which are then cut, rotated or combined to generate a new shape. These visual investigations are a very effective way of creating ideas.

3. **Brainstorming.** This is usually a group activity where everyone thinks of ideas to solve the problem. The ideas are shared, which often stimulates further ideas or adaptations.

4. **Checklists.** The use of a checklist can provide more starting points to stimulate ideas. A word or phrase in a checklist can help you think about the problem from another viewpoint. The checklist may be as at the top of this page or it may be in the form of questions:

What is the purpose of what I am trying to design?

Who may use it?

Where is it going to be used?

Can it be modified?

What is the important part of the design?

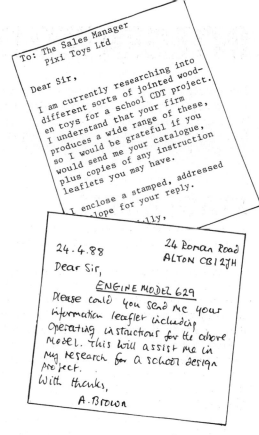

fig 1.44. Letters requesting information

fig 1.45. Use nature as a source for ideas

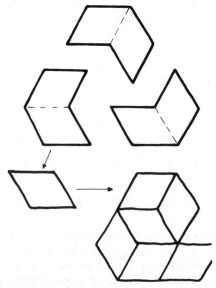

fig 1.46. Ideas from drawing

STAGE 4: EVALUATING

The evaluation of ideas is a critical phase, because it is at this stage that the proposed solution is first identified. It is wise to look carefully at all the ideas, but you need to be clear what you are looking for when choosing an idea to develop. These points may be helpful:

1. Does the idea meet the brief you started with?
2. If not, does it satisfy the need better?
3. Does it meet the specification?
4. Is it possible for the proposed solution to be made with the resources of time, materials and equipment available?
5. Is it financially viable?

In your design work it is wise to write down your reasons for making choices. At the end of the project it may be interesting to know the exact reasons for the decision-making at this critical stage.

STAGE 5: DEVELOPING

Developing and refining the proposed solution is the stage when you convert the idea into reality. A key part of this stage is the modelling of the proposal to see how it works and how it can be improved. The models can use specialist kits or modelling materials. There is no doubt that a good model can be most helpful in developing and refining a proposal. At this stage, a number of factors are likely to arise and require you to make a decision.

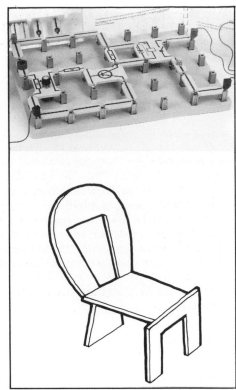

fig 1.47. Modelling solutions

Materials

Materials provide a major constraint. First, you must know how you wish the various parts of your solution to behave. You can then begin to identify an appropriate material for each part. Properties of materials which you might consider are:

weight   strength   toughness   feel   resistance to heat/corrosion

colour   hardness   conductivity   appearance   flexibility

Having identified the properties of the material, you should then consider its availability. This will depend on both the material (e.g. acrylic, mild-steel, beech, card), and also its form (e.g. sheet, tube or block). When you specify the form you should give accurate sizes. In choosing materials you should also consider the cost. For example the cost of precious metals or specialist electronic components might lead you to reconsider.

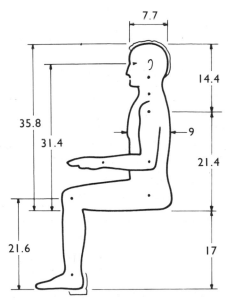

fig 1.48. Anthropometric data

Sizes and shape

These key points will greatly influence your final design. You will almost certainly need to consider how your proposed solution will come into contact with people. This will affect sizes, ranging from printed letters that can be read easily, to the height of a table.

The study of how objects, systems, and the environment can be designed to fit in with people is called **ergonomics.** It is important for deciding such things as the best height for a computer screen, or the smallest size for calculator buttons which can easily be pressed one at a time.

In order to design solutions which fit in with people, you will need to know human body measurements. These are called anthropometric data.

It is also important to consider how your proposed solution will look in its environment. When designing your solution you will therefore need to consider its overall size in relation to other objects, and to assess this constantly.

Appearance

A highly functional product which looks awful is unlikely to sell, as is an attractive product which doesn't function. The visual qualities which give a sense of beauty to a product are called **aesthetics.** Aesthetic values vary with different cultures and within cultures, and fashion and styles change. It is wise to recognise fashion and style, but remember that there will always be differing tastes and opinions.

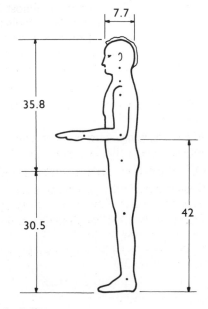

fig 1.49.

Safety

When developing any product, it is important that safety is considered throughout. Appropriate safety standards must always be applied to the design.

STAGE 6: PLANNING

Once the developing and refining of the proposed solution is completed, it is necessary to plan the realisation. Planning is done in two parts.

The first is concerned with the creation of working or production drawings, and the second involves planning to realisation. The working drawings are usually of a formal nature, perhaps in orthographic projection. They should show each part and how it fits together, and give details of all dimensions. This detailed planning through drawing is crucial, and it is essential that such drawings can be understood by others. As well as the working drawings there may sometimes be a presentation drawing which helps to convey the complete idea in its final form. With the final drawings there should be a list of materials to be used, and their sizes. This was traditionally called a **cutting list** and is now called a **parts** or **component list**.

Planning and organising the realisation requires considerable thought. At this stage it is wise to recognise the amount of time available for realisation, because working to a time limit is crucial in stage 7. It is important to write out a procedural flow chart for realisation and a time schedule. These may then need adjusting to fit your time limit. It may help to set a short time limit for each part. Planning can help you identify in advance materials and specialist equipment required.

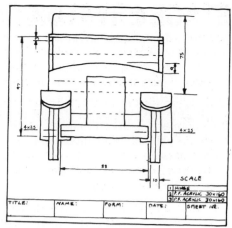

fig 1.50. A working drawing

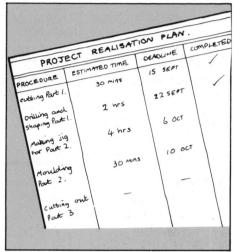

fig 1.51. Project plan

STAGE 7: REALISATION

This is one of the most exciting but time-consuming stages. It can also be one of the most frustrating if the planning stage has not been done thoroughly. The methods of realisation in CDT will vary depending on the particular course or problem. The medium will vary from paint and ink on some dimensional graphics, to heavy construction in perhaps timber, to an electronic system using mass manufactured components. Good design will often involve the use of several different media together to create a sound solution.

The realisation of the solution could include models, prototypes, artefacts or systems. Throughout the realisation there are likely to be problems which were not envisaged, and this can often lead to redesigning parts of the solution.

In the realisation stage it may become necessary to design special tools to help you make the solution. The following are common examples:

Templates are made so that they can be marked around or cut around to repeat a shape several times.

Jigs are tools which are made to allow an operation to be repeated accurately, for example drilling or sawing.

Formers are shapes which are made to allow materials to form around them. This is especially common in plastics.

Moulds are shapes into which materials are usually poured to repeat the shape. It is often necessary to make a pattern first from which the mould can then be made. The pattern is almost identical to the required component.

The making of these specialist tools takes time, but if they are well made it is usually worthwhile. If a project is part of the course work for your examination, you must keep these tools for assessment.

When carrying out the realisation there are some common ground rules:

1. Use tools, equipment and processes in a careful, safe manner.
2. Use materials economically, for example, do not cut material from the centre of a sheet.
3. Always measure and mark out materials accurately.
4. Aim for a high quality finish at all times.
5. On completion, always treat the end product with care.
6. Record briefly the procedures for making in a diary. This will help you learn from your errors and should help you in the future.
7. Try to set yourself small tasks within the project, so that you can assess your progress more easily.
8. Realisation of your solutions should be exciting, so enjoy it.

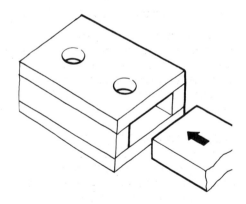

fig 1.52. A jig

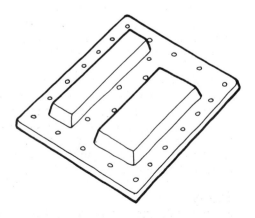

fig 1.53. Former for moulding acrylic

11

STAGE 8: TESTING

Testing the solution is an important part of designing. It will discover whether your solution works, and if so, how well. Testing may be functional, seeing how well your solution works by trying it out, or it may involve repeated tests, checking your solution's reliability. This can be done by carefully setting up an experiment to discover whether the solution meets the requirements in the brief. Testing should place the solution in its intended environment, and observe how it works.

However, if the test could cause an accident, it may be wise to carry out a simulation. This involves testing in an artificial way which is similar to the real situation.

Testing can also concern the appearance of your solution. Here, good testing will involve getting opinions. You might find it helpful to draw up a list of questions on a response sheet.

When you have completed your testing, your results may include the need to start designing again, to improve the solution further still.

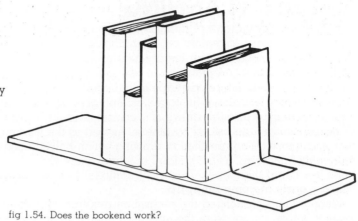

fig 1.54. Does the bookend work?

STAGE 9: EVALUATION

This final stage is concerned with assessing the whole process, from deciding upon the task, creating ideas, and leading to a fully realised design which has been tested. The evaluation should be critical in identifying faults in the process, lessons you have learnt for the future, and possible improvement to your design. Throughout an evaluation, it is wise to be constructive. The following questions may be helpful:

1. Did I use my time effectively?
2. What are the strengths and weaknesses in my design?
3. How can I improve my design?
4. Did I manage to overcome the problems which arose during the project?
5. Were the planning and working drawings adequate?
6. What are the views of others about the solutions?
7. How would I tackle it again doing the same or similar projects?

On completing the project it is clear that you are now ready to begin again, because there is no doubt the solution could be improved. This shows clearly that designing is a fully integrated process and this framework should assist you in solving your design problem.

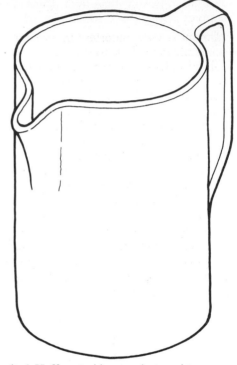

fig 1.55. How would you evaluate and improve this product?

DESIGN FOLDER LAYOUT

Examination boards are likely to suggest a layout for design folders and this should be followed. If no structure is provided, the layout opposite may help you organise your work so it can form a piece of effective communication.

Throughout the design folder, all pages should be named, numbered, and different sections identified.

The presentation is important, but rough sketches should be included to show your thoughts. Do not put research booklets or leaflets in without explaining their value to your design work. Do put letters written and received in the folder. If possible use photographs to explain stages of modelling and making which may be lost in a final solution.

1. Title page — your name, title of project, school and year.
2. Contents page.
3. Design brief.
4. Investigation — analysis, research data and specification.
5. Ideas and their evaluation.
6. Development.
7. Planning.
8. Working drawings.
9. Making — may be shown with sketches or photographs.
10. Testing.
11. Evaluation — including report diary if used.

BASIC GRAPHICS

Basic graphics refers to the graphic skills and techniques used in Technology. It involves drawing, using colour, displaying information and presenting ideas.

Drawing has many purposes, ranging from recording visual information to expressing ideas or feelings. In Design and Realisation you are concerned with drawings as a means of **communication**. You may want to communicate with yourelf, clarify your own thoughts, try to visualise an idea or explain to someone else how someting works or how it is made.

Colour is very important in terms of communication. It is used to help highlight ideas or to show graphically the type of material to be used.

You often need to display information or give instructions. This can be done graphically using drawings or diagrams. Details of electronic circuits can be shown schematically, methods of manufacture can be shown in simple stages.

Presentation is important in Design and Realisation. Ideas need to be well presented in order for them to be easily understood. Finished project work also requires a high standard of finish and presentation. Good work can often be spoilt by poor presentation.

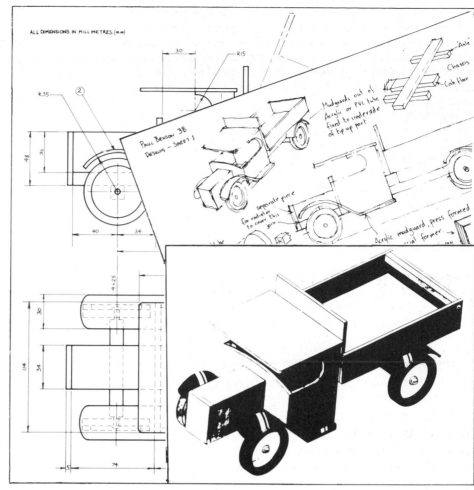

fig 2.1. Examples of graphics related to designing and making

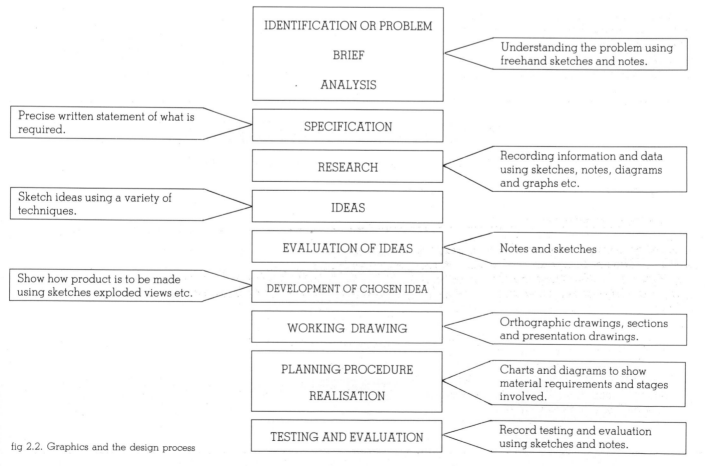

IDENTIFICATION OR PROBLEM BRIEF ANALYSIS	Understanding the problem using freehand sketches and notes.
SPECIFICATION	Precise written statement of what is required.
RESEARCH	Recording information and data using sketches, notes, diagrams and graphs etc.
IDEAS	Sketch ideas using a variety of techniques.
EVALUATION OF IDEAS	Notes and sketches
DEVELOPMENT OF CHOSEN IDEA	Show how product is to be made using sketches exploded views etc.
WORKING DRAWING	Orthographic drawings, sections and presentation drawings.
PLANNING PROCEDURE REALISATION	Charts and diagrams to show material requirements and stages involved.
TESTING AND EVALUATION	Record testing and evaluation using sketches and notes.

fig 2.2. Graphics and the design process

MATERIALS AND EQUIPMENT

Graphic work in Design and Realisation does not require vast amounts of material and expensive equipment. A very high standard of work can be achieved with relatively inexpensive equipment.

PAPER

Drawings can be made on a variety of surfaces, but in Design and Realisation paper and card are normally used. There are many different types of paper available, ranging from expensive hand or mould made papers to machine made papers. Two types of paper commonly used in Design and Realisation are, **layout paper** and **cartridge paper**.

Layout paper is very thin, rather like white tracing paper. It is ideal for sketching because it is thin enough to trace through when you need to redraw, yet it is white enough to draw on with pencil, ink or felt-tipped pen. However, as it is rather fragile, it is not suited to final drawing work or presentation drawing.

Most of our drawings are done on cartridge paper which is heavier and not as fragile as layout paper. Cartridge paper can be used with pencil, ink and a little colour wash, but if large amounts of water colour or other forms of 'wet' colour are to be applied then it may be necessary to use a much heavier watercolour paper.

Layout paper and cartridge paper are both available in the standard A sizes. This system of paper sizing is very easy to remember. It ranges from A6 to A0, A6 being the smallest. A5 is twice as big as A6, A4 twice as big as A5 and so on. You are likely to use A4 or A3 for most of your graphic work.

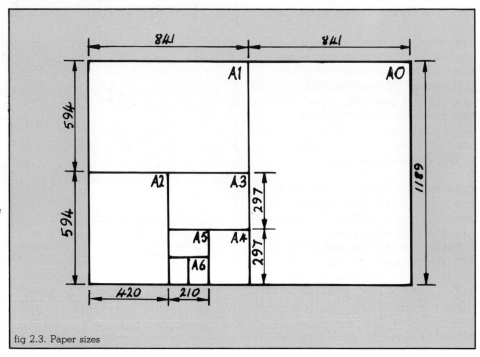

fig 2.3. Paper sizes

PENCILS

The most common piece of drawing equipment is the pencil. The traditional wood and graphite pencils are available in nineteen different grades, ranging from the very hard **9H** to the extremely soft **EE**. You will only need two pencils, a 2H and an HB. Use the 2H for construction lines and layout and the HB for sketching and the final lining in of the drawing.

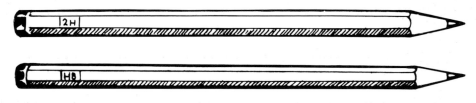

fig 2.4. Traditional pencils

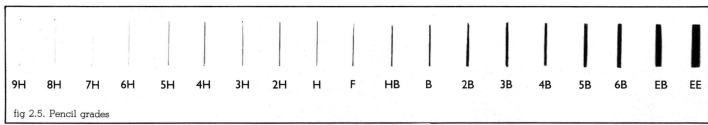

| 9H | 8H | 7H | 6H | 5H | 4H | 3H | 2H | H | F | HB | B | 2B | 3B | 4B | 5B | 6B | EB | EE |

fig 2.5. Pencil grades

Some people prefer to use a **clutch pencil**. This has a plastic barrel rather like a 'biro', but inside there is a continuous length of graphite.

The **automatic fine lead pencil** is very similar to the clutch pencil except that it contains a polymer based 'lead' which may be less than half a millimetre in diameter in order to give a very fine, consistent line.

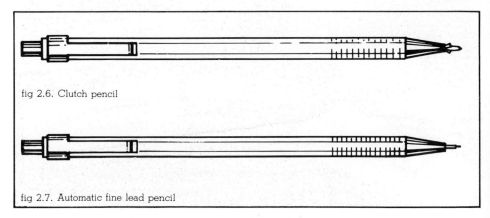

fig 2.6. Clutch pencil

fig 2.7. Automatic fine lead pencil

All pencils except the automatic line lead pencil need to be sharpened. There may be a desk mounted sharpener in your classroom or you may have a pocket sized sharpener of your own. Clutch pencils usually have a detachable sharpener on the end of the barrel. Many designers like to keep their pencils really sharp by occasionally rubbing the point on a piece of very fine glass paper. If you try this take care not to get the graphite dust on your drawing.

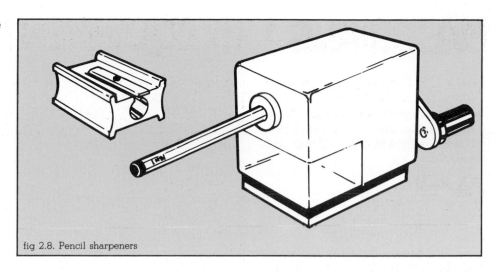

fig 2.8. Pencil sharpeners

PENS

Some designers prefer to use pens, especially if their work has to be copied or printed. There are some very fine line **fibre-tipped** pens available, but they do wear out in time and cannot usually be refilled. If you are doing a lot of drawing in ink it may be worth buying a **technical pen**.

Technical pens have a very fine, hollow nib which gives a consistent line. They are available in a variety of line widths, but the most common sizes are 0.35mm, 0.5mm and 0.7mm. Technical pens can also be used with a wide range of stencils for either lettering or symbols.

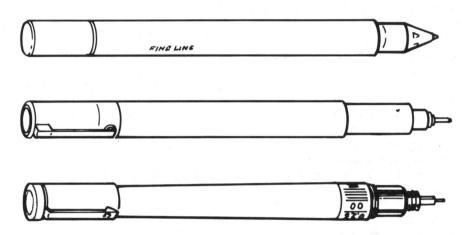

fig 2.9. Pens

fig 2.10. Technical pens

fig 2.11. Erasers

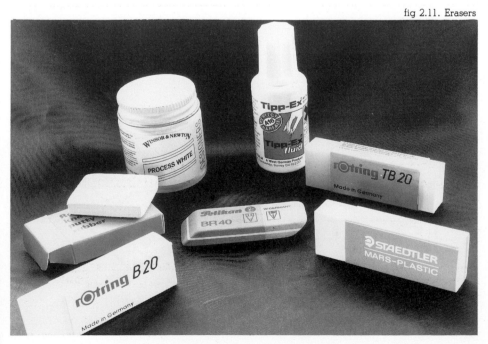

ERASERS

At some time you are bound to make mistakes. Pencil lines can be rubbed out in the normal way with a rubber, but you may find it less messy to use a **plastic eraser** instead of the traditional rubber. A **kneaded** or **putty rubber** is also useful for cleaning your paper after the drawing is finished, and for removing graphite dust which has been rubbed into your paper.

Mistakes in ink are much more difficult to remove. An ink rubber can sometimes be used, but be careful not to damage the surface of the paper. If a mistake cannot be removed with a rubber then you may need to cover it with either white ink or poster paint.

If you use correcting fluid to cover mistakes, make sure you read the instructions on the label carefully.

SKETCHING

Sketching is very important in this subject. It is extremely useful when you are getting your thoughts down on paper quickly. Ideas can be explained far more easily with sketches than with words.

Sketching is usually done **freehand**. Using a ruler or a straight edge takes too long, breaks up the flow of your ideas and prevents you from getting your thoughts down quickly.

START SKETCHING

If you have not sketched before, take a pencil and a piece of paper, and practice drawing a series of horizontal lines. Draw the lines about 50mm long and aim to keep them as straight as possible without using a ruler. Try to draw with your **arm** and not just by moving your wrist. Work quickly and freely.

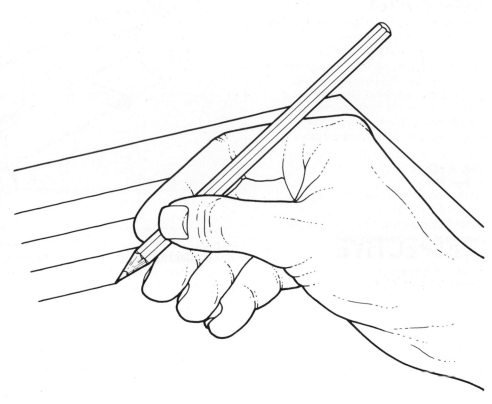

fig 2.12. Holding the pencil correctly

When you have drawn horizontal lines try doing the same with vertical lines. Work from the top of the page downwards and try to keep the lines as vertical as possible. Once you feel confident with vertical lines, you can practise drawing diagonal lines too. Work in both directions and try to keep your lines at approximately 45°. Don't forget to keep your pencil sharp!

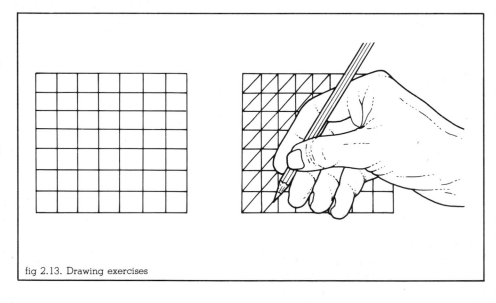

fig 2.13. Drawing exercises

When working freehand there are several traditional drawing techniques which are useful to help you produce a realistic three-dimensional drawing.

OBLIQUE DRAWING

A simple way of making three dimensional drawings is the method known as **oblique drawing**. This method is used when it is important to show the front view of an object. The oblique lines are usually drawn at 45° to the horizontal.

fig 2.14. Oblique

ISOMETRIC DRAWING

Isometric drawing is also useful when sketching freehand. It is best imagined as the object being turned until the horizontal lines appear to be at 30° to the horizontal. This method shows more of the top of the object.

Both these methods of drawing distort the view of the object slightly. If a more realistic view is required then it is best to draw it in **perspective**.

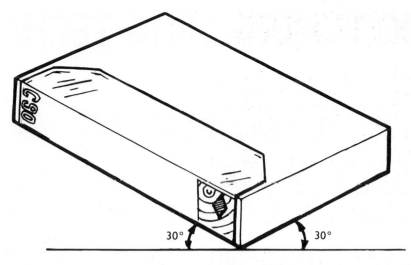

fig 2.15. Isometric

PERSPECTIVE DRAWING

Perspective drawing is based on the fact that lines appear to converge and meet at the **vanishing point**. You have probably seen this visual effect when looking down a railway line or a very straight road.

There are two types of perspective drawing: **single-point** and **two-point perspective**.

Single-point

In single-point perspective all horizontal lines converge and meet the one common vanishing point.

In the example shown, single-point perspective shows the front and one side of the object. If we want to show the top surface, then it is best to use two-point perspective.

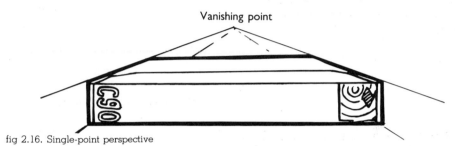

fig 2.16. Single-point perspective

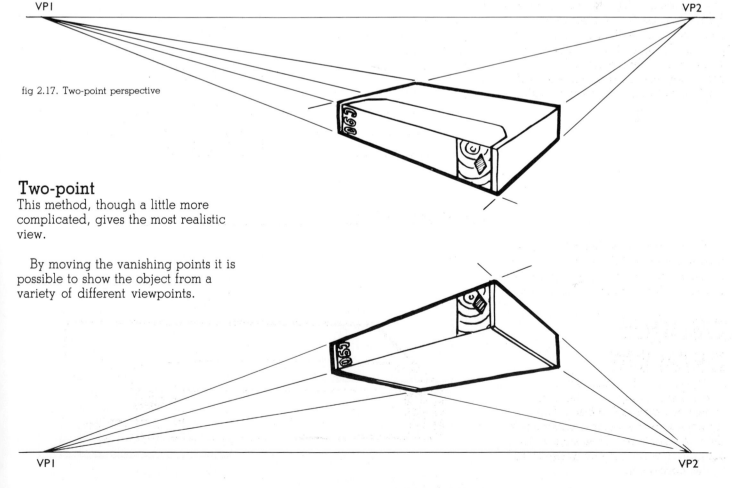

fig 2.17. Two-point perspective

Two-point

This method, though a little more complicated, gives the most realistic view.

By moving the vanishing points it is possible to show the object from a variety of different viewpoints.

fig 2.18. Changing the viewpoint

MORE SKETCHING TECHNIQUES

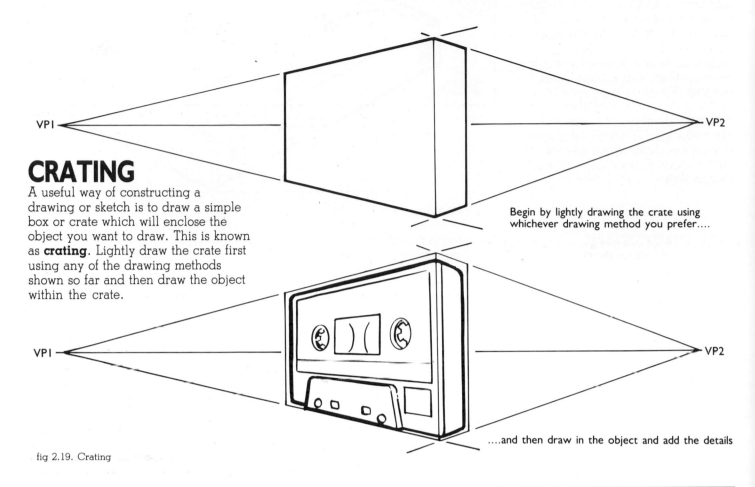

CRATING

A useful way of constructing a drawing or sketch is to draw a simple box or crate which will enclose the object you want to draw. This is known as **crating**. Lightly draw the crate first using any of the drawing methods shown so far and then draw the object within the crate.

VP1

VP2

Begin by lightly drawing the crate using whichever drawing method you prefer....

VP1

VP2

....and then draw in the object and add the details

fig 2.19. Crating

BACKING SHEETS

Grids printed on to a backing sheet and used underneath your paper are very useful in helping you to learn to sketch. They work particularly well with layout paper and can be seen through most medium cartridge paper.

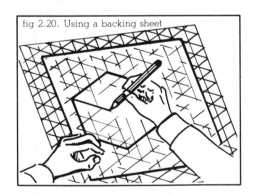

fig 2.20. Using a backing sheet

A backing sheet consisting of horizontal lines is also useful for making sure that your lettering or handwriting is level and evenly spaced on your design sheets.

If there is a photocopier in your school it may be possible (with your teacher's help) to produce a selection of backing sheets for your own use. When freehand drawing remember ... Do not use a ruler or a straight edge and try to work quickly and freely.

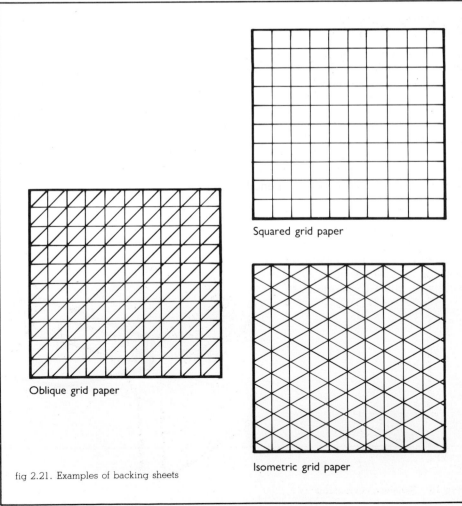

Squared grid paper

Oblique grid paper

Isometric grid paper

fig 2.21. Examples of backing sheets

ELLIPSES

Freehand sketching of objects made up from straight lines is simple, but when curves and circles are introduced it becomes a little more complicated.

As soon as circles are viewed from an angle they have to be drawn as **ellipses**. They no longer appear round, but oval or **elliptical**.

Sketching ellipses is not difficult. The method is illustrated in fig 2.23. This method of sketching ellipses will work whichever drawing method you use, as shown in fig 2.24.

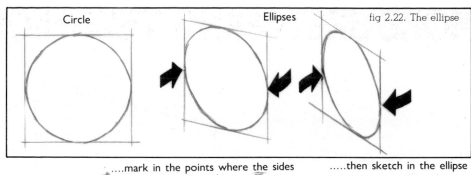

Circle   Ellipses   fig 2.22. The ellipse

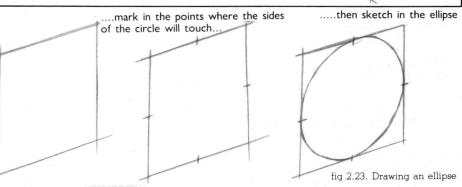

....mark in the points where the sides of the circle will touch...   .....then sketch in the ellipse

Begin by drawing a rectangle which will enclose the circle.....

fig 2.23. Drawing an ellipse

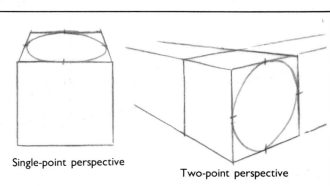

Oblique   Isometric   Single-point perspective   Two-point perspective

fig 2.24. Sketching ellipses using different drawing methods

SKETCHING CURVED SURFACES

Curved surfaces can be drawn quite easily using the same technique.

Begin as before, marking the points where the curved shape will touch the box and then lightly sketch the shape. When you are happy that the shape is correct go over it with your HB pencil to line it in.

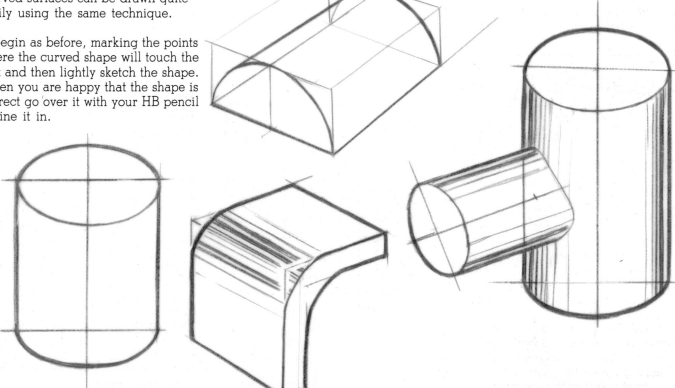

fig 2.25. Sketching curved surfaces

COLOUR

Colour is very important in presentation, it can improve a piece of work or it can ruin it. It is also important to consider the colour of your finished product while still at the design stage. An unsuitable colour could ruin a good design.

There is a great variety of materials available to use, but it is better to keep to those which you can use with confidence. Pencil crayons, felt-tipped pens and watercolours are probably the most suitable.

PENCIL CRAYONS

Pencil crayons are available in a wide range of colours and tones, and are simple and clean to use. By varying the pressure of the pencil on the paper it is possible to produce a good range of **tones** and graduated effects.

FELT-TIP PENS AND MARKERS

Using **felt-tip pens** requires a little more care. Some of the inexpensive types are often only available in a limited range of bright colours which are not really suitable for Design and Realisation work. However, the more expensive designer's graphic markers are excellent, especially when used in conjunction with pencil crayons. Graphic markers are available in a variety of subtle colours and tones. The grey colours are very useful for showing shadows and representing metal.

When using graphic markers, always replace the cap immediately after use as they can dry out very quickly. It is also important to use a sheet of scrap paper under your drawing as the ink tends to soak through. It is best to work from light to dark with markers, leaving the paper white to represent the lightest areas in the drawing and putting in the dark areas last.

WATERCOLOURS

Watercolour can be used as a wash on drawings, but it does require practice to apply well. It can only be used on a fairly heavy paper, and cannot be successfully applied to layout paper. Cartridge paper is suitable, but in order to prevent it from wrinkling, needs to be soaked in water, stuck down to a drawing board with gummed paper tape and allowed to dry. As it dries it will shrink and tighten, and will not then wrinkle when watercolour is applied.

When working with watercolour, work with your paper taped to the board, held at a slight angle. The paint can then be allowed to run down the paper and can be controlled with the brush. Any surplus paint can be lifted off the paper with either the brush or a piece of tissue. This technique may take a little practice to master.

It is essential when using watercolour to keep your water clean, otherwise the colour will appear muddy. Keep a separate jar of water for washing your brush.

fig 2.26. Colour materials

USING COLOUR

Colour can be used as a highlighter by applying a small area of colour around the idea or object drawn on the paper (fig 2.27). Alternatively, the object itself can be coloured.

fig 2.28. Colour combinations can show texture

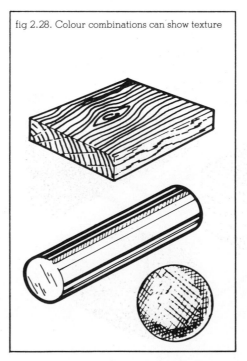

fig 2.27. Colour can highlight sketches

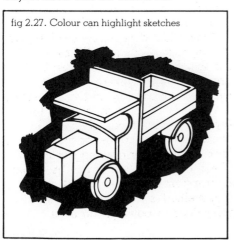

Another excellent use of colour is to use it to show the type of material to be used. A combination of watercolour or graphic marker and pencil crayons is very successful for this. Apply a wash or a background colour and then pick out the details such as woodgrain or reflections with pencil crayons. A white pencil can be very effective when used to show reflections or highlights on shiny surfaces.

The use of colour on a sheet of ideas can improve them enormously or ruin them if not properly applied. Take care with your choice of colour, do not use bright, striking colours such as purple or bright green and avoid using fluorescent markers. Keep to subtle, earthy colours such as browns, yellows or oranges and take care when using other stronger colours. The object is to make the ideas stand out, not the colour itself.

RENDERING

In Design and Realisation, rendering refers to the techniques used to make simple drawings look more realistic and interesting. It can be done quite simply using shading or texture in the form of lines or dots.

SHADING

Shading is usually done using a soft pencil to create an area of tone. By varying the pressure of the pencil it is possible to create a variety of tones ranging from light grey to dense black. It is not possible to shade successfully using a pen. Lines, dots and hatching are used instead. Darker tones can be created using dots or lines close together.

Another method is to use weighted lines to give the impression of light and dark. Weighted lines are simply heavier, darker lines. Fig 2.29 shows the use of this technique.

LIGHT AND SHADE

When shading, it is a good idea to think about the direction of the light falling on the object you are drawing. Apply the shading to the side furthest from the light. This technique adds depth to simple shapes and makes them look more interesting. Drawing the position of shadows will also add to the realism of a drawing.

First determine the position of the light source and estimate where the shadows will fall, then lightly draw in the outline of the shadow and fill in with any of the shading techniques.

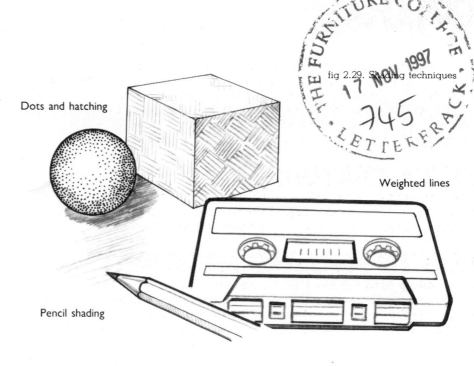

Dots and hatching

Weighted lines

Pencil shading

fig 2.29. Shading techniques

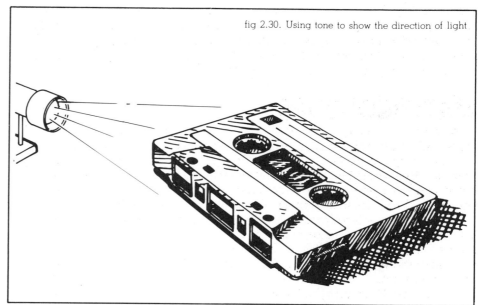

fig 2.30. Using tone to show the direction of light

fig 2.31. Using rendering to show materials

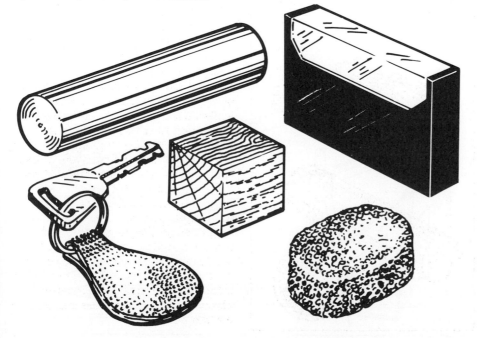

REPRESENTING MATERIALS

Tone, lines and dots can also be used to show the surface texture of an object and suggest the material that it is made from. For example, parallel lines can be used to suggest a shiny surface, while dots can be used to give the impression of a smooth, matt surface. Alternatively, dots can be used to show a stippled, textured surface such as foam rubber or plastic.

A variety of lines can be used to represent wood grain, while small circles positioned close together will look like a leather grained surface. Metal tubes or cylinders can be shown by using broad stripes of dark tone. This method is also used to show reflections in polished surfaces.

WORKING DRAWINGS

Working drawings contain the information needed to make the object you have designed. They need to convey details such as dimensions, materials to be used, construction details or assembly instructions.

Working drawings usually use orthographic projection, but they could also include other views in oblique or isometric projection. You will have to decide what is the best method for the object you have designed.

ORTHOGRAPHIC DRAWING

There are two types of orthographic drawings: **first angle projection** and **third angle proejction** (see fig 2.33). Both types show three separate views of the object: front view, end view, plan view. The difference between first and third angle projections is simply the way the views are arranged on the paper.

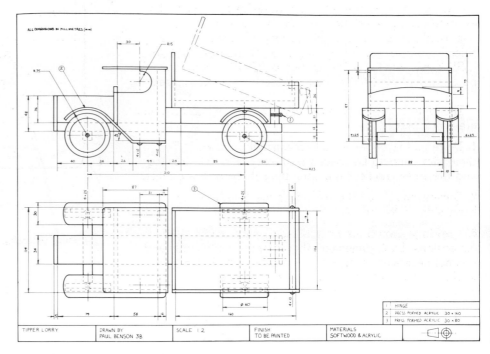

fig 2.32. An example of a working drawing

First angle is mainly used in Britain, but third angle, used in the USA and the continent, is becoming more popular. Third angle has the advantage that the adjoining views appear next to each other on the drawing.

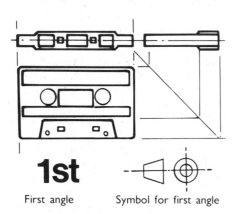

1st

First angle   Symbol for first angle

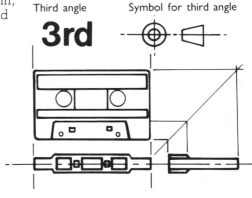

Third angle   Symbol for third angle

3rd

fig 2.33. First and third angle drawings

EQUIPMENT

In order to make accurate working drawings you will need several simple items of equipment. You will need a drawing board and a tee square or a drawing board fitted with parallel motion.

In addition to your HB and 2H pencils you will need two set squares, a 30°/60° square and a 45° square, a pair of compasses and either clips or tape to hold your paper on the drawing board.

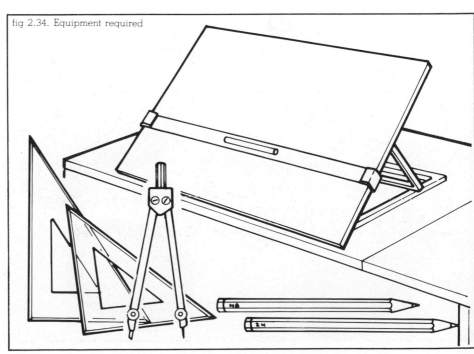

fig 2.34. Equipment required

DIMENSIONING

As working drawings are used to provide information for construction, they are usually drawn to scale and contain the necessary measurements or **dimensions**. In order that everyone can understand the dimensioning used, it is important that a standard set of rules is followed. These rules have been set out by the British Standards Institute (BSI) and are in a booklet known as *BS7308*. There should be a copy of *BS7308* in your school for you to look at.

The main points to consider when dimensioning drawings are as follows.

1. Do not allow dimensions to confuse the drawing. The dimensions should be spaced well away from the drawing and the lines should be lighter than those of the outline.

2. Dimensions should be read from the bottom or right hand side of the sheet.

3. Drawings should not be confused by too many dimensions. Each dimension should appear once only and it is not necessary to include dimensions which can be worked out by adding or subtracting others.

4. Arrowheads should be small, sharp and neat.

5. All dimensions should be shown in millimetres.

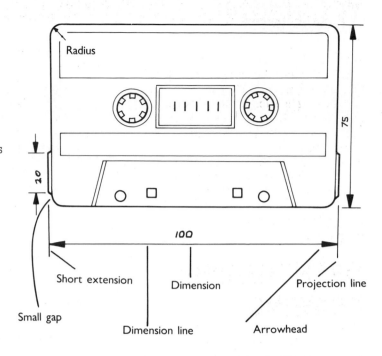

fig 2.35. Dimensioning

LETTERING

You may need to include some written information on your working drawing. This can be done in handwriting, stencils or dry transfer lettering.

It is not difficult to develop your own handwriting style for notes and instructions. Titles and dimensions need to be printed in block capitals. The size of the letters depends on the importance of the information. General information is usually about 6mm high, while titles are 8mm high. Main headings can be up to 10mm high.

Plastic lettering stencils can be bought in a variety of different sizes and styles. Special stencils are available for use with draughting pens which correspond with the size of the nib.

Take care when using stencils to ensure that the lettering is level. Some stencils can be rested on a tee square or a parallel motion straight edge.

Dry transfer lettering gives very professional results and is available in a wide range of lettering styles. The main disadvantage is cost. It can work out rather expensive if used on every drawing.

HANDWRITTEN LETTERING
Develop your own handwriting style and use it to put information on the drawings

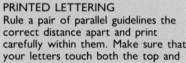

PRINTED LETTERING
Rule a pair of parallel guidelines the correct distance apart and print carefully within them. Make sure that your letters touch both the top and the bottom lines

fig 2.36. Lettering

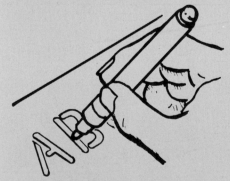

STENCILS   DRY TRANSFERS

fig 2.37. Lettering techniques

SEQUENTIAL DRAWINGS

One way of planning how to make the object you have designed is to work out a planning procedure. This usually consists of a list of the materials and parts required and step-by-step details of construction. A planning procedure will help you to plan and organise your work from cutting up the material or obtaining the components, to the final assembly of the finished product.

This type of information is usually conveyed with the use of **sequential diagrams**. Instructions for self assembly furniture are often given in this way. In Technology it is a good method of clarifying your thoughts and making sure that you know exactly what you are doing.

Sequential diagrams can be drawn as simple block diagrams to show the various processes to be used, or they can use pictorial views when more detailed information is required. Written information can also be added in the form of titles and notes. This is known as **annotating**. **Exploded drawings** can also be useful at this stage to show how the various parts are assembled.

SCHEMATIC DIAGRAMS

In the case of project work involving electronics, details of circuit designs and other systems can be shown diagrammatically. Standard symbols or conventions are used to represent the components. This type of drawing is known as a **schematic diagram**.

The circuit diagram shown in fig 2.40 is an example of a schematic drawing. It is much easier and less time consuming to draw the internationally agreed (British Standard) symbols than it is to draw the actual components and connections. Full details of these symbols can be found in the BSI booklet *PP7303 'Electrical and Electronics Graphical Symbols For Schools And Colleges'*.

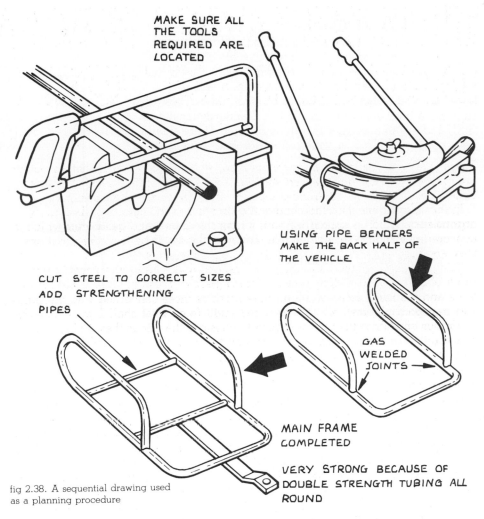

MAKE SURE ALL THE TOOLS REQUIRED ARE LOCATED

CUT STEEL TO CORRECT SIZES ADD STRENGTHENING PIPES

USING PIPE BENDERS MAKE THE BACK HALF OF THE VEHICLE

GAS WELDED JOINTS

MAIN FRAME COMPLETED

VERY STRONG BECAUSE OF DOUBLE STRENGTH TUBING ALL ROUND

fig 2.38. A sequential drawing used as a planning procedure

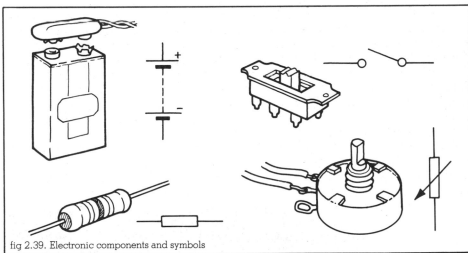

fig 2.39. Electronic components and symbols

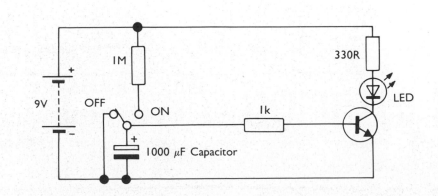

fig 2.40. A circuit diagram

THE HUMAN FACTOR – DESIGNING FOR PEOPLE

There is no such person as the average man, woman, boy or girl. Human beings are different in their physical, artistic and intellectual abilities, as well as their general health. These differences must be thought about when designing.

In this chapter we shall look in detail at two important aspects of design: **ergonomics,** which is concerned with function and use, and **aesthetics** which is concerened with appearance. While they may appear to be two considerations, they are best thought of as different sides of the same coin.

Design is about change and the art of the possible. Our environment is the result of billions of decisions taken by many people. Some of these decisions are large and the result lasts for a long time (such as those concerned with buildings and transport systems), while others are small (e.g. what shall I wear today?).

Various emotions affect the way people consider the things they make, use and handle. This cannot simply be reduced to arguments about style or aesthetics, although appearance is very important.

As technology advances and human activities become more complex, there is a need for the closest possible relationship between people and technology. This close relationship is represented by ergonomics, the name given to the scientific study of human abilities and characteristics which affect the design of equipment systems and control of the environment in a wide variety of situations. It involves engineering 'psychology' as well as physical and physiological factors. Its aims are to improve effectiveness, safety and individual well-being.

The American designer Henry Dreyfuss, in collaboration with Bell telephones (fig 3.1), paid careful attention to the impact of products on the user long before ergonomics was studied. His approach made it clear that designers should not only be concerned with appearance, but also with function.

In his contribution to the High Speed train (fig 3.2), Kenneth Grange took the radical step of designing a cab without buffers. His expertise in combining form with function is also to be found in a wide range of British goods, including Kenwood kitchen appliances and Wilkinson razors.

A designer must bring enjoyment and pleasure and give character to the things people buy and use. He or she can do this by making them more attractive to see, touch and, where appropriate, hear and smell. The Pompidou centre in Paris (fig 3.3), designed by the Richard Rogers architect partnership, is a controversial attempt to humanise design.

Design is very much a juggling act; it is the designer's responsibility to arrive at the best balance of priorities. This includes ergonomics in determining the needs of the user and the appearance of products. Finally these are integrated with other specialist requirements into an overall design solution.

1937

1951

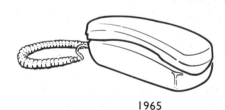

1965

fig 3.1. Three generations of Bell telephone handsets

fig 3.3. Pompidou Centre, Paris

fig 3.2. British Rail's 125 High Speed train

DESIGNING FOR PEOPLE – ERGONOMICS

Ergonomics is an essential resource at the disposal of the designer. It is a particular approach to design which relates the design of an object to its users.

We must constantly remind ourselves to consider the needs of the user. For example, which way is a control moved? What happens if this is done incorrectly? Is it safe? Can a component be easily replaced if it fails? Can both young and old use it?

Ergonomic implications should be considered throughout the design activity especially the early stages. Make use of a **checklist:**

1. Begin with a systemic analysis of the situation from a functional viewpoint i.e. identify the necessary characteristics of the user, those of the equipment or environment and the inter-relationship between the two.
2. Consider the important criteria which ensure the health, safety, convenience and comfort of the user.
3. Examine the design proposals with reference to these criteria (e.g. construct mock-ups and prototypes using ergonomic data to test ideas).

A starting point can often be made by studying people. They come in all shapes and sizes – short or tall, thin or fat. Human differences are obvious if we look at anatomical (body size) variations. These cover

1. human physique – height, weight, range of reach and movement.
2. human **abilities** – strength, associated with posture and range of movement.

Designers normally use sizes taken from both men and women, but also have to cater for people with special needs, for example children or handicapped individuals. Human abilities must also be taken into account, as they limit performance. How much force can be applied with a finger or arm, or how far it can reach, all affect the design of handles and controls.

ANTHROPOMETRY

The science concerned with measuring people is called **anthropometry**. A great deal of anthropometric information is now available from reference books such as the *Compendium of British Standards for Design and Technology in Schools* (PD7302). Data is usually given in the

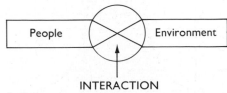

fig 3.4.

form of figures or tables (see fig 3.5). There are two types of measurement:

1. **Static dimensions** – taken when a person's body is in a fixed position (e.g. standing, holding tools).
2. **Dynamic dimensions** – taken during movement. These mainly concern the area covered by the reach of arm or leg.

The human body is a very complex, three-dimensional form. It may not always be possible to obtain the exact information you need, so you may have to measure people yourself.

Determining the needs of an individual and taking the necessary measurements is fairly straightforward. In contrast, designing for groups is much more complex. It is necessary to identify the **target population** (e.g. children aged 7-9 years) and measure a sufficiently large representative sample.

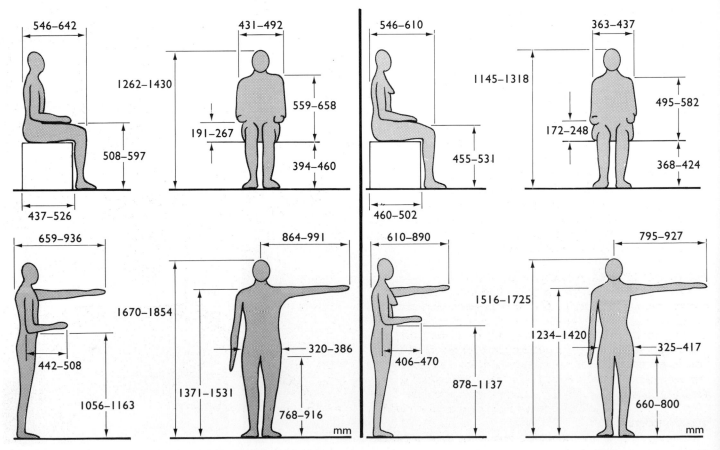

fig 3.5. Male and female body dimensions (5th - 95th percentile value)

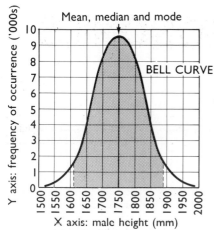

Mean, median and mode

BELL CURVE

Y axis: frequency of occurrence ('000s)

X axis: male height (mm)

fig 3.6. Normal frequency distribution curve

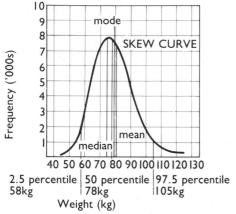

mode

SKEW CURVE

Frequency ('000s)

mean

median

2.5 percentile 58kg | 50 percentile 78kg | 97.5 percentile 105kg

Weight (kg)

fig 3.7. Skew curve resulting from differences in weight

Treatment of measurement

Scientists and designers use complex statistics to examine ranges of measurements in order to make observations about their distribution and how frequently they occur.

Information can be plotted on graphs (fig 3.7). Axis X represents the scale of measurement (male height) and axis Y represents the number of times a measurement occurs. This example produces a symmetrical or bell shaped curve which means that the more frequent scores cluster round the centre or mean value. The extreme values are rarer and spread out on either side of the centre or mean value.

In statistical terms there are three types of average:

mean: arithmetical average of all plotted values
median: middle, 50th percentile
mode: most commonly occurring value, maximum point on the curve (most commonly used average).

Where normal frequency distribution occurs as in fig 3.6, all three coincide. However, when growth is not uniform, when differences in weight may be due to age, sex or diet, then a skew curve results (fig 3.7).

Bar charts and **histograms** can also be used to show the importance and significance of chosen class divisions (e.g. men's heights in the case of fig 3.8). A series of rectangles are drawn to represent each class in a frequency distribution.

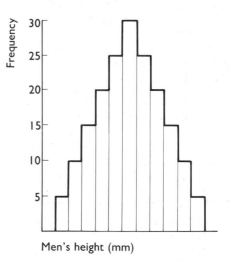

Frequency

Men's height (mm)

fig 3.8. Histogram constructed from men's height

Percentiles are given in fractions of 100 and can be found by dividing any number of measurements into 100 equal groups in sequential order of size, from smallest to largest. The 5th to 95th percentile values are the most used in applying anthropometric data. It is usually both uneconomic and impractical to design for the extremes. When designing for a group of people it may be possible to design an object which can be adjusted to suit different needs.

If an adjustable solution cannot be developed, then it is necessary to compromise to satisfy the average person. The 50th percentile (median) would therefore be used in simple situations (e.g. the height of a wall thermostat). Remember:
1. Aim to accommodate as many people as possible.
2. Design for a range of users, not just the average, as this often excludes up to half the user population.
3. Team work can generate a large amount of anthropometrical data. Calculators and computers can be used to help in the analysis of the many variables.
4. Data, such as body size, cannot be used without thought of the activities to be carried out, including such factors as frequency, duration and posture.

Arrangement of workspace

The efficient layout of workspace is important in order to prevent fatigue and strain. The work position (sitting or standing) and the task should be designed for comfort and to avoid stress and damage to the body (e.g. the back).

Safety : When using a machine the operator must be able to move easily and see clearly. It is necessary to remove potential hazards (e.g. electrical, chemical) so that the operator is protected. Government Acts stipulate certain regulations and standards and these must be taken into consideration.

However, it is in and about the home that most accidents occur!

fig 3.9. Kitchen workspace layout

WORKSPACE LAYOUT

Ideally, work areas (such as a kitchen, workshop or office) should be custom built. By observing a kitchen in use over a reasonable period of time, it is possible to find ways in which efficiency might be improved. For example, make a scale plan of a kitchen layout and record the number of journeys made between particular objects (e.g. cooker–sink–fridge, fig 3.10). These can be recorded as flow lines which will increase in width according to use.

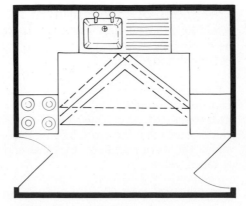

fig 3.10. Kitchen layout

fig 3.11. Comfortable reach

Most objects that need to be handled should be placed within the workspace **envelope** where they can be reached without stretching (figs 3.11 and 3.12). Within the workspace, basic tools and equipment should be located in a definite place so that habitual movements can be established.

Horizontal reach is determined by the height of the work surfaces. Ideal working heights will vary, but where no one height is suitable, it is best to choose the lowest.

For **kitchen worktops,** elbow height is probably the most comfortable, but for working conditions (e.g. sink heights), 100-300 mm below the elbow is best.

For **precision work** (e.g. writing or drawing) the work surface should be higher so that elbows can be rested.

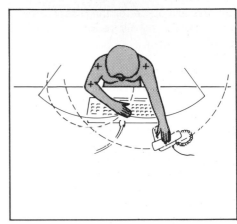

fig 3.12. Workspace envelope

Seating

Seats are used for a variety of purposes (such as working, relaxing, specialist types such as car seats) and there are many different types of seating available.

When sitting, people tend to shuffle around changing position, which is necessary if body tiredness is to be avoided. The position (posture) needed will vary according to use. That needed at a desk or dining table is very different from that adopted in an easy chair.

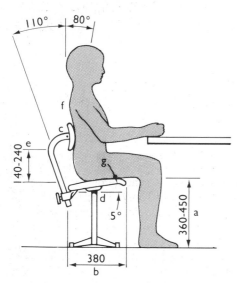

fig 3.13. Seating considerations and measurements

Measurements and considerations include:
Seat height (a) – suited to work level.
Seat depth (b) – provide clearance, avoid trapping blood vessels.
Seat back and angle (c) – should support the natural curve of the spine.
Seat angle (d) – horizontal or sloping backwards.
Back rests (e) – should preferably be adjustable.
Work chair (f) – shoulder blades should be free and not restricted.
Surfaces (g) – hard only for short periods, otherwise padding needed.

Where the seat involves a worktop or work station (e.g. car driving, fig 3.14), it should be considered as a single system. In complex cases, a mock-up or prototype may be used to gather information and test ideas.

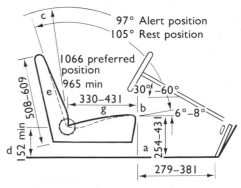

fig 3.14. Specialist seating for car

Hand grip

People use mechanical aids, including tools, to extend and reinforce their strength and effectiveness. User actions involve pulling, pushing, lifting and carrying. These need to be assessed in terms of dimensions and layout.

Simulation can show the effect of size, range and training. For example, consider carrying the typical supermarket wire basket illustrated fig 3.15. How is the grip affected by the different positions of the handles? Which is the most comfortable? The answer may be to use a trolley!

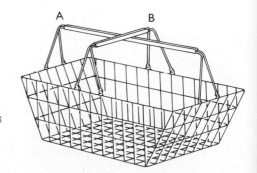

fig 3.15. Consider handle positions A or B on this wire supermarket basket

Hand movement allows both delicate control and the application of pressure (fig 3.16). The index finger is best suited for actions that involve pointing and the middle finger for flexing. The thumb is more suitable for pushing buttons and triggers.

Handles do not always fit the hand well, but the hand can usually adapt to their use. Tools (e.g. screwdriver) are often an unsuitable shape for using over a long period of time. The result can be muscular fatigue and bruising of the soft tissue of the palm.

Tool handles, or the parts grasped, should be between ∅18–50, and the force distributed over as wide an area as possible. The better ones are those with a lot of contact between the hand and the handle. Individual specialist handles are made for the disabled or sports person to ensure balance and precision.

When designing a handle, remember the following points:

1. A textured surface helps to improve grip and avoid slippage.
2. Guards or shaping can also prevent the hand slipping forward in dangerous situations (e.g. with a knife or soldering iron, fig 3.17).
3. Plasticine and clay are ideal materials to model and experiment with form and ideas.
4. Prototypes can be cast in plaster of Paris, polyester or aluminium.

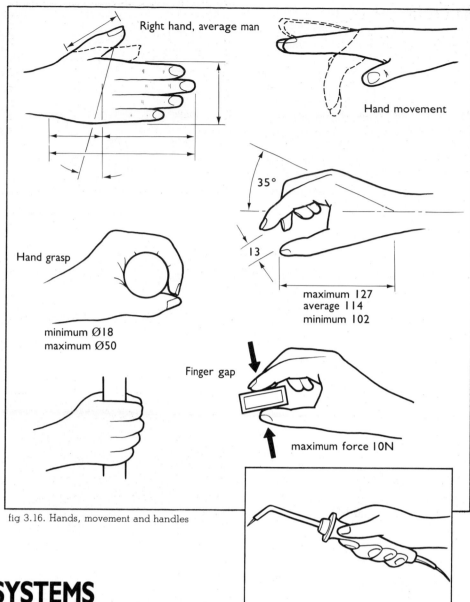

fig 3.16. Hands, movement and handles

PEOPLE – MACHINE SYSTEMS

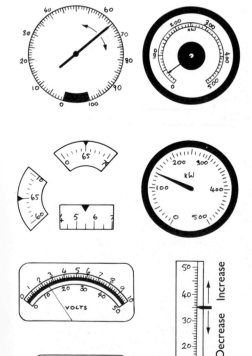

Information and display

Instruments provide detailed information about an event or situation. This information should be displayed in the simplest way possible. Types of information include:

Visual indicators. These are the most common because eyes are the best sense organs for receiving information (e.g. speedometer, thermometer).

Auditory or noise indicators (e.g. bells buzzers and sirens). These attract attention and feature in warning situations. They are especially good at night and as a relief if the visual system is overloaded.

Tactile – shaped and textured controls help identification but generally this type of information is undeveloped.

Displays may be **qualitative** (e.g. a flashing light, indicating whether or not a particular function is being carried out) or **quantatitive** giving information by numbers which can be in either analogue or digital form (fig 3.18). **Analogue** types are best for quick visual checks, as positions are more easily noticed. **Digital** (e.g. mileometer) displays give a precise reading, but may be misread.

Providing they conform to accepted practice, **scales** can be used in a variety of forms (see fig 3.19). To make the information clear, the designer must consider colour, tone markings, the style of pointers and whether there is good illumination with an absence of glare or reflections. Sometimes schematic or pictorial diagrams are used (e.g. location maps). Symbols do have advantages over language.

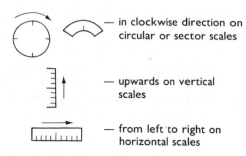

fig 3.17. Shaped guard on soldering iron

fig 3.18. Analogue and digital scales

— in clockwise direction on circular or sector scales

— upwards on vertical scales

— from left to right on horizontal scales

fig 3.19. Conventional use of scales

Controls

There are many types of control devices used to regulate machines. For example, switches, buttons, knobs, infra-red and touch controls (see fig 3.20). They can be used to switch a machine on or off, set a point or value, provide continuous adjustment or control data entry, as in computers. Fingers allow fine, delicate adjustment. Legs and feet can exert a much larger force and relieve the hands for other tasks. When designing a control, or control system, remember:

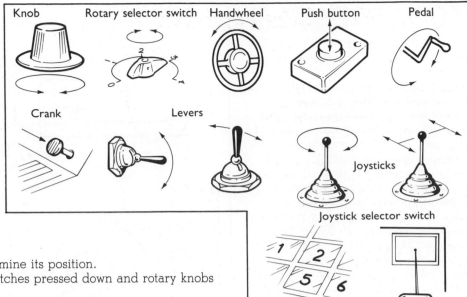

fig 3.20. Control devices

1. Controls should be easily understood.
2. The function of a control should determine its position.
3. Follow accepted conventions (e.g. switches pressed down and rotary knobs turned clockwise for ON).
4. Large diameter knobs are better for fine adjustment.
5. Resistance should be sufficient to prevent accidental use.
6. Shape and size help you to recognise the switch by feel alone.
7. Labelling and colour assist identification.

Layout of control panels is important. It makes them easier to use, and avoids errors.

1. The most important controls and displays should follow a fixed sequence and layout.
2. Emergency controls should be within easy reach.

Environment

A good environment is one which helps people to achieve their objectives, keeping effort, stress and errors as small as possible. We will look at three separate aspects of the designed environment, noise, lighting and temperature.

1. Sound

Noise is unwanted sound. Its effect can be quite dramatic. It irritates people, interferes with communication, reduces working efficiency, disturbs sleep and damages hearing. People's levels of tolerance vary.

Intensity (loudness) and **frequency** (pitch) are two characteristics of sound. The intensity is measured in **decibels** (dB). The human ear responds to 0 – 140 dB; at 120 dB discomfort is felt. dB (A) takes account of the ear's sensitivity to frequency (see fig 3.24). Remember that ear defenders or ear plugs reduce **all** sound, including warning signals and speech.

2. Light

Lighting is important if people are to see clearly.

Illuminence is the amount of light falling onto a surface. The unit of measurement is **lux** . The minimum light needed for work is 300 lux.

fig 3.21. Ease of use and safety are important in car controls

fig 3.23. Luminance levels

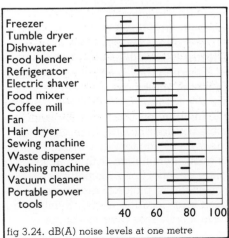

	40	60	80	100
Freezer				
Tumble dryer				
Dishwater				
Food blender				
Refrigerator				
Electric shaver				
Food mixer				
Coffee mill				
Fan				
Hair dryer				
Sewing machine				
Waste dispenser				
Washing machine				
Vacuum cleaner				
Portable power tools				

fig 3.24. dB(A) noise levels at one metre

KEY TO CONTROL POSITIONS
A Mainly visual displays
B Mainly controls and some related displays
C Controls and set up

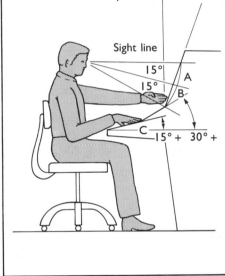

fig 3.22. Workstation

Luminance is the amount of light emitted by a surface. A luminance ratio of 10:3:1 between task and immediate background to the general surroundings is recommended for comfort (fig 3.23). Excessive luminance causes glare (areas of high brightness). Artificial lighting can affect colour rendering as well as human emotions and moods.

3. Temperature

Temperature links comfort with working efficiency. The legal requirement, established by government legislation, sets the minimum working temperature at 16°C. However, a much higher minimal level is needed by both the elderly and young babies.

PEOPLE WITH SPECIAL NEEDS

Sensitive design can make very big improvements in the lives of various groups (e.g. the disabled, the left-handed, babies and the elderly). Special aids can often help restore some of the loss of mobility, strength and flexibility, suffered by the old and disabled.

Industry generally has been slow to respond, because people think that design for such 'minority' groups involves high risks and low returns. However, often their needs are identical to other large groups. For example, arthritis sufferers have difficulty manipulating round door knobs or taps as opposed to levers (fig 3.25), yet at some stage, most people need to open a door with their arms full of parcels or to turn off a tap with wet hands.

The ergonomist has to take into account what people can or cannot do.

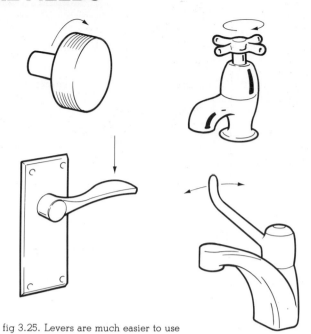

fig 3.25. Levers are much easier to use

AESTHETICS

Aesthetics is concerned with the perception and understanding of the world which we acquire through our senses. We need to consider elements such as appearance and style.

APPEARANCE

The appearance of an artefact is the characteristic that most people notice first. The way an object looks arouses different feelings in people. Appearance is the result of many things, including the function of the object, the use of different materials and type of finish.

It is important that products should have visual appeal. In a world where many new products are similar in function, components and even performance, the shape, look and above all image of a product can make all the difference. Quality will be enhanced by an overall effect which is aesthetically pleasing.

Over the centuries many people have tried to find out just what it is that makes beautiful things beautiful. Aesthetics, rather like creative thinking, is a part of design which is difficult to analyse and describe in words. Yet all the many theories about beauty depend on visual thinking. This involves arranging in space, constructing or otherwise manipulating items so they are in the appropriate relationship to one another.

The following aspects are important factors.

Line

Lines are the basic starting point in our attempts to organise space and represent design ideas. We use lines to enclose space and create shapes, but they can also be used expressively.

Lines may be thin or thick, solid or dotted, straight or curved. By changing the width or weight, length, closeness and direction, many visual effects can be created (see fig 3.26). Straight or wavy lines can express movement and rhythm, give the impression of light and shade as well as texture. A feeling of anxiety, depression and calm can be created. Lines can also be used to deceive the eye.

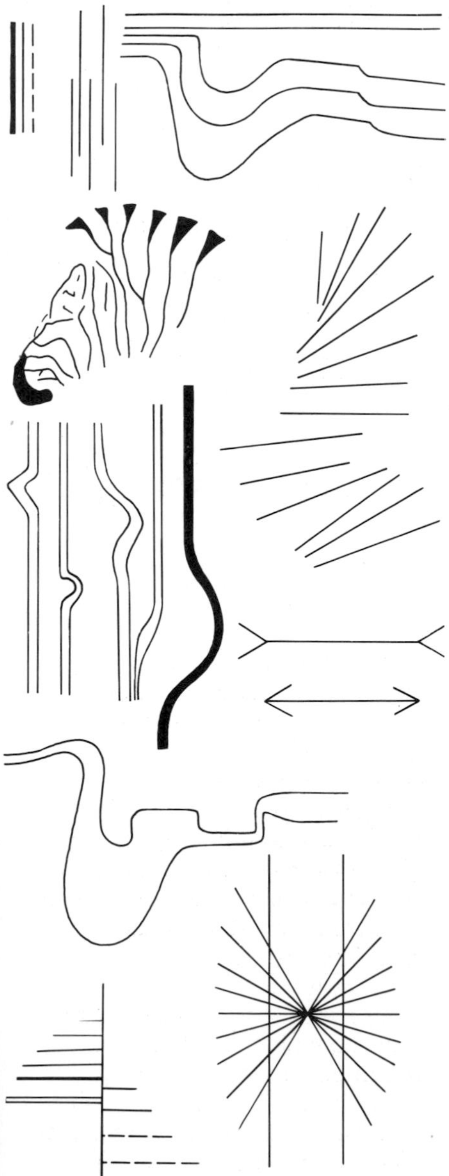

fig 3.26. Varieties of line

Shape and form

These terms are often confused in everyday speech.

Shape is created when lines overlap and cross, so that they enclose space. Shape defines the overall outline of the object.

The possibilities are endless. **Free shapes** can be created by doodling with random lines to see what emerges. (fig 3.27).

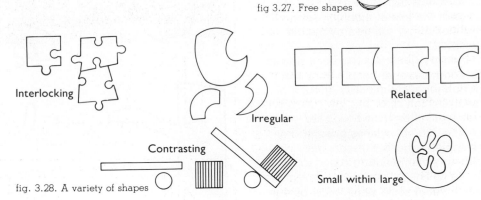

fig 3.27. Free shapes

The following offer an excellent source of ideas (fig 3.29):
(a) Geometrical shapes (e.g. circles, hexagons, polygons).
(b) Natural shapes (e.g. flowers, fruit, insects, fish)
(c) Man-made shapes (e.g. houses, bridges, vehicles, structures)

Other associated terms include interlocking, irregular, related, contrasting and small arranged within large (see fig 3.28).

Interlocking

Irregular

Related

Contrasting

Small within large

fig. 3.28. A variety of shapes

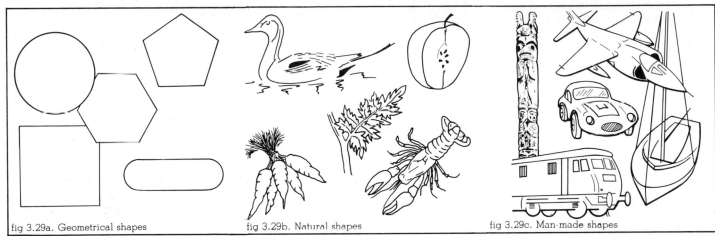

fig 3.29a. Geometrical shapes

fig 3.29b. Natural shapes

fig 3.29c. Man-made shapes

fig 3.30. A variety of forms

Form is when another dimension is added to shape making it three-dimensional. To describe form fully it is necessary to give details of all its characteristics including shape, size, proportion, colour and texture. The source ideas illustrated in fig 3.30 are equally suitable for form.

Experimenting with form is best done by starting with basic shapes (e.g. geometrical) and developing form from these.

Sizes – proportion

The size of an object is found by measuring various parts such as length, width and height (or thickness). These are known as the **dimensions.**

Proportion is the relationship between these various sizes, for example, how the height compares to the width. The manner of dividing a surface area or volume can affect the proportions.

fig 3.31. Proportion, the relationship between sizes

A sense of proportion can be developed by looking at models in which mathematics, ratios and progressions play a part.

The **golden section** dating back to the buildings of ancient Greece (e.g. Parthenon, fig 3.32 was thought to be a perfect shape). It involved a specific ratio of 1:1.62 in the construction of a rectangle, and the further sub-division of areas within it.

However, designers tend to use the eye to divide and proportion areas until they 'look right' rather than rely on numbers or rules.

The relative positions of parts within a design also need to be considered to create a **visual balance.**

Symmetry is concerned with relating one part to its mirror image. More visual interest is usually achieved when something is not symmetrical, but **asymmetrical.**

Positive and negative shapes can be used to create both interest and balance (fig 3.33).

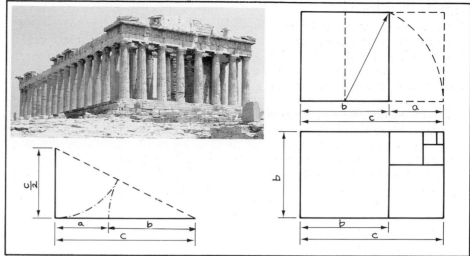

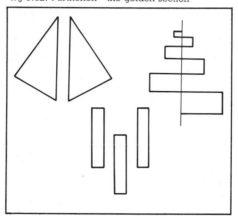

fig 3.32. Parthenon - the golden section

fig 3.33. Visual balance

Pattern

Pattern also involves the division of area. Such arrangements add visual attraction to what would otherwise be plain surfaces, giving a decorative aspect to design work.

The basic element of a pattern is a **motif.** This can be a simple or stylised organic shape, a regular or irregular geometric shape.

Repetition of the motif in patterns can be used to create rhythm and movement (fig 3.34). The idea of repetition can be developed into **tessellations.** These are geometrical shapes which interlock, leaving no gaps. Bricks in a wall and tiles on a roof (fig 3.35) are examples of tessellating patterns.

Drawing a grid will help both the development of individual sub-units, called **tesserae,** and overall arrangement (fig 3.36). A template can help with possible rotations.

This idea can be extended to produce **modular units.** An example of such a standardised unit is the tile or paving slab (fig 3.27).

fig 3.34. Patterns create rhythm and movement

fig 3.35 Roof tiles

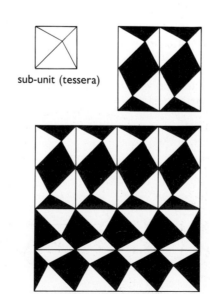

sub-unit (tessera)

fig 3.36. Tessellations

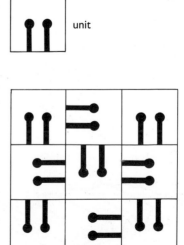

unit

fig 3.37. Modular design for paving

Colour

Colour has no form in itself, but is the complement of form. Used badly, it can spoil good shapes turning everything into a meaningless jumble. On the other hand, it can highlight good shapes and convey qualities of mood and emotions.

Colour is reflected light; fig 3.38 shows the spectrum. The quality of daylight or artificial light affects colour.

Colours can be mixed. Mixing the **primary** pigments at the centre of the colour wheel (fig 3.39) produces **secondary** colours. These in turn when mixed with the primaries will give **tertiary** colours.

Colours closely related to each other produce **harmony**, while opposites give **contrast.**

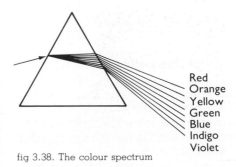

Red
Orange
Yellow
Green
Blue
Indigo
Violet

fig 3.38. The colour spectrum

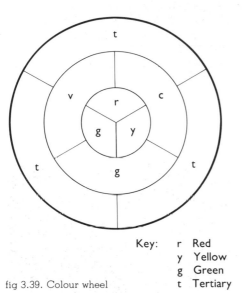

Key:
r Red
y Yellow
g Green
t Tertiary

fig 3.39. Colour wheel

Colour has three properties:
Intensity – brightness, its sensation of blueness or redness, for example.
Temperature – referring to warmth (e.g. reds, oranges) or coolness (e.g. blue, green).
Tone – the lightness or darkness of colour. Neutral colours include greys, beiges and creams. Small quantities of white or black mixed with basic colour create shades or tints. These can be used to give emphasis or provide contrasts.

Texture and finish

The surface of an object is the part which is most often seen, touched and subjected to wear and weathering. The surface finish serves to protect the object. Texture gives 'feel' and creates differences in light and shade by its surface relief. Both texture and finish are used on consumer goods to aid function and provide a decorative feature.

Areas of coarse texture provide grip and give non-slip surfaces (e.g. handles and control knob on the binoculars in fig 3.40). Visual interest is added by contrasting rough and smooth areas. Parts may also be linked by the patterns created.

All materials have their own particular texture. In fig 3.41, the smooth, cold stainless steel pan contrasts with the not so smooth, warm wood. Textures can be added and surfaces altered. Synthetic textures are sometimes applied to suggest other materials.

STYLE

What is meant by the term style, and why is it important? Style is the designers language and its vocabulary is made up of the factors we have been considering, i.e. hue, form, colour, texture and material. The final style is the combination of these elements.

There is no magic formula, but successful designers tend to operate within a particular style. This provides both a stimulus and framework and makes their work recognisable.

All design solutions are particular to time and place. An historical look at the style of housing shows how it relates to the availability of materials, but also to what at the time was socially acceptable and appealing. Style does not stay still, it develops in response to social, political, economic and technological changes in society.

Twentieth century styles: there have been many twists and turns in the styles used this century. They have been classified under such headings as, Art Noveau, Bauhaus, Art Deco, Modern, Pop and High-tech.

Analysis reveals how some of the visual factors have almost been filtered out while others have gained in importance. Our attention will be concentrated on the most important, in terms of modern industrial design.

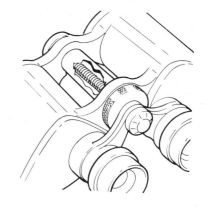

fig 3.40. Textured controls

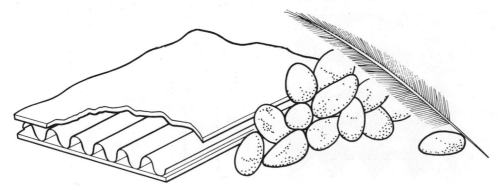

fig 3.42. Contrasting surface textures

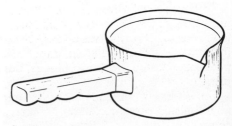

fig 3.41. Purpose designed surface textures

fig 3.43. Bauhaus chairs

Functional style

Ornamentation was a feature of the early industrial products, which were often direct copies of classical or traditional craft styles of the past. Only gradually did this give way to a new machine aesthetic based largely on the simplicity of production technique. Characteristics included use of angular forms, with industrial materials and methods of fabrication providing their own decoration. As far as appearance was concerned simplicity, often stark and undecorated, was the aesthetic of functionalism, with the claim that 'form should follow function'.

The Bauhaus, a school of design established in Germany between the wars, has a tremendous influence on this style. The examples in fig 3.46 show a formal approach to chair design by two of its members. Marcel Breuer used tubular steel, inspired by the strength and lightness seen in the bicycle while Ludwig Mies van der Rohe used elegance, space and perfection of form to good effect.

The functional style was adopted and developed by designers and paralleled by architects in the modern style (e.g. Le Corbusier). Some spectacular and beautiful products have resulted from this approach, especially in machinery, scientific equipment and electronics. However, this style has been less successful in satisfying emotional desires for exclusive objects i.e. those not necessitated by function.

Decoration verses function?

This argument continues even today. There has always been an element of decoration in functional products. The ratio between an artefact and the extent of its decoration is shown quite clearly in the motor car. The American automobile gave rise to streamlining (fig 3.44) with an apparently greater concern for style than anything else. Even the latest Jaguar (fig 3.45) attempts to capture a sense of feline power.

Modern industrial design is more than just styling, it is about integrating the elements into a visually direct whole. In the world market, appearance is vitally important in creating distinctiveness in all kinds of products. Good examples include Audi and Porsche cars from Germany, Olympus cameras and Sony hi-fi (Japan), Swatch watches (Switzerland), Olivetti typewriters (Italy) and Phillips compact disc players (Holland). Large companies such as these see the importance of establishing a corporate design image. Sony is identified with technological innovation and, through products like the Walkman, well designed goods which meet consumer preference for compactness and convenience.

In consumer electronics (e.g. radios, dishwashers), technology has become miniaturised and standardised, often consisting of little more than a few microchips. In such cases, the product's function has little influence on its form. Endless possibilities are presented when it comes to giving the product a visual identity.

Appearance, therefore, plays an important role in helping to meet the needs of manufacturing industry for ever-increasing production and consumption. Today, there is a complexity of styles and a wide range of available products.

fig 3.44. American streamlining

fig 3.45. Feline power, Jaguar Sovereign

Durability or low first cost?

Built-in obsolescence, in terms of function, quality and changes in fashion, is very much a feature of our age. It often makes if difficult to decide what to buy: should it be something cheap and easily replaced? or something more expensive and durable?

Planned obsolescence is one aspect of convenience and mass taste which is increasingly influencing designers. Materials such as plastics have made more goods available to more people through mass production in large numbers. Whether through its buckets, brushes or the disposable cutlery in fig 3.47, our throw-away economy is shown to be still expanding.

The craft aesthetic: amongst other available options, there is still a place for individual crafts where things are made by hand in the traditional way. However today craftwork is justified on aesthetic rather than economic grounds. Few individual craft objects are bought for use, and none from necessity. Batch production is cheaper than one-offs, but still more expensive than mass production.

The quality of craftmanship is still very much part of durability. Traditionally, workmanship was associated with time, skill and effort. This seems hardly compatible with mass production which is concerned with making more in less time with less effort.

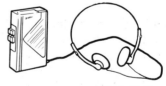

fig 3.46. Sony Walkman

fig 3.47. Plastic disposable cutlery

Which way forward?

Design is concerned with change. Our lifestyles and expectations are different even from those of our parents. At the present time we are involved in a revolution in process technologies, design development and production. Computer aided design and manufacture (CAD/CAM) has far reaching implications; it offers the opportunity to develop new and more varied products faster than ever before.

It is important, however, that technical and commercial considerations do not come before human needs. Ergonomic considerations in making things easy to use and understand, as well as aesthetics and marketing, are needed in order for people to get pleasure from the things they buy. We can do no better than follow the American industrial designer Henry Dreyfuss' thorough approach to design:

'What we are working on is going to be ridden in, sat upon, looked at, talked into, activated, operated, or in some way used by people individually or en masse. If the point of contact between the product and the people becomes a point of friction, then the industrial designer has failed. If on the other hand, people are made safer, more comfortable, more eager to purchase, more efficient – or just plain happier – the designer has succeeded.'

EXERCISES

1. (a) What is an ergonomist? What special skills are needed?
   (b) List the types of problems associated with growing old.
2. (a) Using thin plastic or card construct the 1:10 scale ergonome of an adult male (fig 3.48).
   (b) Use the model to help evaluate different kinds of seating.
3. (a) Make a study of motorway signs and evaluate them from a foreign driver's viewpoint.
   (b) Design a signposting system for visitors to your school.
4. Design a layout for a work-study/bedroom which will also be suitable for hobbies like sewing or model making.
5. Design a computer workstation suitable for use in junior schools.
6. (a) Sketch a range of different types of handle e.g. used for gripping, pushing, pulling).
   (b) Model a handle suitable for a potato peeler.
7. Sketch and give an example of the use of each of the following types of instrument display (a) qualitative; (b) quantitative; (c) representational.
8. (a) Make a drawing of the instrument display used in a family car.
   (b) Analyse the design from an ergonomic point of view.
   (c) What improvements would you make?
9. Devise a scheme to help you find out the range of pedalling movements needed to design a pedal driven toy suitable for 4 year old children.
10. (a) Study and sketch 10 different types of control operated by fingers.
    (b) Design a control knob for a specific function.
11. Design a logo to be used by a shop selling (a) sports equipment; (b) gardening materials; (c) toiletries.
12. (a) What functions can textures perform?
    (b) Illustrate three examples of how textures can be used decoratively.
13. Design a pattern for the lid of a box, based on one motif.
14. (a) Draw a range of products which are based on tessellations or modular units.
    (b) Design a tessellation suitable for wall tiles for either a kitchen or bathroom.
15. Design a printed pattern to be used on wrapping paper and/or bags to illustrate the wares sold by a shop or store of your choice.
16. (a) Explore and research a range of interesting shapes and forms.
    (b) Show how a symmetrical pattern differs from an asymmetric pattern.
    (c) Illustrate the difference between positive and negative shapes.
17. (a) Make a study of a specific design style of this century.
    (b) Make sketches to illustrate its main features.
18. What are the main features of the functional aesthetic style? Sketch examples to illustrate your points.

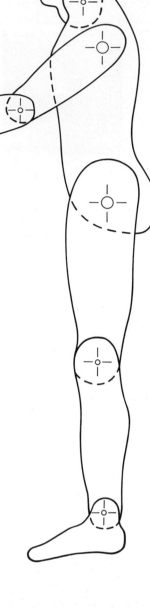

fig 3.48. Ergonome

fig 3.49 Advertising motifs

MATERIALS

An historical background

The earth's abundance of energy resources and natural materials have been used for human survival since the dawn of civilisation. At first, wood, bone and stone were used to make tools and weapons to provide food, clothing and shelter. The use of these natural materials in a variety of forms has persisted throughout the centuries, but new materials have also been introduced. For example, the art of alloying or mixing several naturally occurring minerals led to the production and use of bronze. The later discovery of iron offered new opportunities to conquer and enrich the environment. Indeed historians use materials to describe and trace the early stages of development, i.e. the Stone Age, Bronze Age and Iron Age.

The Industrial Revolution brought about an enormous increase in the use of natural resources. There were considerable changes and developments in the techniques used in mixing and refining as well as in processing materials. The impact of increasing scientific knowledge about the nature of materials led development away from a trial and error approach, to a science based technology. This resulted in new methods being used to work traditional materials and to the introduction of new ones. By the end of the nineteenth century, the visual impact of the increasing use of cast and wrought iron was clear for all to see. It resulted in new forms and designs for bridges, buildings (fig 4.1) and methods of transportation.

The twentieth century has seen the widespread use of concrete, with special reinforcement, to build roads, bridges and high-rise buildings (fig 4.2). However, modern materials are increasingly of the synthetic, manufactured type. Plastics are the materials phenomenon of the age, and affect every aspect of our lives from toiletries to food-packaging and from buildings to transport. The use of such material helps to ensure that comfortable living standards are both maintained and advanced.

Knowledge of materials is the basis of understanding modern technology, just as the technology of material is essential to design activity. This chapter aims to provide a useful guide to the different types and groups of materials available and to form a helpful basis by which comparisons and assessments can be made. It should enable you to make informed choices and successful decisions in terms of materials when designing and making projects.

fig 4.1. 19th century use of cast iron

fig 4.4. Use of GRP

fig 4.5. High tech stacking system

figs 4.2, 4.3. 20th century use of concrete

SELECTION – CHOICE OF MATERIAL

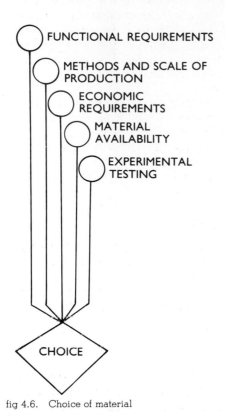

FUNCTIONAL REQUIREMENTS

METHODS AND SCALE OF PRODUCTION

ECONOMIC REQUIREMENTS

MATERIAL AVAILABILITY

EXPERIMENTAL TESTING

CHOICE

fig 4.6.   Choice of material

Choosing those materials which are most appropriate to a particular task is essential in any designing activity. From earliest times people have tried various ways of carrying out tasks using different materials and methods so that improvements can be made. Today the problem is more complex, but more interesting because of the increased possibilities offered by the ever widening range of materials available.

Selection is not usually easy and depends very much upon the skill and experience of the designer. To make successful choices requires knowledge, understanding and experience of working a wide range of materials. There are several factors to be considered before any decision is taken. These can be grouped under five main headings, as shown in fig 4.6 and below.

FUNCTIONAL REQUIREMENTS

In order to meet specific demands, it is necessary to match the task a component or device may have to perform, with the material resources. It is important to consider a whole range of service requirements that are likely to arise, such as hardness, rigidity, flexibility, smoothness, colour, weight and texture. These can be explored and matched with the properties and chacteristics of suitable materials. The requirements are often needed in varied combinations and forms. Electrical, thermal or heat resistance may be linked with resistance to wear and corrosion in order to improve reliability and increase life-span. These and other aspects can be explored and tested across a range of materials and comparisons made. Some narrowing of choice should then be possible.

METHODS AND SCALE OF PRODUCTION

Linked with the consideration of material, is the method, means and scale of manufacture. These are important in order to achieve maximum effect with economy, and precision with high standards of finish. Materials should not be considered in isolation, but with awareness for the scale of production, the methods of working and suitability for manufacturing techniques.

Some materials have the ability to change state which makes them suitable for deforming, casting and moulding. The strength and section of material, together with the method of fabrication, influence both shape and form. The various industrial processes used to manufacture components need to be compatible with and suitable for the materials. For example, modern window frames use a lot of extruded section and are made in either aluminium or uPVC (plastic), rather than the more traditional wood. The choice will also determine the method of fabrication and type of finish.

ECONOMIC REQUIREMENTS

Cost is a vital consideration in the manufacture of any product. It is necessary to compare the overall costs of a range of materials. Total costings must include not only the purchase, but also the working and processing of materials, i.e. machining, joining and finishing. Expensive materials can often be justified because of the low cost of processing. The cost effectiveness of working materials can affect the economic viability of the product dramatically. The aim is to keep costs low, either to maximise profit, or to ensure sales at a realistic market price.

The quality of an artefact is often determined by the choice of material. It can also be dictated by the scale of manufacture or the need to find a cheaper means of production. Some of the variable factors involved can be illustrated by looking at the range of materials/solutions used to provide 'drinking vessels' (fig 4.7). A wide range of alternatives are on offer, including wine glasses, china cups, pottery mugs, silver goblets, pewter tankards, plastic beakers and waxed paper cups. Some items are more suited to large volume mass-production, while others cover the more traditional means of solving the problem, and some match the convenience requirements of our disposable, throw-away age.

fig 4.7.   Drinking vessels

MATERIAL AVAILABILITY

Materials are often classified as **natural** or **synthetic** and **metallic** or **non-metallic**. Each of these groups can be further sub-divided and this is covered later in the section dealing with specific materials.

As well as being of different types, most materials are available from suppliers in many regular forms. These include wire, sheet, plate, flat strip, round and square bar, tube, angle, extruded section, granular, chips, pellets and viscous fluids. They are also in standard preferred sizes which have been established by traditional practice and demand. Standardisation affecting both quality and size is now applied to the specification of most types of material. The need for non-standard sizes or quantities can increase costs considerably. Therefore, it is common practice to work from standard sizes.

It is necessary to decide which forms will be most suited to a particular job and to check that they can be obtained easily and are not too expensive. Supplier's catalogues contain this type of information, as well as details of special items and new developments. However, specialist information is not usually presented in a simple manner and requires careful research. It is essential to check the availability with stockists and ensure that your materials specifications can be met.

EXPERIMENTAL TESTING

Designers should be encouraged to experiment and investigate the increasing possibilities offered by new combinations of materials now available. The experience gained from working and testing a range of different materials will help to reinforce the ability to make successful decisions. Exercises and tests can be a useful means of exploring the limitations, such as strength, of unusual material combinations.

CONCLUDING HINTS

The final choice is often a compromise. In some cases functional demands will dominate, while in others cost may prove to be the main factor. It is only when all the information is collated that decisions can be made. There is rarely one correct answer or 'best' material, usually there are several alternatives or 'appropriate' materials depending on the circumstances.

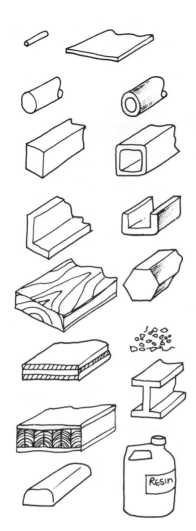

fig 4.8. Materials available in a wide range of forms

PROPERTIES OF MATERIAL

The designer and engineer need to have a thorough knowledge and understanding of the properties and terminology associated with materials in order to select and use them effectively. Every material has certain properties which make it more suitable for some situations than others. Constructional materials in general must be able to withstand the action of forces without undergoing significant distortion. They must incorporate a high level of operational safety; this is particularly important where structures such as bridges and aircraft are concerned.

In manufacturing, however, different requirements are needed. Properties which permit the permanent deforming of materials enable components to be shaped easily and produced cheaply using the least amount of energy. Other **mechanical properties** are associated with the behaviour of material when linked to the application of force. It is these properties that designers are concerned with when considering a material for a specific duty. Testing can also be undertaken to determine mechanical properties. Those properties determined by other methods are called **physical properties** and it is these that we shall consider first.

PHYSICAL PROPERTIES

Fusibility

Metals and some plastics have the ability to change into a liquid or molten state when heated to a certain temperature, known as the **melting point**. This varies considerably between materials (fig 4.9), but is an essential feature in casting, moulding, welding, soldering and other related processes.

Density

Density is defined as the mass per unit volume. Relative density is the ratio of the density of a substance with that of pure water at a temperature of 4°C.

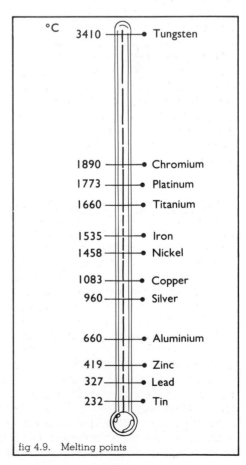

°C	
3410	Tungsten
1890	Chromium
1773	Platinum
1660	Titanium
1535	Iron
1458	Nickel
1083	Copper
960	Silver
660	Aluminium
419	Zinc
327	Lead
232	Tin

fig 4.9. Melting points

Electrical conductivity

All materials resist the flow of electricity to some extent.

Electrical conductors offer a very low resistance to the flow of an electric current. Metals, especially silver, copper and gold, are generally good electrical conductors. Liquids (electrolytes) and some gases also allow current to pass through them easily.

Electrical insulators offer a very high resistance to the flow of electricity. Non-metals are generally good insulators, but vary in their ability to resist the flow of electricity. Wood is comparatively poor, while ceramic materials and mica are very good, as are glass and many plastics, such as PVC and nylon.

Semi-conductors range between the two previous extremes and allow electric current to flow only under certain conditions. Silicon and germanium in their pure state are poor conductors, but their electrical resistance can be altered by the addition of small quantities of impurities.

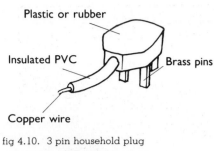
fig 4.10. 3 pin household plug

fig 4.11. Part of pylon showing ceramic insulator

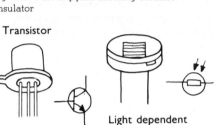
fig 4.12. Light dependent resistor and transistor

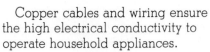
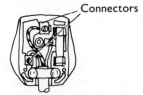

Copper cables and wiring ensure the high electrical conductivity to operate household appliances.

Insulators are used to isolate the electricity for reasons of safety thereby making the best use of conductors.

Semi-conductors, because they are affected by heat and light energy, are used in a wide range of electrical circuits and devices (e.g. alarms).

Thermal properties

The term thermal comes from the Greek word meaning heat, so the thermal properties of a material relate to its reaction to heat. For example, spacecraft have to endure extremely low temperatures in space, but on re-entry to the earth's atmosphere extremely high temperatures are created. Asbestos and other fire resistant materials such as silica tiles are used to prevent vaporisation.

Thermal conductivity is about how heat travels through material. It is measured in watts per metre degree celcius (W/m°C). Metals, especially copper, possess high thermal conductivity.

In the pan illustrated (fig 4.14), possible alternatives would include aluminium, enamelled pressed steel and cast iron.

Thermal insulators are those materials with low value thermal conductivity, generally non-metals. They are used to prevent heat gains or losses (e.g. pan or coffee pot handles). Air is one of the best thermal insulators. The materials illustrated (fig 4.17, 4.18) trap air and are used to reduce heat loss in the home.

fig 4.13. Space shuttle

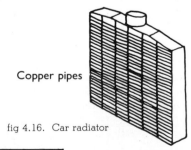
fig 4.14. Apollo capsule

fig 4.15 Should heat quickly and evenly

fig 4.16. Car radiator

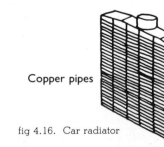
fig 4.17. Loft insulation

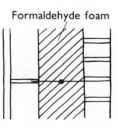
fig 4.18. Cavity wall insulation

Thermal expansion: materials generally expand as they get hot and shrink upon cooling. A material's coefficient of linear expansion is the fractional change in length due to changes in temperature. It varies considerably with different materials.

In large civil engineering structures such as bridges, allowance has to be made for this movement caused by seasonal variations in temperature.

Control mechanisms also use this effectively (e.g. car thermostat or the automatic kettle, fig 4.20).

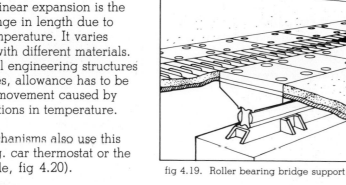

fig 4.19. Roller bearing bridge support

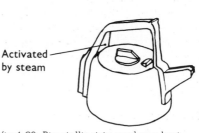

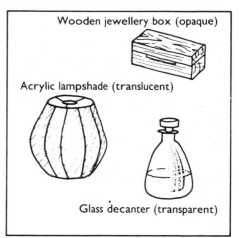

fig 4.20. Bimetallic strip used as a heat sensor in automatic kettles

fig 4.21. Reflectors

fig 4.22. Solar panel

Optical properties

Materials react in different ways to light and heat by reflection, radiation and absorption. Materials can be opaque, translucent or transparent. **Colour** is a particularly significant factor; it can be a means of identification and can also determine how suitable a material is for decorative work.

Colour can be modified or changed using paints or dyes.

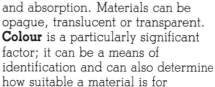

fig 4.23. Opacity and translucence

MECHANICAL PROPERTIES

These properties are associated with how a material reacts towards the application of force. A sufficiently strong force will produce some definite amount of deformation, either temporary (**elastic**) or permanent (**plastic**) in the material.

Strength

Strength is defined as the ability of a material to withstand force without breaking or permanently bending. Different forces require different types of strength to resist them.

Force per unit is called **stress**. Displacement (either distortion by extension or compression) per unit length is called **strain**.

$$Stress = \frac{Load}{Area}$$

$$Strain = \frac{Extension}{Original\ length}$$

Tensile strength is the ability to resist stretching or pull forces. It is an essential property of all cables, chains and ropes.

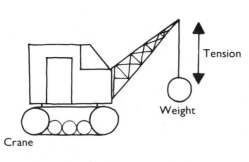

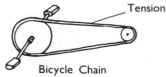

fig 4.24. Tension

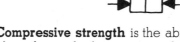

Compressive strength is the ability to withstand a pushing force which tries to crush or shorten.

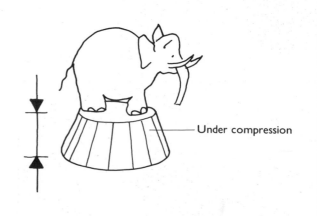

fig 4.25. Compression

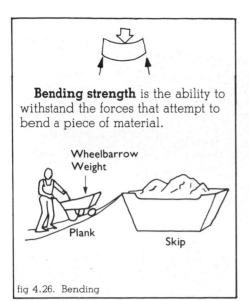

Bending strength is the ability to withstand the forces that attempt to bend a piece of material.

fig 4.26. Bending

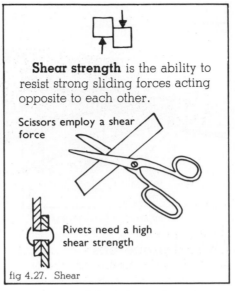

Shear strength is the ability to resist strong sliding forces acting opposite to each other.

Scissors employ a shear force

Rivets need a high shear strength

fig 4.27. Shear

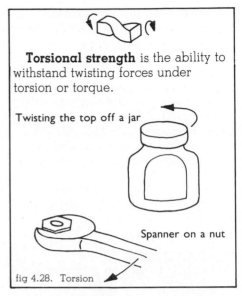

Torsional strength is the ability to withstand twisting forces under torsion or torque.

Twisting the top off a jar

Spanner on a nut

fig 4.28. Torsion

Elasticity

This is the ability to flex and bend when subject to loads and forces, and regain normal shape and size when these are removed (rather like an elastic band).

Most structures need to possess some degree of elasticity.

Plasticity

Plasticity is the ability of a material to be changed permanently in shape, by external blows or pressure, without cracking or breaking (e.g. plasticine). Some materials are more 'plastic' when heated. Two other properties are associated with this term.

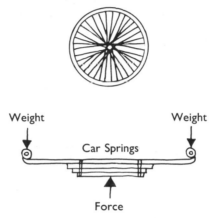

fig 4.29. More likely to bend than fracture

fig 4.30. Car body shells being pressed

Malleability refers to the extent to which a material can undergo permanent deformation in all directions under compression (i.e. by hammering, pressing or rolling) without rupture or cracking.

Plasticity is essential, but malleable materials need not be strong.

Ductility is the ability to undergo cold plastic deformation by bending, twisting or more usually by stretching, i.e. in tension.

Permanent reduction in cross-section can be achieved by pulling through a die without rupturing.

All ductile materials are malleable,

but malleable materials are not necessarily ductile, since a soft material like plasticine may lack strength in tension and tear apart easily when stretched.

A comparative table of common metals is shown below:

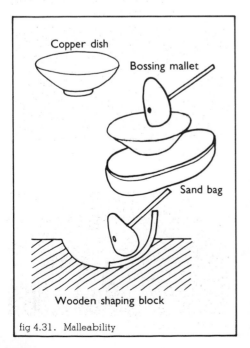

fig 4.31. Malleability

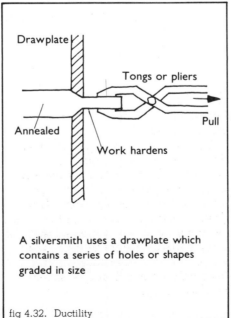

A silversmith uses a drawplate which contains a series of holes or shapes graded in size

fig 4.32. Ductility

Order	Malleability	Ductility
1	Silver	Silver
2	Copper	Iron
3	Aluminium	Nickel
4	Tin	Copper
5	Lead	Aluminium
6	Zinc	Zinc
7	Iron	Tin
8	Nickel	Lead

Hardness

Hardness is a complex property. It is the ability of a material to resist abrasive wear and indentation or deformation.

It is an important quality in all cutting tools (e.g. drills, files). Abrasives also depend upon hardness to be effective.

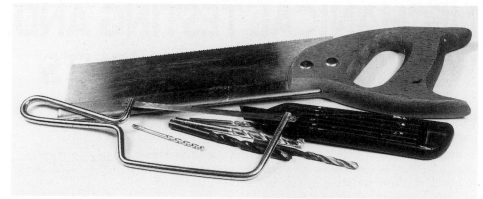

fig 4.33. Cutting tools

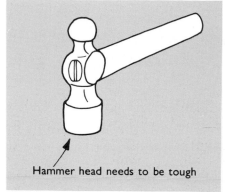

Hammer head needs to be tough

fig 4.34. Toughness

Toughness

Toughness is usually used to denote the ability of a material to withstand sudden shocks or blows without fracture. It also includes resistance to cracking when subjected to bending and shear loads.

The opposite of toughness is **brittleness**, which is a tendency to show little or no strain (i.e. plastic deformation) before fracture.

If a material is brittle it is not ductile and will not allow pressing or bending, but will simply break.

fig 4.35. Brittle material

Fatigue

Fatigue is caused by repeated or reversed stress cycles, bending or tension. It is frequently found in engineering structures (e.g. flexing of aircraft wings).

Fatigue is also affected by corrosion, temperature and surface finish.

Stress cycle caused by bending

Aluminium fracture due to fatigue

fig 4.36. Stress cycles

fig 4.37. Aircraft stress point

Durability

This is the ability to withstand wear and tear and weathering and the deterioration or corrosion this may cause. It often involves changes in appearance, but the changes in properties which can occur, resulting in mechanical weakening, are of more concern.

Corrosion is common in metals with the notable exception of gold. Steel structures are vulnerable to **oxidation** (rust). When this is combined with electrolysis the results can be disastrous.

Ultra-violet light also causes deterioration. It causes wood to deteriorate over a period of time, can cause colour changes affecting shade and pigments, and may also cause some plastics to crack or become brittle.

The properties of plastics generally are less prone to decay, which has led to their widespread use.

fig 4.38. Rusting cars in a scrapyard

fig 4.39. Plastic bottles washed up on a seashore

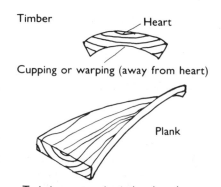

Timber

Heart

Cupping or warping (away from heart)

Plank

Twisting occurs in timber length

fig 4.40.

Stability

Stability is resistance to changes in size and shape.

Timber tends to **'warp'** and **'twist'** due to changes in humidity. Metals and some plastics gradually **deform** when subjected to steady force or steady stress for long periods. This gradual extension under load is known as **'creep'**. It is very important that turbine blades are made from creep-resisting materials because high temperatures and rotational speeds produce creep.

fig 4.41. Gas turbine blades

MECHANICAL TESTING AND WORKSHOP EXPERIMENTS

Elaborate standardised tests are carried out in industry to determine mechanical properties. These are done by deformation or destruction and are carried out for two main reasons: either to determine the properties of a material or to check that raw materials are of the required standard and that processes (e.g. heat treatment) have been completed satisfactorily. The main routine tests cover tensile strength, hardness, toughness and ductility.

In the workshop situation it is sometimes helpful to devise tests to measure and compare materials using simple apparatus rather than expensive equipment. Some suggestions are given after each standardised test.

Hints

In any form of testing it is important to remember the following points:

1. Conditions are the same for all specimens.
2. Observations and measurements are taken and carefully recorded.
3. Plotting findings in the form of a simple graph often helps to illustrate the results in a more interesting and effective manner.

TENSILE TESTS

Tensile tests measure the properties of tensile strength and ductility. A standardised test piece (fig 4.42) is gripped in the jaws of a testing machine and an increasing force is applied.

The graph in fig 4.43 shows the relationship between force and extension and also the nominal stress against strain. If a small force is applied, extension is proportional to the force. If the force is removed before point **A** is reached, the material will return to its original shape and size (**elastic**), but when the elastic limit is reached, a small permanent extension will remain (**plastic**). Further force causes the sample to stretch rapidly. 'Necking' or wasting occurs shortly after the maximum force **M** has been reached and just before final fracture occurs.

If a nominal stress/strain curve is drawn from informaton recorded in the test, Youngs Modulus of Elasticity '**E**' can be determined. (E is the slope of the straight portion O-A).

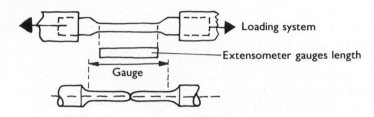

fig 4.42. Test piece machined to British Standards (flat or round)

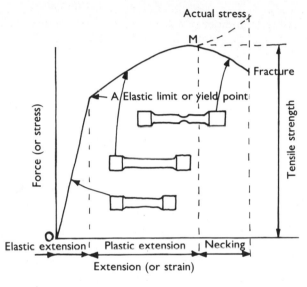

fig 4.43. Typical tensile test curve

Factors of safety

All components must be designed to withstand forces well below the material's elastic limit.

$$E = \frac{\text{increase in STRESS}}{\text{increase in STRAIN}} \quad \text{where STRESS} = \frac{\text{force}}{\text{original area}} \quad \text{and STRAIN} = \frac{\text{extension}}{\text{original length}}$$

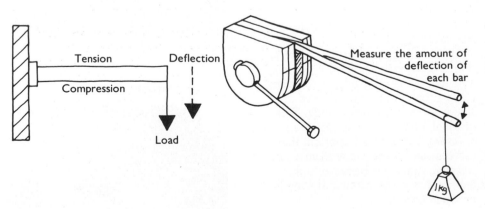

fig 4.44. Assessing the design requirements for a typical cantilevered towel rail

Similarly, in the workshop, strength can be measured and compared. The experiment illustrated (fig 4.44) could be carried out in a vice using bars of different materials, but of the same length (e.g. 750 mm).

In all cases deflection is proportional to the load. If this experiment can be further undertaken over an extended period of time, the phenomenon of **creep** (showing increased deflection) may be seen with some materials. **Stiffness** is the term applied to how little distortion or deflection occurs.

In any experiment of this type the weight of the material itself needs to be considered.

Different cross-sections of material might also be tried and compared (fig 4.45). Whatever material is chosen, it must be used in a manner where it offers the most resistance to stress.

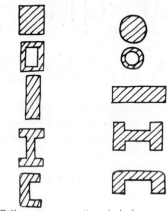

fig 4.45. Different cross sections to test

HARDNESS TESTS

All hardness tests involve comparison between the material under test and some other material. There are a large number of hardness tests because of the different aspects and definitions of hardness.

Scratch tests

These tests show the resistance to scratching. In Moh's scale, used by mineralogists, a number of substances are arranged in rank order so that each will scratch the one coming before it. In this scale a diamond has a hardness index rating of 10.

Such tests can easily be duplicated in the workshop by scratching the surface of small samples of material with a scriber, a diamond (old glass-cutter), tungsten carbide (top of an old masonry drill) or even abrasives.

Observe the size and depth of the marks produced.

Indentation tests

Hardness is usually considered as the resistance to plastic deformation. There are several standardised tests giving universally accepted scales of hardness (fig 4.47).

They involve forcing an indenter into the surface of the test specimen. The hardness value is then based either upon the surface area of the impression or the depth to which the indenter enters the specimen material.

fig 4.46. Hardness testing machine

The **Brinell test** uses a hardened steel ball as the indenter, pressed under a constant load.

F ↓ kg

Brinell Hardness Value

$$= \frac{\text{Force}}{\text{Area}}$$

fig 4.47a.

The **Vickers Pyramid hardness test** uses a pyramid diamond indenter.

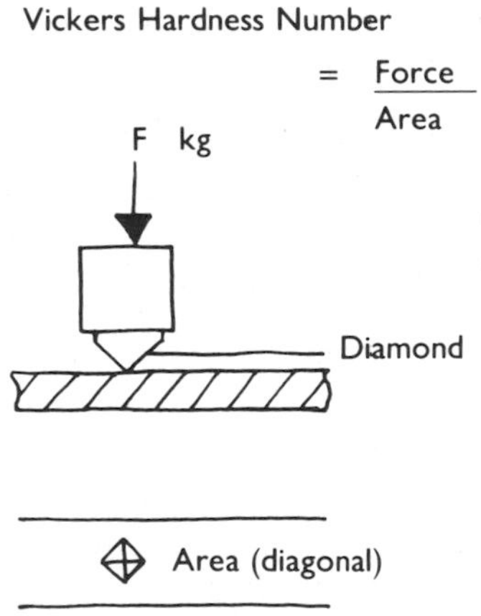

Vickers Hardness Number

$$= \frac{\text{Force}}{\text{Area}}$$

F kg

Diamond

⊕ Area (diagonal)

fig 4.47b.

In the **Rockwell hardness test** the indenter can be either a steel ball (B scale) or a diamond cone (C scale).

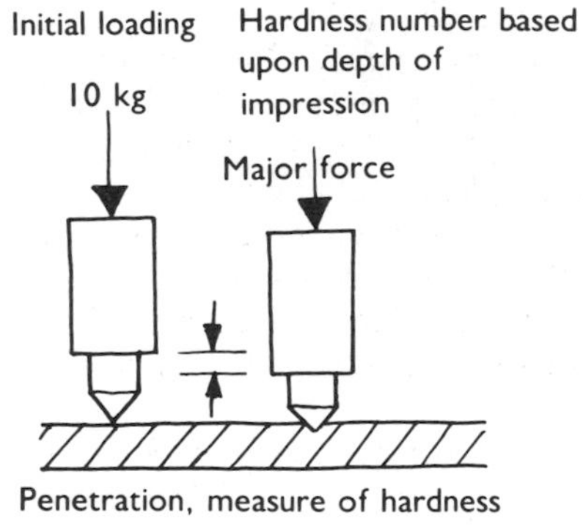

Initial loading   Hardness number based upon depth of impression

10 kg

Major force

Penetration, measure of hardness

fig 4.47c.

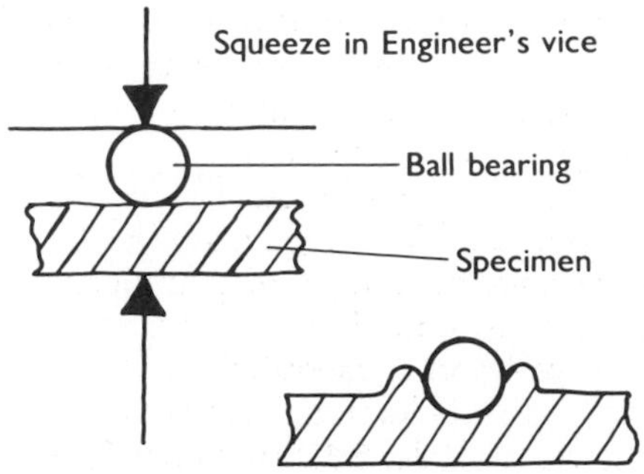

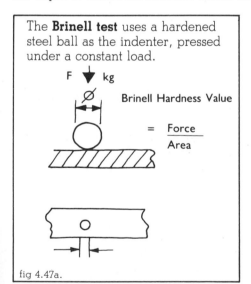

Squeeze in Engineer's vice

Ball bearing

Specimen

Simple workshop tests can be used to cut and dent a range of materials. They can be placed in rank order of hardness or softness. Hard ball-bearings (tungsten-carbide), letter or number stamps, or even a centre punch can be used. The size or depth of the impression can also be observed or measured. Will this be directly proportional to the force used?

fig 4.48. Workshop test to assess hardness

TOUGHNESS TESTING

The **Izod impact test** is used to compare the shock resistance of different materials.

A notched specimen machined to specific sizes, is struck by a heavy pendulum falling under gravity. The extreme swing position is used to show impact strength. The tougher the material, the more energy is absorbed in breaking it and the smaller the extent of the swing after fracture.

In the workshop situation, toughness cannot be expressed in simple numerical terms. However, a similar test can be used which allows some simple comparisons to be made (see fig 4.50).

Using constant hammer blows, 'feel' the amount of force necessary to bend or break samples.

The more bending which takes place, the less tough the material.

Note: Safety — take care! Brittle materials are likely to fracture.

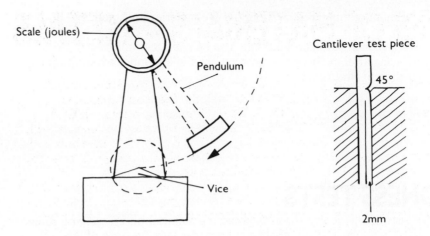

fig 4.49. A 1300 impact tester

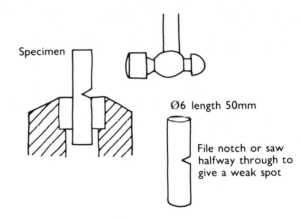

fig 4.50. Workshop test to assess hardness

DUCTILITY TESTS

A bending test provides a simple test of ductility that requires neither specialist equipment, nor specially prepared test pieces.

1. Bending backwards and forwards past the neutral position will measure the toughness of the material (fig 4.51). It will also work harden the material past its point of fatigue.

2. Bending around a former or mandrel will measure the plastic deformation in one direction. Ideally it should be unbroken and free from visible surface cracks.

3. The specimen is pressed between shaped formers. The amount of force needed to tighten the vice is measured. Surface quality will also need careful checking.

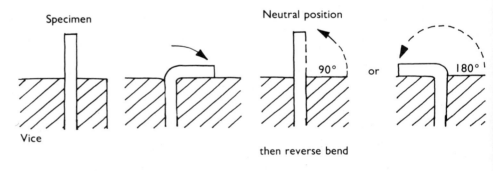

fig 4.51. Ductility tests

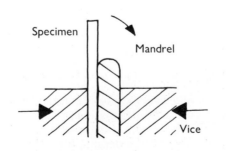

fig 4.52. Bending around a former

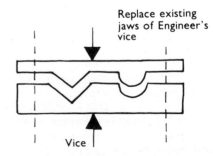

fig 4.53. Pressing between shaped formers

TYPES OF MATERIALS – METALS

Of the known, naturally occurring elements, the major proportion are metals. They form about 25% of the earth's crust by weight. The most common is aluminium (8%), followed by iron (5%). Others such as chromium (0.02%), copper (0.007%) and silver (0.00001%) are much more scarce. All metals, with the exception of gold, are found chemically combined with other elements in the form of oxides and sulphates. These ores are not distributed evenly. Substantial deposits tend generally to be found in localised areas.

Exploitation by open cast working or deep mining depends on commercial considerations. These include such matters as size of deposit, ease of location, scarcity and demand. The history of Cornish tin mining illustrates how these circumstances continue to fluctuate.

Metals are divided into three basic categories:

1. **FERROUS** — the group composed mainly of ferrite or iron with small additions of other substances (e.g. mild steel, cast iron, tool steel). Almost all are magnetic.

2. **NON-FERROUS** — the group of metals that contain no iron (e.g. copper, aluminium, tin, lead).

3. **ALLOYS** — metals that are formed by mixing two or more metals and sometimes other elements to create a new metal which has improved properties. The process is called alloying. An almost limitless range of combinations is possible, with widely differing properties. They may be grouped into ferrous alloys, e.g. stainless steel (steel and chromium), high speed steel (steel and tungsten) and non-ferrous alloys e.g. brass (copper and zinc), duralumin (aluminium and copper).

fig 4.54. Cornish tin mine

THE PRODUCTION OF FERROUS METALS

This group has played a most important part in our developmental history and remains vital to everyday life even today. Iron ore is widely distributed over the earth's crust and is found in different forms, each containing different amounts of iron. A workable ore may yield from 20–65%. The basic types are iron oxides:

Magnetite ores contain the mineral magnetite, are black in colour and the richest known ore, yielding up to 65% iron. It is found in Sweden, USA and USSR.

Haematite ores contain the mineral haematite, are reddish-brown in colour, yielding between 40 and 60% iron and found in Spain and USA.

Although Britain has some very small deposits of haematite, concentrated high grade ore has to be imported. To convert the ore into usable material involves a number of processes. The first steps involve **washing**, **grading** and **crushing**. It is crushed to produce a suitable lump size (100mm cubes) or 'sintered' (small loose particles fused with coke), into a hard porous mass of similar size. Magnetic ores can be concentrated by magnetic means. Graded ores undergo a process of **roasting** by which some of the carbon, sulphur and water are driven off.

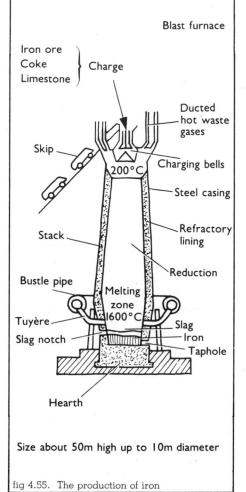

Size about 50m high up to 10m diameter

fig 4.55. The production of iron

The production of iron

The iron ore is refined in the **blast furnace** to produce **pig-iron** (fig 4.55). The charge is made up of three parts, **iron ore**, **coke** and **limestone** in variable proportions according to the grade of ore. It is taken to the top of the furnace by skips and emptied continuously into the double bell arrangement. This valve system prevents heat loss.

Heated air is blasted into the bottom of the furnace from the bustle pipes through the tuyères, the oxygen making the coke burn fiercely. The limestone starts to decompose and the iron and impurities begin to separate. This is called '**reduction**'.

The limestone absorbs the impurities into a molten waste called **slag**. The heavy liquid falls to the bottom of the hearth, while the lighter slag floats on top.

Periodically, the slag and iron are tapped off separately. The slag which is run off first is used for ballast and road making. The waste gases are collected and passed through a cleaning plant before being used to pre-heat the blast. The process runs continuously for years, stopping only when the fire-brick lining needs replacing.

From the blast furnace, the molten iron is used in one of two ways. It is either fed into a casting machine, producing small bars of iron termed 'pigs', known collectively as 'pig-iron', for future resmelting in an electric arc furnace or refining into cast iron or, in the modern integrated steelworks, it is conveyed in molten state by brick lined steel ladles, straight to the steel-making furnace.

The pig iron produced has a carbon content of about 3–4% together with small quantities of impurities.

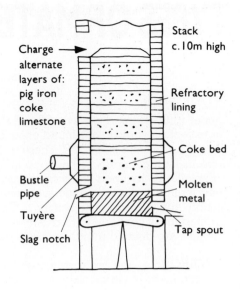

fig 4.56. Section of a cupola furnace

Cast iron

This is produced by smelting selected pig iron and scrap iron in a much smaller furnace called a **'cupola'** (fig 4.56). This process refines the iron by reducing the amount of carbon and controls other elements, especially phosphorus, sulphur and silicon. It is cast into specially constructed sand moulds formed from wooden patterns.

Cast iron can differ widely in its properties and uses. White cast irons are hard and brittle and used in crushing machines. Grey cast iron is used in most of the cast shapes and includes lathe beds and wood vices. (Wrought iron, previously produced by puddling in a reverberatory furnace, has been almost totally replaced by steel).

The production of steel

To make steel, the carbon content of pig iron is reduced from over 3% to less than 1.5% and often to below 0.25% in the case of mild steel. Other impurities are removed and small amounts of other elements are added.

A great deal of reorganisation has been undertaken in British steel making in recent years. Basic production is concentrated in about five main plants, which use the basic oxygen process to produce 14 million tonnes annually. An alternative process uses the electric arc furnace to produce special alloy steels and much of this is based in Sheffield.

The basic oxygen furnace

This is the principal production method and is used for making large tonnages. The furnace is tilted and charged with molten iron, from the blast furnace, and up to 30% scrap metal. It is then brought to a vertical position.

A water cooled oxygen lance is lowered to just above the surface of the metal ready for the blow. This consists of blowing oxygen into the melt at high speed to combine with the carbon and other unwanted elements. During the blow, lime is added as a flux, so that the impurities form a slag on the surface. Once the steel has been checked it is tapped out into ladles.

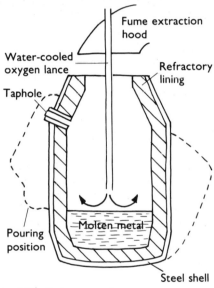

fig 4.57. Basic oxygen furnace

The electric arc furnace

This process produces high quality or high 'alloy' steels in the furnace illustrated in fig 4.58. The charge, pig-iron of known composition and selected scrap, is placed in the shallow refractory lined bath and carbon electrodes are lowered through the lid. Powerful arcs are struck between the electrodes and the metal, producing high temperatures (over 3000°C) to melt the metal. Lime and other deoxidisers are used to remove the impurities in the form of slag, which is poured off through the surface door by tilting. Alloying elements are added and samples analysed before it is tapped into a ladle.

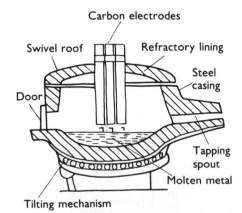

fig 4.58. Electric arc furnace

Alloy-steels

The properties of steels, including hardness, can be increased by alloying them with other metals, i.e. **chromium**, **tungsten**, **nickel** and **vanadium**. Compared with carbon

steels which lose their hardness at high temperatures, **high speed steels** maintain their hardness and cutting edge even at red heat and are used for such things as milling cutters and drills.

Other improved qualities, such as resistance to corrosion are evident in stainless steel, which contains 12% chromium and some nickel.

Converting the steel

Once the molten steel is produced it is shaped for use in one of three ways.

1. It may be poured directly into sand moulds to make steel castings.
2. It may be cast into ingots and allowed to solidify. The red hot ingots are then passed between rollers to make square blooms or flat slabs, billets and heavy girder sections, or forged into shape by hammering or pressing.

   Standard forms are produced by passing the reheated large billets through finishing rolling mills to form flat bars, strips, tubes, rods, wire and also sections (angles, tees and channels) (see fig 4.59).
3. It may be poured directly into a continuous casting machine to produce billets, blooms and slabs then water cooled and cut to length. This method aims to increase efficiency and reduce production costs.

The result of rolling steel when hot, is a black oxide finish. **Black mild steel** as it is called, is generally used for forging.

To produce a bright finish and make accurate sizes, the steel is cleaned, oiled and re-rolled cold. The bright steel is then drawn through graded dies to make the accurately shaped, **bright drawn mild steel** used in the workshop.

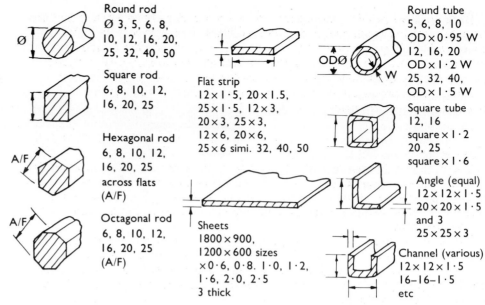

Round rod
Ø 3, 5, 6, 8, 10, 12, 16, 20, 25, 32, 40, 50

Square rod
6, 8, 10, 12, 16, 20, 25

Hexagonal rod
6, 8, 10, 12, 16, 20, 25
across flats (A/F)

Octagonal rod
6, 8, 10, 12, 16, 20, 25 (A/F)

Flat strip
12 × 1.5, 20 × 1.5, 25 × 1.5, 12 × 3, 20 × 3, 25 × 3, 12 × 6, 20 × 6, 25 × 6 simi. 32, 40, 50

Sheets
1800 × 900, 1200 × 600 sizes × 0·6, 0·8. 1·0, 1·2, 1·6, 2·0, 2·5 3 thick

Round tube
5, 6, 8, 10 OD × 0·95 W 12, 16, 20 OD × 1·2 W 25, 32, 40, OD × 1·5 W

Square tube
12, 16 square × 1·2 20, 25 square × 1·6

Angle (equal)
12 × 12 × 1·5 20 × 20 × 1·5 and 3 25 × 25 × 3

Channel (various)
12 × 12 × 1·5 16–16–1·5 etc

fig 4.59. Commonly available forms and sizes of metal

THE PRODUCTION OF NON-FERROUS METALS

Aluminium
This is the most plentiful metal in the earth's crust. The increasing demand for lightness and strength has also now made it by far the largest, in terms of production output, in this group.

The only commercial source is **bauxite**, a hydrated form of aluminium which is found in the USA, France, Guyana, Australia and parts of Africa. Unfortunately it is difficult to decompose and no cheap chemical is available for reduction purposes. Therefore, an expensive **electrolytic process** is needed for production, which consumes large quantities of electrical energy.

As much as 5 times more electrical energy is needed to produce 1 tonne of aluminium compared with that required to produce 1 tonne of steel.

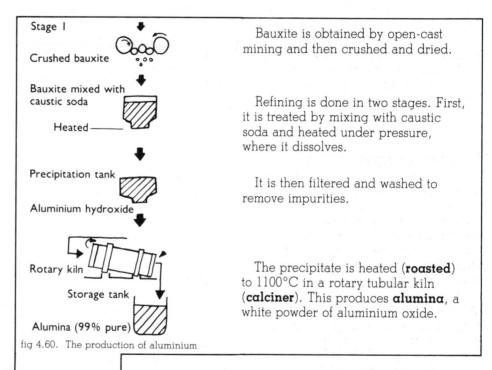

Stage 1

Crushed bauxite

Bauxite mixed with caustic soda

Heated

Precipitation tank

Aluminium hydroxide

Rotary kiln

Storage tank

Alumina (99% pure)

Bauxite is obtained by open-cast mining and then crushed and dried.

Refining is done in two stages. First, it is treated by mixing with caustic soda and heated under pressure, where it dissolves.

It is then filtered and washed to remove impurities.

The precipitate is heated (**roasted**) to 1100°C in a rotary tubular kiln (**calciner**). This produces **alumina**, a white powder of aluminium oxide.

fig 4.60. The production of aluminium

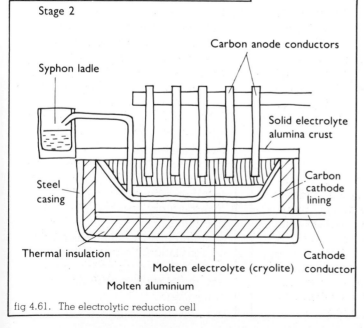

Stage 2

Syphon ladle

Carbon anode conductors

Solid electrolyte alumina crust

Steel casing

Carbon cathode lining

Thermal insulation

Molten electrolyte (cryolite)

Cathode conductor

Molten aluminium

fig 4.61. The electrolytic reduction cell

The reduction of alumina to oxygen and aluminium is achieved by an electrolytic process.

The reduction cell consists of a shallow steel box with a carbon lining which acts as the negative electrode. Suspended above the box are a number of carbon rods which act as anodes. Mixing with **molten cryolite** reduces the melting point and dissolves the alumina.

A powerful electric current is passed though the mixture causing aluminium to be liberated. It then sinks and is deposited on the carbon lining of the furnace. Periodically the very pure (99%) aluminium is syphoned off and cast into ingots for further processing and shaping.

In order to improve the properties of hardness and strength, a large proportion of this pure metal is used in alloyed forms containing other metals (e.g. copper, manganese and magnesium). Like steel, it is available in a variety of forms (see fig 4.59).

The production of copper

The use of this ancient metallic material pre-dates the Bronze age. Due to scarcity and high production costs, it has been overtaken by aluminium in terms of world output and is now ranked in third place after iron and aluminium.

In the past copper was mined and smelted in Wales, but today USA, Chile, Canada, Zambia and USSR, are the leading producers.

Ores usually contain less than 4% copper. One of the most common ores is **chalcopyrite**.

Other useful metals include:

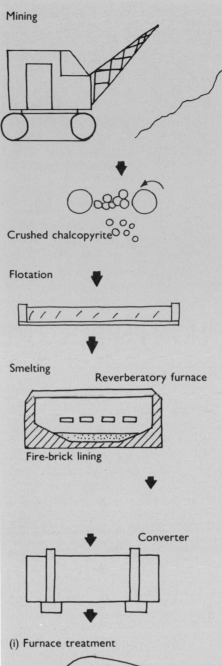

Mining

Crushed chalcopyrite

Flotation

Smelting

Reverberatory furnace

Fire-brick lining

Converter

(i) Furnace treatment

Poling

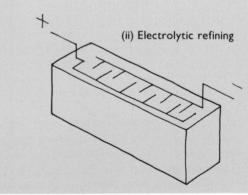

(ii) Electrolytic refining

fig 4.62. The production of copper

After open cast or deep shaft mining, the ore is converted into a more concentrated form by crushing.

The concentrate is then separated by **flotation**, a process used in the treatment of metal ores where the grains of copper are carried in a froth on the surface of the liquid, and the rock particles sink.

The resulting copper concentrate is smelted in a **reverbatory furnace** and lime is added as a flux. The impurities form a slag which is then tapped off.

The mixture or 'matte' of copper and iron sulphides is taken to a **converter** to remove the iron and sulphur. The blister copper is cast into cakes or slabs.

The copper is finally refined by one of two processes.
1. Remelting or **fire refining** in a furnace where the charge is melted and the impurities oxidised and lost as a slag. This is followed by a 'poling' operation in which poles of green timber are used to remove oxygen by combustion.
2. **Electrolytic refining** in which lead lined tanks are filled with a mixture of copper sulphate and sulphuric acid. Thick slabs of pure copper act as anodes. These are interleaved with cathode starter sheets (thin copper) on to which the refined copper is deposited. The impurities containing small quantities of gold and silver are deposited at the bottom of the bath.

Lead
Ore: galena
Lead ores are closely associated with zinc and usually smelted at the same time. Smelting takes place in a blast furnace, using limestone as a reducing agent.

Molten lead is poured through a layer of molten zinc, the impurities remaining with the zinc in the form of slag.

Zinc
Ore: zinc blonde
Zinc blonde is crushed and then concentrated by flotation, before being smelted in a blast furnace. Zinc is removed as a vapour and condensed when in contact with molten lead.

A very pure form is obtained by electrolysis.

Tin
Ore: cassiterite
Cassiterite is crushed, washed and then roasted, before being smelted in either a blast furnace or a reverberatory furnace. The tin is cast into slabs.

Refining is by either electrolysis or liquidation, because the melting point is influenced by impurities and therefore temperature controlled.

METALLIC STRUCTURE

To help in understanding the behaviour of materials, it is necessary to look at their physical make up or structure.

An **atom** is the smallest part into which an element can be divided and still retain the chemical properties of that element. The atoms of all elements have the same basic structure and differ mainly in size and weight. The nucleus or centre of an atom consists of an association of protons and neutrons. Orbiting around the nucleus are light particles with a negative electrical charge known as **electrons** (see fig 4.63). It is the electrons which largely determine how an element behaves, both physically and chemically.

All atoms and molecules are attracted to one another by electrical forces. Material is held together by the positively charged nucleus and negatively charged electrons.

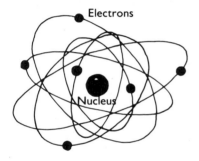

fig 4.63. The atom is rather like a solar system

Metallic bonding

Metals usually have only one or two electrons attached very loosely in their outer electron shell. Unlike non-metals which are bound more strongly, these electrons come off fairly easily.

The metal crystal exists as a regular arrangement of positive ions immersed in a cloud of free moving electrons which latch on to any atom for a short time. The crystals are held together by the electrostatic attraction between the cloud of negative electrons and positive ions (fig 4.66).

It is this free movement of electrons which gives metals their high thermal and electrical conductivity. This mobility also gives rise to plasticity in metals in terms of malleability and ductility. As soon as a bond between ions is broken another is formed.

Key • Sodium electron
× Fluorine electron
Transferred electron

Sodium cation   After transfer   Fluorine anion
Na+   F−

fig 4.64. Ionic transfer

Hydrocarbon (e.g. Methane)

Key • Carbon electron
× Hydrogen electron

fig 4.65. Covalent bonding

Positively charged ions

Negatively charged electron cloud

fig 4.66. Metallic bonding

Arrangement of atoms

fig 4.67. Face centred cubic (FCC) structure

Ionic bonding

This is achieved after the metallic atom donates its outer shell electron(s) to fill the outer shell of a non-metallic atom (fig 4.64).

An electrically charged atom is known as an ion. Forces attracting the positive and negative ions are termed ionic bonds, which form the building blocks of some crystal structures.

Covalent bonding

A covalent bond is a different type of bond used to hold many types of non-metallic materials together (e.g. sand and organic materials, such as wood, oil and natural gas (fig 4.65)).

It is structurally more complex with atoms sharing some of their outer electrons, but they are not electrically charged.

Crystal (lattice) structures

All metals, with the exception of mercury, are solid at normal atmospheric temperatures. In their molten or liquid form, the atoms of metals are highly energised and move around at random.

When the atoms solidify or 'freeze', they adopt a regular structure. They group together and pack closely in regular geometric patterns or **crystal lattice**.

Most metals crystallise into one of three basic types of lattice. The basic unit cells which make up each lattice are illustrated in fig 4.68.

Iron* is an important metal because it changes from a BCC structure to one which is FCC when heated to 910°C. Taken beyond 1400°C it reverts to BCC once more. When cooled, the changes take place in reverse. It also absorbs carbon in the FCC form, an important factor in steel making.

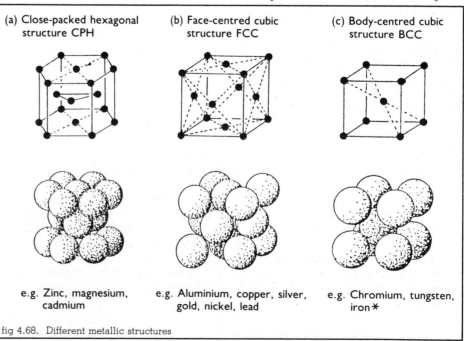

(a) Close-packed hexagonal structure CPH

(b) Face-centred cubic structure FCC

(c) Body-centred cubic structure BCC

e.g. Zinc, magnesium, cadmium

e.g. Aluminium, copper, silver, gold, nickel, lead

e.g. Chromium, tungsten, iron*

fig 4.68. Different metallic structures

fig 4.69. Quartz crystals

Crystallisation

A crystal is simply a substance with an organised structure. Familiar crystalline structures include gemstones (e.g. rubies) or rocks (e.g. quartz) (see fig 4.69). Other materials also include graphite (pencil lead) and plastic such as nylon or polypropylene. All true solids are crystalline in nature. However, glass, which might at first be thought of as crystalline is, in fact, 'amorphous'. This is where the atoms or molecules are distributed in an arbitrary, jumbled way.

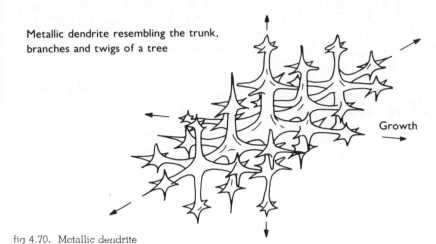
Metallic dendrite resembling the trunk, branches and twigs of a tree

Growth

fig 4.70. Metallic dendrite

Pure metals solidify at a fixed temperature and begin with the formation of minute **seed crystals** or **nuclei**. These form when energy is lost and are simple units, either basic unit cube or hexagonal structures (fig 4.67).

The cell units begin to grow in all directions, forming small, skeletal crystals called **dendrites** which are tree-like growths (fig 4.70). Each dendrite continues to develop independently until contact is made with neighbouring growths.

Finally small crystals or **grains** are formed as the atoms between the arms of individual dendrites become attached to the structures. Dendrite growth always causes irregularities or misfits at the grain boundaries because of the different orientation of the original nuclei.

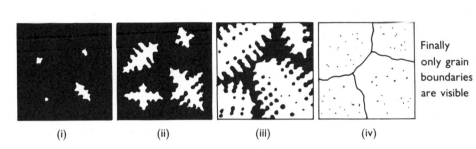
(i) (ii) (iii) (iv)

Finally only grain boundaries are visible

fig 4.71. Solidification of metal

fig 4.72. Crystalline structure of zinc

Zinc clearly shows the crystalline nature of the material (fig 4.72). However, some crystals are so small that they need to be examined under a microscope. Specimens can be prepared by polishing a flat surface and then etching with dilute acid. Only the crystal boundaries will be visible because, in the case of pure metals, all atoms are similar. The presence of impurities also helps to reveal the pattern.

Deformation of metals

The physical properties of a metal depend not only on the crystal and grain structures, but also on the presence and concentration of defects within the grains. These flaws or faults, caused by interruptions in the pattern, are called **dislocations**.

Atoms can be completely missing or misaligned. Experiments with ball-bearings in an acrylic tray show how atoms pack with the formation of grain boundaries and dislocations (fig 4.73).

Applying force or mechanical stress near a dislocation causes the atoms to slip and resettle into a more regular position. Balanced and stable bonds are formed which make the metal harder and stronger.

The grain boundaries form natural barriers which prevent further change or movement without fracture. The metal has now become hard and brittle. Introducing changes by applying stress is known as '**work hardening**'.

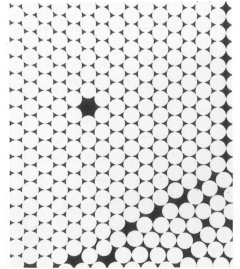 
fig 4.73. Dislocations in the crystal lattice

HEAT TREATMENT

Heat treatment is the term given to the process of heating and cooling metal in a controlled manner, to alter its properties in order to obtain certain desired characteristics. From our knowledge of the structure of metals, we learn that the properties which occur at the grain boundaries are different from those within the grains. At low temperatures the reverse is true. Therefore, to obtain maximum strength, fine grains with many boundaries are needed for low temperature work, and large grains with fewer boundaries for work at higher temperatures. The rate of cooling also controls the size of grains, giving rise to a weak or strong metal.

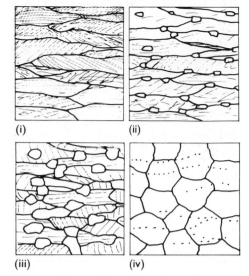

(i)   Metal after cold rolling
(ii)   Recrystallisation has started, new seed crystal forming
(iii) Growth by absorbing old crystals
(iv) Recrystallisation is complete

fig 4.75. Recrystallisation stages during the annealing process

ANNEALING

When the structure has been deformed by **cold working** (hammering, bending and rolling), work hardening results. Before further work can take place, there must be some restoration of the crystal structure.

The introduction of heat energy during the annealing process allows sufficient mobility of the atoms, so that dissipation of the strain energy can take place. This relief of internal stress takes place at relatively low temperatures.

However, most annealing involves complete recrystallisation of the distorted structure. As the temperature increases, a point is reached where new crystals begin to grow. Grain growth and ultimately grain size depends on the length of time and the temperature of the treatment.

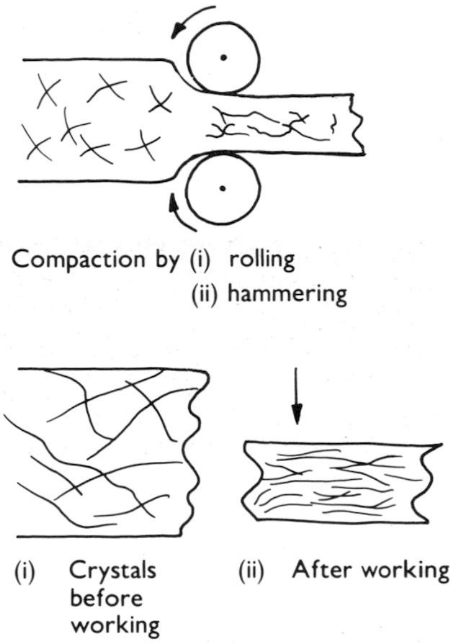

Ferrous metals

Bright steels need to be annealed before or after working. This involves heating the metal (fig 4.76) to **bright cherry red** (about 725°C), retaining the temperature for the required length of time (**soaking**) and then allowing it to cool very slowly. This may be achieved by leaving it in a dying fire or placing it in sand to retain the heat. Large, coarse grains are formed which gives the metal a soft, workable quality.

Compaction by (i) rolling
               (ii) hammering

(i)   Crystals before working   (ii)   After working

fig 4.74. Work hardening

Hot metal left to cool should be clearly marked with a warning notice.

Non-ferrous metals

Aluminium is first rubbed with soap because of the danger of overheating due to its low melting point (660°C). It is then **heated gently** until the soap blackens (about 350–400°C) and left to cool.

Copper is heated to **dull red heat** (500°C) and is then either quenched in water or allowed to cool in air.

Brass is heated to **dull red heat** and allowed to cool slowly.

Both copper and brass form scales when heated. These can be cleaned off chemically by placing the cooled metal in a bath of dilute sulphuric acid. After 'pickling', the metal is removed with tongs and washed carefully in water (fig 4.77).

An alternative would be to clean off the scale **mechanically** by rubbing with pumice powder and steel wool.

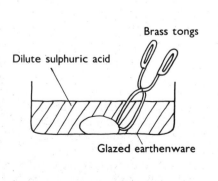

Brass tongs
Dilute sulphuric acid
Glazed earthenware

fig 4.77. Pickling

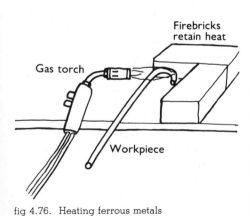

Firebricks retain heat
Gas torch
Workpiece

fig 4.76. Heating ferrous metals

NORMALISING

This process is confined to steel. It is used to refine the grain of a steel which has become coarse-grained through forging or work-hardening. Refining the grain improves its ductility and toughness. This entails heating the steel to just above its upper critical point (see fig 4.78). After a short period of soaking, it is allowed to cool in still air. Small, fine grains are formed which give a much harder and tougher metal.

Normal tensile strength results, and not the maximum softness achieved by annealing.

HARDENING

The physical properties of steel vary considerably, depending upon the amount of carbon present with the iron. It exists in a number of forms. Steel made up of pearlite gives maximum strength with good hardness. Cutting tools are made from this range of steels.

As well as cutting itself in its softer forms, steel is used to cut other metals and a wide range of other materials. It has to undergo changes to make this possible including hardening.

To obtain maximum hardness together with the smallest grain size, the steel must be heated uniformly, heating to just over 720°C for steels with 0.87% or more carbon, and to just above the upper critical point for steels with less than this amount (see fig 4.78).

It is retained or soaked at that temperature long enough for the whole mass of metal to change into austenite. If it is quenched immediately in water it becomes very hard and brittle.

The structure of the iron has changed back to BCC (from FCC in austenite) before the carbon has time to escape. In this frozen state the metal is called **martensite**.

In order to prevent cracking and to minimise distortion, quenching should be done vertically (see fig 4.79) in cold water, or brine (salt water) for heavier sections or plain carbon steel, or in oil in the case of most alloy steels.

If quenching is less fierce or delayed, the complete transformation to martensite does not take place.

The degree of hardness depends upon the amount of carbon present in the steel and the form in which it is trapped on quenching.

The full hardening effects are only possible in steels with a carbon content above 0.8%. Such steels are known as high carbon or plain carbon steels.

With mild steels below 0.4% in carbon content, no noticeable change takes place, and they cannot be hardened in this way.

Between the two are the medium carbon steels which gain a degree of toughness rather than hardness.

Ferrite — a solid solution in (BCC) iron which is soft and ductile.

Cementite — a chemical combination called iron carbide which is hard and brittle.

Pearlite — made up of alternative layers of ferrite and cementite with 0.87% carbon, and very strong.

Austenite — a solution of carbon in (FCC) iron with a maximum content of 1.7% carbon. Soft, it normally only exists at about 700°C.

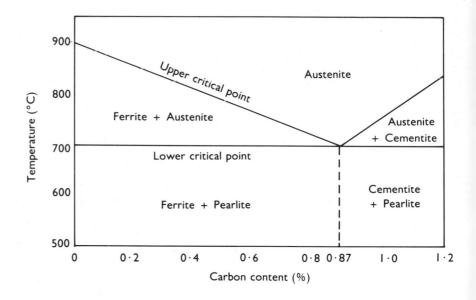

fig 4.78. Heat treatment of steel

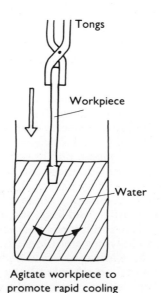

Agitate workpiece to promote rapid cooling

fig 4.79. Quenching

SAFETY
If oil is used for quenching there is a danger of firing the oil. Therefore, use only oil which has a high flash point.

TEMPERING

After hardening, the metal is very hard and capable of resisting wear when cutting other metals. It is also brittle and will break under load. By reducing the hardness slightly, a more elastic, tougher material that will still maintain a cutting edge is produced. The process by which this is achieved is called tempering.

In the workshop this is done by cleaning the hardened steel to brightness with emery cloth so that the colour of the oxide will be seen.

The work is raised to 230–300°C depending on the tool or article used. For example, a lathe tool subject to steady pressure can be left harder than a chisel receiving intermittent blows or a screwdriver which has to withstand torque stresses (see fig 4.80).

If bright steel is heated well behind the cutting edge by a gas/air torch (fig 4.81) coloured oxides develop. These range from pale straw, changing to darker brown, then through shades of purple and finally to blue.

As the temperature rises, both the brittleness and hardness are reduced. When the desired colour reaches the tip, it is quenched in cold water.

In industry, temperature controlled ovens are used which make quenching unnecessary.

Colour	Hardest	Approx temp (°C)	Uses
Pale straw	Hardest	230	Lathe tools, scrapers, scribers
Straw		240	Drills, milling cutters
Dark straw		250	Taps and dies, punches, reamers
Brown		260	Plane irons, shears, lathe centres
Brown-purple		270	Scissors, press tools, knives
Purple		280	Cold chisels, axes, saws
Dark purple		290	Screwdrivers, chuck keys
Blue	Toughest	300	Springs, spanners, needles

fig 4.80. Tempering guide table

CASE HARDENING

Mild steels which do not contain sufficient carbon to enable them to be hardened can be given a hard skin or case by heating in a carbon-rich material (fig 4.82).

The metal is heated to **cherry red** and dipped in **carbon powder**, then reheated and dipped two or three times more, increasing the degree of hardness. Finally, it is reheated to cherry red then quenched in water, which hardens the skin.

Superficial case-hardening is used where only the surface is subject to wear and a soft core is needed to withstand sudden shocks (e.g. tool holders, and equipment generally).

Another process called **carburising**, involves placing the mild steel specimen in a box packed with charcoal granules (fig 4.83).

The lid is sealed and the box is heated in an oven to 950°C and soaked for several hours. The outer skin thickens and becomes hard, but the inner core remains soft.

The carburising method also permits a degree of normal hardening and tempering to be carried out.

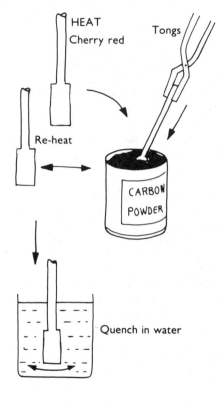

fig 4.82. Case hardening

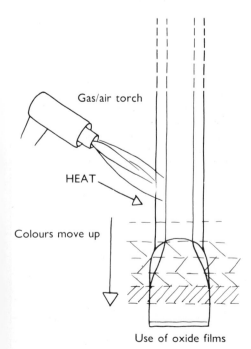

Use of oxide films

fig 4.81. Tempering a cold chisel

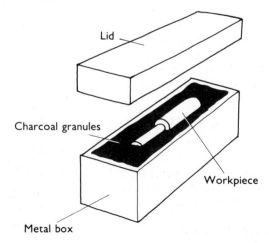

fig 4.83. Carburising

TABLE OF METALS

(a) Ferrous metals

NAME AND MELTING POINT	COMPOSITION	PROPERTIES AND WORKING CHARACTERISTICS	USES	
Cast iron 1200°C	Iron + 3.5% carbon wide range of alloys white, grey and malleable forms	Hard skin, brittle soft core, strong under compression, self lubrication cannot be bent or forged	Heavy crushing machinery Car brake drums or discs Vices or machine parts	●
Steel Mild steel 1600°C	Alloys of iron and carbon 0.15–0.35% carbon	Tough, ductile and malleable, high tensile strength, easily joined, welded, poor resistance to corrosion, cannot be hardened and tempered, general purpose material	Nails, screws, nuts and bolts Girders Car bodies	●●●
Medium carbon steel	0.4–0.7% carbon	Strong and hard, but less ductile, tough or malleable	Garden tools (trowel, fork) Springs Rails	●●
High carbon steel (silversteel) 1800°C	0.8–1.5%	Very hard, but less ductile, tough or malleable, difficult to cut, easily joined by heat treatment, strength decreases above 0.9% carbon	Hand tools (hammers, chisels, screwdrivers, punches)	●●
Alloy steels Stainless steel	Alloys 18% chromium 8% nickel 8% magnesium	Hard and tough, resists wear, corrosion resistant, different forms affect malleability (types 18/8), difficult to cut or file	Sinks Cutlery Dishes, teapot	●
High speed steel	Medium carbon steel + tungsten + chromium + vanadium	Very hard, resistant to frictional heat even at red heat, it can only be ground	Lathe cutting tools Drills Milling cutters	●
High tensile steel	Low carbon steel + nickel	Corrosion resistant, low rate of expansion, exceptional strength and toughness	Gears/engine valves Turbine blades	●
Manganese steel	1.5% manganese	Extreme toughness	Chains Hooks and couplings	●

(b) Non-ferrous metals and their alloys

NAME AND MELTING POINT	COMPOSITION	PROPERTIES AND WORKING CHARACTERISTICS	USES
Aluminium 660°C	Pure metal	High strength/weight ratio, light, soft and ductile (FCC), work hardens in cold state, annealing necessary, difficult to join, non-toxic, good conductor of heat and electricity, corrosion resistant, polishes well	Kitchen cooking utensils (pans) Packaging, cans, foil Window frames
Casting alloy (LM 4) (LM 6)	3% copper 5% silicon 12% silicon	Casts well, sand and die casting, good machineability, tougher and harder, increased fluidity	Engine components, cylinder heads
Duralumin	4% copper 1% manganese + magnesium	Almost the strength of mild steel but only 30% of the weight, hardens with age, machines well after annealing	Aircraft structure
Copper (Cu) 1083°C	Pure metal	Malleable, ductile (FCC), tough, suitable for hot and cold working, good conductor for heat and electricity, corrosion resistant, easily joined, solders and brazes well, polishes well, rather expensive,	Hot water storage cylinders Central heating pipes/tubing Wire electrical Copper clad board (circuits)
Copper alloys Guilding metal	15% zinc	Stronger, golden colour, enamels, easily joined	Architectural metalwork Jewellery
Brass 900–1000°C	35% zinc	Corrosion resistant, increased hardness, casts well, work hardens, easily joined, good conductor of heat and electricity, polishes well	Castings (e.g. valves) Boat fittings Ornaments
Bronze 900–1000°C	10% tin	Strong and tough, good wearing qualities, corrosion resistant	Statues Coins Bearings
Tin (Sn) 232°C	Pure metal	Soft and weak, ductile and malleable, excellent resistance to corrosion even when damp, low melting point	Bearing metals Solder
Tin plate	Steel plate tin coated	Bends with mild steel core, non-toxic	Tin cans
Lead (Pb) 327°C	Pure metal	Very heavy, soft, malleable and ductile but weak, corrosion resistant, even by acid, low melting point, casts well, electrical properties	Roof coverings — flashings Plumbing Insulation against radiation
Zinc (Zn) 419°C	Pure metal	Very weak, poor strength/weight ratio, extremely resistant to atmospheric corrosion, low melting point, ductile (cph) but difficult to work, expensive	Galvanised steel, dustbins Corrugated iron sheet roof Die casting alloys and rust proof paints

TYPES OF MATERIAL — WOOD

Wood is one of the most adaptable and versatile of materials. It has been used for almost every conceivable purpose, as fuel for fires, weapons for protection and hunting, tools, utensils and even footwear.

Structural uses for housing show a remarkable range including crude shelters, large sophisticated Japanese temples (fig 4.84), to the mass produced timber framed units of today.

The first machines including clocks and windmills (fig 4.85) were made in this material. In terms of transportation, wood has seen a wide divergence of use (e.g. carts, wagons, canoes and ships). Throughout history human needs have been met by perfecting ways of working this material.

fig 4.84. Horyuji temple

fig 4.86. Crook barn

Original oak beams and rafters are still to be found in the roofs of many old buildings (fig 4.86). However, it is perhaps in the realm of furniture, that we most associate this material. Locally grown woods such as beech, elm, ash, apple, cherry and oak were used in furniture making as well as for many other country crafts (e.g. hurdle making, basket weaving).

fig 4.85. Wooden windmill

The **Windsor chair** (fig 4.87) first produced in quantity around Buckinghamshire, best summarises the diverse nature of the material. Elm is used for the seat, ash for the bent bows, arms and back and beech for the turned legs and sticks.

Fashionable timbers were also imported and gave rise to distinctive designs of style and elegance which contributed to a golden age of furniture making in the eighteenth century.

The Victorian period (1830–1900) saw the introduction of new materials and new ways of working as machinery was introduced to meet increasing demands.

fig 4.87. Windsor chair

By contrast, the amount of solid wood used in today's furniture industry is small in comparison to that of machine-made timber. Nevertheless, it still holds its own against newer timber as better ways of using it, as well as improved fabrication techniques continue to be developed. This is illustrated in fig 4.88 by the structural use of laminated timber for building purposes.

fig 4.88. Laminated timber for building purposes

The changing conditions of supply and demand continue to affect this important resource. The problem has been partially met by schemes of reafforestation, undertaken on world-wide scale, in order to safeguard future supplies.

Forests are one of the few natural resources capable of self-renewal within a short period of time. Their importance in converting carbon dioxide into oxygen, preventing soil erosion, providing habitat for wildlife and recreational areas of outstanding natural beauty is undeniable. Nevertheless, vast areas of forest continue to be destroyed at an alarming rate in order to provide roads and industrial development.

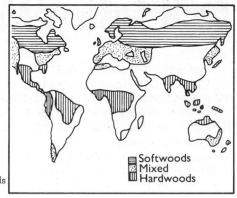

fig 4.92. Distribution zones of hardwoods and softwoods

fig 4.89. Broadleaf woodland

Britain is one of the least wooded countries in Europe. In spite of the work of the forestry commission, Britain still imports 90% of its timber needs. Even with recent replanting of mainly fast growing soft woods, there remains both a commercial and environmental need to improve and extend our derelict broadleafed woodland (fig 4.89).

Not only does the tree have a beauty which is uniquely its own, but it can also provide a beautiful material with which to work. Each tree provides timber peculiar to its own species. The characteristics include colour, grain pattern, texture, strength, weight, stability, workability and durability.

It is necessary to find out as much as possible about wood, its structure, properties and characteristics in order to meet your particular needs before selecting one from the choice of hundreds available. Only then can the technical restraints imposed by grain patterns be appreciated and harnessed to make individual pieces.

TREES

Trees are the most highly developed plants and are made up of an immense number of minute cells. They are mainly composed of **cellulose**. Certain changes take place in the cells as they age, some form the wood of the tree. This thickening and hardening of the cell walls is known as **lignification**.

Although wood is a **cellular structure**, the cells are not all alike, and vary considerably in number, form and function. It is this variation which enables timbers to be identified and distinguished from one another by timber technologists.

Trees can be designated into one of two groups.

1. **ENDOGENS** (monocotyledon) are trees where most of the growth takes place inwardly in a hollow stem (e.g. bamboo, palms, yucca and tree ferns).
This group has little or no commercial value.

2. **EXOGENS** (dicotyledons) are outward growing and increase in size by adding new tissue in each growing season in the form of individual layers of concentric growth rings.
The valuable exogens are divided into two classes: angiosperms, better known as deciduous, and gymnospersms, better known as coniferous.

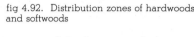

Fruit acorn

fig 4.90. English Oak (deciduous)

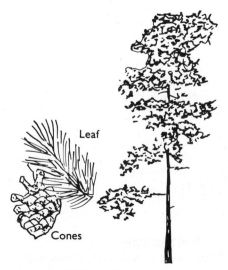

Leaf

Cones

fig 4.91. Scots Pine (coniferous)

Broadleaf or deciduous trees

Deciduous (meaning leaf losing) trees (fig 4.90) have broad leaves and covered seeds, often enclosed in fruits or nuts (e.g. apple, acorn).

Although commonly called **hardwood**, this is a botanical division and not always a true guide to softness or texture. Some hardwoods (e.g. balsa) are notably lighter in weight and softer than yew or pitch pine (classified as softwoods).

Broadleaf trees grow in warm, temperature climates (fig 4.92) such as Europe (British Isles), Japan, New Zealand and Chile, as well as in the tropical and sub-tropical regions of central and south America, Africa and Asia.

They are generally slow growing, often taking 100 years to reach maturity and are, therefore, expensive.

Although most deciduous trees shed their leaves annually, hardwoods such as holly and laurel are evergreen. The tropical hardwoods keep their leaves all year and tend to grow more quickly and to a greater scale.

Coniferous trees

Coniferous (meaning cone bearing) trees (fig 4.91) are commonly classified as **softwoods**. They have thin, needle-like leaves and are usually evergreen. (Exception: larch).

They grow in the colder temperate climates (fig 4.92) of Scandinavia, Canada, Northern Russia and at high altitudes in Europe and elsewhere.

Growth is quick, maturity is reached in about 30 years, making them relatively cheap and commercial.

GROWTH AND STRUCTURE

Although hardwoods and softwoods have different types of cell and differ in formation of tissue, their growth and overall structure are sufficiently similar to allow a combined study of how a tree grows.

Fig 4.93 shows the structure of a typical tree, together with a cross-section of the trunk. The function of each labelled part is given below.

Roots

The root structure begins to grow as the seed sprouts and continues to develop through the sapling stage.

Roots serve two basic purposes:

1. Root hairs absorb water and dissolve mineral salts to make crude sap.
2. They support and anchor the tree.

Sapwood

Sapwood is the newly formed wood made up of **xylem** cells. Sap water and mineral salts are carried through these cells up the tree by suction pressure to the leaves, where they are manufactured into food.

Often light in colour and quite soft, it is least resistant to decay and is prone to attack by insects and fungi.

In the young tree, all the stem and branches are required for conveying sap, but as the girth of the trunk increases the proportion of sapwood becomes progressively smaller.

Heartwood

Heartwood was once sapwood, which has matured and become inactive. Heartwood is made up of lignified (hardened) cells which serve to give strength and support the tree and provide storage for waste products such as resin.

It is much harder, stronger and often darker in colour than sapwood, and provides the most commercially useful part of the tree.

Pith or (medulla)

The pith is the centre of the trunk. It is the remains of the earliest growth of the sapling and is often soft. It is to be found throughout the length of the tree, forming in the crown or leading shoot as it extends upwards.

Medullary rays

These thin sheets of tissue or rays extend from the cambium to the pith (medulla) like the spokes of a wheel. They conduct and distribute waste products horizontally for storage, in the mature cells. They vary considerably in thickness and visibility, forming figure or silver grain, in oak.

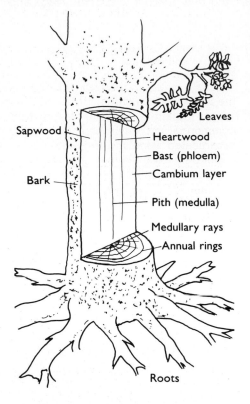

fig 4.93a. Structure of a tree

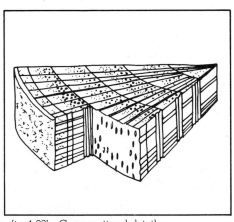

fig 4.93b. Cross-sectional detail

Annual rings

These are commonly called growth rings, because they represent one season's growth. Each ring or band is made up of two distinct layers, the spring wood and the summer wood. The inner most spring wood consists of large, soft, thin-walled cells which help the flow of sap. In summer, with less sap, the cells are smaller, thicker walled and more dense. It is this density which often accounts for darker variations in colour and texture. Viewed in cross-section, this growth cycle gives distinctive bands, by which the age of the tree can easily be determined.

By contrast, some tropical timbers show no visible annual rings because growth takes place uniformly throughout the year.

Cell structure

Wood cells vary in size, shape and function. This permits a botanical distinction to be made between hardwoods and softwoods based on the arrangements and type of cells.

Leaves

Leaves take in carbon dioxide from the atmosphere and sunlight is absorbed by the **chlorophyll** (green pigment) in the leaves. The energy from the sun is used to synthesise organic compounds (in the form of sugars and starches) from carbon dioxide and water. This complex chemical reaction is known as **photosynthesis**.

The leaf surface has tiny vents or pores (**stomata**). Oxygen and carbon dioxide enter and leave through the stomata, and water vapour is also lost through the stomata, a process known as **transpiration**.

During daylight hours, when photosynthesis is taking place, carbon dioxide is absorbed and any excess oxygen is expelled.

At night when photosynthesis stops, excess carbon dioxide is expired through the stomata. In this way trees help to maintain the delicate balance of oxygen and carbon dioxide in the atmosphere.

Bark

Bark is a skin or protective coating which prevents transpiratioin from the trunk and serves to protect the tree from damage and the extremes of temperature. It is made from the outer layers of bast or phloem as they die, and expands as the tree grows, with the outer, corky layer becoming hard.

Bast or phloem

Bast or phloem is the inner bark made up of living tissue (**phloem cells**) which carries food in the form of sugars, amino acids to make up proteins, and hormones which control growth. These are mainly carried downwards from the leaves to other parts of the tree.

Cambium layer

This completely surrounds the sapwood and is where growth takes place by cell division. New wood cells (xylem) are formed on the inside and, to a lesser extent, new phloem (bast) cells on the outside.

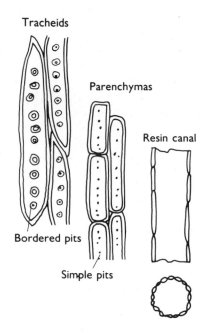

Tracheids

Parenchymas

Resin canal

Bordered pits

Simple pits

fig 4.94. Softwood cells

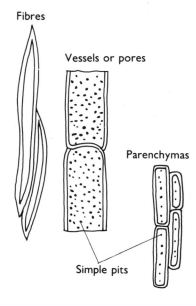

Fibres

Vessels or pores

Parenchymas

Simple pits

fig 4.95. Hardwood cells

Softwood structure is more primitive than hardwood.

The main types of cells are:

Tracheids — these form the bulk of the timber. They are thin, elongated tubes sealed at the ends and spliced together in the direction of growth. Communication between the cells for the passage of sap and food takes place through small openings in the walls known as **pits**.

As they age, the cells harden and serve to support the tree. They form in radial rows and it is the direction in which these cells lie that makes up the grain of the wood.

Parenchymas — smaller than tracheids, with simple type pits, make up the remaining cells. These include rays, which in the case of softwoods are usually thin, only one or two cells thick. Rays are almost invisible, but they are a reliable means of identification between species when magnified.

Resin canals — occur in most conifers and are evidence of the function of the rays, i.e. the means by which resins and gums (waste products) are carried.

Hardwood structure

Fibres — make up the bulk of hardwoods. They correspond to the tracheids in conifers, but they are very much smaller and sharper, giving mechanical support to the tree. However, they do not carry sap and are not arranged in any form of pattern.

Vessels or pores — found only in hardwoods, they provide a positive means of identification. They form ducts or tubes and extend the whole length of the tree carrying food. They are numerous and often clearly visible, and appear in two different forms dividing hardwoods, into two groups:

1. Diffuse porous — when they are evenly spread throughout the tree (e.g. beech, birch, sycamore, limes are typical and the tropical hardwoods, ebony, mahogany).

2. Ring porous — when they appear quite large in the early spring growth and much smaller in the summer growth (e.g. ash, elm and oak).

When the pores are only slightly larger than those produced later, they are called 'semi-ring porous' (e.g. walnut).

Parenchymas — are also found in hardwoods, forming radially in the rays which are often more prominent. In oak especially they can be 20 to 30 cells thick, producing the familiar silver grain.

In some timbers these cells mark the end of each season's growth. Much rarer, in Burma teak, they form at the start of the growth ring.

FELLING

Trees are felled when they reach maturity and this normally takes place in winter, when there is less sap and moisture in the tree. The top and main branches are removed to leave logs which can then be cut to standard lengths to help in transportation.

They are collected together and stacked near road or railway for taking to the saw mill. In some countries (e.g. Canada), a more economic method and one which also avoids rapid drying out is available: the spring tides of flowing rivers are used to float logs downstream for processing (fig 4.97).

fig 4.96. Tree-felling

fig 4.97. Logging

CONVERSION

Conversion is the term given to sawing the log into marketable timber. Many factors affect how this is achieved, such as the type of timber and market requirements, including eventual use. It can also promote features likes grain pattern and figure, and can increase stability in use.

Home grown hardwood is rarely stripped of bark at the sawmill because it helps to protect against drying out too quickly. Most imported timbers are debarked before shipping to avoid insect contamination, and are exported square edged.

Baulks of timber are sometimes produced, which involves removing the unwanted sapwood (fig 4.99). Two basic methods are used in conversion.

fig 4.98. Inside a sawmill

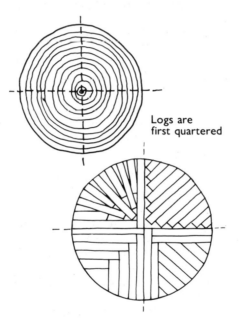

fig 4.99. Saw cuts to form a baulk

Slab, plain or through and through sawn

All these terms refer to the simplest, quickest and cheapest method by which the log is cut into parallel slices or slabs of variable thickness (fig 4.100). This makes handling and seasoning much easier and is used mainly for softwoods.

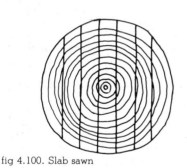

fig 4.100. Slab sawn

fig 4.101. Alternative radial methods

Logs are first quartered

Quarter (radial) sawn

This method involves first sawing the log into quarters and then cutting it again (fig 4.101). It produces excellent quality, stable timber which is less likely to 'move' (expand or contract). However, it is costly in time and sometimes wasteful in material.

Ideally in quarter sawing all the boards should be cut radially, making the annual rings as short as possible and at 90° to the exposed surface of the board. This shows the 'figure' (notably in oak with its silver grain) when the medullary rays are exposed on the surface.

In practice, several near radial methods are used to reduce waste and simplify sawing.

SEASONING

A growing tree contains more than its own dry weight in water. The object of seasoning is to remove excess, unwanted sap and moisture from the timber.

Timber is an **hygroscopic** substance, taking in moisture from a damp atmosphere, but giving up moisture in a dry one. Consequently damp wood shrinks in dry air and dry wood swells in damp air (e.g. doors sticking). Although slightly affected by temperature, wood is considerably influenced by humidity.

If unseasoned **'green' timber** is placed in a room, it twists badly when drying out and any jointing opens up leaving gaps. It is important when seasoning to reduce the moisture content to less than 20%. This has a number of effects.

1. It makes it immune from decay and increases resistance to rot.
2. It increases timber strength and stability.
3. It helps preservatives to penetrate (wet wood does not take finishes easily).
4. It makes timber considerably less corrosive to metals.

Timber should retain some degree of moisture. **Moisture content** is the technical description of the amount of moisture contained in the wood and is expressed as a percentage of its dry weight.

Seasoning aims to reduce the moisture content to below 18% for general outdoor use, falling to below 14% for indoor use, and to around 10% in centrally heated homes.

There are two basic seasoning methods, air and kiln seasoning.

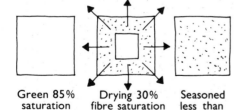

Green 85% saturation | Drying 30% fibre saturation point | Seasoned less than 20% moisture

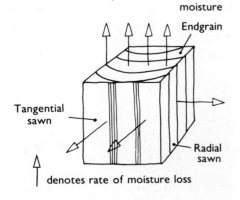

Endgrain

Tangential sawn

Radial sawn

↑ denotes rate of moisture loss

fig 4.102. Evaporation of moisture during seasoning

Natural (air) seasoning

Although this traditional method is fairly cheap to operate, it is very dependent upon weather conditions.

The timber, converted from the log, is stacked carefully in piles within an open or louvre sided shed. The sloping roof protects against direct sun and rain.

The boards are separated by **sticks** of a standard size placed one above the other and at regular intervals along the timber (fig 4.103). Air is allowed to circulate freely resulting in moisture evaporation.

fig 4.103. Timber stacked for seasoning

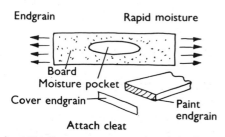

fig 4.104. Preventing moisture loss through endgrain

To help prevent rapid, uneven evaporation through the ends of boards, the end grain can be covered by either paint or cleats of wood or metal (fig 4.104). This generally reduces splitting and degrading.

Disadvantages of this method are:

1. The moisture content can only be reduced to that of the surrounding atmosphere (maximum 15–18%).

2. It tends to be very slow and inaccurate. The time taken varies according to the type of wood and thickness of planks. A general guide is approximately one year for every 25 mm of thickness (e.g. 3 years for 75 mm thick planks). This is uneconomic in terms of stock turnover.

In practice most softwoods are air seasoned because they are used in conditions where a low moisture content is not required. They also dry out in less time than hardwoods and generally, imported smaller sections have time to dry before use.

Artificial (kiln) seasoning

Kiln seasoning provides a quicker, more controlled and reliable method. It offers a more rapid turnover, and is therefore used by manufacturers to process most hardwoods.

The timber is stacked as for natural seasoning, but on trolleys, before being put in the kiln (fig 4.105). After sealing the kiln, steam is introduced which soaks and penetrates the timber. After a time, pressure and humidity are reduced and the steam is drawn out by fans.

Heat is gradually introduced and the temperature raised. Finally, hot, dry air circulates until the moisture content is reduced to the required level.

By carefully recording temperature and humidity, changes can be made and schedules adjusted to meet specific requirements.

As the required moisture content level approaches, sampling is undertaken at intervals to determine and meet exact moisture requirements.

This involves removing and weighing test pieces and making calculations based on the formula:

$$\% \text{ moisture content} = \frac{\text{initial weight} - \text{dry weight}}{\text{dry weight}} \times 100$$

There is some danger of overheating, which can case harden the wood making it brittle on the outside.

Advantages of this method:

1. Precise moisture content can be obtained in only a few weeks, i.e. from 1–2 weeks per 25 mm thickness, depending upon the density of the timber.

2. It has the added benefit of killing insects/eggs in the process.

3. Although expensive to operate, less space is required for stacking, improving stock turnover.

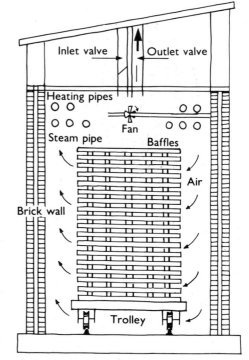

fig 4.105. Cross section of a drying kiln

MOVEMENT — SHRINKAGE

Shrinkage is closely associated with seasoning. It occurs as the wood dries out. Wood cells contract, which often results in splitting and twisting. Fig 4.106 shows where most shrinkage occurs.

(a) Maximum shrinkage occurs along the direction of the annual rings, tangentially, the medullary rays close like a fan.

(b) Some, though minimal, shrinkage takes place in a radial direction across the grain (about half the amount of (a)).

(c) There is negligible shrinkage in length.

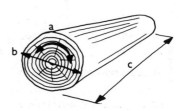

fig 4.106. Where shrinking occurs

DEFECTS IN TIMBER

Defects or faults in the structure of timber not only affect appearance, but also reduce strength, durability and usefulness considerably.

They can be caused by a variety of factors including abnormal growth, wind damage, poor seasoning and attacks by fungi and insects.

Shrinkage

After conversion and seasoning, shrinkage affects the shape and movement of the board, depending on the part of the log it is cut from and how it was converted (see fig 4.107). Movement cannot be eliminated entirely, as changes in humidity and temperature continue to affect wood even after seasoning. This important characteristic must be considered carefully when working this material.

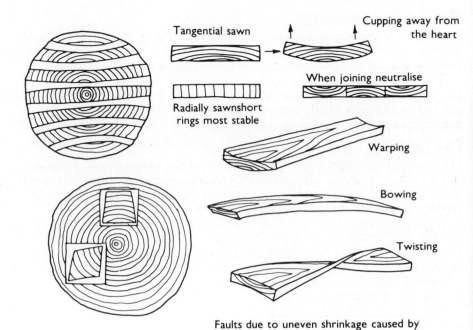

Faults due to uneven shrinkage caused by poor seasoning and bad storage/stacking

fig 4.107. Movement

fig 4.108. Live knots

Irregular grain

Knots can also contribute to variations in the direction and pattern of the grain. This can add visual interest, but in constructional terms, it can also lead to areas of weakness, seriously decreasing strength. The short grain (fig 4.110) makes it unsuitable for load bearing.

Irregularities, such as spiral twisted grain, are caused by distorted growth. These weak areas are more liable to distort and twist. Interlocking grain generally causes difficulties in working, i.e. tearing.

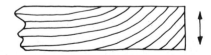

fig 4.110. Short grain

Knots

These may be considered natural irregularities formed at the junction of branches. All knots weaken the structure, but are considered in two groups.

1. Live knots (fig 4.108) are sound, healthy and firmly jointed to the surrounding wood. They are only regarded as a major defect if they are large in size or present in sufficient number.
2. Dead knots (fig 4.109) showing evidences of decay, will be loose and likely to fall out and are an obvious source of weakness.

Splits

Logs form radial splits if allowed to dry out before conversion (fig 4.111a). Similar splits which occur during seasoning in converted timber are called 'checks' (fig 4.111b). They follow the line of the medullary rays and are caused by too rapid drying out through the end-grain.

fig 4.109. Dead knots

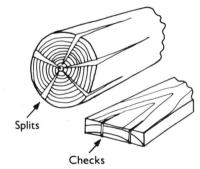

fig 4.111. Splits and checks

Shakes

Shakes (fig 4.112) are separations in adjoining layers of wood and are the result of faulty growth or, in the case of **Heart and Star** shakes shrinkage, where splits occur along the medullary rays.

Cup and Ring shakes are the result of strains by wind, poor felling or bad seasoning. In such cases the annual rings fail to join up properly causing fibre separation.

Thunder shakes are thin, air-line cracks, which form across the grain in some African timbers (e.g. mahogany, mansonia).

 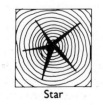  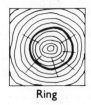 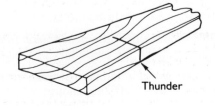

Heart   Star   Cup   Ring   Thunder

fig 4.112. Shakes

Fungal attack

Fungal attack causes wood to decay, resulting in loss of strength and weight, together with increased ability to absorb water (sponge-like). Fungi are parasitic plants whose spores cause the wood cells to collapse.

Certain conditions are necessary for fungi to develop, i.e. oxygen and low-cold temperatures. More importantly, a moisture content of above 20% is needed for the spores to germinate. Even seasoned timber can meet those conditions easily because of its ability to absorb available moisture.

fig 4.113. Dry rot

Dry rot

The sponge-like fungus, *Merulius lacrymans*, is the most common in timber (fig 4.113). It thrives in damp, unventilated situations where there is a lack of circulated air. It is known as dry rot because it reduces wood to a dry, soft, powdery condition, with a pungent musty smell.

Dry rot is extremely dangerous in buildings because of the speed with which it spreads. The spores can be transmitted easily by wind and animals. The fine strands of hyphae can even penetrate masonry in the search for further food supplies.

Prevention:
1. Use sound, well seasoned timber.
2. Instal in dry, well ventilated situations.

Treatment:
1. The complete removal and burning of infected timber.
2. Sterilisation of the area.
3. Chemical treatment of replacement timber.

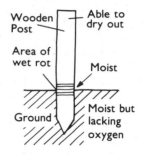

fig 4.114. Area vulnerable to wet rot

Wet rot

Timber subjected to alternate wetness and dryness begins to decompose. Outside woodwork (e.g. window ledges) and posts at ground level (fig 4.114) are vulnerable. The timber becomes spongy when wet and brittle when dry.

Prevention: treat with a water repellent finish.

Treatment: affected timber can be cut out and replaced. Cut back to sound wood because, unlike dry rot, it does not spread.

Stains

Some staining can be caused by otherwise harmless fungi. They affect mainly sapwood, though lighter coloured hardwoods (e.g. sycamore) can also be affected. Strength is not impaired, as fungi lives on the contents, and not the cells themselves.

fig 4.115. Common woodworm

Insects

Unlike warmer climates where many insects including termites (white ants) are a serious menace (fig 4.115), in this country attacks are mainly restricted to:

1. **Wharf borers**, or **weevils**, which affect underwater installations.

2. **Pin hole borers**, which only attack certain types of timber in its green state and do not persist after seasoning. Appearance is spoilt by small holes with dark surrounding stains which appear across the grain.

3. Four varieties of **beetle** (fig 4.116), which attack during and after seasoning.

Common furniture beetle (woodworm)	Death watch beetle	Powder post or lyctus beetle	House houg horn beetle
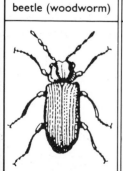	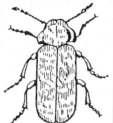		
responsible for most attacks in hardwood and softwood makes a honeycomb of tunnels	prefers to attack large structural timbers e.g. oak, found in historic buildings and churches	damages the sapwood of hardwoods e.g. oak, ash, elm which have large pores to receive the eggs	once rare in Britain, it devours softwoods, especially roof structures

fig 4.116. Insects that attack wood

Life cycle of beetle

1. Eggs are deposited in convenient crevices.
2. The resulting grubs (larvae) eat into the wood cellulose, tunnelling for up to two years or more.
3. They then return to a cavity near the surface for pupation.
4. Finally the beetle eats its way out through a small flight or exit hole, to begin the life-cycle once again.

fig 4.117. Life cycle of a beetle

Prevention: it is impossible to achieve complete immunity from attack. Some degree of protection and discouragement is given by finishes (e.g. sealing crevices and joints with wax and polishing surfaces with aromatic oils/creams).

Avoid using sapwood in timbers such as oak.

Treatment: proprietary chemicals squirted into holes disrupt the life-cycle and prevent further infestation. In severe cases fumigation needs to be undertaken by experts.

IDENTIFICATION AND CHARACTERISTICS OF HARDWOODS AND SOFTWOODS

Trees can be identified in their growing state by reference to appearance (e.g. general shape, leaf form) (fig 4.118).

Once converted, trees can be identified by careful microscopic examination of the end grain and cell structure.

It is useful to be able to recognize the different types of timber available in the workshop in order to help selection and determine suitability for various jobs. Experience gained in observing, but more especially from working, the material is of enormous benefit. Equally, consideration of the characteristics of the material can be useful in identifying and classifying different kinds of wood.

fig 4.118. Shape and leaf form

Commercial forms and sizes of timber

After conversion and seasoning, timber is reduced again into smaller sections of common shapes and sizes.

It is sold either **rough sawn** (also called nominal or full-size) or **ready machined** (planer thicknessed).

Planing can be **PBS** (planed both sides) or **PAR** (planed all round).

The size of planed timber is described as the nominal (rough sawn) size, but will actually be approximately 3 mm smaller.

Buying timber, especially the selection of hardwood boards, can be an enjoyable experience. However, do remember about planed thicknesses and the need to allow extra for things such as saw cuts and split ends.

Weight Weight varies considerably, but hardwoods tend to be heavier than softwoods. However, there are exceptions (e.g. yew (s), balsa (h)).

Odour Many timbers have a distinctive smell (e.g. pine). This fades with time, but can be revived by heat, friction or planing.

Colour It can be misleading to say softwoods are generally lighter in colour than hardwoods. This is frequently not the case (e.g. sycamore, holly, willow). Some woods do change when exposed to light. Many fade, while others, such as teak, darken.

Grain It is the nature of the 'grain', i.e. straightness or irregularities, which is the key to both identification and attractiveness in timber (e.g. silver, figure, striped, ripple).

Hardwood is more decorative than softwood and where appearance is concerned (e.g. furniture), is to be preferred.

Texture Since there are more varieties of hardwood than softwood available, they offer more choice. Their closer grain formation also provides better surface when in contact with food.

Durability Hardwoods generally are more resistant to surface marking and being more durable have a longer life span than softwoods.

Outdoor use Selection is linked with rot-resistance as well as durability. Most softwoods deteriorate rapidly outdoors; western red cedar is an exception.

Ease of working Hardwoods are generally stated to be more difficult to work than softwoods, blunting cutting edges more quickly. However, each piece of timber offers unique qualities and no certain rules apply. For example, yew is very hard and knotty pine presents problems.

Cost Softwoods are considerably cheaper than hardwoods. Commerical investment has led to the intensive forestry of individual varieties. Their long straight trunks make them available in longer boards.
By comparison, hardwoods are expensive, taking much longer to mature.

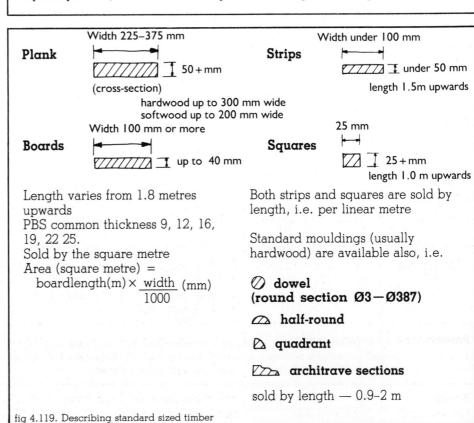

Length varies from 1.8 metres upwards
PBS common thickness 9, 12, 16, 19, 22 25.
Sold by the square metre
Area (square metre) =
$$\text{boardlength(m)} \times \frac{\text{width}}{1000} \text{ (mm)}$$

Both strips and squares are sold by length, i.e. per linear metre

Standard mouldings (usually hardwood) are available also, i.e.

⊘ **dowel**
(round section Ø3—Ø387)

⌒ **half-round**

◁ **quadrant**

▱ **architrave sections**

sold by length — 0.9–2 m

fig 4.119. Describing standard sized timber

TABLE OF COMMON TIMBERS

(a) Hardwoods

NAME	ORIGIN/COLOUR	PROPERTIES AND WORKING CHARACTERISTICS	USES
Beech	Europe White to pinkish brown	Close-grained, hard, tough and strong, works and finishes well, wears well but prone to warping	Functional furniture (e.g. chairs, toys, tools, veneer, turned work, steam bending)
Elm	Europe Light reddish brown	Tough, durable, cross-grained which makes it difficult to work, does not split easily, has a tendency to warp, good in water	Garden furniture (when treated), turnery and furniture
Oak European English Japanese	Europe Light brown Japan Yellow brown	Very strong, heavy, durable, hard and tough, it finishes well, open-grained, it contains tannic acid which corrodes iron/steel, fittings leaving dark blue staining in the wood, expensive Slightly milder, easier to work but less durable	High class furniture, fittings, boat building, garden furniture, posts, veneer Interior woodwork and furniture
Ash	Europe Pale cream colour and light brown	Open-grained, tough and flexible, good elastic qualities, works and finishes well	Tool handles, sports equipment, traditional coach building, ladders, laminating
Mahogany African (e.g. Sapele, utile)	Central-South America, West Indies, West Africa Pink reddish brown	Easy to work, fairly strong, medium weight, durable, available in long, wide boards, some difficult interlocking grain, prone to warping	Indoor furniture and shop fittings, panelling, veneers
Meranti	S.E. Asia Dark red, also white-yellow	Fairly strong, durable and fairly hard to work	(Mahogany substitute) interior joinery and furniture, plywood–red and white forms
Teak	Burma, India Golden brown	Hard, very strong and extremely durable, natural oils make it highly resistant to moisture, acids and alkalis, works easily but blunts tools quickly, darkens with exposure to light, very expensive	Quality furniture, outdoor furniture, boat building, laboratory equipment, turnery, veneers
Iroko	East/West Africa Yellow but darkens to dark brown	Like teak it is oily and durable, cross-grained, heavy	(Teak substitute) furniture cladding, construction work, veneers
Walnut African	Europe, USA, West Africa Yellow, brown, bronze, dark lines	Attractive, works well, durable, often cross-grained which makes planing and finishing difficult, available in large sizes	Furniture, gun stocks, furniture veneer
Obeche	West Africa Pale yellow	Straight, open grained, soft, light and not very durable, sometimes cross-grained	Constructional uses, hidden parts of furniture, plywood core

(b) Softwoods

NAME	ORIGIN/COLOUR	PROPERTIES AND WORKING CHARACTERISTICS	USES
Scots pine (red deal)	N Europe, Russia Cream, pale brown	Straight grained, but knotty, fairly strong, easy to work, cheap and readily available	Mainly constructional work, joinery, paints well, needs outdoor protection
Western Red Cedar	Canada, USA Dark, reddish brown	Light in weight, knot free, soft, straight silky grain, natural oils make it durable against weather, insects and rot, easy to work, but weak and expensive	Outdoor uses, timber cladding of external buildings, also wall panelling
Parana Pine	South America, Pale yellow with red/brown streaks	Hard, straight grained, almost knot free, fairly strong and durable, smooth finish, tends to warp, expensive	Best quality interior joinery, i.e. staircases, built — in furniture
Spruce (whitewood)	N Europe, America, Creamy-white	Fairly strong, small hard knots, resistant to splitting, some resin pockets, not durable	General indoor work, whitewood furniture i.e. kitchens

MANUFACTURED BOARDS

Veneer

Veneering, the art of applying a thin sheet of decorative wood on a plain ground core or base, can be traced back to ancient civilisation. However, it was not until the seventeenth century, a period also linked with the importation of exotic timbers, that the development of this process took place.

Veneers were first produced by sawing decorative wood into slices which were then glued on to less attractive timbers, often softwoods. This made furniture not only stronger, but considerably more attractive in appearance.

The mass-produced furniture of today is almost totally based around this material and technique, as is the manufacture of man-made boards. Considerable developments have taken place in the machinery used to produce veneer and the adhesives required for bonding. The reasons for its extensive use can be summarised as follows:

1. It permits the economic use of highly decorative exotic woods which are in limited supply.

2. It extends the usefulness of many woods which are weak, but in this form can be used to give interesting variation in grain and colour.

3. In terms of appearance, effects can be created by use of pattern, 'matching veneers', cross-banding and marketry.

4. It is essential for mass-produced furniture and the manufacture of man-made boards (e.g. plywood).

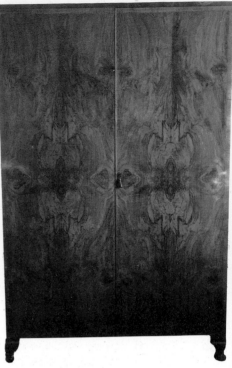

fig 4.120. Veneering

The manufacture of veneer is a highly specialised business. It is produced in several forms.

Saw cut is the oldest method, producing a lot of waste (sawdust). It is still used for difficult and highly figured hardwoods (e.g. ebony) which cannot be knife-cut.

The veneers, produced by special saws, are generally thicker and more expensive, but of high quality with little damage caused to the wood fibres.

The majority of veneer is **knife cut**. The log is prepared by steaming in water in order to condition (soften) the wood and give a clean cut.

There are two basic types, **rotary peeling** and **slicing**.

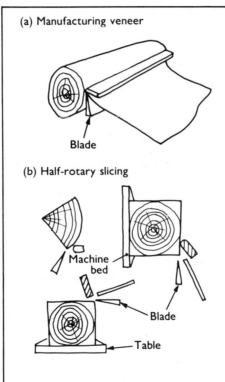

(a) Manufacturing veneer

Blade

(b) Half-rotary slicing

Machine bed

Blade

Table

fig 4.121. Manufacturing veneer

Rotary peeling: after steaming, the log is mounted on a machine similar to a lathe and rotated slowly. Once it is cylindrical, a long knife is fed automatically into the log (fig 4.121a). This action results in a thin, continuous sheet peeling off, and this is then trimmed, cut, dried and graded.

This is the cheapest method with little waste, but it produces the plainest veneer, 90% of which is used for plywood manufacture.

Slicing is used to produce the finer, more decorative face veneers.

Fitches, which may be either quarter, flat or half round are prepared. After steaming, they are secured on a movable frame which is brought down or rolled against a knife.

Automatic resetting gives accurate, successive veneers, with closely matching grain. They are carefully stored in order to allow special grain effects by 'matching'. Veneer is used extensively for the manufacture of man-made boards (e.g. plywood, blockboard, chipboard and hardboard).

Constructional veneer is also available. This is usually thicker (1.5, 2.3 mm) and used for laminating.

All veneer is sold by the square metre.

Plywood

The principle of plywood is an important process in improving the physical properties of timber. It was not until the 1890s, with the introduction of rotary cut veneers, that its qualities began to be exploited, and early uses included tea chests and piano frames.

Plywood is formed using an odd number of thin layers (veneer approximately 1.5 mm thick) called **laminates**, with the grain of each running at right angles to its neighbour (fig 4.122). This interlocking sandwich gives plywood its high uniform strength and resistance to splitting. The odd number of layers balance the stresses around the central core, cancelling out any chance of shrinkage across the grain. It also means that the grain on the outer layers runs in the same direction.

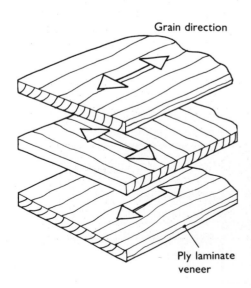

Grain direction

Ply laminate veneer

fig 4.122. Plywood construction

Some of the common forms of plywood are illustrated in fig 4.123. It is manufactured in large presses. Rollers apply adhesive and then extreme pressure and controlled heat (or radio frequency) are used to cure (set) the adhesive. Waterproof or highly water resistant glue is used, making the bond stronger than the wood itself.

The faces are cleaned, then graded by appearance quality, and defects are repaired by circular plugs. The quality is shown by the letters A, B, BB, i.e. B/BB would have one face better than the other making it less expensive than B/B.

A variety of timbers is used (e.g. birch, alder, beech and gabon), depending upon the country of manufacture. Standard plywood is commonly available white or red faced. Birch or cheaper white meranti and gaboon or cheaper red meranti are the most popular.

Veneered plywood is produced with a decorative face veneer in a variety of timbers, including oak, mahogany, afromosia and teak. The reverse face usually has a less expensive veneer to balance and compensate for the extra stress.

Marine plywood made from makoré veneers and phenolic resin adhesive (WBP) offers special protection for outdoor use including boat building.

Pre-formed plywood is also available where rigidity and curved forms are required (e.g. to provide seating).

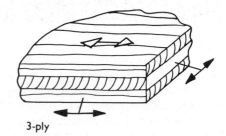

3-ply

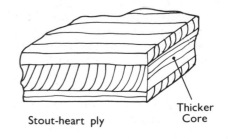

Stout-heart ply

Thicker Core

Available: Standard sheet sizes 1525 × 1525 mm, 2440 × 1220 mm
N.B. It is always quoted with the length of the face grain given first
Graded — A, B, BB. Best quality Birch, Gaboon
Metric thicknesses (0.8, 1.5) 3, 4, 6, 9, 12, 18 mm
Related term: WBP, weather and boil proof, highly resistant to weather
        BR,   boil resistant, not suitable for prolonged exposure to weather
        MR,   moisture resistant
        INT,   interior use only
Basic uses: wide ranging, from decorative panels to furniture (e.g. backs, drawer bottoms, carcases, boat building)

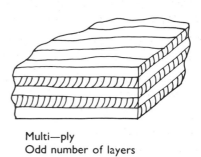

Multi—ply
Odd number of layers

fig 4.123. Types of plywood

Blockboards

Plywood is expensive to manufacture in thicknesses over 12 mm. Blockboards are often used as substitutes when built up boards of greater thickness are required. Although not of the same uniform strength, they possess many of the qualities of plywood. Blockboard is used as a collective term for a group of boards of similar construction.

Lamin board consists of a solid timber core made up of parallel strips of softwood, 5–7 mm in width, sandwiched between two outer facing veneers (about 3 mm thick) whose grain runs at right angles to the core (see fig 4.124a). These thin strips make a stable, strong slab core and are usually of pine or spruce, though in some countries hardwood is used. The facing veneer can be of birch or gaboon.

Blockboard is similar, except that the core strips are wider (see fig 4.124b), up to 25 mm. It is not as stable as lamin board and a slight ripple can often be detected on the surface because of the increased core width. However, it does provide strength and stability at reasonable cost. 18 mm is a common thickness in this material.

Superior 5 ply: the quality of both core and veneers can vary considerably, but more expensive, superior kinds of blockboards are available (fig 4.124c). These have additional veneers where the grain direction runs parallel to that of the core.

Lamin board

5–7

Blockboard

up to 25

Second thinner veneer parallel to core

First veneer at right angles to core

Core

Superior 5-ply

fig 4.124. Types of blockboard

Available: standard sheet size 1525 × 1525,
    1525 × 3050, 1220 × 2240 mm
    Thicknesses 12, 16, 18, 25 mm
    Best quality 5-ply construction (Birch)
Uses: carcases, knock-down furniture, flush doors, table tops, work surfaces

---

Chipboard (particle board)

This type of engineered board is made in large, flat sheets or panels in a variety of sizes. It is made from wood particles, including flakes, chips and shavings from all commercial hardwoods and softwoods bonded with synthetic phenolic resin.

The small particles give no grain direction and make these boards equally strong in all directions. The boards are produced by highly automated processes, either flat pressed under heat and pressure, or extruded between parallel metal patterns to produce core boards. These are less strong than the flat pressed type.

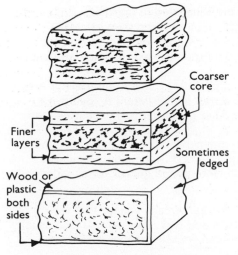

fig 4.125. Different forms of chipboard

The various market forms are illustrated in fig 4.125.

1. **Single (one-type)** layer has interlocking, similar sized particles which give uniform appearance on all surfaces.
2. **Sandwich construction** has coarse particles sandwiched between finer, smaller chips on the face layers which give a smoother surface finish.
3. **Veneered** chipboard, sometimes called conti-board, has both sides covered with hardwood veneer, which increases costs compared to standard chipboard. The material provides an excellent stable core for plastic laminates as well as veneer.

Available: standard grade, graded density or veneered
Sizes 2440 × 1220 mm
Thicknesses 12, 15, 18 mm
Uses: interior use only, including shelving, work tops and mass produced furniture, core-stock for plastic laminates, sub flooring

Hardboards

Hardboards provide a cheap, light material which is often used as a substitute for plywood, where space-filling rather than strength is required. The raw material, wood fibre, is obtained from wood chips or pulped wood waste. During manufacture it is exploded under high pressure heat and steam to leave a fine, fluffy mass of brown fibres. These are refined and formed into mats, thick felted blankets of loose fibres held together by natural lignum and other bonding agents.

It is then pressed between steam heated plates to give large, flat grainless sheets with one smooth, glossy face and a rough patterned, textured surface formed in manufacturing. This is followed by conditioning, which involves adding moisture in a humidification chamber to help prevent warping.

Hardboard has no regular grain and is equally strong in all directions. The standard grade absorbs moisture very easily, especially through its textured side and is unsuitable for outdoor work.

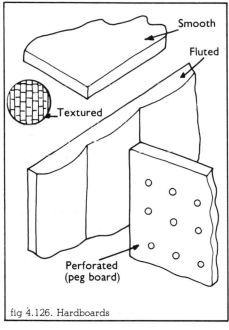

fig 4.126. Hardboards

Tempered hardboard is stiffer with a harder finish which offers more resistance to cuts, scratches and moisture. This form is impregnated with oil and other chemicals during the pre-finishing process.

Special hardboards with different surface finishes are available, including types which are perforated (peg board), embossed, veneered and plastic faced (fig 4.126).

Medium density fibre board is becoming increasingly popular. It is more dense and has smooth faces, and is generally thicker and heavier than hardboard. It is very stable, being unaffected by changes in humidity. It is also a good electrical insulator and takes paint and other finishes extremely well.

Insulation board is similar to hardboard, but not so compressed. It has a low density, and is both light and weak. It is particularly suited to use on interior walls, where it is a good insulator for both heat and sound (e.g. accoustic tiles, notice boards).

Available: graded according to density
Standard sizes 1220 × 2240 mm Thicknesses 3.2, 4.8, 6 mm;
Medium density fibre board 9, 12, 16, 18 mm; insulation board 12–25 mm
Uses: flexible, but needs supporting, e.g. drawer bottoms, backs of cabinets

By using wood economically, manufactured boards help to relieve the demand for prime quality timber. However, they should not be regarded as cheap substitutes. Cost comparisons and properties such as strength can be misleading. Many have no grain and must be considered separately from those which have.

Man-made boards are valuable materials in their own right, with a part to play alongside solid timber. They present their own problems of working which are summarised and illustrated in figs 4.127 and 4.128.

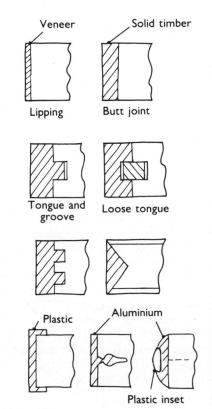

fig 4.127. Edge treatment of manufactured boards

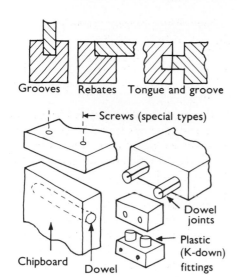

Grooves   Rebates   Tongue and groove

← Screws (special types)

Chipboard   Dowel

Dowel joints

Plastic (K-down) fittings

fig 4.128. Simple constructions

Advantages of man-made boards:
1. Available in large, standard sheets of uniform thickness and quality.
2. Extremely stable, not affected by humidity and temperature.
3. Those with grain, have uniform strength and good strength/weight ratio.
4. Large, flat surfaces are ideal for finishes, providing a base for veneering.
5. Difficult to split and flexible in thin sheet form, allowing forming (bending).
6. Special adhesive bonding gives resistance to decay (some waterproof, others heatproof).
7. Simple construction techniques are required (often using less joints) (fig 4.128).

Disadvantages of man-made boards:
1. Some form of edge treatment is needed (see fig 4.127).
2. Many thin sheets do not stay flat unless in some kind of frame.
3. Difficult to joint compared to traditional construction techniques.
4. Problems of working vary, but sharp cutting edges are easily blunted by adhesives.

Costs vary considerably according to type and grading.

TYPES OF MATERIAL – PLASTICS

Plastic is not an easy term to define, because it covers a wide range of diverse substances. To be included in this group, the material must at some stage be plastic or putty-like, a state which is neither solid nor liquid, but somewhere in between. During this stage it can be shaped and moulded by pressure and heat, before setting in the desired form.

Plastic materials have been used in their natural form for centuries (e.g. resins, clays, cowhorn, amber, bitumen and shellac). The Egyptians and Romans made use of natural waxes and resins as seals for documents, appreciating one of the most important properties of plastics, its ability to be moulded.

It was not until the use of rubber in the 1820s, with the later discovery of vulcanisation enabling it to be moulded into shape, that the possibilities of chemical development arose. This gave the lead in synthetic plastic materials. The first to be introduced was **cellulose nitrate** (parkensine) (fig 4.130) made from natural cellulose and nitric acid producing a horn-like material. **Celluloid** was also developed from ordinary cellulose fibre (wood or cotton). Further experiments led to other materials, such as casein (milk), being used to imitate natural materials (e.g. horn, ivory, tortoise shell and coral). However, by the turn of the century only a few plastics were commercially available and these were largely based on natural materials.

Although the development of 'bakelite', a thermosetting synthetic plastic based on phenol and formaldehyde, had some commerical success in the electrical industry, it was the period leading to the second world war which led to most change. It provided the stimulus needed for the mass-production of synthetic plastics to replace more traditional materials.

Substitutes for materials such as rubber led to the development and processing of a wide range of synthetic materials which form the basis of today's plastics industry. Styrene, used in synthetic rubber, led to the development of **polystyrene**, one of the most widely used of all modern plastics. **Vinyl** provided a whole range of versatile plastics including **PVC**. The clear, glass-like material **acrylic**, was first introduced in aircraft canopies. Scientific research also resulted in the development of **polythene**. The man-made fibre **nylon**, which is very strong, resilient to corrosion and able to be spun when molten, offered a wide range of uses (e.g. stockings, clothings and propellers and bearings).

All of this contributed to a thriving plastics industry and development has continued at a rapid pace. Starting life as substitutes to replace expensive raw materials has unfortunately led to the association of the term 'plastic' with cheap, imitation commercial products. This is far from being the case today. Many high quality items could not be made from anything else. The unique range of properties this group of materials has to offer is now being recognised, appreciated and exploited.

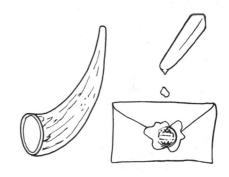

fig 4.129. Natural plastic

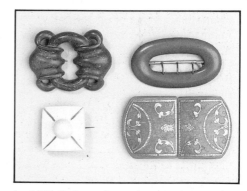

fig 4.130. Early synthetic plastic

fig 4.131. Early use of bakelite

PLASTICS — THE MATERIALS PHENOMENON

A wide variety of plastic products are to be found in every modern home (e.g. kitchen equipment, toothbrushes, floor coverings, telephones, electrical products). The scope and potential of plastics means that they will continue to affect every part of our lives from space exploration to healthcare (fig 4.132).

More things than you realise are made from plastic, and there are now hundreds of different types of plastic. Many have very long and complicated chemical names, for example, polymethyl methacrylate, more commonly known as acrylic.

How many others are you able to recognise and identify? This is no easy task, as some are hard and brittle, while others are soft and flexible. Even the same type of plastic can differ in appearance and texture. Polystyrene, for example, is found in expandable blocks and sheets as well as high density moulded forms.

Plastics are very much at the forefront of modern materials. Therefore, we must increase our knowledge of the sources, structure, types, properties, forms and uses of this group of materials.

There are two mains sources of plastics (fig 4.133).

fig 4.132. Typical use of modern plastic

Natural resources

Modified forms of these natural materials play only a small part in the plastics industry.

Synthetic resources

These materials, especially oil, are the major suppliers of raw materials for the production of plastics.

The refining of crude oil in a **fractioning tower** (fig 4.134) is the process by which liquids of varying densities and valuable petroleum gases are separated. The oil is heated, changing it to gases, which rise up the tower and pass through various liquids, causing separation or breaking into fractions. Many of these are ready for use after cleaning (e.g. heating oil, aviation fuel).

'**Cracking**' is one of the most important activities of oil refineries. This involves breaking up heavy particles of oil into lighter particles of petroleum. This can be done by applying heat and pressure (thermal cracking), but more usually it is heated and made to crack by catalytic cracking. (A catalyst is a substance which speeds up chemical change in the oil). The fraction used for the production of plastics is the **hydrocarbon naphtha**. This liquid is heated with steam to break up its structure, or crack it into fragments, the most important of which are ethylene and propylene.

It was through organic (carbon) chemistry that complex compounds were built from simple units to make substances not found in nature, i.e. polymers or plastics. These simple units were obtained from what had previously been considered waste products, produced by destructive processes such as the distillation of coal gas.

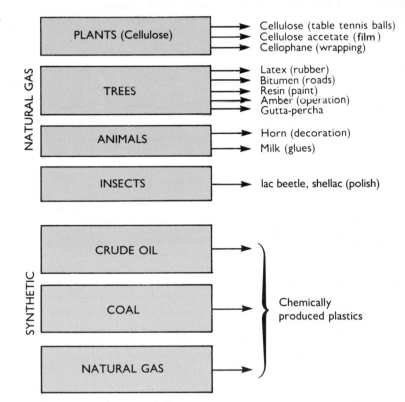

fig 4.133. Two main sources of plastic

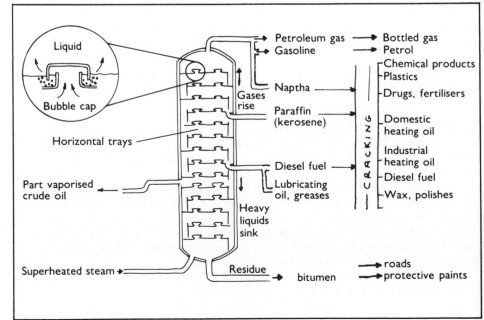

fig 4.134. Fractioning tower

THE STRUCTURE OF PLASTICS

Matter can be broken down into elements which have the ability to combine with one another to form **molecules**. These are the smallest units which form the building blocks for various chemical compounds.

In naturally occurring compounds these building molecules consist of only a few atoms joined together, making molecules short and compact.

Water, H_2O, is a good example. It can also exist in three different forms: gas (steam), liquid and solid (ice).

The absorption of heat leads to the absorption of energy which causes the molecules to vibrate and try to separate. In the case of plastics, the change of state from solid to liquid is gradual; the material becomes plastic or putty-like before melting into a liquid. It is this unique characteristic that make plastics such a valuable moulding material.

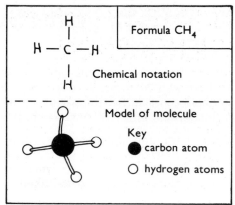

fig 4.135. Methane

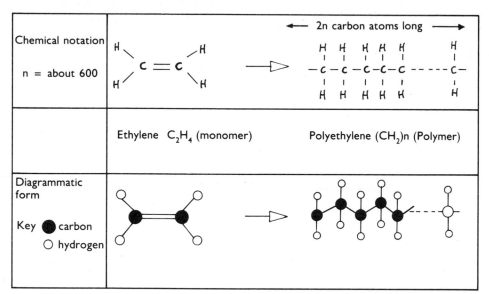

fig 4.136. Polymerisation of ethylene

The element carbon forms the backbone of polymer (plastics) chemistry, but other elements notably hydrogen, oxygen, nitrogen, fluorine and chlorine, play a part.

Hydrocarbons, combinations of hydrogen and carbon, include **methane** (CH_4), **propane** (C_3H_8) and **butane** (C_4H_{10}).

In the case of methane (fig 4.135), the carbon atom forms the central core and bonds with hydrogen atoms which attach to its four arms. This is a stable compound which is saturated, i.e. unable to take more atoms.

With plastics, molecules do not stay as single units, but link up with one another to form long chains of **giant molecules**. The smaller units which form the links (similar to those in a bicycle chain) are known as **monomers**.

The process of linking the units to form the chain is called **polymerisation**. The prefix 'poly' means many, and 'mer' is greek for unit. A **polymer** (many units) consists of between 200 and 2000 units in the molecule.

Compounds with one or more carbon atoms linked chemically by double bonds are called **unsaturated compounds**. They are ideal for linking together to form polymer chains in a process known as **additional polymerisation**.

In ethylene (fig 4.136), a by-product of petroleum cracking, the carbon atoms link with two hydrogen atoms, but have spare electrons to link themselves together (double-bonding).

Under pressure and at an elevated temperature, or with the aid of a catalyst, two molecules may be joined together by opening the double bond. The resulting molecule also has a double bond allowing the units to link up repeatedly, building up a long chain. As the chains form, they become entangled and bond together by weak forces (known as Van der Waals forces) to form solid material.

Ethylene is the monomer, but several hundred links results in the formation of the polymer polyethylene or polythene as it usually called.

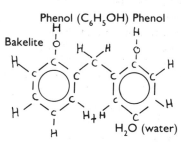
Formaldehyde (HCHO)

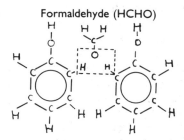
Phenol (C_6H_5OH) Phenol
Bakelite

H_2O (water)

fig 4.137. Condensation polymerisation

Condensation polymerisation

In this method, two different monomers react to give a larger chain molecule (**macromolecule**). Parts of the reacting smaller molecules are split off and eliminated as a by-product, usually water (H_2O).

One of the first patented synthetic plastics, 'bakelite', is an example of this process. This thermosetting material was made from phenol and formaldehyde (fig 4.137).

In this case, the formation of cross-links (fig 4.138) means the chain molecules are joined by covalent bonds which are very strong compared to the Van der Waals forces of thermoplastic materials.

Condensation polymerisation is also used to produce thermoplastics, notably nylon (polyamide). Again water is the by-product.

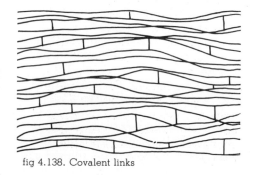

fig 4.138. Covalent links

How plastics can be changed

The characteristics of polymer material can be changed in three ways:

1. The molecular chain can be lengthened or shortened. Substances with less than 5 carbon atoms are gases, those with between 5 and 11 are liquids, and those with 20 or more are solids. In the case of the ethylene monomer, a short chain consisting of 15 links would produce paraffin wax polymer, a much longer one with 1200 links would produce polythene.

2. The basic unit, the monomer, can be altered. In the vinyl chloride monomer (fig 4.139), one atom of hydrogen has been replaced by an atom of chlorine. This links up to form the polymer polyvinyl chloride (PVC) (fig 4.140), which has a more complex, **cross-linked** pattern.

3. Two or more different monomers can be combined to form a new material. This is called **co-polymerisation** and the new material a **copolymer**. For example, vinyl chloride monomer mixed with vinyl acetate monomer (fig 4.141) makes PVAC (vinyl chloride, vinyl acetate copolymer) which is easier to process than PVC because it is stable when heated.

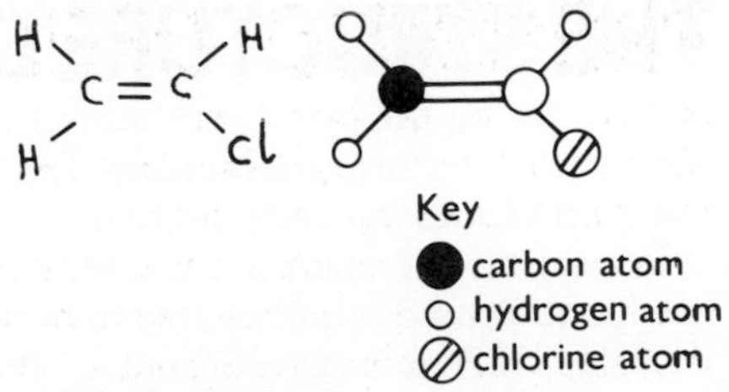

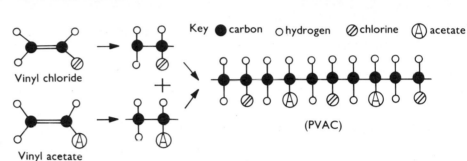

Key
- ● carbon atom
- ○ hydrogen atom
- ◐ chlorine atom

fig 4.139. Vinyl chloride

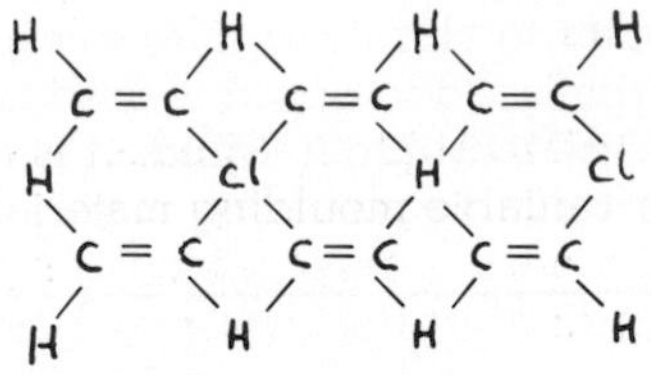

fig 4.140. Polyvinyl chloride

Plastics are divided into two main groups, each with their special types of chain formation. The key factor which identifies each group is how they react to heat.

Thermoplastics

Thermoplastics are made from long chain molecules which are entangled but flexible, similar to cooked spaghetti (fig 4.142). The polymer chains are held together by mutual attraction, known as Van der Waals forces.

This attraction can be lessened by introducing heat energy which increases the distance between molecules, but decreases the forces between them. As the molecules move, they untangle and become soft and pliable and easy to mould into shape.

When the heat is removed, the cooling chains reposition and the material becomes stiff and solid.

This ability to soften under heat, even after moulding, and then return to its former state is called '**plastic memory**'. It can be repeated many times providing no damage or decomposition has occurred through overheating.

The thermoplastic group range from rigid to extreme flexibility and account for the vast majority of plastics in common use. They include polythene, polypropylene and polystyrene.

Low and high density polythene are chemically the same, the differences are caused by different amounts of branching in the chains.

Low density has a lot of branching, while in high density the molecules are almost linear (fig 4.143). The degree of branching has important effects on the **crystallinity** of the material.

Branching hinders close packing, while linear molecules move more readily and become more aligned and ordered. Increased crystallinity, as in high density polythene, increases stiffness and hardness.

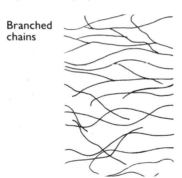

Key ● carbon ○ hydrogen ◐ chlorine ⓐ acetate

Vinyl chloride

Vinyl acetate

(PVAC)

fig 4.141. Co-polymerisation

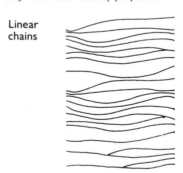

Branched chains

fig 4.142. Low density polythene

Linear chains

fig 4.143. High density polythene

fig 4.144. Covalent 'cross-links'

Thermosetting plastics

This group also begins as long, chain-like molecules, but become chemically tied together by **covalent bonds** and are '**cross-linked**' when the polymer is heated, usually under pressure. They set with heat and then have little plasticity.

The molecules link side to side as well as end to end (fig 4.144). Once the rigid network structure has formed, it cannot be reheated and changed.

Thermosetting plastics are therefore rigid and non-flexible even at higher temperatures. They include polyester resin and urea formaldehyde.

Elastomers

Elastomers form a third group which lies between the two basic groups of polymers. They have similar properties to natural rubber and include the synthetic rubbers.

They form rather loose structures with only a limited number of cross-links which allows considerable movement between chains.

74

PROPERTIES OF PLASTICS

A walk along any beach or coastline reveals many of the important properties of plastics. Low density and resistance to corrosion contribute to pollution of the environment by plastic containers.

Each group of plastics show particular characteristics: **thermo-plastics** are easily moulded and any waste is re-used making for economic use. However, they are less useful where heat is concerned. Many soften and lose rigidity at temperatures just over 100°C. (An exception is PTFE). By contrast, **thermosets** withstand higher temperatures without loosing rigidity and are good thermal insulators.

Mechanical properties

1. **Strength** is generally much lower in plastics than other structural materials, but lightness gives good strength/weight ratio. Strength does vary considerably according to temperature.

2. **Corrosion resistance** is a valuable consideration in selecting these materials. Although they are not indestructible, many have the ability to withstand impact and misuse.

3. **Specific properties:** nylon and PTFE have very low coefficients of friction and make ideal materials for bearings.

Disadvantages of plastics

1. They are prone to deformation, especially a tendency to 'creep', i.e. they elongate slowly under load.

2. Deformation depends upon temperature, deterioration is rapid above 200°C.

3. Many polymers become brittle and develop surface cracks on exposure to ultra-violet light.

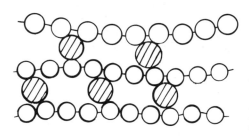

fig 4.145. Plasticisers act as spacers

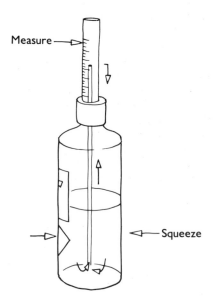

Measure

Squeeze

fig 4.146. Special catalyst dispenser

Use of additives

The mechanical properties are increased by the use of **additives**. Many polymers/resins cannot be processed into plastics without further modification by the use of additives; some are detailed below.

Plasticisers are normally liquids added to polymers to improve flow properties. They lower the softening temperature and make them less brittle. Adding an oily plasticiser to PVC makes it soft and flexible and more suitable for use in packaging and wall coverings than that used in, for example, drainpipes. It provides mechanical spacers (fig 4.145) which separate the polymer chain reducing the Van der Waals force of attraction.

Catalysts are chemical peroxides used to increase or decrease the speed at which molecules link up. They are used in resin casting and are available either in paste or liquid form. The liquid form is easier to use. A special dispenser (fig 4.146) avoids any danger of contact with skin.

Accelerators are chemical additives (cobalt naphthanate) used to shorten the setting time of resin. Normally most resins are already pre-activated (denoted by PA) and are recommended wherever possible. Special resins, however, cannot be pre-activated as different work requires different amounts of activator.

Fillers and other additives are usually in the form of powdered solids which do not mix chemically. They are most often used with thermosetting compounds of the phenol-formaldehyde type and serve two purposes:

1. To reduce costs, low cost bulk means using less expensive polymer.

2. To improve properties (e.g. strength) by reducing brittleness and increasing resistance to impact and dimensional stability.

Additives such as mica improve electrical resistance, asbestos improves resistance to temperature and graphite reduces friction.

Colour pigments in the form of liquids or pastes can be mixed (<10%) with resins. They are available as translucent or opaque colourants and offer help in protecting source polymers from light.

Antioxidants are used to prevent oxidation.

Stabilisers help to prevent polymer damage by long exposure to ultra-violet light. This can reduce transparency and cause deterioration to mechanical properties.

STRENGTHENING PLASTICS

Thermosetting plastics produce a hard, but brittle material. This can be made much stronger and tougher by using other materials for reinforcement.

Layers of paper and cloth

Layers of paper, cloth and other cheap materials can be bonded with resin to give a sandwich or laminated form. Impregnation with melamine resin produces decorative sheets used for kitchen work surfaces (e.g. formica) and also functional printed circuit boards (PCB) used in electronics (fig 4.146).

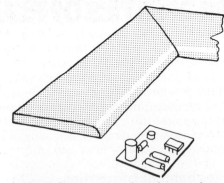

fig 4.147. Thermosetting plastic laminated surfaces

Glass reinforced plastic

Glass reinforced plastic (GRP) is the reinforcement of polyester resin using stranded glass which gives the materials high tensile and compressive strength. It provides a light, hard-wearing surface of thin section which has excellent resistance to corrosion (fig 4.148).

Glass fibre or mat is available in different forms. Chopped strand mat is the cheapest, the material is loosely bonded with polystyrene glue and becomes soft and pliable when wetted with resin.

Surface tissue made from finer, more closely spaced strands provides better surface finish.

Woven glass fibre is stronger, but more expensive and is available in cloth or tape form. It is used in places of stress (e.g. corners), where greater tensile strength is needed.

All forms are sold in different weights (e.g. 300, 450, 600 grams per square metre) and different widths (e.g. 25 mm in the case of tape).

Carbon fibres

Carbon fibres are a more recent development. They are spun into cord and give exceptional strength when laminated. They are spaced to withstand strain in special items like sports equipment.

fig 4.148. GRP work

AVAILABLE FORMS OF PLASTICS

Manufacturers supply a wide range of different forms (fig 4.149). Powders, granules, pellets and viscous 'liquids' provide the raw material for fabrication into finished products.

They are also available in standardised forms, i.e. films, sheets, tube, rod and extruded mouldings.

Many plastics are available in several different forms. For example, PVC is used as a powder when dip-coating metals, as film when packaging or as sheet for vacuum forming. Equally, a plastic like polypropylene can serve many different purposes.

Expanded plastics

A wide range of expanded plastics and foams are available which are light in weight, good thermal and electrical insulators and provide energy absorption and flexibility. They involve the inclusion of gas pockets to form a cellular structure. Two main varieties are manufactured which give either **open, interconnecting cells** (these are known as sponges or foams) or **closed cellular structures** (referred to as expanded plastics).

The **polyurethanes** are a good example of thermosetting polymers used in this way. In its open cell form, polyurethane foam is flexible and used in upholstery sponges. However, polyester polyurethane foam has a closed cell structure making it rigid and buoyant and suitable for use as internal reinforcement in such things as boats and aircraft wings.

In industry, the foam mixture is poured into closed moulds (e.g. chairs), and the foam then fills the enclosed space.

In the school workshop, it is used in ready made slab or block form. For example, it provides a core material for GRP work.

Expanded polystyrene is well known as a lightweight packaging material. Because 90% of its volume consists of air bubbles, it is a good thermal insulator and has excellent flotation qualities.

It is made by adding a volatile hydrocarbon liquid to the polystyrene formation of tiny beads. When heated, usually by steam, it changes to gas and the beads expand into spheres. This is often done in two stages. First it is pre-expanded to a set volume and then it is confined in a mould where the expanded beads fuse together to form the mass of material familiar in shaped packaging (fig 4.150).

In the school workshop, polystyrene foam is used in the ready formed slab variety.

fig 4.149. Packaging

NEW DEVELOPMENTS

Many new plastics continue to be developed and marketed. Foamex is the brand name of one such product. It is a foamed PVC sheet which is available in 3–9 mm thickness and has the advantage of being worked hot or cold. It can be bent quite easily and is ideally suited to the packaging of electronic circuits.

Corriflute is another light, rigid sheet material available in a range of primary colours (fig 4.151). It is made from polypropylene and is heat and impact resistant. It cuts and models well, making it suitable for a wide range of design structures and prototypes.

Futuristic materials include unusual developments with rubber. 'Anti-rubber' expands if stretched and shrinks when squeezed, what is known as the negative, poisson effect. The key to its bizarre properties apparently lies in its microscopic structure, which resembles irregular, buckled-in cubes.

These re-entrant foams promise a wide range of applications ranging from shock absorbers because of their resilience, to filters because their pores tend to open when pressure increases, so they clog less easily.

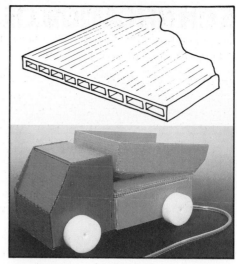

fig 4.150. Corriflute

SAFE USE AND STORAGE OF PLASTICS

1. **Skin protection:** polyester resins contain styrene which is a grease solvent and may cause skin irritation. Contact should be avoided and if it does occur, should be washed off immediately.

   Hands should be protected by using a **barrier cream** before starting work. This is a necessary precaution even with the use of polyethylene or PVC gloves. Use a proprietary cream to cleanse the skin afterwards, together with washing in warm water.

   Note: the use of solvents (e.g. acetone) for this purpose should be avoided, as degreasing can be harmful.

2. **Eye protection:** catalysts (sometimes called hardeners) are usually organic peroxides and will irritate the skin. Use special dispensers to avoid spillage and splashing. These substances will cause damage if in contact with eyes, hence the need for goggles or glasses. Any catalyst in contact with skin should be washed off immediately with warm water. When using power tools (i.e. drills) on resin/glass fibre laminates, goggles must be worn.

3. **Handling hot plastics:** plastics have a high heat capacity and burn in contact with the skin, especially in their softened or molten state. They also stick to skin readily and are difficult to remove.

   Hands should be protected by using dry industrial **leather gloves**.

4. **Respiratory (nose and throat) protection:** there are obvious dangers from the inhalation of toxic gases. GRP work gives off styrene fumes into the air, and quantities need to be carefully monitored. **Adequate ventilation**, with fresh supplies of air should be maintained at all times.

   Harmful vapours build up through the use of solvents and the breakdown of plastic material. Concentrations must be kept at a low level especially in hot weather. When cutting or cleaning up polymers, including glass fibre laminates, a **gauze mask** should be worn.

   Remember any form of dust is dangerous.

5. **Combustible materials and storage:** rags or paper which have been in contact with resin, catalyst or cleaners should be placed in metal bins and disposed of regularly. They must be kept away from naked flames!

   Resins should be stored in cool, dry conditions, preferably in metal cupboards. Shelf-life is limited so storing small amounts of stock (i.e. 3 months supply) is both economic and safe.

   Catalysts and accelerators should be stored separately in metal cupboards. **Never mix them directly** as this can promote a violent reaction with danger of explosion.

   Foamed and other highly flammable material should be stored well away from naked flames and other sources of heat.

Polythene gloves

Safety spectacles

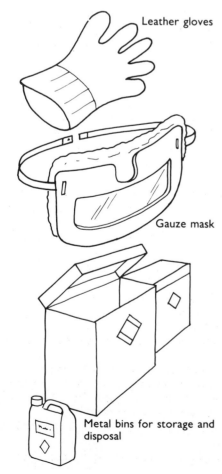

Leather gloves

Gauze mask

Metal bins for storage and disposal

fig 4.151. Safety equipment

SAFETY

All work with this type of **expanded material** should only be carried out under strictly controlled conditions. Avoid crumbling the material as it is inert and dangerous if breathed into the lungs. It is best moulded with low voltage, hot wire cutters, but fumes can still be hazardous (see safety with plastics).

IDENTIFICATION OF COMMON PLASTICS

It is possible to identify most types by using the following workshop tests. Record and analyse your findings using one specimen or several samples. Do not rely on just one test.

1. Appearance

- Is the specimen (a) stock material (b) raw polymer (c) a finished product?
- If (c) try to establish the method of manufacture or processing techniques. Look for tell-tale flow lines, sprue or ejector pin marks.
- What is the colour? Is it pigmented, transparent, translucent or opaque?
- Try to establish the basic group i.e. thermoplastic or thermoset.

2. Rigidity and feel

- How hard is the sample? Try to scratch it.
- How does it cut? Cleanly into slivers indicates a thermoplastic, if it flakes, powders or chips then a thermoset is indicated.
- Drop the sample on a hard surface. Styrenic thermoplastics (e.g. polystyrene) give a metallic ring, mouldings made from co-polymers and high impact material do not.

3. Bending

- Try to bend the sample and note the reaction and recovery.

4. Heating

- Heat a metal sheet over a bunsen flame or electric plate and place the sample on it. Does it soften, remain hard, flow, bubble, swell or char? Thermoplastics soften rather than melt, thermosets do not melt. If the sample softens then hardens with continued heating, it indicates an uncured compound which has heat-cured.
- Try to describe the odour of any fumes, relate to familiar smells (e.g. burning rubber, sweet-fruity, marigolds, burning paper, acid, rancid butter).

5. Burning

- Hold a small piece in a flame, when ignited withdraw it.
- Inflammability, does it burn? Is it self extinguishing?
- What colour is the flame?
- Note the type of flame (e.g. steady, short, tall, spluttering).
- Note the type of smoke (e.g. none, black, thick black, shot streamers).
- Is the burning accompanied by a distinct smell?

6. Density/specific gravity

- Put a sample into water. Stir to remove air bubbles. Does it float/sink?
- Specific gravity results can be found by relating weight to weight of water displaced. Remember to consider the presence of fillers and reinforcements.

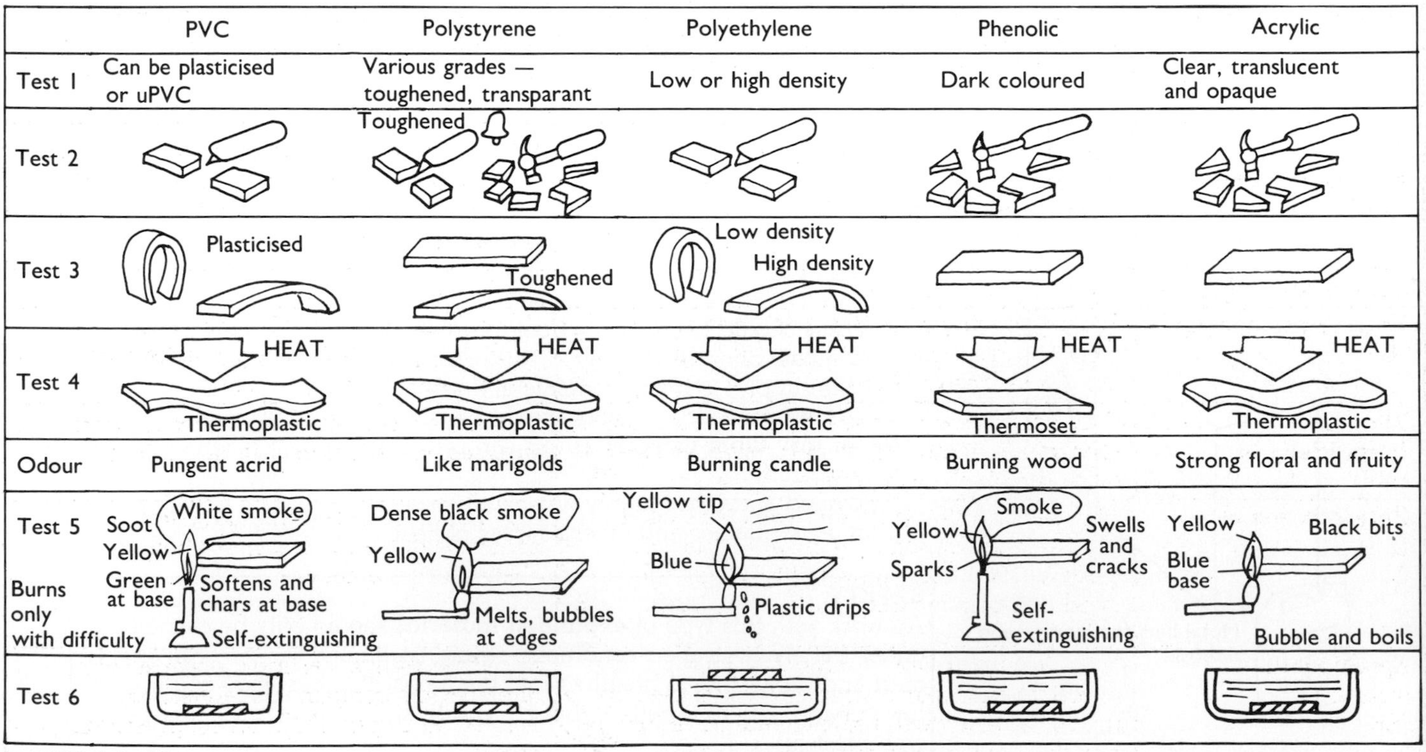

	PVC	Polystyrene	Polyethylene	Phenolic	Acrylic
Test 1	Can be plasticised or uPVC	Various grades — toughened, transparent	Low or high density	Dark coloured	Clear, translucent and opaque
Test 2		Toughened			
Test 3	Plasticised	Toughened	Low density / High density		
Test 4	HEAT — Thermoplastic	HEAT — Thermoplastic	HEAT — Thermoplastic	HEAT — Thermoset	HEAT — Thermoplastic
Odour	Pungent acrid	Like marigolds	Burning candle	Burning wood	Strong floral and fruity
Test 5	Soot, White smoke, Yellow, Green at base, Softens and chars at base, Self-extinguishing, Burns only with difficulty	Dense black smoke, Yellow, Melts, bubbles at edges	Yellow tip, Blue, Plastic drips	Smoke, Yellow, Sparks, Swells and cracks, Self-extinguishing	Yellow, Blue base, Black bits, Bubble and boils
Test 6					

fig 4.152. Identification tests

TABLE OF COMMON PLASTICS

Key: Suitability for project work
- • poor
- •• average
- ••• good

(a) Thermoplastics

MATERIAL	PROPERTIES AND WORKING CHARACTERISTICS	USES
Polythene (polyethlylene) (LDPE)	**Low density:** tough common plastic good chemical resistance, flexible, soft, attracts dust, electrical insulator, wide range of colours,	Detergent squeezy bottles, toys, packaging film, carrier bags, TV cable
(HDPE)	**High density:** stiffer, harder, higher softening point, can be sterilised, waxy feel ••	Milk crates, bottles, pipes, bowls houseware, buckets, bowls.
Polypropylene (PP)	Light, hard, impact resistant even at low temperatures, good chemical resistance, can be sterilized, easily joined, welded, good resistance to work-fatigue, bending, hinges, good mechanically •••	Medical equipment, syringes, containers with integral hinges, string, rope, nets, crates, chair shells, kitchenware, film
Polystyrene (PS)	(a) **Conventional:** light hard, stiff, colourless, transparent, brittle, low impact strength, safe with food, good water resistance	Model kits, packaging, disposable plates, cups, utensils, TV cabinets, containers
	(b) **Toughened:** increases impact, strength, pigmented	Toys, refrigerator linings
	(c) **Expanded/foam:** buoyant, lightweight, crumbles, good sound/heat insulator •••	Sound and heat insulation, packaging
Polyvinyl chloride (uPVC) **Plasticised** (PVC)	Good chemical, weather resistance, stiff, hard, tough, lightweight, wide colour ranges, needs to be stabilized for outdoor use Soft, flexible, good electrical insulator •••	Pipes, guttering, bottles, shoe soles, roofing sheets, records, window frames Underseal, hosepipes, wall coverings
Polymethyl methacrylate (Acrylic) (PMMA)	Stiff, hard, clear, very durable, IOX impact resistance of glass, but scratches easily, excellent light transmission, fibre optic qualities, safe with food, good electrical insulator, colours well, easily machined, polishes well •••	Light units, illuminated signs, record player lids, aircraft canopies, windows, rear car lights/reflectors, furniture, sanitary ware
Polyamide (Nylon)	Creamy colour, hard, tough, resilient to wear, low co-efficient of friction, bearing surfaces, self-lubricating, resistant to extremes of temperature, good chemical resistance, machines well, difficult to join except mechanically •••	Bearings, gear wheels, casings for power tools, curtain rail fittings, combs, clothing, stockings, hinges, filaments for brushes
Cellulose acetate	Tough, hard and stiff (can be made flexible), resilient, light in weight, transparent, non-flammable, easily machined, absorbs some moisture •	Pen cases, photographic film, cutlery handles, knobs, lids, spectacle frames, containers
Acrylonitrile butadienestyrene (ABS)	High impact strength and toughness, scratch resistant, light and durable, good appearance, high surface finish, resistant to chemicals •••	Kitchen ware, cases for consumer durables (e.g. cameras), toys, safety helmets, car components, telephones, food processors/mixers

(b) Thermosetting plastics

MATERIAL	PROPERTIES AND WORKING CHARACTERISTICS	USES
Urea-formaldehyde (UF)	Stiff, hard, strong, brittle, heat resistant, good electrical insulator, wide range of light colours, adhesive (Aerolite) •	(White) electrical fittings, domestic appliance parts (e.g. knobs), adhesives (wood), coating paper, textile
Melamine-formaldehyde (MF)	Stiff, hard, strong, scratch resistant, low water absorption, odourless, stain resistant, resists some chemicals, wide range of colours ••	Tableware, decorative laminates for work surfaces, electrical insulation, buttons
Polyester resin (PR)	Stiff, hard, brittle (resilient when laminated GRP), good heat and chemical resistance, electrical insulator, resists ultra-violet light, good outdoors contracts on curing, takes colour well ••	Casting, encapsulation, embedding, panels (with GRP), boats, car bodies, chair shells, containers
Epoxy resin (epoxide) (ER)	High strength when re-inforced, good chemical and wear resistance, resists heat up to 250°C, electrical insulator, adhesive for bonding unlike materials, low shrinkage ••	Surface coatings, castings, encapsulation of electronic components, adhesives, laminating paper, PCB, tanks, pressure vessels

MATERIALS –
WHAT OF THE FUTURE?

Too many variable factors make it extremely difficult, if not impossible, to predict the likely materials of the future. However, the increasing population and the development of third world countries serve to increase consumer demand for manufactured goods. Material shortages have already been created and the continued extraction and exploitation of accessible resources, whether ores, timber or oil, cannot be unlimited.

This realisation has increased the need to look for new developments. Even plastics, which fill many for the requirements previously met by more traditional materials, is largely dependent on oil. Consequently, the polymers may not be able to fulfil all future demands.

Technological developments are taking place, many allied to nuclear energy. Space stations offer tremedous potential for refining and processing new materials outside the earth's gravity, and who knows what moon rocks will reveal?

Nevertheless, we need to curb our wasteful use of existing resources. Our throw-away age of built-in obsolesence increases the problem. Every year, the average family of four will throw away the equivalent of six trees, 50 kg of metal and 40 kg of plastics.

Surely there is not only a need to conserve, but to use more effectively and recycle the world's existing resources for future generations.

fig 4.153. Cylindrical pencil container

EXERCISES

1. (a) Outline the physical and mechanical properties of a material of your choice.
    (b) Give two uses which your material is ideally equipped to tackle.

2. (a) Why is it necessary to test materials?
    (b) Give examples of different types of testing which can be carried out.
    (c) Illustrate and explain one such test in detail.

3. By means of flow diagrams, show the production of (a) ferrous metal and (b) a non-ferrous metal, from ore to useable form.

4. Explain each of the following terms used in heat treatment, giving an example of when each might be used: (a) annealing (b) normalising (c) hardening and tempering (d) case-hardening.

5. Construct a table or chart to show the difference between hardwoods and softwoods, in (a) their growing state and (b) their converted state.

6. (a) By means of sketches and brief notes, explain the terms 'conversion' and 'seasoning'.
    (b) Show how moisture content can affect 'movement' in timber.

7. (a) Outline the defects to be found in timber.
    (b) Suggest ways of avoiding these and treating/eliminating them.

8. (a) Sketch three different forms of man-made board.
    (b) What are the advantages of manufactured board when compared to timber?
    (c) Show details of how edge treatment of man-made boards can improve appearance and durability.

9. (a) Name two sources for the manufacture of plastics.
    (b) Show, by giving examples, how polymerisation produces synthetic plastics.

10. (a) Explain the difference between the two groups of plastics
        (i) thermoplastics and (ii) thermosetting plastics.
    (b) List the properties which make plastics suitable for such a wide range of applications.
    (c) How can these properties be further improved?

11. (a) Illustrate the various raw materials and standard forms of plastic to be found in the school workshop.
    (b) What special precautions need to be taken when using plastics?

12. (a) How can you identify different types of plastic?
    (b) Show simple tests and explain how these might assist identification.

13. The cylindrical container for pencils and brushes (fig 4.153) could be made in a wide variety of materials.
    What factors would determine your final choice of material?

14. The pressure to recycle materials is mounting. The energy saved from recycled aluminium is as high as 95%, with pollution also reduced.
    (a) What are the difficulties facing the introduction of any recycling programme?
    (b) Show how you would attempt to recycle any suitable materials.

15. Although we have concentrated upon three distinct groups, there are lots of other materials from which to choose, i.e. fabrics, leather, glass and ceramics. Cements, sand, aggregate and water chemically harden to give another valuable material, concrete.

    Research and collect information on one of these, noting
      (i) properties and characteristics
     (ii) available forms
    (iii) possible uses.

WORKING WITH MATERIALS

Craft skills, especially those involving hand tools, have evolved over many hundreds, even thousands of years. The 18th century craftsmen who created the beautiful furniture that has become so prized today, would have used tools very similar to those found in any school workshop.

These people had developed the ability to use tools and materials to the full without the advantage of electrically powered machinery, electric lighting, modern materials or modern adhesives.

Before you can achieve a high standard in your work it is vital that you understand the various methods of working with materials. You will then be able to select a suitable material and plan your project efficiently, using the most appropriate tools.

You will avoid many problems by adopting a thoughtful approach to your work, and making early decisions about the tools and processes that you are intending to use.

This chapter deals with the workshop processes you are likely to use while involved in realisation, and the tools you will need to carry them out. We shall deal with processes that make use of familiar hand tools and also processes utilising sophisticated machine tools. You will soon find that the correct, safe method of using any tool is the method that is also the most efficient and usually demands the least physical effort.

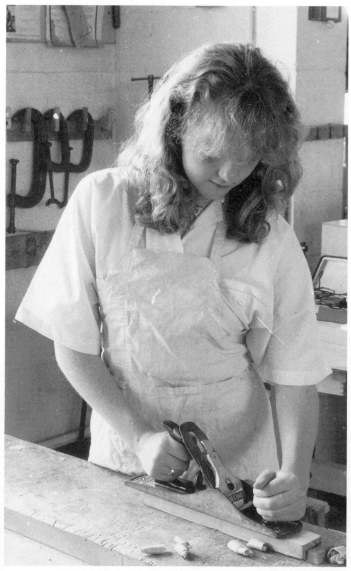

fig 5.1.   Pupil planing

fig 5.2.   Carpenter's workshop

SAFETY

The first and most important part of realisation is a proper regard for safety and safe working practice. More working days are lost in manufacturing industries as a result of accidents than for any other reason. Millions of pounds are spent annually in an attempt to make people more aware of the dangers that exist all around them, and even so, two out of every three industrial accidents are caused by individual carelessness. Some accidents are very serious, and occasionally fatal. A few seconds disregard for safety can result in an accident that could permanently change your life. So take notice of all safety instructions.

BEHAVIOUR

Accidents in school workshops can very easily result from silly behaviour. Never suffer fools in a workshop. Somebody else's foolish behaviour could result in your injury. Move around and carry tools and materials in a safe manner. Never run or cause other people to have to hurry.

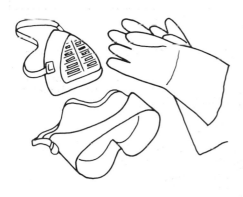

fig 5.3. Safety clothing

DRESS

Loose clothing of any sort is dangerous as it can become tangled in machinery. Before starting work you should remove jackets, remove or tuck in ties, roll up sleeves, remove jewellery and tie back long hair. You should wear protective clothing, an apron or laboratory coat, at all times, and always wear eye protection when instructed. Sensible, stout shoes should also be worn.

HOUSEKEEPING

Keep your workshop tidy. Gangways are your escape route in an emergency and must always be kept clear. The areas between benches and around machines must be kept clear to avoid tripping and falling.

Tools and protective clothing should be put away when not in use, and any breakages or losses reported.

Machines should be cleaned after use with a brush or swarf rake, not your hands. Any loose features on machinery should be secured.

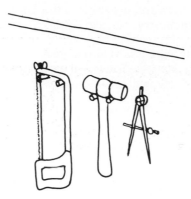

fig 5.4. Hand tools

TOOLS

See that tools are kept sharp and correctly set. They are more likely to slip and cause injury when blunt than when working efficiently.

Report any damages, such as chipped cutting edges, loose or split handles on files and chisels, and loose heads and split shafts on hammers and mallets.

When using sharp edged tools always keep both hands behind the cutting edge.

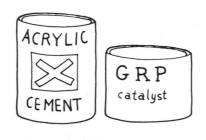

fig 5.5.   Chemicals used in the workshop

CHEMICALS

Many modern materials have a chemical base or use chemical based adhesives. Always heed the warnings given, use only in well ventilated areas and be sure to wash well after use even if you have been wearing gloves.

Wear a face mask when sawing, filing, or sanding GRP. Always consult your teacher before disposing of any chemical waste.

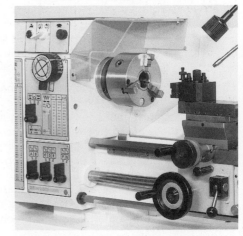

fig 5.6.   Centre lathe headstock with guard over the chuck

MACHINERY

Be confident that you understand how to operate any machine that you intend to use and always get permission before starting to use it. Never use machinery if you are in a room alone.

You should always use both the eye protection and the guards provided and check that all is secure on the machine and with your clothing before starting work.

Do not distract or stand talking to anybody who is operating a machine. Accidents with machine tools can happen very quickly so it is important that you concentrate at all times.

ACCIDENT PROCEDURE

It is important that you know what to do in the event of an accident. Make sure you know where to assemble in the event of fire and where the emergency stop buttons are located.

Do not run about or shout, as this can lead to panic. Inform a responsible adult immediately any accident occurs.

Never administer first aid unless you are trained to do so.

WORK HOLDING

There are holding devices to assist with all processes from marking out to finishing. Some holding devices restrict movement when large cutting forces are being applied, while other devices are less rigid and only restrict accidental movement. Figure 5.7 shows a heavy machine vice that could be used for holding work on a milling machine where the cutting forces are considerable. In this situation the vice needs also to be bolted down securely to the machine table. G-cramps and sash cramps (fig 5.8) are used to hold work together whilst glue is allowed to set. Here the holding forces required are much less.

fig 5.7.   Heavy machine vice

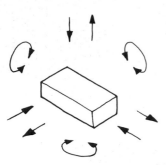
fig 5.9.   Six ways in which movement can take place

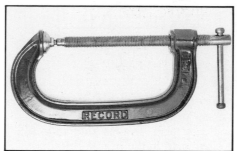
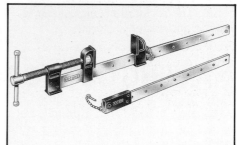
fig 5.8.   G cramp and sash cramp

The principles of holding

The principles of holding are simple, but first it is necessary to see how things can move.

Movement can take place in six ways, as shown in fig 5.9, and it can be restricted by two methods.

1. By positive location, this means against a solid object.

2. By frictional resistance, this means being gripped.

Fig 5.10 shows how all six ways in which movement takes place are restricted by the jaws of a vice.

When holding work against cutting forces, it is a good idea wherever possible to arrange for positive location to act against the cutting action.

A sawing-board provides positive location against the cutting force of a tenon saw. A bench-stop provides positive location against the cutting force of a plane.

Fig 5.12 shows a hand vice being used to hold a piece of work for drilling. Here the drill is exerting both a downwards force and a rotational force. The drill table provides positive location against the downwards force and the person holding the vice handle provides positive location against the rotational force.

Positive location prevents this rotation

Frictional resistance prevents this movement

Frictional resistance prevents this rotation

Positive location prevents this movement

These forces would be produced by sawing or filing

Frictional resistance prevents this movement

Positive location prevents this rotation

fig 5.10.   Movement restricted by jaws of vice

Cutting force

Sawing board

Cutting force

Bench stop

fig 5.11.   Positive locations acting against cutting action

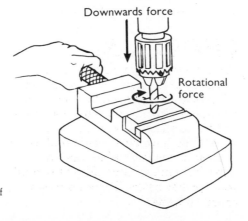
Downwards force

Rotational force

fig 5.12.   Hand vice used to hold a piece of work for drilling

Hints for work holding

1. Select a holding device that is sturdy enough to withstand the cutting forces involved.

2. Arrange for cutting forces to be restricted by positive location if possible.

3. Do not over tighten with flimsy work and remember that some vice jaws mark.

MARKING OUT

Careful, thoughtful marking out is essential to avoid wasting both material and time.

Consider the examples in fig 5.12. Both are alternative ways of marking out the development of a sheet metal tray. Fig 5.12a results in a slightly less waste than fig 5.12b, but consider the usable material remaining. The 'L' shape in fig 5.12a, though larger in area, is less likely to find an application than the rectangle in fig 5.12b. The rectangle is also easier to handle and easier to store.

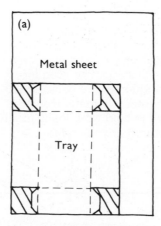
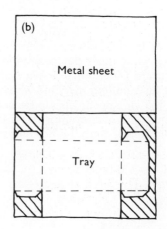

fig 5.13. Marking out

MARKING OUT TOOLS

The tools used tend to be governed by the material involved. Wood can often be adequately marked with a **pencil,** but when saw or chisel cuts are to be made across the grain, then a **marking knife** should be used. The marking knife will cut the surface fibres of the wood giving a clean start to the saw or chisel cut. Acrylic sheet is normally supplied with a protective paper covering. This paper should be left on for as long as possible to protect against scratching. A pencil can be used when marking out acrylic with the paper on. If the paper has been removed, then a **chinagraph pencil** or a **spirit based felt tip pen** is needed. **Scribers** are used for marking out on metal. The scriber has a hardened tool steel point that scratches the surface. The bright surface of many metals, for example, bright mild steel, make it difficult to see scriber marks, and it is necessary to coat the surface with **marking blue** before marking out. Marking blue is a quick drying, spirit based liquid applied with a small brush or from an aerosol can. The top should always be replaced when using liquid blue to avoid evaporation of the spirit. Evaporation results in the blue becoming too thick to use.

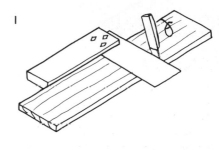

DATUMS

It is important to establish datum faces or edges and to make all measurements from these. This will prevent errors creeping in. When working with wood, an edge is planed square to an already planed side to create the **face side** and **face edge.** The stock of the try square or the marking gauge is then held against one of these datum faces. With metals and acrylic sheet, datum edges at 90° to each other should be established before marking out.

The four stages involved in squaring a line around a piece of wood are shown in figure 5.14. The tools in use are a **try square** and a **marking knife.** Notice how the stock is held against either the face side or the face edge. These are the datum faces.

Figure 5.15 shows the correct method of marking the position of a series of holes along a steel strip. **Odd leg calipers** are used to mark a line parallel to datum face 'A'. The position of each hole is then measured from datum face 'B'. The positions should not be stepped along, as any small initial error would become exaggerated. This is known as an **accumulative error.**

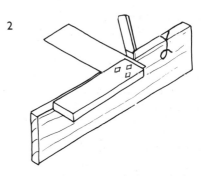

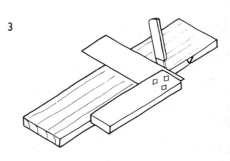

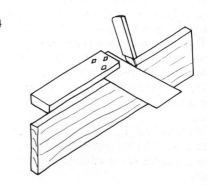

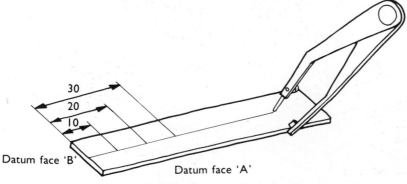

fig 5.15. Correct method of marking the position of a series of holes

fig 5.14. Try square and marking knife

84

Marking gauges

The marking gauge has a similar function to the odd leg calipers. Marking gauges are used on wood to mark lines parallel to the face side and face edge.

The gauge is set as shown in 5.16 using a steel rule. All rules used in the workshop must have a zero end. Variations on the marking gauge are the **cutting gauge** and the **mortise gauge**.

Cutting gauges have a cutter instead of a spur and are used for marking across the grain. The mortise gauge has two spurs and will mark two parallel lines. It is used for marking out mortise and tenons.

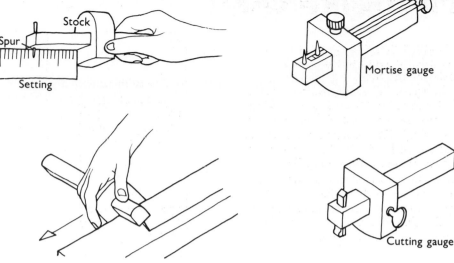

fig 5.16. Marking gauge, mortise gauge and cutting gauge

HOLES AND CIRCLES

Centre marks for holes to be drilled in metal are achieved using a **centre punch** and an engineer's hammer. The indentation produced provides a start for the drill. Centre punches have a 90° point angle.

Dot punches are similar to centre punches, but they have a 60° point angle. They are used to add witness marks to a scribed line that may be in danger of being rubbed off. Dot punches are also used to mark the centre of an arc and provide anchorage for **spring dividers**.

Spring dividers are used to scribe arcs on metal and acrylic surfaces. A **drawing compass** should be used on acrylic with the protective paper intact. Either dividers or compasses may be used on wood and man-made boards.

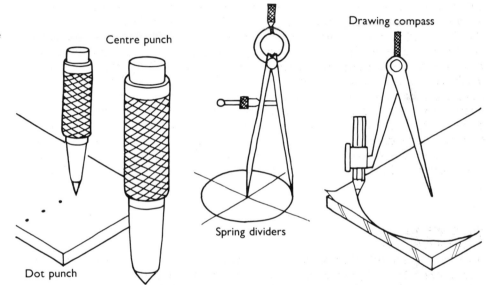

fig 5.17. Tools for marking holes and circles

PRECISION MARKING OUT

For very accurate marking out it is necessary to work from a **surface plate.**

Surface plates are made from cast iron and have an accurately ground or planed top surface. This surface should be protected by a cover when the plate is not in use.

The plate forms a datum and measurements are transferred from a rule using a **surface gauge** (see fig 5.18). Surface gauges have a fine adjustment and also a fine scribing point.

Work is held precisely vertical by clamping it to an **angle bracket,** a heavy accurately machined iron casting.

Vee blocks and **clamps** are used to hold cylindrical work for marking out.

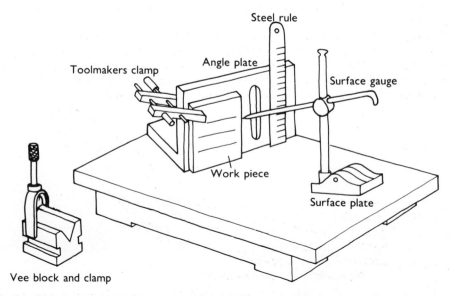

fig 5.18. Surface gauge

MEASUREMENT

Choice of measuring device is determined by the degree of accuracy required, not by the material.

In many situations the rule is the easiest tool to use and is sufficiently accurate. In some cases it is necessary to measure to a standard beyond that of a rule, in which event a **Vernier caliper** or a **micrometer** may be used.

RULES

All rules used in the workshop should be zero ended. The most common type of rule is the 150 mm or 300 mm **steel rule.** These are graduated in millimetres and are precision instruments. Extending **steel tape** rules are useful when measuring long lengths of material and when fabricating frames and carcases.

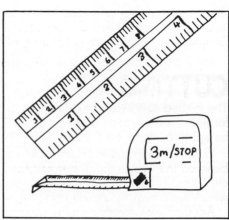

fig 5.19.   Steel rule and steel tape

VERNIERS

The Vernier scale, named after the inventor, is a method of sub-dividing a main scale into smaller parts. This principle is applied to **calipers, height gauges** and **protractors.**

For example, the main scale of a pair of calipers graduated in millimetres has a Vernier scale as part of the moving jaw. The Vernier scale is 49 mm long, divided into 50 equal parts. Each part is therefore 0.98 mm long or 0.02 mm shorter than the 1 mm divisions of the main scale. This means that as the Vernier scale moves past the main scale, each 0.02 mm of movement will cause a line on each scale to coincide, thus an accuracy of 0.02 mm is achieved.

MICROMETERS

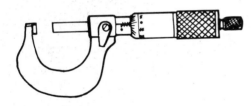

To understand the principle of the micrometer you need only to look at a G cramp. Turning the thimble closes the gap between the measuring faces through the action of a precision internal screw thread. The pitch of the thread is 0.5 mm, thus one revolution will close the gap by 0.5 mm. By marking the thimble with 50 equal divisions, an accuracy of 0.01 m (0.5 divided by 50) is achieved. The barrel is graduated in half millimetres, whole millimetres above the line and 0.5 millimetres below.

To read the micrometer:

1. Read the number of whole millimetres exposed.

2. Add on any visible ½ millimetre.

3. Add on the reading from the thimble 0 — 0.49 millimetres.

The most common workshop micrometer has a range of 0 — 25 mm. The same principle is also applied to **internal micrometers, depth micrometers** and a full range of **large framed micrometers** up to those reading 575 mm — 600 mm.

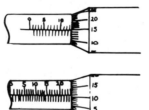

fig 5.21.   0 - 25 mm micrometer

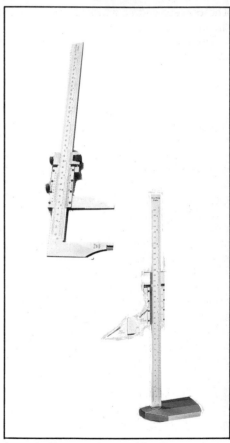

fig 5.20.   Vernier caliper and height gauge

Electronic digital micrometers provide direct digital readout, reducing the chances of reading errors. They can be switched from metric to imperial and can be zeroed at any point to enable them to be used as a comparitor.

fig 5.22.   Electronic micrometer

WASTING

Wasting processes are those that produce waste or unusable material by cutting bits out or cutting bits off. They include sawing, drilling, planing, chiselling, centre lathe turning, wood turning, filing, milling and screw cutting.

CUTTING

The cutting action involved is the same for all wasting processes. In its simplest form it can be likened to driving a wedge into the material causing the waste to be split off, as in fig 5.23a.

With this simple wedge action a large amount of friction is encountered between the wedge and the workpiece. A large amount of energy is needed to overcome this friction. The friction can be reduced by lifting the back of the wedge and creating a clearance angle (fig 5.23b).

Another way of reducing the friction is to make the wedge angle smaller, but this also makes it weaker and in practice it wears more quickly.

The cutting angles of tools have to be varied to suit the material being cut. The correct angles will ensure efficient cutting and a good resultant surface finish.

The basic wedge cutting action can be identified in all of the processes shown in fig 5.24.

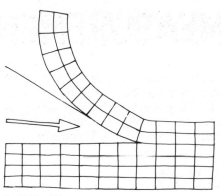

fig 5.23a. Wasting process

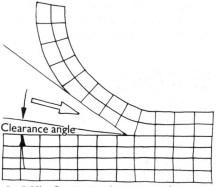

fig 5.23b. Creating a clearance angle

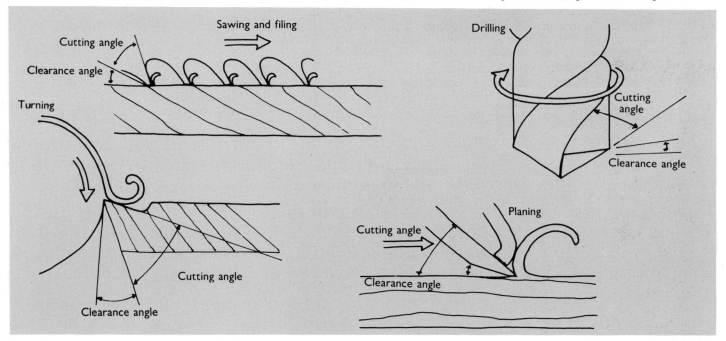

fig 5.24. Basic wedge cutting action

SHEARING

The exception to cutting using a wedge or a toothed cutting action, is shearing. Scissors, tin snips and guillotines shear waste from the workpiece without creating filings, swarf or sawdust. In this process two cutting edges come together or pass by each other, separating the waste from the work (fig 5.25).

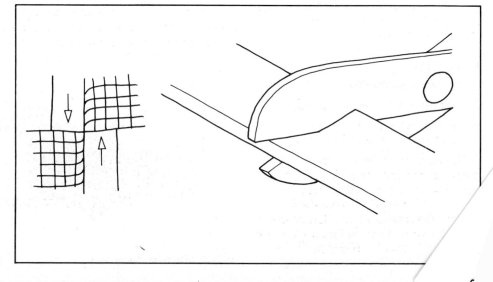

fig 5.25. Shearing

SAWING

Sawing is a method of separating material that is needed, from the material that is not.

The cut or gap that a saw produces is called the **kerf.** The kerf is wider than the blade so that the blade does not jam and get stuck. This is usually achieved by bending alternate teeth to the left and right. This is called the **set.** The set of hacksaw blades is sometimes in the form of a wavy cutting edge (fig 5.26).

Always cut to the waste side of the line when sawing and allow a small amount of waste for finishing (fig 5.27).

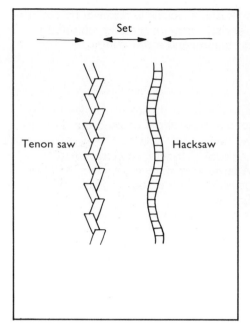

fig 5.26. Set of saw blades

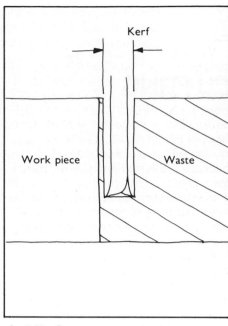

fig 5.27. Cutting to waste side of the line

Choice of saws
The choice of saw is governed by the material to be cut. Saws designed for woodworking are not hard enough to cut metal and should never be used for this purpose. Metal working saws will cut wood, but not very efficiently. Plastics can be cut with either, though handsaws should not be used.

SAWING STRAIGHT

Handsaws
Large pieces of wood require large saws. **Rip saws** are used for sawing along the grain. The blade is about 650 mm long with 4 or 5 teeth per 25 mm. Hold short lengths vertical in a vice and longer boards between trestles. Sawing across the grain and sawing manufactured boards requires a **cross cut saw.** These are similar in length to rip saws, but the teeth are sharpened differently to cut across the wood fibres more cleanly. The teeth are slightly finer, 6 to 8 teeth per 25 mm. The **panel saw** is a shorter version of the cross cut saw (approximately 500 mm). Having finer teeth (10 per 25 mm), the panel saw is suited to thinner wood and sheet ply wood. Hand saws should be used on wood only.

Backsaws
Saws with stiff backs are more suitable for detailed work than those with blades that flex. The **tenon saw** is the most used backsaw for both wood and plastics. The blade is 250 mm to 350 mm long with 12 to 14 teeth per 25 mm. It is used mostly with a sawing board on small work, including most joints. The **dovetail saw** is 200 mm long with 20 to 25 teeth per 25 mm. It is used for small, very accurate work, such as cutting dovetails and small tenons.

Hacksaws
Hacksaws and **junior hacksaws** have a replaceable blade held in tension in the frame. The blade should be put in with the teeth facing forwards to cut on the forward stroke. Hacksaw frames are adjustable to accommodate 250 mm or 300 mm length blades. The blade can also be turned through 90° for long cuts where the frame would collide with the work. Blades have a pitch of 14, 18, 24 or 32 teeth per 25 mm. Selecting the correct blade is important. Soft materials require a coarse pitch and hard materials a fine pitch, but an overriding requirement is that three teeth should be in contact at all times. This means that a fine pitch is needed for tubes and thin sections.

Sheet saws can be likened to a panel saw with a hacksaw blade attached. Standard 300 mm or special 400 mm blades are screwed to the sheet steel blade. Sheet saws are used to cut sheet metals and plastics, and are especially useful for corrugated sheet.

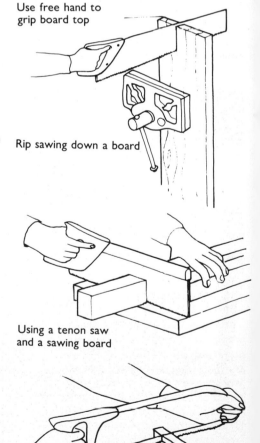

Use free hand to grip board top

Rip sawing down a board

Using a tenon saw and a sawing board

Hacksawing

fig 5.28. Sawing straight

SAWING CURVES

Sawing curves requires a saw with a narrow blade so that it can turn within its kerf. Unfortunately, narrow blades break easily so great care must be taken.

Coping saws are the most commonly used saws for curves in wood and plastics. The replaceable blade is held in a frame with the teeth pointing backwards to cut on the pull stroke. This is because the blade is too flexible to be pushed. The blade can be angled in the frame similarly to a hacksaw if the frame impinges upon the work.

Piercing saws are similar to coping saws, but have very thin blades and are used for fine curves in thin metal and plastics.

Abrafiles are toothed circular blades that fit, into a hacksaw frame using a pair of small adaptors. Coarse, medium and fine grades are available.

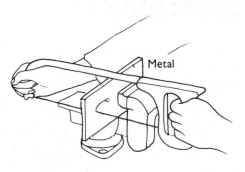

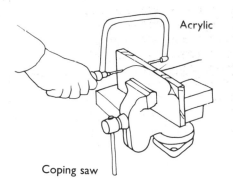

Metal

Abrafile

Blade passed through pre-drilled hole

Acrylic

Coping saw

fig 5.29. Coping saw and abrafile

Portable, electric **jig saws** make easy work of cutting curved shapes in sheet materials. Jig saws have short, reciprocating, interchangeable blades allowing for the selection of a blade which, along with the adjustable speed, will enable the saw to tackle most types of material.

The base plate of the saw can be tilted to produce a sloping cut and some jig saws can be fitted with a fence so that straight cuts parallel to an edge are possible.

The absence of any frame, unlike the coping saw and abrafile, means that jig saws can work deep into large sheets.

fig 5.30. Black and Decker jig saw

MACHINE SAWS

Electrically powered machine saws are a great asset in any busy workshop. They are also very dangerous and must only be used by a suitably qualified adult.

Circular saws can be fitted with either rip or cross cut blades for 'with the grain' and 'across the grain' sawing of wood. Very large sheets of manufactured board can be accommodated by extending the saw table. Correct blade guard setting is essential.

Powered hacksaws make light work of steel up to 150 mm diameter. Many are fitted with a re-circulating coolant supply to assist efficient cutting, and most have automatic switch-off after each cut.

Bandsaws can be fitted with blades suited to wood, plastics or metal. The blade is a continuous loop, with narrow blades enabling the cutting of complex profiles with sharp radii.

> **SAFETY**
> Accidents happen very quickly with machine saws. Never distract anybody who is operating a machine saw.

fig 5.31. Circular saw

DRILLING

Drilling is the process that produces holes by rotating a drill or boring bit in a hand powered or electric powered device. Drilling on a lathe is the exception to this and is dealt with later in the chapter.

TWIST DRILLS

Twist drills are the most common tool for producing holes and are suited to wood, metal and plastics. Twist drills with tungsten carbide cutting tips will drill brick, concrete and; with extreme care, glass and ceramics.

The twist drill has two cutting edges that work together with a basic wedge type of cutting action. The twist or helix of the drill forms flutes that carry the waste, called swarf, up and out of the hole.

Some drills are made of carbon steel, but better quality, harder wearing drills are made from high speed steel (HSS). There are two main types of twist drill.

1. **Straight shanked,** sometimes called **jobber drills.** These are made in sizes up to 20 mm diameter, though few chucks can accommodate more than 13 mm.

2. **Taper shanked** These have **morse taper-shanks** that locate directly into machine spindles or lathe tailstocks. They are readily available in sizes up to 37.5 mm diameter. Industrial size No. 6 morse tapers can take 100 mm diameter drills.

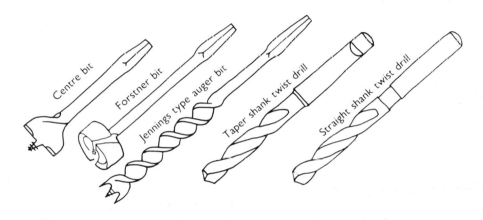

fig 5.32. Straight shank drill

BORING BITS

For holes in wood larger than 8 mm, a twist drill tends to leave a rough finish. Wood boring bits have a **spur** to cut the fibres cleanly. The centre screw point pulls the bit into the wood and the helix or auger on the Jennings type bit clears the waste from deep holes.

fig 5.33. Twist drill and boring bits

Centre bits, from 6 mm to 50 mm in diameter, are suitable only for shallow holes as there is no auger to remove the waste nor parallel sides to guide it in the hole.

Jennings type auger bits are similar to centre bits, but are suited to deep holes of 6 mm to 38 mm in diameter.

Forstner pattern bits do not have a centre screw point and are guided by an outer cutting ring. They are able to produce clean, flat bottomed holes.

Wood boring bits usually have tapered square shanks. Centre and Forstner bits however, may be cylindrical for use in drilling machines. The **Carpenters ratchet brace** is designed for square shanked bits. It is best used horizontally, so that body weight can be applied. The ratchet means that a full rotation of the handle is not required where space is limited. When boring through wood or manufactured board, such as blockboard, the bit should just pierce through and then be removed. The hole is then completed from the reverse side (fig 5.34). This avoids splitting on the back and ensures a clean hole.

fig 5.34. Carpenter's ratchet brace

PILLAR DRILLS

These are either bench or floor mounted (fig 5.35). The chuck has a 13 mm capacity, but can be removed from the spindle to facilitate the use of Morse taper shanked drills.

The table is adjustable for height and often angle of inclination. A chuck guard is provided and this must be used at all times.

The speed at which a drill is run is governed by the material and the drill size. Soft materials and small drills run fast and harder materials and larger drills run slow. Fig 5.36 gives a guide to drilling speeds. Drilling speed is varied manually by adjusting the belt drive.

The chuck is lowered via a rack and pinion mechanism and sensitive pressure should be applied to encourage efficient cutting. Do not force it or allow it to rub. When the drill breaks through, especially with acrylic and thin sheet metal, there is a danger that it will snatch. At this point it is important to reduce the downwards pressure.

fig 5.35. Floor mounted pillar drill

SAFETY – Wear eye protection when using any power drill.

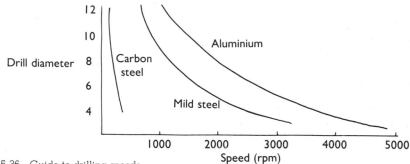

fig 5.36. Guide to drilling speeds

Hand drills

The **hand drill** or **wheel brace** has a chucking capacity of 8 mm. It can be used vertically or horizontally and the side handle can be removed when access is a problem.

The **breast drill** is a larger hand drill. It has a 13 mm chuck and is used horizontally against the chest with body weight providing additional force.

Portable power drills

Electric powered portable drills vary greatly in their degree of sophistication. The most basic type have a single speed and an 8 mm chuck. More expensive models have 13 mm chucks, depth stops, two speeds and a percussion facility for masonry.

fig 5.37. Portable electric drill

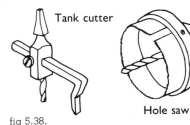

fig 5.38.

Large hole cutters

Tank cutters are used in a carpenter's brace for holes from 25 mm to 125 mm diameter. They are intended for cutting holes in thin metal steel, but are equally effective on plastics.

Hole saws are used in power drills and have interchangeable toothed cutting rings to give a range from 20 mm to 75 mm. Both tank cutters and hole saws remove a disc of material rather than swarf and are, therefore, trepaning and not drilling.

COUNTERSINKS AND COUNTERBORES

It is often desirable to have screw heads finishing flush with the surface. A head that stands proud may obstruct movement and spoil the appearance. **Countersinks** have a 90° point angle to provide a conical seat for countersunk screw heads. There are two types, light **'rose' countersinks** for hand drill use, and **machine countersinks** for power drills.

Counterbores provide a seat for the head of cheese head screws or bolt heads. Counterbores are not tapered and so require a pilot to provide location in the hole.

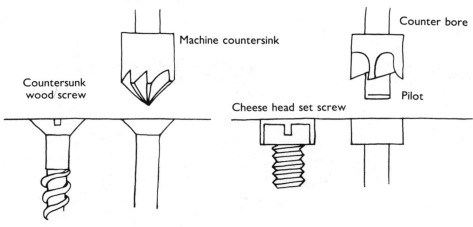

fig 5.39. Countersinks and counterbores

CHISELLING

Chiselling is a process applicable to wood and metal only. **Wood chisels** are used for wood and **cold chisels** for metal.

Chiselling is essentially a basic wedge cutting action (see page 87).

CHISELLING WOOD

There are four types of wood chisels (fig 5.40).

Firmer chisels are used for general purpose work. They have a square-edged blade and can withstand light mallet blows. They are available in widths from 3 mm to 50 mm.

Bevel edged chisels have a less strong bevelled blade to get into corners easily. They should not normally be driven by a mallet. Widths are the same as for firmer chisels.

Mortise chisels have thick blades in widths from 6 mm to 13 mm. They are designed to withstand heavy blows and an amount of levering.

Gouges are really curved bladed firmer chisels, used for carving and concave profiles.

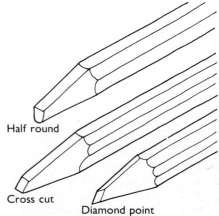

fig 5.40. Chisels

Firmer chisel

Bevel edged chisel Mortise chisel Gouge

Shock absorbing washer

Paring

Paring is the process of removing small shavings using hand pressure. One hand pushes the chisel while the other hand is used to control and guide the cutting edge. Paring can be either horizontal or vertical. Always keep both hands behind the cutting edge.

Chopping

Chopping is driving the chisel using blows from a mallet or hammer. A hammer should not be used on a wooden handled chisel. Chopping is carried out when removing large quantities of waste such as when cutting mortises. The chisel should be held firmly and the work clamped down.

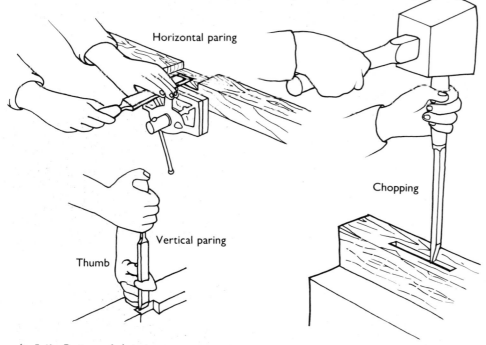

Horizontal paring

Chopping

Vertical paring

Thumb

fig 5.41. Paring and chopping

CHISELLING METAL

Cold chisels have a hardened and tempered cutting edge. The other end is left soft to withstand hammer blows. Cutting sheet metal is carried out in one of two ways: shearing across the top of an engineer's vice, or by vertical chiselling with the material supported on a soft steel cutting block. Half round, cross-cut and diamond pointed cold chisels are used for shaped grooves and awkward corners.

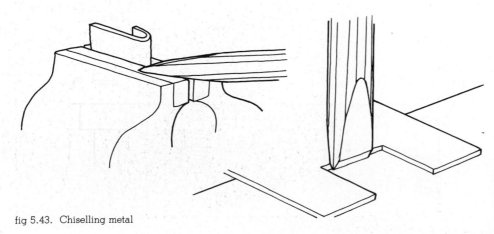

fig 5.43. Chiselling metal

Half round

Cross cut

Diamond point

fig 5.42. Cutting edges

SAFETY — Keep chisels sharp. Keep both hands behind the cutting edge. Chisel away from your body.

PLANING

Planing is a process that is best restricted to wood. Acrylic can be planed, but not easily.

The wedge cutting action of the plane is very similar to that of the wood chisel, but where a chisel tends to split the wood when working with the grain, the plane is ideally suited for this purpose.

The two types of plane most frequently found in school workshops are **Jack planes** and **Smoothing planes.**

Jack planes are 350 mm long and are used for planing wood flat and to size.

Smoothing planes are shorter, 250 mm long, and lighter. They are used for finishing, planing end grain and are generally easy to handle.

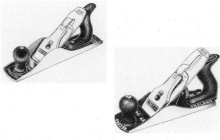

fig 5.44. Jack plane and smoothing plane

Hints for planing

1. Check that the plane is sharp and correctly set.

2. Stand firm and comfortable without having to over reach.

3. Press down on the front and push from the back.

4. When planing with the grain, plane in the direction that lays it, rather than the direction that lifts it.

5. On narrow edges, to avoid wobbling, hold the toe rather than the knob (fig 5.46).

6. To avoid splitting when planing across end grain, plane through onto some waste or plane from alternative sides (see fig 5.47).

7. If shavings jam, then remove them with care from above. Never use a rule or chisel from beneath.

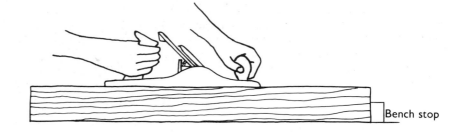

fig 5.45. Planing with the grain

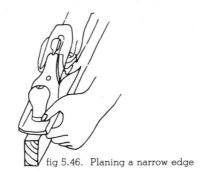 

fig 5.46. Planing a narrow edge   fig 5.47. Planing end grain

Special purpose planes

There are numerous special purpose planes designed for very specific operations.

Plough planes are for cutting grooves parallel to an edge.
Routers are for finishing housings and grooves across the grain.
Shoulder planes, which are narrow with full width blades, are for finishing against a shoulder, such as on tenons.
Rebate planes are for rebating along the grain.
Spokeshaves are for working curved surfaces.

fig 5.48. Plough plane

SURFORM TOOLS

Surforms are an example of traditional tools evolving to suit modern requirements. This range of tools consists of a body or frame onto which a replaceable blade is fitted. The blade has hundreds of cutting edges with a hole behind each to clear the waste and thus avoid clogging.

Surforms are available in a variety of shapes and sizes. There are short and long 'plane' types with flat or curved cutting faces, a 'file' type also with a flat or curved surface and a round 'file'.

The blades are graded: standard cut, for rapid shaping of softwoods and soft plastics such as nylon; fine cut for finishing and for hardwoods, soft metals and acrylic; special cut for mild steel and plastic laminates.

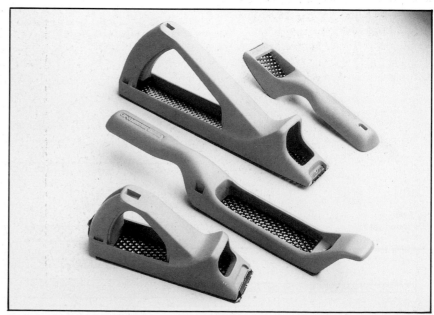

fig 5.49. Range of surform tools

FILING

Filing is a very versatile wasting process. Files are made of high carbon steel. The body is hardened and tempered with the tang left soft. Cutting is achieved by rows of teeth removing small particles called filings.

Engineers files

Engineers files are the largest group of files and these are classified by length, shape and cut.

File length is selected according to area of work.

The shape of the work will determine the shape of the file.

General surfacing work is carried out with a **hand file, a flat file** or the flat surface of a **half round file.** The flat file is a general purpose file, which tapers towards the end. Hand files are flat, parallel and have one uncut safe edge, to prevent cutting into one face of a square corner while the other is being filed. The curved surface of a half round file is for concave curves.

Square files are used for slots and tight corners; if the corner is less than 90°, then a **triangular file** should be used. **Round files** are for enlarging holes and for round-ended slots. Narrow slots require the thin **warding file.**

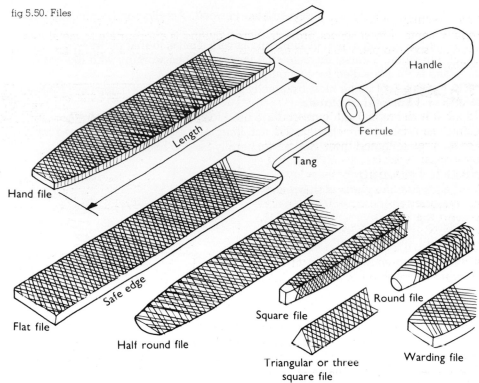

fig 5.50. Files

Handle
Ferrule
Length
Tang
Hand file
Safe edge
Flat file
Half round file
Square file
Triangular or three square file
Round file
Warding file

Most files are **double cut,** the cuts in the face running in two directions producing small diamond shaped teeth. **Single cut** files have cuts in one direction only and are most suited to light finishing work. Five grades of cuts exist. Rough and bastard cuts for coarse work, second cut files for general use and smooth and dead smooth files for fine cuts prior to finishing.

Other types of file

Dreadnought files (fig 5.53) have a curved cut and are used for the rapid removal of soft and fibrous materials (e.g. copper, aluminium and glass fibre).

Rasps (fig 5.54) have individual teeth instead of cuts and are most suited to working wood.

Needle or **Swiss files** (fig 5.55) are very small precision versions of engineers files. They have dead smooth cuts and are available in a large range of shapes.

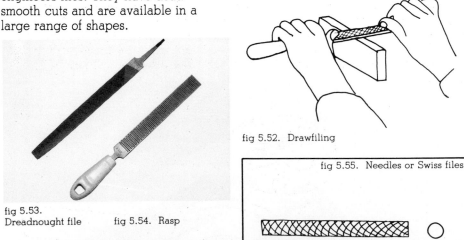

fig 5.53.
Dreadnought file   fig 5.54. Rasp

fig 5.51. Crossfiling

fig 5.52. Drawfiling

fig 5.55. Needles or Swiss files

Hints for filing

1. **Crossfiling** (see fig 5.51) is for the rapid removal of waste down to a line.

2. Always stand firm, but comfortable, with your feet apart and your thumb on the top of the handle.

3. Use a firm left hand grip for coarse crossfiling and a lighter grip for light work.

4. Keep your forearm and the file in a horizontal straight line. This is made easier by holding your work in a fixed vice at a comfortable height.

5. When crossfiling, use the whole length of the file and a downwards forwards pressure to make it cut. Files only cut on the forward stroke.

6. **Drawfiling** (see fig 5.52) is to remove the marks left by crossfiling to obtain an improved surface finish.

7. Always use a smooth file for drawfiling and keep your hands as close to the work as possible.

8. Finer finishes can be achieved by wrapping a strip of emery cloth around the file and then repeating the process.

SAFETY — Never use a file without a handle.

SCREW CUTTING

Screw cutting by hand using ISO metric threads from M3 to M14 will satisfy the requirements of most school projects. Screw cutting is appropriate to metal and plastics (see also page 133 'Nuts and bolts' and page 99 'Screw cutting on the centre lathe').

TAPPING

Tapping is the term used to describe cutting an internal or female thread. For all sizes of thread there is a set of three taps: taper tap, second tap and plug tap. The **taper tap** has a long 'lead in' taper to assist in starting the cutting true to the axis of the hole. The **second tap** has a shorter taper and the **plug tap** only a chamfered end. They should be used in sequence until a full thread is achieved. On thin material it is only necessary to use the taper tap.

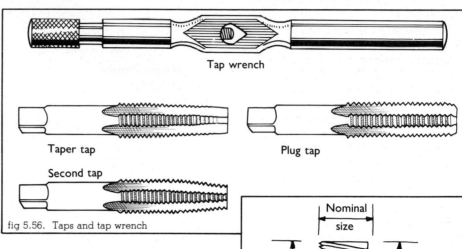

fig 5.56. Taps and tap wrench

fig 5.57. Tapping

It is essential that the drilled hole to be tapped is the correct size. This tapping drill size must be taken from a chart of tapping sizes. The size is smaller than the nominal size to allow for material to be cut out. For example, an M10 thread needs a 8.5 mm diameter hole.

Taps are driven by a **tap wrench** and the method of operation is important. Taps are usually high speed steel (HSS) and are hardened and tempered making them brittle and easy to break. Each clockwise cutting turn should be followed by a half turn anti-clockwise to break off the swarf. Failure to do this will result in the flutes becoming clogged and the tap jamming.

Nominal Diameter	Pitch (mm)	Tapping drill size (mm)
M3	0.5	2.5
M4	0.7	3.3
M5	0.8	4.2
M6	1.0	5.0
M8	1.25	6.8
M10	1.5	8.5
M12	1.75	10.2
M14	2.0	12.0

fig 5.58. Tapping drill sizes

Blind holes

Blind holes are those that do not go right through the material. The tapping size hole is drilled deeper than the required depth of thread to accommodate the chamfered end of the plug tap, and also any swarf that falls to the bottom. It is easy to break a tap in a blind hole, but very difficult to get a broken tap out, so care should be taken.

THREADING

Threading is used to describe the process of cutting the external or male thread. The tool used is a **split die.** This is held in a **die stock.** Die stocks have three screws to provide location and adjustment for the die. Tightening the centre screw will open the die resulting in a tighter fitting thread. Tightening the two outside screws will close the die to provide a looser fit. Dies have a tapered lead on the side with the writing on to help them get started. Filing a taper on the end of the rod to be threaded will also help. The rod should be nominal size (e.g. 10 mm diameter for an M10 thread). Dies are used in a similar way to taps. For the same reason, a turn clockwise must be followed by a half turn anti-clockwise.

Hints for screw cutting

1. Always use a suitable lubricant. For steels use a proprietary cutting compound. For aluminium and copper use paraffin. No lubricant is needed for brass and plastics.

2. Check for squareness when starting taps and dies since this cannot be corrected later.

3. When cutting both internal and external threads, cut the internal thread first. The die being adjustable enables the external thread to be cut to provide the fit required.

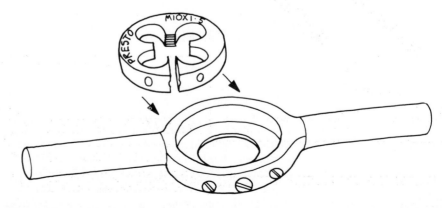

fig 5.59. Split die and die stock

CENTRE LATHE
TURNING

It is difficult to imagine a mechanical device that does not contain a cylindrical component. Projects of a mechanical nature will nearly always require the use of a centre lathe to turn components. Wheels, axles, pistons, pivots and similar mechanisms are all produced by turning. Care and precision will ensure good fits and result in a long working life for parts that must work together.

Lathes are amongst the earliest forms of machine tools. Centre lathes that were able to cut metals in the same way as those common today, were developed in the 19th century. The most recent developments in turning with the whole process being controlled by computer are dealt with in chapter 7.

The principle of turning is straightforward. Work is held firmly and rotated while a cutting tool held in a tool post cuts the work using a simple wedge cutting action. The shape of work produced is dependent on the path taken by the tool. It will be of either cylindrical form or it will be flat (fig 5.60).

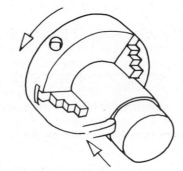
Parallel turning producing a cylindrical form

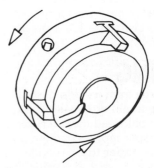
Facing producing a flat surface

fig 5.60. Parallel turning and facing

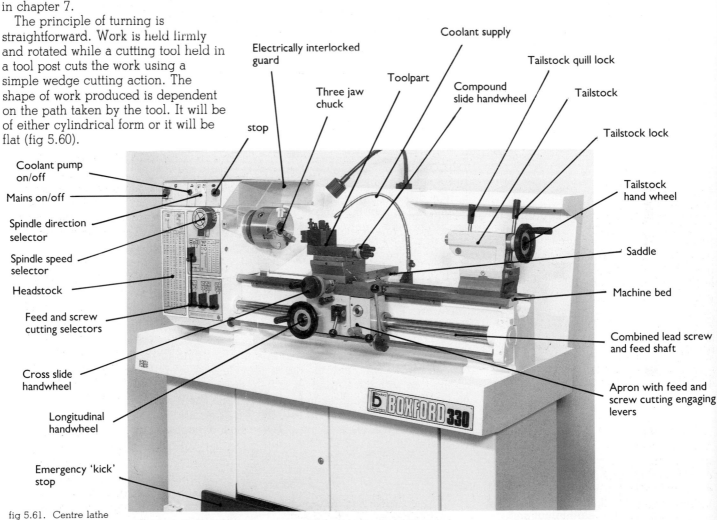

fig 5.61. Centre lathe

Centre lathes, like the one shown in fig 5.61, have four main elements: a rigid bed, a headstock containing the gearbox and most of the controls, a saddle that travels along the bed, and a tailstock. The size of a lathe is determined by the swing and the distance between centres. The swing is the largest diameter that the lathe can accommodate; in the machine shown this is 330 mm. The distance between centres is the distance measured along the axis between a centre in the headstock spindle nose and a centre in the tailstock in its rearmost position. This would represent the longest possible length of material that could be held between centres (see opposite page). The Boxford 330 lathe shown is available with either 750 mm between centres (the one shown), or with 1000 mm between centres.

HOLDING WORK

Holding work on a centre lathe can be a problem. The important point to remember is that your piece of work is going to rotate at high speed and may be subjected to large cutting forces. Therefore, the work must be held very firmly and securely.

The **self-centring 3 jaw-chuck** is the most common work holding device, but it is only suitable for short cylindrical work. Turning the chuck key causes all three jaws to close together, ensuring that the centre line of the work remains on the rotational axis of the machine. The jaws are stepped to enable bored work to be held on the inside (see fig 6.62). A second set of jaws with the steps in the opposite direction further increases the versatility of the 3 jaw-chuck. Care must be taken when changing from one set to another. Do not mix up the sets and ensure that the number on the jaws (1, 2 and 3) coincides with the number next to the slots in the chuck body. Although regarded as self-centring, repeatability cannot be relied upon. It is good practice to complete all of the operations on one end of a workpiece before altering its position in the chuck.

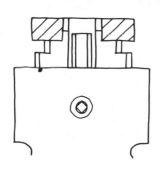
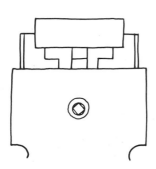

fig 5.62. Self-centring 3 jaw chuck

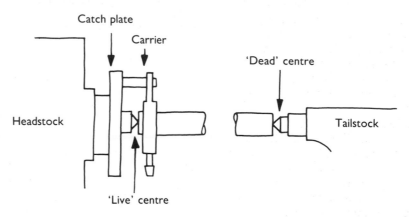

fig 5.63. Between centres

Long pieces of work should be held **between centres** (fig 6.63), one in the headstock spindle nose and one in the tailstock. This is the most accurate method of work holding, in terms of repeatability. Work can be removed from the lathe and replaced in the knowledge that it is returning to precisely the same position. This enables small batches of the same component to be machined by carrying out one operation on each component before moving on to the next operation, unlike when using the 3 jaw-chuck.

Work must be prepared by facing and centre drilling both ends in order to accommodate the centres. The headstock spindle requires a reducing bush so that the 'live' centre can be located. The appropriate sized carrier or 'driving dog' should be clamped to the workpiece. If the diameter of this end is already finished, a small piece of soft material, such as aluminium, should be used to protect the finished surface. Drive is transmitted from a catch plate screwed onto the spindle, to the carrier. The 'dead' centre in the tailstock provides support for the other end of the work. Ideally, this will be a revolving centre that rotates freely on an internal ball race. Alternatively a centre, or if it is necessary to work right up to the end, a half centre can be used, but these require lubrication to reduce friction.

fig 5.64. 4 jaw chuck

The **independent 4 jaw-chuck** (fig 5.64) is designed for holding square and rectangular sectioned material and irregular shapes. Each jaw on a 4 jaw-chuck is tightened independently. This enables more force to be exerted and firmer holding to be achieved. The jaws are independently reversible to assist in holding awkward, irregular shapes. Although more versatile than the 3 jaw-chuck, the 4 jaw-chuck can be time consuming to set up.

Awkward shaped work may be clamped to a **face plate** (fig 5.65), if necessary using an angle bracket.

Counterweights should also be added. An out of balance face plate will damage the lathe's headstock bearings and could be dangerous.

fig 5.65. Face plate

TURNING TOOLS

Centre lathe tools need to be both hard and tough. Solid tools are high carbon steel or high speed steel (HSS). High speed steel 'bits' are available for purpose made holders. Carbide tips are extremely hard and resistant to wear and are available brazed onto shanks or as 'throw away' inserts for special holders.

Tool profiles

Selection of a tool is determined by the operation to be carried out. Roughing down to within 1 mm of finished size is carried out with a roughing tool. Fine finishing cuts are best done using a tool with a small radiused point. Knife tools (left or right) enable the cutting of sharp corners. The parting-off tool is used to produce undercuts and grooves and for cutting your work off from the material that remains in the chuck. Screw-cutting tools have a profile to suit the required screw thread. Internal turning requires the use of boring bars which may have any of the above profiles.

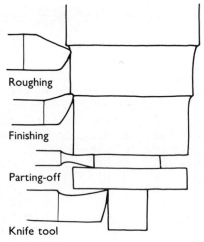

fig 5.66. Tool profiles

Tool geometry

Tool geometry refers to the angles that make up the wedge shape of the turning tool. Efficient cutting of any material demands that these angles are correct for that material. The term used for the top angle of the tool measured along the line of cut is **rake. Clearance angles** are those that enable only the cutting point of the tool to be in contact with the work (see fig. 5.67).

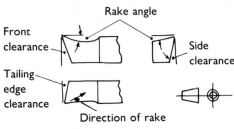

fig 5.67. Clearance angles

fig 5.68. Setting tool to the correct height

Tool setting

For efficient cutting, the tool point must be located on centre height (see fig 5.68), and it should be as far back in the tool post as possible. Excessive overhang creates vibration or chatter, resulting in a poor quality finish.

> **SAFETY** – Never use a centre lathe without permission. Always use the eye protection provided.

Turning speed

The speed at which the lathe should rotate is determined by the material and the diameter of the work. The cutting speed for materials using a high speed steel tool is given in the table below. This is the speed (in metres per minute) at which the work should pass the tool cutting edge. It is clear, therefore, that small diameters should rotate faster than larger diameters. The following formula is used to calculate the correct turning speed:

$$N = \frac{1000S}{\pi d}$$

Where N = Speed of the lathe in revs per minute (rpm)
S = Cutting speed (from the table below)
d = Diameter of work in mm

For example, the turning speed for a 40 mm diameter mild steel bar:

$$N = \frac{1000 \times 25}{\pi \times 40} \simeq 200 \text{ rpm}$$

Cutting lubricant

Most machining processes benefit from the use of a cutting lubricant, depending upon the material being cut. Lubrication is provided to help the chip slide easily across the top of the tool reducing wear and increasing the life of the tool. The cooling properties of a cutting lubricant mean that higher speeds may be used as the heat generated is carried away. Refer to the table below for recommended cutting lubricants.

Material	Rake Angle	Cutting speed m/min with H.S.S. tool	Cutting lubricant
Aluminium	40°	200	Paraffin
Brass	2°	90	none
Cast iron	2°	20	none
Hard steel	6°	18	Soluble oil
Mild steel	20°	25	Soluble oil
Nylon	30°	170	none

In addition to the two basic turning processes, facing and parallel turning (see fig 5.60), centre lathe turning includes drilling, knurling, boring, turning tapers and screw cutting.

Drilling

Drilling on a centre lathe differs from drilling using a pillar drill in that the workpiece rotates and the drill remains stationary. The speed of rotation is determined by the size of the drill, rather than the size of the work. The drill may be held in a chuck, located in the tailstock by its morse taper, or morse taper shanked drills may be used.
Centre drilling is necessary to provide a start for any drilling operation on the lathe.

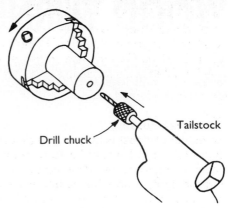

Drill chuck   Tailstock

fig 5.69. Drilling

Knurling

Knurling is the process that presses a pattern into the surface of cylindrical work to provide grip. This may be straight or diamond patterned. The hardened wheels that make up the knurling tool are pressed into the slowly rotating work and then traversed slowly along the surface.

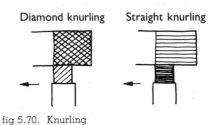

Diamond knurling   Straight knurling

fig 5.70. Knurling

Boring

Boring is internal turning, used to enlarge drilled holes. This is a process that requires great care, as it is not possible to see precisely what is happening. Boring bars tend to flex when cutting so only light cuts should be used.

Pre-drilled hole   Boring bar   Tool post

fig 5.71. Boring

Taper turning

The shortest most common form of taper is a **chamfer.** This is produced by the tool being ground or set to the appropriate angle (usually 45°) and simply fed into the workpiece. The work takes on the form of the tool. Slightly longer tapers can be machined by turning the compound slide through the required angle and using the compound slide handwheel to effect the cutting.

Long tapers, when turning between centres, are generated by off-setting the tailstock. the degree and direction of taper is determined by the amount and direction of movement of the tailstock.

Some centre lathes are fitted with a taper-turning attachment.

Compound slide

Machine axis   Tailstock centre offset to produce taper

Tool path parallel to machine axis

fig 5.72. Chamfering

Screw-cutting

Screw-cutting on the centre lathe is a way of cutting very precise screw threads.

A single point tool ground to the profile of the thread being cut, is mounted accurately in the tool post using a setting gauge. The appropriate gearing is selected to provide the correct pitch of the thread and, using a very slow speed, the tool is traversed repeatedly along the work to cut the thread.

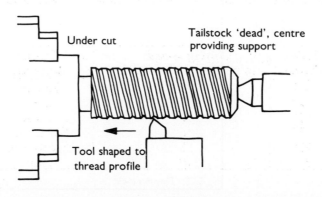

Under cut   Tailstock 'dead', centre providing support

Tool shaped to thread profile

fig 5.73. Screw cutting

99

WOOD TURNING

Turned woodwork ranges from traditional turned projects, such as bowls, table lamps and chair legs, to patterns for casting and vacuum forming and formers for glass reinforced plastic (GRP).

The wood-turning lathe provides two work stations. However, these are not to be used simultaneously. The outside or left hand face plate accommodates large diameters and the inside of the headstock can be fitted with either a smaller face plate or a forked driving centre for turning between centres. Alternatively, either side of the headstock can be fitted with a sanding disc.

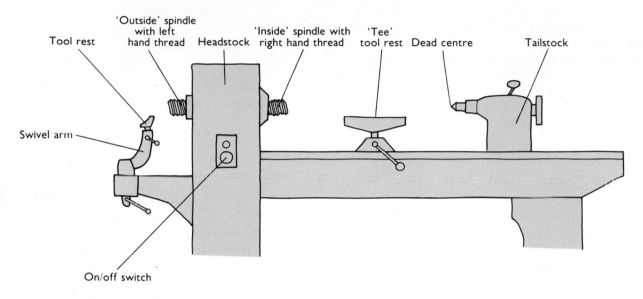

fig 5.74. Wood turning lathe

TURNING TOOLS

The lathe provides the work holding and the rotation; the cutting is carried out by a range of hand held tools. These fall into three broad categories: **Turning gouges, turning chisels** and **scrapers.**

Gouges and chisels cut with a proper cutting action, whereas scrapers actually scrape the surface away. It is for this reason that the tool rest height and the approach angles differ (fig 5.75).

Gouges are able to remove large quantities quickly and are therefore suited to truing up and rough shaping. Chisels are used for final shaping and fine finishing, but they are not easy tools to use and require a lot of practice.

Scrapers remove wood slower and are easier to use than chisels. The finish achieved is not as good as with a chisel in experienced hands, and will require sanding.

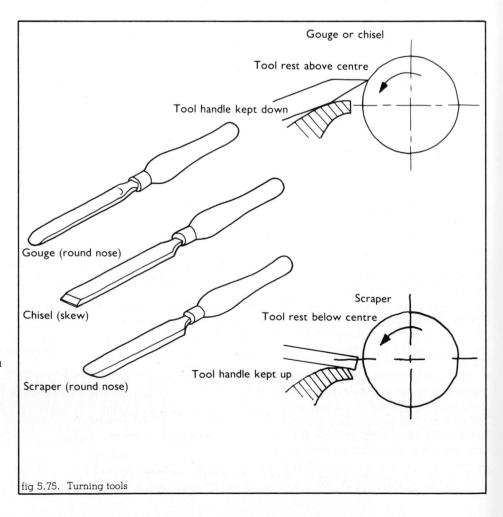

fig 5.75. Turning tools

FACE PLATE TURNING

Wood turning on a face plate is often called bowl turning, and is the method by which bowls, dishes, plinths, bases and formers are turned.

Preparation

Select a piece of wood that is large enough and that is free from splits. it is possible to buy prepared, fault free hardwood discs specifically for turning. Wood cut from a plank should be marked with the required diameter and the corners cut off (fig 5.76). The wood is then screwed, along with a spacing disc if needed, onto a face plate. A spacing disc is required if there is a danger of the tool hitting the face plates. The screws used must be long enough to hold firmly and yet not so long that it breaks through on the inside if the work is to be hollowed.

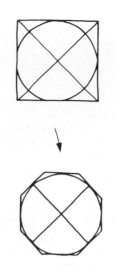

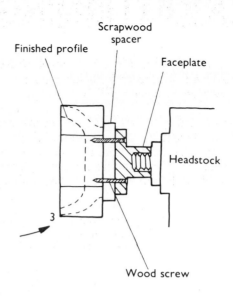

fig 5.76. Preparing wood for turning

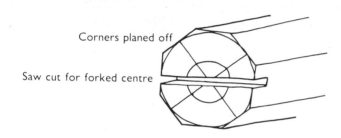

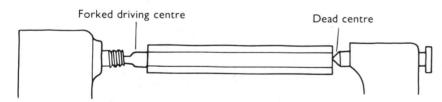

fig 5.77. Preparation for turning between centres

Templates and calipers

It is important to be able to check work being turned against the original design. With a bowl or table lamp this may not be critical, but for legs that have to be made identical, or for formers, for example, a check is necessary.

A **template** made from stiff card or hardboard should be cut to a full size half profile for this purpose (fig 5.78).

Calipers are used to compare diameters of a finished piece with one being turned, or to transfer measurements from a rule to the workpiece. Calipers should be used to check wall thickness when hollowing bowl shapes.

Hints for woodturning

1. Have the tool rest as close as possible without catching and remember to readjust it as the diameter reduces. Rotate by hand before turning on lathe.

2. Use high speeds for smaller diameters and slow speeds for larger ones.

3. Use a tool that is the correct shape for the area being turned and change tools as appropriate.

4. Hold the tool firmly. The long handles on turning tools provide a lot of leverage. A firmly held tool will be able to withstand any accidental snatches.

TURNING BETWEEN CENTRES

Turning between centres, or spindle turning, is for long pieces of work that need to be supported at both ends. A forked centre is located in the headstock and this transmits the drive to the wood. The other end is supported by a 'dead centre' located in the tailstock. Friction burning can be reduced by using grease or tallow.

Preparation

Find the centre of each end of the wood using intersecting diagonals. Punch the centre and draw a circle. Plane off excess waste (fig 5.77) and make a saw cut across one end. Tap this end onto the fork centre. Now move the tailstock up to support the other end, forcing the dead centre into the wood while rotating by hand.

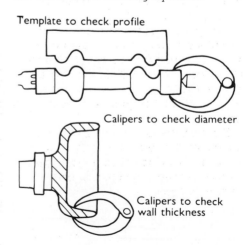

fig 5.78. Templates and calipers

MILLING

Milling is a process that uses rotating multi-toothed cutters to shape metals and plastics.

Milling machines are robust pieces of equipment with powerful drive motors and all work must be clamped securely to the machine table.

There are two types of milling machine, **horizontal** milling machines and **vertical** milling machines, the name being derived from the axis of rotation of the milling cutter.

Cutters on horizontal machines are mounted on a horizontal arbor that is supported within the body of the machine at one end, and by a support bracket on an overarm at the other. Vertical milling machines have cutters mounted either on a short vertical stub arbor or, more commonly, in a chuck designed specifically for the purpose. Fig 5.79 shows both a horizontal milling machine being used to machine a horizontal flat surface and a vertical milling machine being used to produce a slot.

The lower half of each type of machine is identical. It consists of either a flat machine table cut with 'tee' slots onto which a machine vice can be bolted, a magnetic vice or, alternatively, work may be clamped directly to the machine table using 'tee' nuts or bolts and clamps.

Milling machine tables move and can be locked in all three axes. Machines are often fitted with a powered traverse in the X axis (along the length of the table). Larger machines have a powered traverse in all three axes.

fig 5.79. Milling operations (guards removed for clarity of illustration only)

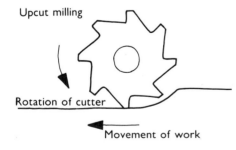

fig 5.80. Upcut milling

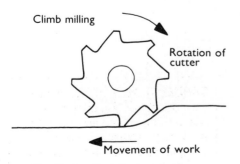

fig 5.81. Climb milling

Cutting action

Milling cutters are multi-toothed, each tooth in turn cutting a chip. There are two types of cutting action depending on the relationship between the cutter's rotation and the direction of movement of the workpiece.

Upcut or conventional milling (fig 5.80) produces a wedge shaped chip that starts fine and becomes thicker. The movement of the work is in the opposite direction to the cutter rotation.

Downcut or climb milling (fig 5.81) demands a very sturdy machine, therefore, it is rarely applicable to the school workshop. There is a tendency for the cutter to keep snatching the work.

MILLING PROCESSES

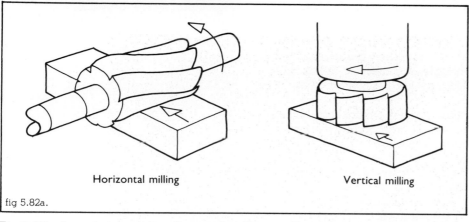

fig 5.82a.

Fig 5.82a shows horizontal and vertical milling machines being used to produce horizontal flat surfaces. The horizontal machine is using a slab mill or roller mill, and the vertical machine is using a face mill. Notice that in all the illustrations on this page, guards are removed for clarity purposes only. See the **safety** note below.

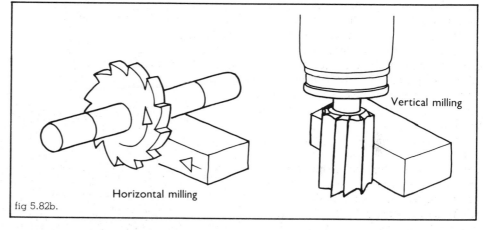

fig 5.82b.

Fig 5.82b shows milling machines being used for vertical flat surfaces. The horizontal machine is using the side of a side and face cutter. Side and face cutters cut on both the side and the diameter.
The cutter being used on the vertical machine is an end mill.

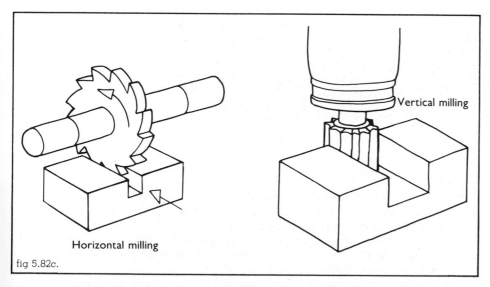

fig 5.82c.

Slots can also be machined on both horizontal and vertical milling machines. Wide slots on a horizontal machine (above 6 mm wide) can be machined using a side and face cutter. The cutter in fig 5.82a is a slotting cutter, these are available from 6 mm to 12 mm wide and have no cutting edge on the side. Slitting saws 1 mm to 6 mm wide are used for the narrowest slots. Slots on vertical machines can be machined using end mills which are available in sizes from 2 mm to 50 mm. End mills cannot cut down into the work unless a hole is drilled first. Alternatively a slot drill can be used. Slot drills are similar to end mills but are able to cut downwards like a drill as well as on the diameter like an end mill.

DEFORMING

Deforming is the name applied to processes that bring about a change of shape, without the loss of material that occurs in all of the wasting processes. However, deforming does not make use of a change of state, such as solid to liquid or liquid to solid. These are reforming processes and are dealt with later in this chapter.

Some materials lend themselves to deforming processes more readily than others. The property that a material must possess in order to be deformed without damage to its structure is **malleability.** This allows a material to be deformed by hammering, bending or pressing without fracture taking place. This is a similar property to **ductility** and though it is true that all ductile materials are malleable, not all malleable materials are ductile. The level of malleability of many materials can be increased dramatically by the introduction of heat. For example, acrylic is a material that is brittle at 20°C and extremely malleable at 160°C.

Malleability can be restored to some materials that have become stressed by **annealing**. This is another process which requires heat, but one in which the malleability remains after cooling. Copper is a material that becomes stressed with working and is annealed to restore malleability.

Materials that are extremely malleable, such as glass fibres and thin wood lamina, are easily formed into complex shapes, but require the addition of an adhesive to fix the shape.

A more detailed definition of the terms ductility, malleability and annealing, and an explanation of the structural changes that occur within material during heat treatment is given earlier in the chapter on Materials.

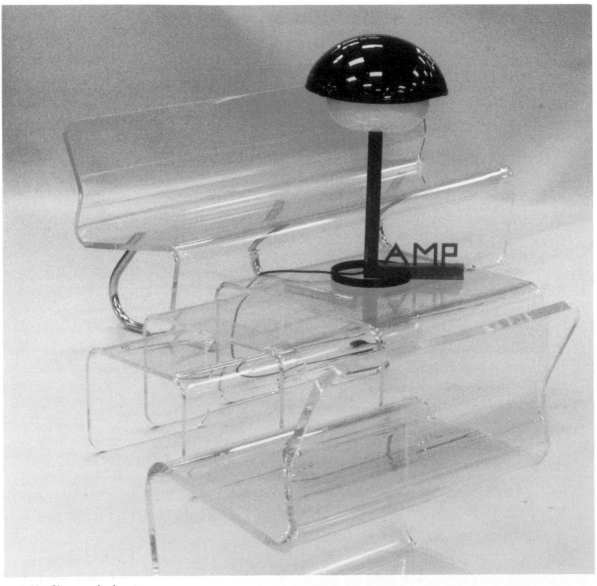

fig 5.83. Clear acrylic furniture

FORMING THERMOPLASTICS

The range of thermoplastic materials is vast, though only a few are generally applicable to school workshop applications. **Acrylic** (ICI trade name 'Perspex') is the most popular thermoplastic material for hand working. It is available in sheet, tube, rod and block form, and may be transparent, translucent or coloured.

Colours range right across the spectrum, offering exciting design possibilities. The degree of translucence varies from smoked pinks and greys to near solid colour. Projects related to light and light sources gain a great deal from researching the effects of different translucent acrylics, some of which have a fibre optic effect when viewed on edge.

Strip heaters are used to provide local heating for line bending. The principle is quite straightforward. An electric element, similar to that of an electric fire, is enclosed in a channel with an opening at the top. Acrylic sheet is placed across supports above the opening. The width of the strip to be heated is determined by the height of the supports. The strip heater shown in fig 5.84 has adjustable support height.

It is difficult to be precise regarding heating times with any radiant heating processes, because it is dependent upon the colour of the thermoplastic. Dark colours absorb heat faster that light colours.

The wider the heated strip, the more gradual is the resultant bend. Thick acrylic should be turned during heating before the strip has become flexible to avoid blistering. Under and over strip heaters do not require the acrylic to be turned.

Ovens enable sheets of acrylic to be heated all over. This is necessary for forming and moulding. Ordinary domestic electric ovens are fine for this operation, though air circulating ovens are available to ensure uniform distribution of heat. The oven thermostat should be set to 170°C. Blistering is caused by overheating and the presence of absorbed moisture. Surprisingly, plastics do absorb moisture, but it can be dried off by subjecting it to heat, approximately 80°C for 24 hours prior to working.

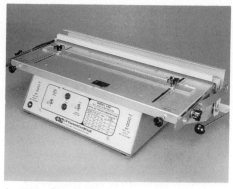

fig 5.84. Strip heater

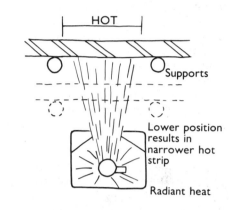

fig 5.85. Use of a strip heater

SINGLE CURVATURE FORMING

Bending jigs
Bending jigs (fig 5.86) should be used to hold the acrylic at the correct angle until it has set. Jigs are not formers; the shape of the bend is determined by the width of the heated strip and not the jig. Avoid sharp bends, as these will result in thinning and weakness.

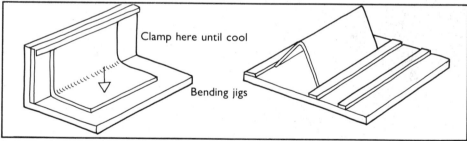

fig 5.86. Bending sheets

Formers
Formers must be well prepared and ready to accept the hot, flexible sheet that emerges from the oven. You must work quickly and have everything to hand, including gloves or tongs for handling the sheet. Good surface finish on formers is essential. Coarse woodgrain, joint lines and countersunk screw heads will all leave permanent impressions in the surface of hot acrylic. Formers need not always be custom made in wood, the enterprising student may well make use of piping, metalworking stakes or cooking utensils, for example.

Drape forming for a single curve requires the simplest of formers and a cloth stretcher to hold the form until it cools. (Do not use a cloth with a coarse weave).

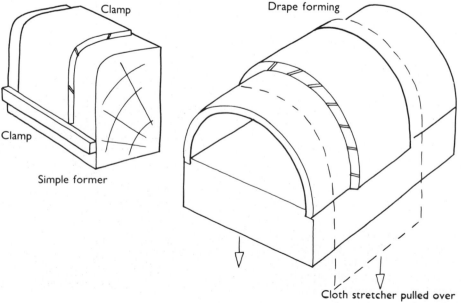

fig 5.87. Formers

DOUBLE CURVATURE FORMING

More complex forms with curves in more than one direction require more complex formers. Formers made in pairs, male and female, are often necessary. They should be simple, but well made, and you must remember to take the thickness of material into account. The forces involved with thick acrylic can be considerable. Solid wood, well braced or thick plywood are suitable materials to use. It is important to have some method of maintaining alignment between the two halves. One method is to have dowel guides fixed in the lower half locating in holes in the upper half, another is to construct a sturdy guide box into which different pairs of formers can be located.

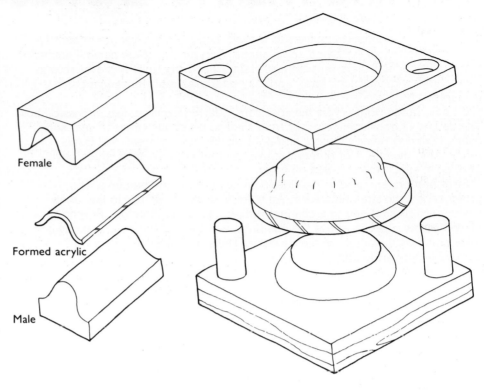

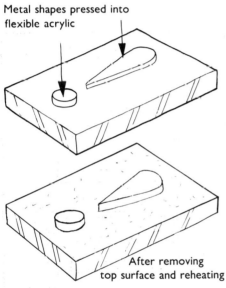

Metal shapes pressed into flexible acrylic

After removing top surface and reheating

fig 5.89. Acrylic memory

fig 5.88. Double curvature forming

ACRYLIC MEMORY

A characteristic of thermoplastics is that when reheated they will endeavour to return to their original shape. This can be a great asset if things go wrong, since returning your work to the oven will restore its sheet form.

The **memory technique** utilises this characteristic for decorative purposes. This involves pressing a shape into the surface of flexible acrylic, machining or filing away the top of the surface after it has cooled, and then reheating to restore the height of the decorative shape. The effect can be quite dramatic, particularly if the filed or machined surface is left textured.

BLOW MOULDING

Blow moulding in its simplest form, **free blowing,** forms flexible, hot thermoplastic sheet into a dome shape using compressed air (fig 5.90). The clamping ring or template will determine the shape of the moulding (sharp corners should be avoided), and the volume of air determines the depth of the moulding.

Speed is essential to this process and the use of fast acting toggle clamps to hold down the clamping ring will help. Air pressure must be maintained until cooling has taken place.

Blow moulded forms are very strong, enabling relatively thin material to be used for most applications.

A restriction former held in the path of the expanding dome introduces other possibilities for this forming process. A simple flat restriction changes a dome into a bowl (fig 5.90).

fig 5.90. Blow moulding

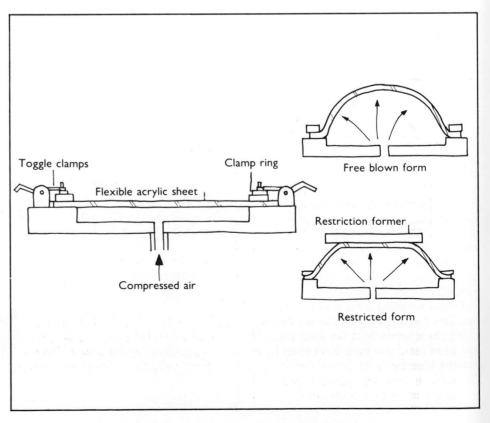

Toggle clamps

Clamp ring

Free blown form

Flexible acrylic sheet

Restriction former

Compressed air

Restricted form

VACUUM FORMING

Acrylic can be formed by vacuum forming, but it is not an ideal material, because of its short plastic range. Acrylic begins to become flexible at 120°C and is ideal for most forming processes between 150°C and 170°C. Plasticity, the desirable quality for vacuum forming, is reached at 180°C, but unfortunately acrylic degenerates at 185°C. It is impossible to maintain this narrow temperature band over the whole area of sheet that is in free air and is also clamped around the edges. Therefore, vacuum formed acrylic lacks the definition possible with more suitable thermoplastics.

Perspex TX (from ICI) is an extruded rather than cast acrylic that goes plastic at 150°C and is, therefore, suited to vacuum forming.

High density polystyrene, ABS (Acrylonitrile-butadiene-styrene), low density forming grade polythene, and flexible PVC (polyvinyl chloride) are also materials suited to vacuum forming.

Complicated deep shapes can be formed by this process.

fig 5.91a. Vacuum former

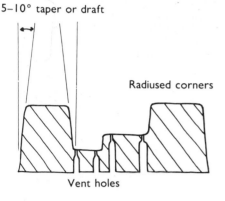

5–10° taper or draft

Radiused corners

Vent holes

fig 5.91b. Mould for vacuum forming

A high quality mould or pattern is required. The sides should taper slightly for ease of removal and there must be no undercuts. Large moulds and moulds with deep internal draws require small vent holes to avoid trapping pockets of air. The vacuum does not suck, the absence of air allows atmospheric pressure to push (fig 5.91b).

The vacuum forming process

The thermoplastic sheet to be formed is clamped around its edges by an air tight clamp plate situated above the mould. Heat is applied by radiant heating elements located in a hinged hood just above the thermoplastic. When plasticity is achieved, air is drawn out and the thermoplastic is forced, by air pressure, onto the mould.

The problem with this basic process is the thinning that takes place when the form is deep. The vacuum forming machine shown in fig 5.91a has two major refinements in order to improve upon the basic process. First the platen, the base upon which the mould stands, can be raised, and second there is a blow facility.

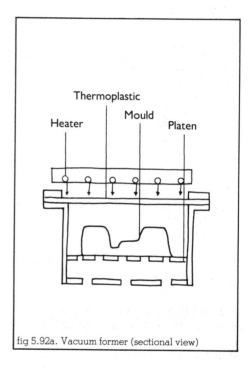

Thermoplastic

Heater   Mould   Platen

fig 5.92a. Vacuum former (sectional view)

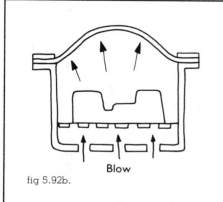

Blow

fig 5.92b.

1. The thermoplastic is heated by the radiant heater in the hood. The blow facility is then used to stretch the thermoplastic over its entire surface area, the thinning effect being more or less uniform.

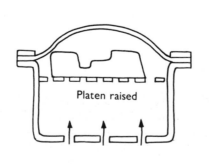

Platen raised

fig 5.92c. Platen raised

2. The platen is now raised into the dome created by the blow. This overcomes the need for a deep draw down the sides of the former.

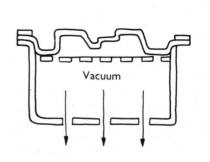

Vacuum

fig 5.92d. Air evacuated

3. Finally the air is evacuated and atmospheric pressure forces the still plastic thermoplastic tightly over the surface of the mould.

107

HOT FORMING METAL

FORGING

Long before industrialization, forging was the only available method for working iron, with blacksmiths practising their craft in every small community. Few blacksmiths exist today and forging of steel has developed into a sophisticated computer controlled industrial process.

Forging has many virtues as a shaping process. Hammering hot metal into shape refines the grain flow of the material resulting in increased strength. Forged components are also stronger because the grain flow follows the shape. Fig 5.95 shows a crank mechanism that has been forged, compared with one produced by a wasting process. The short grain that remains following the wasting process is an area of weakness. It is for this reason that crankshafts for car engines are produced by drop forging (see 'Manufacturing technologies' pages 163–190).

Forging offers great opportunity for creative design. The techniques for hand working hot metals may have changed little over the centuries, but the ingenuity of craftsmen and women has led to the creation of many beautiful pieces of work.

fig 5.93   Forge work

Forging tools

The **forge** is the source of heat. In many schools, traditional coke burning forges are being replaced by ceramic chip forges. These are much easier to light, reach a working temperature much quicker and avoid the problems created by smoke, dirt, fumes and clinkering. Chip forges are fuelled by gas, thus saving on fuel storage space.

The main workspace for forging is provided by the **anvil** (fig 5.96). This is a more versatile tool than it would at first appear. Anvils have a hardened working face with a radiused edge for bending over and a soft cutting face for cutting onto. The beak or bick is used for forming curves and for drawing down. The hardie hole is for locating fullers and swages and the punch hole is for punching into when punching holes.

Fullers are tools in two parts. The bottom fuller locates in the hardie hole and the top fuller is held by its handle and struck, usually with a heavy hammer. Hot metal between the fullers is drawn down (fig 5.98).

Swages are forming tools for finishing circular sections of various sizes. They are made in pairs, the bottom swage fitting the hardie hole and the top swage having a handle and a striking face. They are used in a similar way to fullers.

fig 5.94. Ceramic chip forge

fig 5.95.

Forged crank with uninterrupted grain flow

Crank produced by a wasting process
Grain flow cut into

Weakness

fig 5.96. Anvil

Hardie hole   Working face   Cutting face

Punching hole

Beak or bick

Fullers

Swaging

fig 5.98. Fullers and swaging

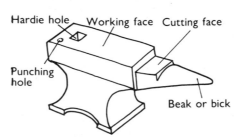

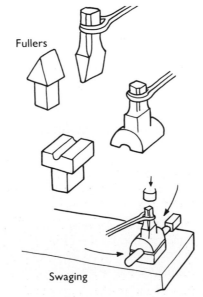

Tongs for holding hot metal have mouths in a large range of shapes. It is important to select a pair that will provide a firm grip and resist movement during forging. Tongs should be quenched in water occasionally during use to keep them cool.

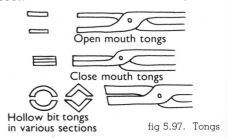

Open mouth tongs

Close mouth tongs

Hollow bit tongs in various sections

fig 5.97. Tongs

Flatters are used to finish surfaces that have been previously worked. They are smooth and have rounded edges to avoid bruising the surface (fig 5.99)

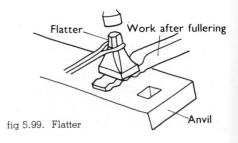

Flatter   Work after fullering

Anvil

fig 5.99. Flatter

FORGING PROCESSES

For any forging process to be effective, it is essential that there is sufficient heat and that it is in the correct place. Maximum deformation will take place at the point of maximum heat.

Mild steel should be worked at around 1200°C, i.e. a bright red heat. The temperature should be hotter for upsetting and punching. The spread of heat is controlled by quenching those areas that do not require working with water. Working material that is not hot enough results in surface bruising and fracturing on bends.

Drawing down

This is the process that increases the length of material by reducing its section. It is usually carried out on the anvil by using a cross-pein hammer, but larger sections require fullering (fig 5.100).

Upsetting

Upsetting, or jumping up, is the process by which a metal section is increased by reducing its length. Heat must be limited to the area that requires upsetting. Upsetting is used to provide additional metal for decorative features, metal from which to form a head on the end of bars and to allow for sharp bends without loss of thickness on the corner (fig 5.101).

Bending

Bends may be sharp or gradual. Sharp bends require upsetting before bending and can be carried out over the corner of the anvil. More gradual bends are achieved using a former in a vice or the anvil beak.

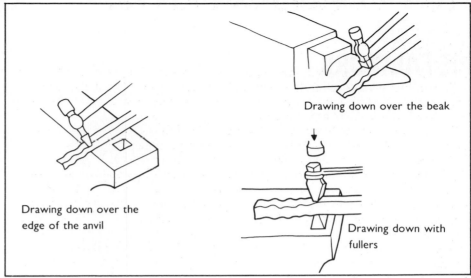

fig 5.100. Drawing down

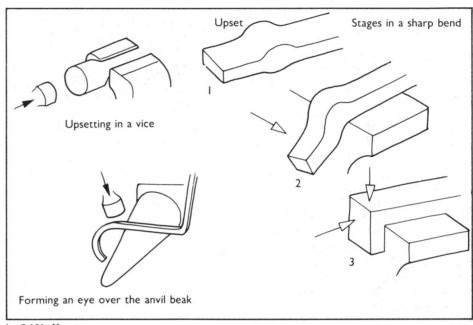

fig 5.101. Upsetting

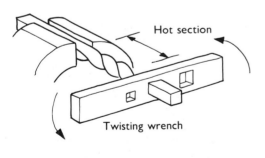

fig 5.102. Twisting and scrolling

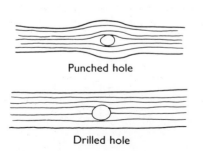

fig 5.103. Punched and drilled holes

Twisting and scrolling

These are much used decorative features of traditional wrought iron work.

To achieve an even twist, it is important to have even heat over the length of the twist and to work quickly (fig 5.102).

Scrolling involves gripping the hot strip to a scrolling iron and simply pulling it around the form. Flattening is then necessary using the face of the anvil.

Punching and drifting

Holes punched through metal reduce its strength far less than drilled holes. The grain flow is diverted rather than being cut (fig 5.103). It is for this reason that punched holes are used at the termination of structural ties rather than drilled holes. Drifts are used to enlarge and to re-shape punched holes.

SAFETY — Hot metal can inflict severe burns. Always wear the eye protection and protective clothing provided. Never take hot metal out of the heat treatment area.

COLD FORMING METAL

BEATEN METALWORK

Copper, brass and guilding metal are the materials most frequently used for beaten metalwork. They are malleable and, when finished, are extremely attractive. Aluminium is a cheaper alternative. Silver is an ideal material for this process, but is very expensive. All of these materials work-harden, therefore, it is necessary to continually anneal the material during any beaten metalworking process.

Surface forming oxides can present problems following annealing. If the oxide layer is not removed, there is a danger of hammering it into the surface, leaving permanent marks.

Pickling in dilute sulphuric acid will remove the oxide layer. If the metal is warm, not hot, the acid will act faster. Use brass tongs and avoid any skin contact with the acid. Always wear eye protection. After pickling, remove acid residue with clean water. An alternative mechanical method is to use abrasive pumice powder and steel wool.

Hollowing

The is a process for forming shallow dish shapes. The process involves thinning to produce the required form and the finished dish is, therefore, only slightly smaller in diameter than the initial blank.

Concentric circles drawn with a pencil and drawing compass should be marked on the surface of the blank disc. These should be approximately 10 mm apart to act as guidelines for the hollowing.

The tools required are a **bossing mallet** and a **sandbag**. Bossing mallets have elongated, egg-shaped heads made from boxwood. Sandbags are leather covered and when using them it is necessary to dry the water from your work following pickling to avoid wetting the leather.

The procedure is to work around the marked circles starting at the outside, and moving inwards, hollowing the metal into the sandbag with the small end of the mallet. The large end of the mallet is used to true up any wrinkles that develop. Do not rush, and remember to anneal at regular intervals.

An alternative method of hollowing is to use a **blocking hammer** and a hard wood block that has been shaped to the correct form.

fig. 5.104. Beaten metalwork

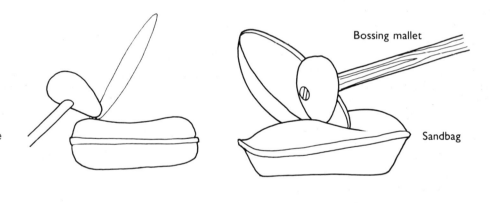

fig 5.105. Hollowing using bossing mallet and sandbag

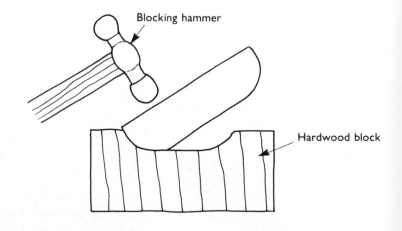

fig 5.106. Blocking hammer

110

Sinking

Sinking is a process for forming shallow shapes when it is required to leave an unaffected rim or edge.

A **sinking block** must be made first. This should have the correct form and depth and two dowels against which to position the rim to ensure a consistent width (fig 5.107).

Concentric circles are marked in a similar manner to hollowing. Sinking commences just inside the inside of the rim and proceeds around the circles, as in hollowing. A sinking or blocking hammer should be used for this process. The rim distorts continually and must be flattened using a flat hardwood block and a flat faced mallet such as a **raising mallet** or a **tinmans mallet.** This is a slow process and requires a greater level of skill than hollowing.

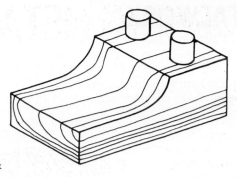

fig 5.107. Sinking block

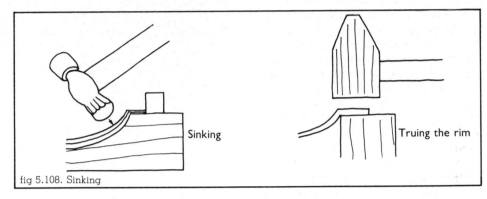

fig 5.108. Sinking

Raising

Tall and steep sided shapes are formed by raising. Hollowing and sinking are both processes that stretch metal downwards thereby causing it to become thinner. Raising is the opposite to this. The metal is raised, and in doing so the thickness is increased in order to accommodate a large circumference of blank into a smaller circumference of work.

As for the other processes, the preparation for raising is to mark concentric pencil circles.

For raising shallow dishes use a **roundhead stake** and a **raising mallet** (fig 5.109). Work starts in the centre and proceeds outwards. It is important to strike the metal above the stake in order to force it to thicken. Trapping metal between the mallet and the stake will thin and stretch it.

Before raising a tall or steep sided shape, the metal should be hollowed slightly. This is a guide for the raising and it starts the metal forming in the correct direction. If a flat base is required the hollowing can be flattened out on a round-bottom stake after raising. A **raising hammer** and a **raising stake** are used for steep sided shapes (fig 5.110). Be sure to hit the metal above the stake and not trap it.

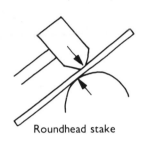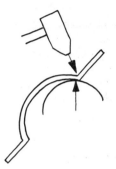

fig 5.109. Raising shallow dishes

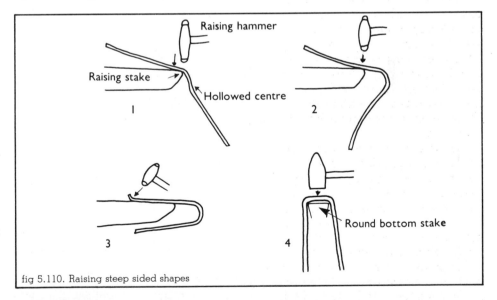

fig 5.110. Raising steep sided shapes

Planishing

Planishing is the conclusion to any of the above processes. After the final shape has been achieved, the work should be annealed, pickled and cleaned using pumice powder. Planishing requires highly polished **planishing hammers** and polished stakes. Take care of planishing hammers and do not use them for any other purpose.

Mark out the workpiece with concentric pencil circles and, starting in the centre, carefully and methodically planish around each circle in turn. Ensure that each tap traps the work between hammer and stake and that each planishing mark just overlaps the previous one. Planishing will true up any small irregularities in the final form and will work harden the material increasing the mechanical strength of the workpiece.

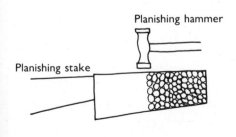

fig 5.111. Planishing

SHEET METALWORK

Boxes, trays, cones and pipework can be formed using sheets of metal. Aluminium, tinplate, mild steel, brass and copper are all materials well suited to this process.

The material involved is bent into the desired shape and other than the unavoidable stretching on sharp corners, deformation in terms of thinning or thickening does not take place.

Developments

The first stage in forming a piece of work from a single sheet of metal is to draw out a full size development on paper or thin card. This can then be cut out with scissors and folded up into shape. Modelling your work in this way enables you to make decisions regarding the position of flaps for riveting or soldering, make alterations and explore the possible bending sequences. Working it through on paper or card is cheap and quick. The development can then be transferred to the metal without fear of it not working out.

Fig 5.112 shows the development of a leaflet dispenser to be made in tinplate. It is to be folded up and then soft soldered. The joint flaps will increase the area of solder. A design criterion here is that no joints should appear on the front.

Safe edges are flaps folded back on themselves to stiffen the edge and avoid the risk of people cutting themselves on thin sheet material. All exposed edges of thin sheet should be made safe.

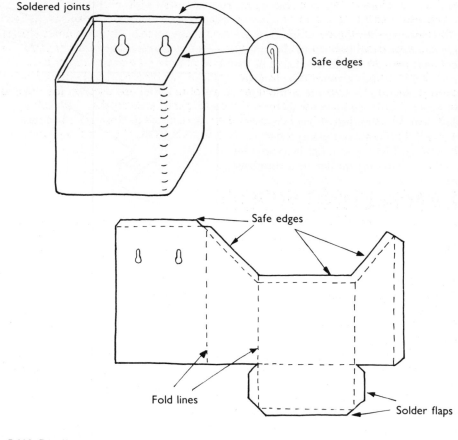

fig 5.112. Development of a leaflet dispenser

Bending

Sheet metal should be supported along both sides of the length of the bend.

Folding bars held in a vice provide edges for bending sheet at 90°. For safe edges use a **hatchet stake** to take the bend further and finish off on a flat bench top (fig 5.114).

Use a rawhide or nylon hammer or mallet to bend sheet metal, and take it over gradually working up and down its length. This avoids stretching and wrinkling the material. For radiused bends use a hardwood former (fig 5.115).

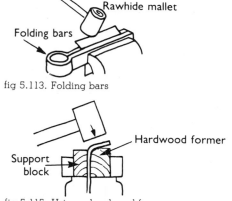

fig 5.113. Folding bars

fig 5.115. Using a hardwood former

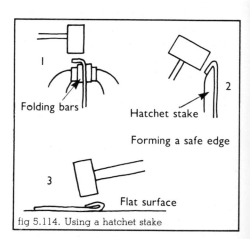

fig 5.114. Using a hatchet stake

Seaming

Cylinders and cones can be joined up using a seam joint. The procedure is quite straightforward, but the width of the seam must suit the **seam set** that is used to finish off and tighten it up (fig 5.116). Use a strip of waste that is the same thickness as the material being worked and be sure to leave an allowance on your development for the material used in the seam. Remember also to form the 'hooks' in opposite directions on each end. If it is necessary for the joint to be water tight then it can be 'sweated' with soft solder.

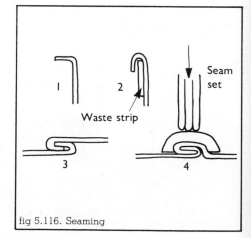

fig 5.116. Seaming

LAMINATING

Thin material deforms easier than thick material. To understand why, we need to look at what happens to material when it is being bent.

Fig 5.117 shows a simple single bend, the outside of the bend has to stretch and is, therefore, in tension, trying to recover. The inside of the bend is compressed and is trying to recover by pushing outwards. The result is that the material will straighten out in order to relax these forces. With thinner material the difference between the outside circumference and the inside circumference is much less, so the forces trying to straighten the bend are also much less.

In laminating, strips of thin, flexible material are deformed or bent to the desired shape. This means that longer strips of material are used on the outside of a bend than on the inside. These strips are glued all over their contacting surfaces. Once the glue has hardened they are unable to straighten because straightening would involve the strips sliding past each other, and they can no longer do this.

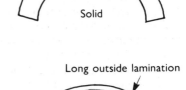

Solid

Long outside lamination

Laminated

Short inside lamination

fig 5.117. Laminating

LAMINATING WOOD

Laminating in wood not only introduces interesting aesthetic possibiliites, but laminated wooden forms are also very strong mechanically. Loaded structures often make use of this technique, chairs, tables, arches, bridges and beams.

Formers

Solid wooden formers are suitable for shallow forms. Fig 5.118 shows a solid former for producing the legs for a sports trophy. Each leg is to be laminated in turn and they must be identical. Formers must be designed to allow for the correct thickness of the laminations. A single cut will not provide a uniform space. Polythene or paper is used to stop the work from sticking to the former. Ideally a layer of rubber should be positioned either side of the lamination to even out any irregularities. Do not use excessive amounts of glue, but thinly coat all of the inside surfaces, then clamp the lamination in a vice or with clamps until it is fully set.

Built up formers are needed for larger, deeper work. Fig 5.119 shows a former built up on a base board. The shape being produced is for chair sides. The inside, or male, part of the former is fixed securely to the base board and each of the outer sections are added in turn, starting from the middle and working outwards. These outer sections are clamped along with the laminate to the inner, using sash cramps or G cramps.

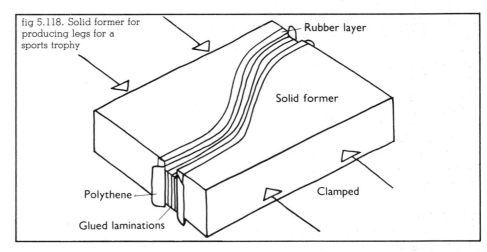

fig 5.118. Solid former for producing legs for a sports trophy

Rubber layer

Solid former

Clamped

Polythene

Glued laminations

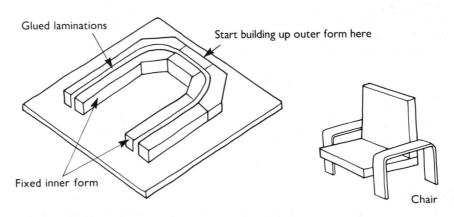

Glued laminations

Start building up outer form here

Fixed inner form

Chair

fig 5.119. Former for chair rest built up on a base board

Flexible formers should be utilised when the shape permits. With flexible formers it is only necessary to manufacture the male part of the former, therefore, the time spent on preparation is reduced.

Fig 5.120 shows a semi-circular lamination being produced using a flexible steel band to pull the work onto the former. This process is limited to curved forms in one direction.

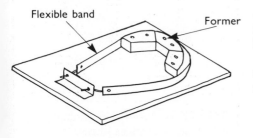

Flexible band

Former

fig 5.120. Semi-circular lamination being produced using a flexible steel band

Air pressure forming

Air pressure is another flexible method of forcing laminations onto a former. In Fig 5.121 air from a hand or foot pump is used to inflate a length of tube. The expanding, pressurised tube presses the lamination onto the former. It is essential to construct a sturdy jig to contain both the former and the tube. A vacuum is used in fig 5.122 to allow atmospheric air pressure to provide the necessary force. The formers and laminates are placed on a base board, which is then placed into the vacuum forming envelope. Adhesive tape is used to maintain the correct relative positions.

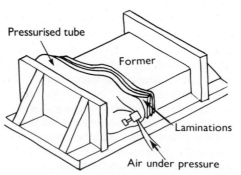

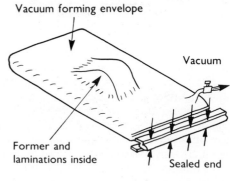

fig 5.121. Pressurised tube

fig 5.122. Using a vacuum

The bag is then sealed using strips of wood and clamps. After evacuating the air, a valve in the pipeline will restrict return flow until it is released. Air pressure processes are only suited to forms using thin, very flexible lamina. Maintaining the pressure in these processes is reliant upon the seals on the bag or tube. A gradual loss of pressure before the glue sets will result in de-lamination.

The quantity of wood used in laminating is relatively small, a great deal of mechanical strength is gained and there is a minimum amount of waste produced. Unfortunately the preparation involved, in both time and material, for the former can be considerable.

Good design will take advantage of the fact that, once made, the former can be cleaned and used a number of times, and for different projects. For example the chair side in fig 5.119 could be shortened and used for a matching coffee table (fig 5.123).

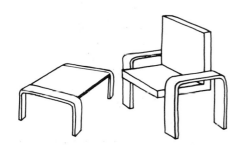

fig 5.123.

LAMINATING GLASS REINFORCED PLASTICS

Glass reinforced plastic (GRP) can be used for a vast range of projects. The main applications are those that make use of its high strength to weight ratio, its high resistance to corrosion, and the ability to produce complex shapes. Canoes, cars and caravans are examples of products made from GRP, but smaller projects, such as model cars, model boats and seats, can all utilise this process.

GRP, sometimes called **glass fibre,** is stranded glass that is set in a polyester resin. The glass fibres are approximately 50 mm long and are bonded together in a flexible mat. The polyester resin is in liquid form. A catalyst, or hardener, is added to the resin to start a chemical reaction and make the resin set. A colour pigment is also normally added. The glass fibres provide strength, while the resin bonds the fibres and provides, in the gel-coat, a smooth surface finish.

fig 5.124. GRP work

SAFETY — Avoid skin contact with resin and glass fibres. Always work in a well ventilated area.

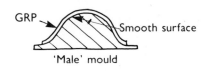

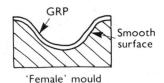
'Male' mould

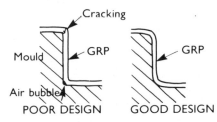
'Female' mould

POOR DESIGN   GOOD DESIGN

fig 5.125. GRP moulds

GRP moulds

A high standard of finish from GRP work can only be achieved with a high quality mould.

The 'finished' side of the work is the side that is in contact with the mould surface and the smallest defect will be mirrored in your work. Moulds can be made from almost any material and are often made from a combination that may include wood, plywood, chipboard, hardboard, sheet metal, wire, plaster of Paris and GRP. If a porous material is used it must be sealed, preferably using a mould sealer.

It is often convenient to make a model of the finished piece of work and to produce a GRP mould from this. This is particularly true where the mould needs to be a deep concave shape. Better results can often be achieved with this approach because the GRP mould provides the opportunity for filling, polishing and making minor adjustments.

To enable work to be removed from the mould, it must be made with tapered sides and have no undercuts. The use of a release agent is essential. The surfaces must be coated with a release agent before lay up begins, or else the work will adhere firmly to the mould.

Mould design should exclude sharp corners and large flat areas. Sharp corners encourage cracking and the formation of air bubbles. Flat areas tend to sink and be weak. Convex curves, even shallow ones, provide structural strength.

Laminating procedure

The actual laminating is carried out in methodical stages. Therefore, it is important to have the tools and materials to hand. You may need some assistance with a large piece of work.

The illustrations show the stages in the production of a 'bucket' type seat for a child's pedal kart. It is important that the inside of the seat has a good finish, thus the mould must be internal.

fig 5.126. Pedal kart with GRP seat

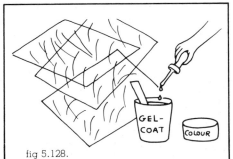

fig 5.127.

1. Polish the mould all over with a releasing agent.

fig 5.128.

2. Cut up the glass fibre mat into the minimum number of pieces that will cover the mould in three laminations. Add colour to the gel-coat and then the hardener to catalyse it.

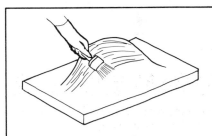

fig 5.129.

3. Wearing polythene gloves, apply the gel-coat to the mould with an even brushing action to achieve a thickness of about 1 mm. Gel-coat is thixotropic and will not run.

fig 5.130.

4. When the gel-coat has cured, about 30 minutes, coat it with a layer of catalysed lay-up polyester resin. On to this lay the first lamination of glass fibre mat. Stipple the mat using a stiff brush until it is thoroughly wetted and all air is driven out. Repeat with successive layers. Use surfacing tissue as the final lamination for an improved rough side.

fig 5.131.

5. Leave for about 40 minutes while you wash all brushes and tools thoroughly. After this time the edges can be carefully trimmed using a sharp knife.

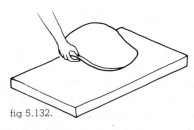

fig 5.132.

6. Wait at least another 3 hours before separating the work from the mould. Full hardness is achieved after curing in approximately 24 hours, after which time it will be possible to work with wood and metal working tools.

REFORMING

Reforming involves a change of state within the material concerned. This usually means forming the material while it is in a liquid state. The methods employed to bring about this change of state depend upon the nature of the material. Many materials become liquid when sufficient heat is introduced, they are said to melt. All metals can be melted using heat. Thermosetting plastics cannot be melted in this way. Polyester resin, for example, is a liquid in its base form. Its change in state is brought about by the addition of a chemical hardener and, once achieved, cannot be reversed. Material in a liquid state can be cast into any desired form. Casting is the process of pouring a liquid material into a mould so that its form can be held until the material becomes solid or set.

fig 5.133. Objects formed by casting

CASTING METAL

Imagine trying to make the body of a bath tap, a bell for a clock tower, or the bed of a centre lathe from single pieces of solid metal. The amount of work that would be involved in removing surplus material would be colossal. Many times more waste would have to be removed from the inside of the bell than would remain in the finished product. These three items are examples of metal products that are made by casting.

The metal is melted at very high temperatures and is then poured into a mould that is the shape of the finished product, rather like making a jelly or a plaster of Paris figure.

Bath taps are cast from brass. Bells are cast from a special alloy of copper and tin, called bell metal. The beds of centre lathes are cast from cast iron. There is very little waste and in most instances any waste and scrap there is can be re-cycled, and cast again.

CASTING RESIN

Polyester resin similar to that used in GRP work (see page 114) can be cast using suitable moulds to form various small items. Best results are gained by using resin developed especially for casting or for encapsulation.

Encapsulation is the process of using clear polyester resin to encapsulate small objects such as stamps, insects or electronic components. This enables personalized novelty 'paper weights', for example, to be made quite simply.

A variety of smooth, cup shaped objects can be used for moulds, and the process is quite simple, but should nevertheless be well planned. Remember that the first object encapsulated will emerge on top when the casting is removed from the mould.

First a layer of clear resin is poured into the mould and the top object is placed face down upon it. This is followed by subsequent layers and objects allowing time for gelling, not fully curing, between layers. The final base layer can have a colour pigment added to enhance the appearance.

CASTING CONCRETE

Concreting is another reforming process. Although never really a proper liquid, wet concrete can be encouraged to act like one. Concrete is a mixture of portland cement, sharp sand and aggregate (stones). These should first be mixed dry and then mixed with water. As the water dries out the concrete sets, though it should be noted that the setting is in fact a chemical action and cannot be reversed by adding more water, this will only weaken the concrete.

Concrete work can contribute to many outdoor projects such as seating, bird baths and sundials.

Concrete is best cast into wooden moulds that are screwed together and so can be taken apart to facilitate removal of the concrete work.

Internal features can be formed using expanded polystyrene. This has the advantage that it can be dissolved out of the finished concrete casting using a chemical agent (acetone) that will react with the polystyrene.

ALUMINIUM CASTING

Casting molten aluminium into sand moulds is the casting process that is most readily applicable to the school workshop. Aluminium is cheap, easy to obtain, and can be cast at 750°C, a temperature that is not difficult to achieve. The process involves five distinct stages.

1. Making a pattern in the form of the required work piece.
2. Completely encasing the pattern in moulding sand.
3. Removing the pattern from the sand leaving a sand mould.
4. Pouring the molten metal or melt into the mould.
5. Removing the sand from around the solidified work piece.

PATTERN MAKING

The quality of a casting is dependent upon the quality of the pattern used. When making a pattern it is important to remember that the metal shrinks when it cools. The pattern should be made slightly larger if the finished size is critical. Industrial pattern makers use contraction rules. These are graduated at an increased scale according to the coefficient of expansion of the metal to be cast. It is also important to add on a machining allowance to areas that will require machine finishing to achieve important dimension or are required to be especially flat.

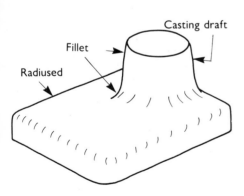

WELL DESIGNED PATTERN

fig 5.135. Quality for pattern making

Split pattern for a hacksaw handle

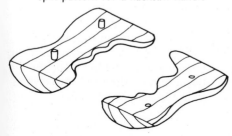

fig 5.136. Split pattern

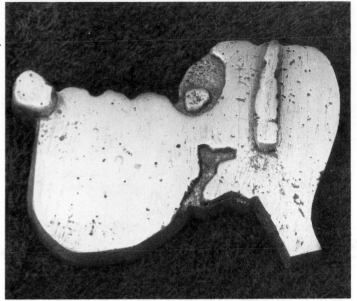

fig 5.134. Work produced by 'lost' pattern cutting

'Lost' patterns

One of the earliest pattern making processes was to shape a pattern in bees wax. The wax pattern was then coated in clay and buried in sand. The sand was heated until the wax could be poured out, and the molten metal could then be poured into the cavity that remained.

The modern equivalent of this process is to use **expanded polystyrene.** This is shaped, buried in sand, and the molten metal when poured in, burns the polystyrene completely away.

Expanded polystyrene is such a common packaging material for electrical appliances, television sets, video recorders, that it can usually be obtained at no cost. A hot wire can be used to shape the material and it can be glued together using PVA (Polyvinyl acetate).

Polystyrene patterns do have two serious disadvantages. They are not re-usable, and the fumes given off are extremely toxic. The fact that the pattern is only used once means that removal from the mould need not be considered. This process lends itself to sculptural art forms that can be quite complex and may well make use of the textured surface that remains. The fumes can be a problem and extractor fans and plenty of ventilation are essential when pouring the melt.

Wooden patterns

The most important consideration when designing a pattern, is the ability to remove it from the mould. This means that there must be no undercuts and all vertical surfaces must have a gradual taper to assist in the withdrawal. This taper is known as a **casting draft**.

Sharp corners should also be avoided. Outside corners must be radiused and inside corners should have fillets, which can be worked into the pattern or added in the form of flexible strips.

An ideal wood from which to manufacture patterns is jelutong. This is a close grained hardwood, which is easy to work and is favoured by most industrial pattern makers.

Patterns must be finished to a high standard. They should be smooth and well sealed using varnish or paint.

The simplest type of pattern is the flat back type. All of the detail is on one side of the pattern, so moulding is a simple process. This type of pattern would be suitable for lamp bases, wheels and wall plaques. Patterns that contain cylindrical forms need to be split patterns. It is not possible to avoid undercutting with a cylinder. Split patterns are made in two halves with pegs providing location between the halves (fig 5.136). Each half must be tapered and free from undercuts.

MOULD MAKING

The procedure for making moulds varies slightly depending on the pattern that is used. The following example shows moulding using a split pattern. The moulding box is in two parts, the halves locating together with two pegs that are fixed into the upper half. This upper half is called the **cope** and the lower half is called the **drag.**

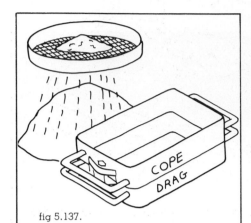

fig 5.137.

1. Preparation of the moulding sand. Damp moulding sand is often called 'green sand'. Before it can be re-used, it must be broken up and riddled with a course sieve to remove stubborn lumps and bits of metal. The sand must be damp enough to hold its shape, but not so damp that it sticks to your hands. Dry sand is best dampened with a spray of water, if it is too wet, dry sand should be added. In both instances a thorough mixing is essential.

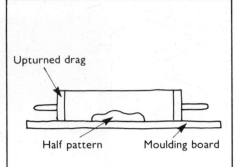

fig 5.138.

2. Place the drag upside down on a stout, flat moulding board. Place the half of the pattern that does not have the pegs flat face down on the moulding board, at least 50 mm away from the drag on all sides.

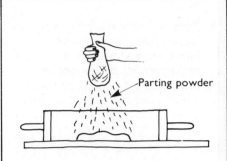

fig 5.139.

3. Sprinkle the moulding board and the half pattern with parting powder. This is a fine powder that is used to coat any surfaces that will later need to be separated, such as the two halves of the mould from each other, and the pattern from the sand.

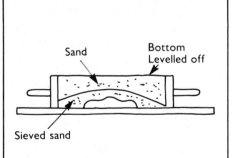

fig 5.140.

4. Sieve the fine sand over the pattern until it is completely covered with a layer at least 25 mm deep, then gently ram this down using a hardwood ram. Be very gentle at this stage. Fill the drag up to the bottom with sand and ram it well. The excess should be scraped off by strickling (levelling off using a metal straight edge.) This surface must be level and free from hollows.

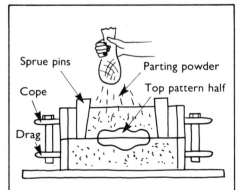

fig 5.141.

5. Carefully turn the drag the right way up. Place the other half of the pattern in place and put the cope onto the drag. Coat the pattern and joint line with parting powder. At this point the **sprue pins** must be added. Sprue pins are tapered, circular sectioned, hardwood pegs that create the **runner** down which the metal flows into the mould, and the **riser**, up which the air escapes and the excess melt rises when the mould is full.

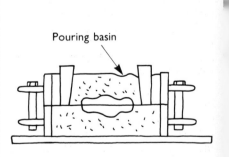

fig 5.142.

6. The procedure is as before. Sieve in fine sand to cover the pattern with a 25 mm layer, then top up with sand and ram solid. Take care not to knock over the sprue pins. Before removing the sprue pins shape the top surface with a spoon or a small trowel and, using your fingers, create a pouring basin and a smooth radiused lead in to the runner and riser.

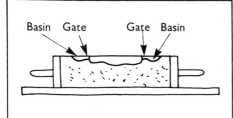

fig 5.143.

7. Remove the sprue pins, a tap will loosen them, and then very carefully separate the two halves of the mould. Before gently removing the pattern halves, shape basins and gates in the lower mould half to allow the melt to flow without turbulence into and out of the mould. Use a spoon and your fingers to ensure smooth surfaces. Take great care when removing the pattern halves.

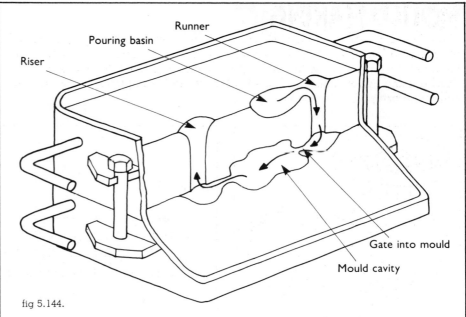

Runner
Pouring basin
Riser
Gate into mould
Mould cavity

fig 5.144.

8. Carefully re-assemble the mould box and place it level on a sand covered casting floor. Be sure that it is in a position convenient for pouring.

Moulds for flat back patterns are produced in an identical manner to that shown above. The only exception is that no upper pattern half is added when the cope is first put on. When using expanded polystyrene patterns the sand must not be rammed too heavily, as it is possible to crush the polystyrene. Runners and risers should be larger to ensure a quick pouring rate and easy escape for the styrene fumes. Additional small vents should be added to help in the venting of the fumes.

POURING

Never pour the melt without the teacher's assistance. Great care is needed when pouring, and protective clothing must be worn. This should include leather gloves, apron, leggings and a full face mask.

A **crucible furnace** is used to melt the aluminium. The crucible is the ceramic pot in which the metal is melted and from which it is poured.

Aluminium will melt at 600°C, but needs to be at around 750°C for pouring. At this temperature the melt has a slight pink colour.

Remove the crucible from the furnace using lifting tongs and place it carefully in the pouring ring.

Gas and impurities present in the melt should be removed at this stage. A de-gassing tablet is dropped in and held down at the bottom of the crucible by the de-gassing plunger. After a few seconds the bubbling will stop and a surface layer of dross or slag will have formed. Remove this with a ladle before pouring begins.

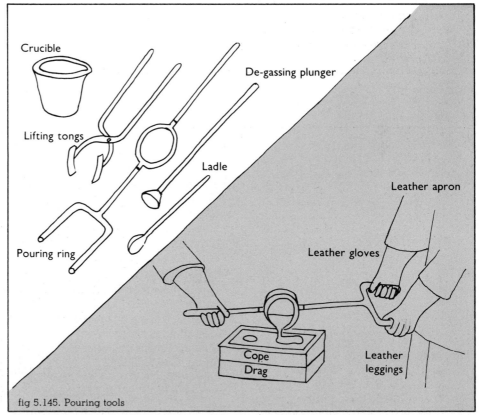

Crucible
Lifting tongs
Pouring ring
De-gassing plunger
Ladle
Leather apron
Leather gloves
Leather leggings
Cope
Drag

fig 5.145. Pouring tools

Pour slowly and continuously into the pouring basin and continue to pour until a pool is formed at the top of the riser.

When the metal has completely solidified the sand can be carefully broken away from around the workpiece. Take care, as the sand and the work may still both be hot.

Finally, the casting will require feltling. The involves sawing off the runners and risers (which can be used again), and filing off the gates and any casting flashes that have formed through leaking at the mould joint line. Any amount of machining and finishing may then follow.

SAFETY — Never pour the melt without your teacher's assistance. Wear the protective clothing. Do not overcrowd the casting area. Ensure plenty of ventilation.

FABRICATING

There are few projects that can be realised using just one piece of material. Most work will involve joining together several different pieces.

These may be pieces of the same material or they may be pieces of different materials.

Look at the photograph (fig 5.146). An oil rig is just one of many industrial examples which illustrate the assembly of numerous different parts in a single, final structure or item.

Joining pieces together, whether or not they are of the same material, is called **fabricating.**

It is essential to have a knowledge of the joining methods available before you can plan the realisation of your design.

fig 5.146. Fabrication in industry

There are two major types of joining process: those that are permanent and those that are temporary.

Permanent joints once made cannot be undone without resorting to means that may cause some damage to the workpiece.

Temporary fixings are not necessarily designed to be taken apart at regular intervals, but disassembly is possible should the need arise.

A major design decision has to be made before any form of fabricating takes place. Should the joints used be permanent or might it not be more convenient to use some form of temporary fixing?

PERMANENT JOINTS

All joints that make use of adhesives are permanent. A guide to suitable adhesives for particular applications is given on the next page. Wood that is jointed and assembled with glue is permanently joined. The purpose of the most simple wood joints, such as lap joints (page 124), is to provide a large glueing area.

Other, more complex joints like dovetails (page 124) have mechanical strength even before glueing.

Permanently joining metal means using either rivets, adhesives or one of the heat processes, soldering, brazing or welding.

A full knowledge of the types of permanent joint available is needed before deciding on which type to use.

TEMPORARY FIXINGS

Most temporary fixings make use of screw threads. This simple principle has been used since early Grecian times and screw threads have evolved to suit a large range of needs.

Nuts and bolts can be found in Swiss watches, on suspension bridges and in orbiting space stations.

Different screws are used for wood, metal and plastics. A great deal of modern furniture makes use of KD or knock down fittings, of which there are a large variety.

The range of temporary fixings is large, but with a knowledge of the different types available you should be able to solve any fixing problem that might arise in your project work.

ADHESIVES

MATERIAL	WOOD	METAL	ACRYLIC	EXPANDED POLYSTYRENE	MELAMINE	POLYSTYRENE	FABRIC	RUBBER	LEATHER
WOOD	PVA or Synth. res.								
METAL	Epoxy resin								
ACRYLIC	Epoxy resin		Acrylic cement						
EXPANDED POLYSTYRENE	PVA								
MELAMINE	Contact adhesive								
POLYSTYRENE	Contact adhesive					Polystyrene cement			
FABRIC	PVA or contact	Contact adhesive					PVA or latex		
RUBBER	Contact adhesive or latex adhesive							Rubber solution	
LEATHER	Contact adhesive or epoxy resin								

PVA Polyvinyl acetate (Evostik Resin W)

This is the most popular wood glue. It is sold ready to use, is easy to apply, non-staining and strong, providing that the joints fit well. Any excess should be wiped off after cramping with a damp cloth. It is not waterproof.

Synthetic resin (Cascamite, Aerolite 306)

This is a stronger wood glue than PVA and also waterproof. It is chemically activated plastic resin that must be mixed with water and a hardener. Cascamite has the resin and hardener ready mixed in the form of a white powder. Aerolite 306 has a liquid hardener supplied in a separate bottle. Synthetic resins will fill small gaps in joints.

Epoxy resin (Araldite)

This is a very versatile, but expensive adhesive that will bond almost any clean, dry materials. Equal amounts of resin and hardener are mixed to start the chemical hardening process. Hardening begins immediately, but full strength is achieved after two or three days depending on the temperature.

Contact adhesive (Dunlop Thixafix)

This is used for glueing sheet material, such as melamine to work surfaces. Both surfaces are coated with a thin layer which is left for approximately 15 minutes to become touch-dry. Adhesion takes place as soon as contact is made between the surfaces, there is no provision for re-positioning. Contact adhesive must only be used in a well-ventilated area.

Latex adhesive (Copydex)

This is a cheap adhesive suited to fabrics, paper, card and upholstery. It is non-toxic and has no fumes and is therefore ideal for younger children.

Acrylic cement (Tensol)

This is an adhesive purpose made for acrylic and available in two forms. Tensol Cement 12 is a solvent adhesive that is supplied ready for use. Tensol Cement 70 is a two part polymerising adhesive that requires mixing before use.

Polystyrene cement

This is a purpose made adhesive for rigid polystyrene and is usually supplied with polystyrene model kits such as 'Airfix'.

Rubber solution

Supplied as part of a bicycle puncture repair outfits, but also manufactured by 'Bostik', rubber solution is a purpose made adhesive for rubber.

Glueing hints

1. Do not apply any form of finish to the glueing surfaces.
2. Ensure that the glueing surfaces are free from dirt, dust, oil and moisture.
3. Assemble all joints dry before re-assembling with adhesive. Have all the clamps and assistance that you will need to hand before you begin to apply glue.
4. Check the above chart for the correct adhesive for the job. Read the adhesive manufacturer's instructions and warnings.

SAFETY — Many modern adhesives are solvent based, they give off fumes that are both addictive and very harmful. Be sure that you have plenty of ventilation. Avoid excessive skin contact. Always take note of the manufacturer's warnings.

JOINING WOOD

When joining and fixing wood it should be remembered that it will always continue to move. Wood will expand and contract across its grain (not along its length) with changes in temperature and humidity. Most man-made boards do not suffer from this problem, but is is something to bear in mind when using wide natural timbers.

Consider your choice of joints carefully, there will often be more than one that will do the job.

Try to plan your joints so that the loading on the finished article will continue to push the joints together, or at least shear them, rather than pull them apart.

Joints can be used to form features and enhance the appearance of products.

fig 5.148. Product with joints

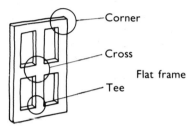

fig 5.149.

FLAT FRAME JOINTS

Flat frames often form parts of items of furniture. They are the basis of doors, picture frames, sides of cupboards and window frames. Flat frames will always require joining at the corners, and other joints are needed if additional members are included to provide increased strength and resistance to twisting. These will be **tee joints** and possibly **cross joints** (fig 5.149).

Butt joints and mitre joints

The simplest form of flat frame joint is the butt joint. This is relatively weak, having only a small glueing area. It is often adequate, however, particularly if the frame is covered with a plywood or hardboard panel using glue and panel pins (fig 5.150).

Picture frames are usually mitred so that the shape of the picture frame moulding flows around the corner without interruption. Mitres must be accurately cut at 45° to ensure a good glueing area. This is not a very strong joint, but can be strengthened by nailing, or on heavy frames by applying a thin plywood reinforcing plate (fig 5.151).

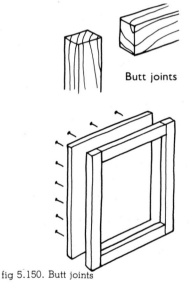

fig 5.150. Butt joints

fig 5.151.

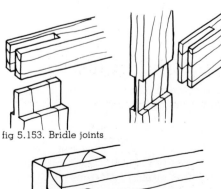

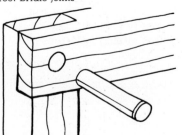

fig 5.153. Bridle joints

fig 5.152. Halving joints

Corner halving joint

Tee halving joint

Cross halving joint

fig 5.154. Increasing strength using a dowel

Halving joints and bridle joints

Halving joints are cut by removing half of the material thickness from each piece of wood to be joined. This is carried out using a tenon saw and a firmer or bevel edged chisel (see pages 88 and 92). This process can be applied to corners joints, tee joints, and cross joints (fig. 5.152). This is stronger than butt jointing and the strength can be further increased using screws or dowels (fig 5.154).

Bridles for corner joints and tee joints have an increased glueing area compared with halving joints and are therefore stronger (fig 5.153). Screws or dowels can also be added to increase the strength.

Dowelled joints

Dowel is circular sectioned hardwood, usually ramin or beech.

Dowelled joints are really butt joints reinforced with dowels and are strong. They are straightforward to make providing that you are careful. Holes, usually two, are drilled in the end of one piece and the side of another in order to form both corner joints and tee joints. Glue is then applied and short lengths of dowel are inserted as shown in fig 5.155.

It is important to use a dowelling jig to position the holes. Dowels will enter more easily if the ends are chamfered slightly using a dowel bit in a carpenter's ratchet brace. A groove along the length of the dowel will allow air and surplus glue to escape from the hole.

When strengthening halving and bridle joints using dowel, it is necessary to drill a hole through the joint. A length of dowel is then glued into the hole when the joint is being assembled. Any protruding dowel should be cleaned off after the glue has dried.

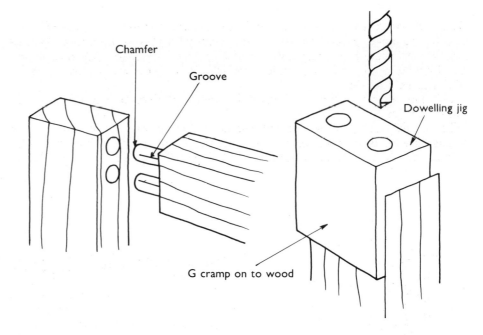

fig 5.155. Dowelled corner

fig 5.156. Mortise and tenon joint

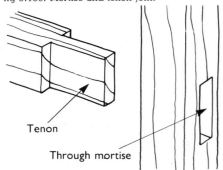

Tenon

Through mortise

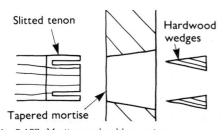

Slitted tenon

Hardwood wedges

Tapered mortise

fig 5.157. Mortise wedged by sawing slits in the tenon

Mortise and tenon joints

The traditional strong joint, the mortise and tenon joint is well worth mastering. The basic mortise and tenon is a tee joint, either through or stopped (fig 5.156). This is cut using a tenon saw and a mortise chisel, and it requires careful marking out using a mortise gauge (see page 85). It can be strengthened using dowel in the same manner as a tee bridle or halving joint. Alternatively, the through mortise can be wedged by sawing slits in the tenon, tapering the mortise and driving wooden wedges in (fig 5.157).

On a corner, a **haunched mortise and tenon** joint can be used, either square or sloping (fig 5.158). This enables a mortise to be used near to the end of a length of wood. Sloping haunches are used where the top of the frame is visible. If this is not critical then a square haunch is adequate.

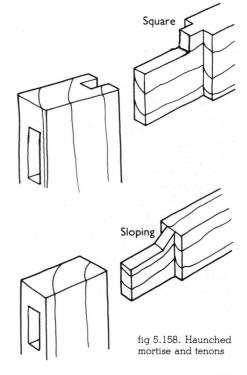

Square

Sloping

fig 5.158. Haunched mortise and tenons

THREE DIMENSIONAL FRAME JOINTS

The occasion often arises, particularly with stools and tables, where it is necessary to joint three pieces of wood at the same place, such as a leg and two rails (fig 5.159). This problem is solved by other variations on the mortise and tenon joint. Mitred haunched mortise and tenons should be used at the top of the leg. The mortises are cut to meet each other, though it is not desirable that the tenons should meet in the middle. Lower down the leg a simple mitred mortise and tenon can be used (fig 5.160).

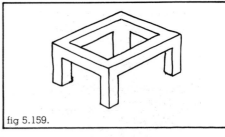

fig 5.159.

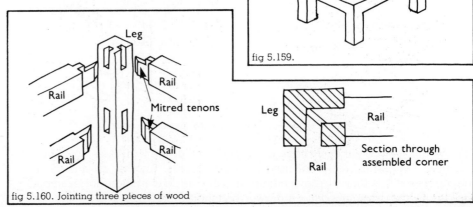

Leg

Rail

Rail

Mitred tenons

Rail

Rail

fig 5.160. Jointing three pieces of wood

Leg

Rail

Rail

Section through assembled corner

BOX JOINTS

Kitchen furniture, bedroom furniture, book shelves, record cabinets, jewellery boxes and cupboard drawers are all things that have a box like form. Products of this type are very often made not from solid wood, but from manufactured board.

Wide, solid wood shrinks, warps and twists, and there is a limit to the available width; 225 mm is the normal maximum width of softwood and 330 mm the maximum for most hardwoods. Manufactured boards also have problems. Chipboard has little mechanical strength, blockboard and plywood are stronger and more expensive than chipboard, but like chipboard are harder to join than solid wood and also require edging.

When designing box or carcase types of structures, manufactured board can often be considered as an alternative to solid wood. An understanding of the methods available for fabricating boxes will help you to make the correct design decisions.

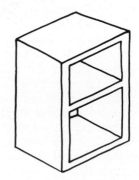

fig 5.161. Box-like structure

Butt joints and lap joints

These joints should be considered alongside the temporary methods of fabricating on page 120.

Butt joints are quick and simple to make, but they lack strength. Using solid timber the joint can be reinforced by dovetail nailing (fig 5.162). Another form of corner reinforcement is to use glue blocks (fig 5.163). These can also be added to manufactured board. The glue block can be triangular in cross section and applied using just glue after assembling the corner.

Alternatively, glue blocks can be square in section and are glued and screwed to one side to provide a positive location for the second side which is glued and screwed to the corner block in turn. Take care that the screws don't run into each other (fig 5.164).

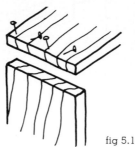

fig 5.162. Dovetail nailing

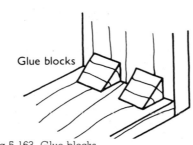

Glue blocks

fig 5.163. Glue blocks

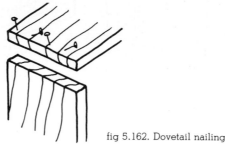

fig 5.164. Using glue and screws

fig 5.165. Lap joint

Lap joints, sometimes called corner rebates, are stronger and neater than butt joints, having a larger glueing area and less exposed end grain (fig. 5.165). With solid timber, dovetail nailing can again be added.

When using plywood and blockboard, cut the depth of the rebate to a complete lamination (fig 5.166).

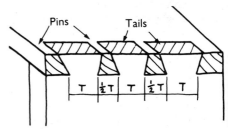

Plywood | Blockboard

fig 5.166. Plywood and blockboard lap joints

DOVETAIL JOINTS

Dovetail joints are the strongest box corner joints. They are also attractive to look at, providing care is taken in the construction (fig 5.167). There are two properties of a dovetail joint that contribute to its strength. First the large glueing area, and second the assembly. Dovetails can only be assembled in one direction and can therefore only be pulled apart in one direction. You should position dovetail joints so that any tendency to force the corner apart is at right angles to the way it was assembled.

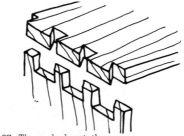

fig 5.167. Through dovetails

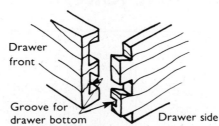

Drawer front

Groove for drawer bottom

Drawer side

fig 5.168. Lapped dovetail

Dovetails can be either through or lapped, so that the joint does not show on one face. Lapped dovetails are used on drawer fronts. Another advantage of a lapped dovetail is that a groove cut around the inside is hidden, for example, the groove that accommodates a drawer bottom (fig 5.168).

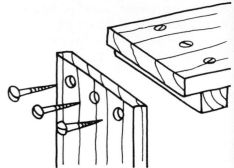

Pins | Tails

fig 5.169. Pins and tails

Hints for dovetailing

1. Use a dovetail template for marking out.
2. The wide part of the pin should be approximately half as wide as the narrow part of the tail.
3. Leave a wider pin at each end of the joint.
4. Mark out and cut the tails first and draw around them to mark out the pins. Remove the waste with a dovetail saw, a coping saw and then a sharp bevel edged chisel.

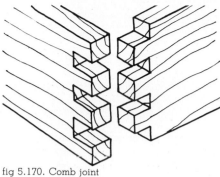

fig 5.170. Comb joint

Comb joints

Like dovetail joints, comb joints, sometimes called finger joints, can be very attractive. The comb joint was developed as a compromise within the furniture industry because of the difficulty of machine cutting dovetails. Comb joints are easy to machine and also easier to cut by hand than dovetails. Strength comes from the large glueing area (fig 5.170).

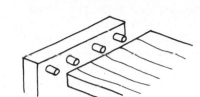

fig 5.172. Veneered chipboard

Dowelled joints

Dowels can be used for both corners and tee joints. This is a particularly useful joint for chipboard and veneered chipboard, which are not normally easy materials to work with. The process is similar to that used with frame joints. The increased number of dowels means that a wider dowelling jig is required and it must be deep enough to provide positive alignment for the drill, especially important on ends of board (fig 5.171).

When using dowelled joints on melamine faced chipboard, carefully remove a strip of melamine to provide a glueing area (fig 5.173). Wood glue will not adhere to melamine.

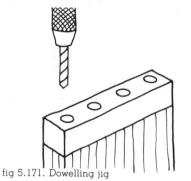

fig 5.171. Dowelling jig

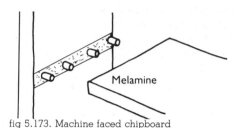

fig 5.173. Machine faced chipboard

Housing joints

Shelves and partitions can be housed into the sides of a box structure. The simplest housing is the through housing. If there is a danger that the side will be pushed outwards then a dovetail housing can be used. This can be through or stopped. If it is desirable that the joint does not show then stopped housings can be used (fig 5.174).

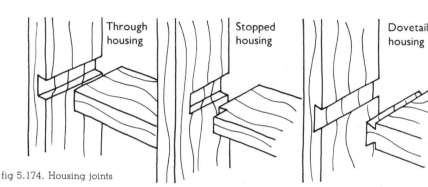

fig 5.174. Housing joints

EDGING AND EDGE JOINTING

Edging

The edges of manufactured boards are not very attractive, are vulnerable to damage and allow absorption of moisture.

Where the edge will not be subjected to physical knocks, a wood veneer can be applied. Pre-glued edging veneer is available in widths and woods to match veneered chipboard. The glue is heat activated using a hot clothes iron, alternatively contact adhesive can be used.

Melamine edging strip is also available to suit melamine faced chipboard. For a harder wearing edge a solid hardwood strip can be applied. It is best to mitre the corners so that no end grain is exposed. Solid edges are fixed by butt jointing or by using a tongue and groove. The tongue may be part of the edge or alternatively a loose plywood strip (fig 5.175). All methods should be securely cramped until the glue has set. Tongued edging is stronger than butt jointed.

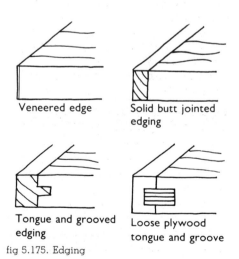

fig 5.175. Edging

Edge jointing

Joining solid wood edge to edge is dependent upon carefully planed, flat and square edges. The methods of joining are similar to those applied to edging, butt jointing, tongue and grooving or by using a loose plywood tongue. Another alternative is to use dowels (fig 5.176).

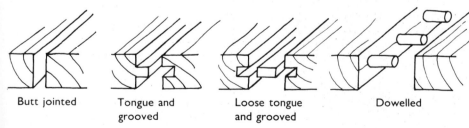

fig 5.176. Edge joining

WOOD SCREWS

Wood screws provide a neat, strong method of fixing. They can be removed and are, therefore, categorised as a temporary method of fixing, unless used with glue. They are used for joining wood to wood, metal and plastic to wood and also for fixing hinges, catches, locks, letterboxes, light switches, door knobs, table tops and other fittings.

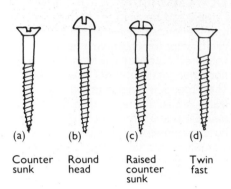

fig 5.177. Types of screws

(a) Counter sunk (b) Round head (c) Raised counter sunk (d) Twin fast

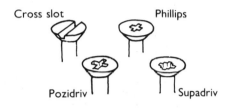

fig 5.178. Screw driver slots

Cross slot   Phillips   Pozidriv   Supadriv

There are many different types of screws and they are specified by length, gauge, material and type of head (e.g. 25 mm No 6, brass, round head). The length of a screw is the total length for a countersunk screw and the length from under the head for a headed screw. The gauge is the thickness, the larger the gauge the thicker the screw (e.g. No 6 is 3.5 mm, No 10 is 7.9 mm).

Screws are usually made from steel or brass, steel for cheapness and strength, brass for appearance and corrosion resistance. Chrome plating, galvanising or black lacquer (black japanning) are common finishes applied to screws. There are various types of head, having different shapes and different screwdriver slots (fig 5.177).

Countersunk heads (a) are the most popular and are used for joining wood, fixing hinges and anywhere that it is desirable to leave a flat surface remaining.

Round head screws (b) are mainly used for thin metal fittings like brackets and gate hinges.

Raised countersunk screws (c) are usually chrome or brass to look attractive and are used for fixing door furniture and other household fittings.

Twinfast screws (d) are used for screwing into chipboard or blockboard. They have two threads and greater holding power in this type of material.

Screwdriver slots are either straight or crossed. The straight slot can allow a screwdriver to slip out and scratch the surrounding surface. Cross slots provide a positive location for crosspointed screwdrivers. The original cross slot was the Phillips, from which evolved Pozidriv and then Supadriv (fig 5.178).

Caps, cups and mirror screws

Screw heads can be hidden or enhanced by plastic caps that cover the head, and by screw cups that provide a form of raised countersink.

Mirror screws are chrome with a slotted countersunk head that has a threaded hole in the centre. After inserting the screw, a domed chrome cap is screwed into the head, completely covering the slot.

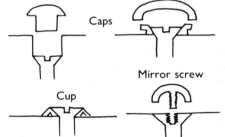

fig 5.179. Caps, cups and mirror screws

Caps   Mirror screw   Cup

Hints for screwing

1. Screw through the thin piece and into the thick.
2. Use a screw two or three times as long as the piece of wood being fixed.
3. Drill the clearance hole slightly larger than the shank diameter of the screw. Screws will not hold very well in end grain. Either drill a hole into the end grain and insert a raw plug, or drill a hole across the path of the screws and insert a length of a dowel (fig 5.181).
4. Start screws with a pilot hole, use a bradawl in softwood and a drill the size of the screws core in hardwood.
5. Brass screws tend to shear off if screwed into hardwood, so use a steel screw to make the joint then remove this and replace it with the brass screw.

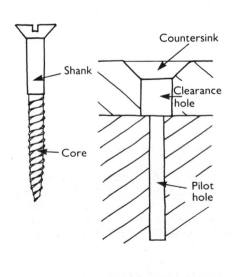

fig 5.180. Hints for screwing

Shank   Core   Countersink   Clearance hole   Pilot hole

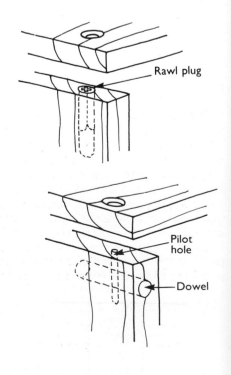

fig 5.181. Using a rawl plug or pilot hole

Rawl plug   Pilot hole   Dowel

KNOCK-DOWN JOINTS

Knock-down or KD fittings are used mainly by manufacturers of flat pack furniture. All the kitchen and bedroom furniture that is sold by MFI furniture stores is sold in flat cardboard packages to be assembled at home using the KD fittings provided.

Some KD fittings can be purchased independently of furniture retailers and are worth considering for design and realisation projects, especially when using manufactured board.

fig 5.182. KD coffee table

Corner blocks

Butt jointed corners and tee joints for shelves can be easily made using neat plastic 'bloc-joint' fittings (fig 5.183). The two piece fitting has one half screwed to each piece of board and the halves are then fixed together using the machine screw provided with the joint. These can be very quickly taken apart again.

The single block is very simple and involves just three screws, two into one piece and one into the other. Using this only on light constructions. Remember with manufactured board to use twin fast screws.

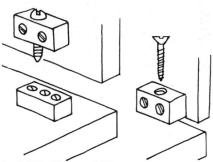

fig 5.183. 'Bloc-joint' fitting

Frame connectors

The tubular steel legs of the coffee table in fig 5.182 are fixed to the wooden rails using a form of frame connector. A short length of aluminium bar with a hole drilled and tapped through it is inserted into a hole in the rail. The end of the rail is drilled to allow access for a machine screw that passes through the tubular steel leg and screws into the aluminium, fixing the leg to the rail. A short pin is also included to stop the rail turning over (fig 5.184).

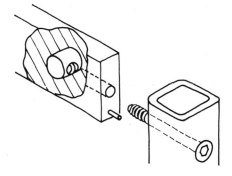

fig 5.184. Short pin used to stop rail turning over

Fig 5.185 shows a variation on this method of using frame connectors, where the cylindrical 'nut' is inserted from the top of the rail so that it will later be covered and not seen. The leg in this case is wood and a dowel is added (without glue) to prevent rotation.

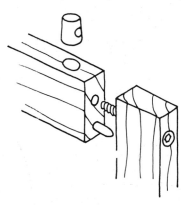

fig 5.185. Using frame connectors·

NAILS

Nailing is a quick and permanent method of joining wood. Nails grip by forcing the fibres of the wood away from the head of the nail so that they then act against withdrawal (fig 5.186). The length of nail used is important. It should be three times as long as the thickness of the wood being fixed. Nails are sold by weight according to the type and length of the nail. Fig 5.187 shows the most common types of nail.

Round wire nails are made from steel wire, are round in section and have a flat head. They are used for general joinery and are available in lengths from 12 mm to 150 mm.

Oval wire nails are made from oval section steel wire and have a head that can be punched below the surface using a nail punch. The hole can then be filled and hidden. Use oval nails with the long axis in line with the grain. Oval nails also range from 12 mm to 150 mm in length.

Masonry nails are hardened steel, round in section and designed for hammering into brickwork to fix wooden battens to walls.

Panel pins may be of a standard type or deep drive. Standard pins have a thin shank up to 50 mm long and a small head that can be punched below the surface. They are used for pinning joints such as mitres and small lap joints. Deep drive pins are made for fixing hardboard. They have a squared point to penetrate the surface better and the specially shaped head does not require punching below the surface prior to filling.

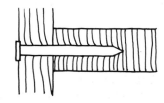

fig 5.186. Nailing

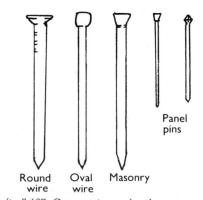

Panel pins

Round wire   Oval wire   Masonry

fig 5.187. Common types of nail

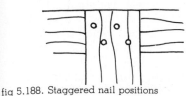

fig 5.188. Staggered nail positions

Hints for nailing

1. Use a hammer that is a comfortable weight.
2. Keep your eye on the nail, not on the hammer.
3. Nailing near to the end of a piece of wood will split it, if you must do this then drill a clearance hole through first.
4. When nailing frames together, stagger the nail positions as in fig 5.188.

JOINING METAL

Heat processes

All of the heat processes used for fabricating metal are permanent. The amount of heat available, the metal involved, the structure of the work, and the stress to which it will become subjected in use are all factors that will affect your decisions when looking at permanent fabrication of metals using heat.

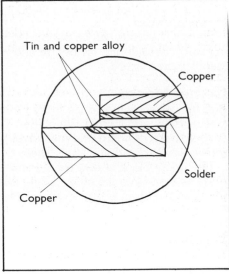

fig 5.189. Soldered joint

SOFT SOLDERING

This is an easy, quick method of making joints in copper, brass, tinplate and steel. It is a process best confined to light fabrication where strength is not required and where the joint is not subjected to vibration or heat. Solder is an alloy of lead, tin and antimony. The joining process relies on local alloying. The tin in the solder forms an alloy with the surface of the metals to be joined. Fig 5.189 shows a magnified soldered joint between two pieces of copper.

Solder for electronics contains more tin than lead, which makes the solder flow quickly at a lower temperature. Solder for sheet metal work and plumbing contains more lead than tin. They melt at a higher temperature and set harder.

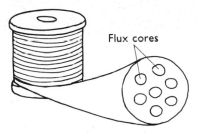

fig 5.190. Multicore solder

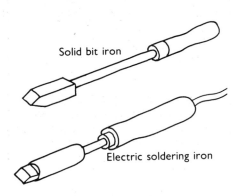

fig 5.191. Copper bit

Joint preparation

The effectiveness of any soldering depends on the joint area being thoroughly clean. This can be achieved using emery cloth or for soft metals like copper, use steel wire wool. After cleaning, avoid touching the joint area, as this will leave oils from your skin on the surface.

Flux, in the form of a liquid or a paste, aids the soldering process by preventing oxidisation of the area around the joint. There are two kinds of flux, active and passive.

Active fluxes, the most popular being zinc-chloride, chemically clean the surface to be soldered, as well as preventing oxidisation, but they are corrosive and the residue must be cleaned off after the joint has been made.

Passive fluxes are non-corrosive, but only protect and do not actually clean. A passive resin flux, should be used for electrical and electronic work. 'Multicore' solder for electronics has fine cores of flux running along its complete length (fig 5.190) and no additional flux is required.

Making a soft soldered joint

A soldering iron or a gas/air torch provides the heat. Soldering irons have a copper bit that is either heated electrically, or is heated by a gas flame (fig 5.191). The iron must be clean and regularly 'tinned'. Tinning means cleaning the iron while it is hot, dipping it in flux and then coating it with a thin film of solder.

There are many variations on the shape of joint, but a close fitting joint is essential so that capillary action can draw the solder in and provide a large joint area.

There are also several ways of applying both heat and solder.

fig 5.192. Apply heat and solder together

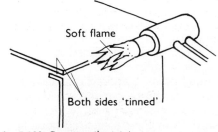

fig 5.193. Sweating the joint

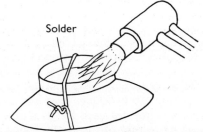

fig 5.194. Placing the solder and using a flame

Applying heat and solder together (fig 5.192). The joint is first fluxed and the tinned iron is then drawn slowly along the joint line. Solder flows from the iron into the heated joint by capillary action aided by the flux. Solder should be added sparingly to the iron as necessary.

Sweating the joint (fig 5.193). Both sides of the joint are tinned with a film of solder. The joint is then brought together and heat from an iron or a flame is applied to the joint area while it is held in place.

Placing the solder and using a flame (fig 5.194). The joint is fluxed and assembled using wire if necessary to keep it together. Small pieces of solder are laid on the joint and the work is heated by a flame. The solder then melts and runs around the joint.

HARD SOLDERING

Hard soldering involves higher temperatures than soft soldering, though the principle of local alloying and the use of flux is the same as that for soft soldering. Soft solder metals at around 200°C, whereas the lowest melting point of hard solder is 625°C. This means that heat cannot be applied by a soldering iron, a gas/air torch or an oxy-acetylene welding torch must be used. Hard soldered joints are much stronger than soft soldered joints.

Silver soldering

Hard solders containing silver alloyed with copper and zinc, are known as silver solders. There is a range of silver solders with differing melting points from 625°C to 800°C. This enables work to be joined in several stages using first a high melting point solder, then lower melting point solders, thus avoiding the risk of the early joints coming apart while applying heat for the later ones.

Joint preparation is equally important with all hard soldering. The joint area must be thoroughly cleaned and an active flux applied. For the lowest melting point silver solder, called 'Easy-Flo', a special 'Easy-flo flux' is used. The other silver solders require 'Borax' flux.

Brazing

The hardest and highest temperature hard solder is brazing spelter, which is an alloy of copper and zinc.

Brazing spelter melts at 875°C which makes it too hot to use with brass or copper, but ideal for mild steel. Borax is a suitable flux for brazing.

Making a hard soldered joint

Butt joints are possible with hard soldering and are common in jewellery and ornaments. All joints should be wired or held securely and fluxed before assembly. The procedure is illustrated below.

fig 5.195. Brazing hearth

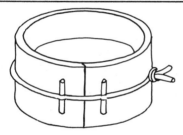

fig 5.196.

1. A copper cylinder, fluxed and wired for silver soldering. Notice how the wire is kept above the surface at the joint line so that it does not get soldered in place.

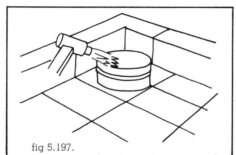

fig 5.197.

2. Place fire bricks all around to reflect heat and maintain an even temperature. Pre-heat the copper with a bushy gas/air flame.

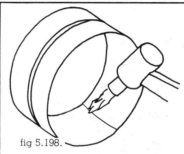

fig 5.198.

3. Concentrate the heat on the joint with a small pointed flame and allow the copper to melt the silver solder. The solder will follow the flame along the joint line.

Joints that must be strong are best made with some form of positive location. Fig 5.199 shows the base of one of a pair of loudspeaker stands. The material is mild steel, a piece of tube and some rectangular section bar. The tube is slotted to accommodate the bar, and the two lengths of bar are cut with a cross-halving joint (fig 5.200). The stand is next assembled and fluxed, surrounded by fire brick and then heated until bright red. The brazing spelter is then introduced and encouraged by the flame to flow in the joints (fig 5.201).

fig 5.199. Base of a loudspeaker stand

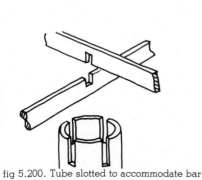

fig 5.200. Tube slotted to accommodate bar

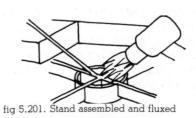

fig 5.201. Stand assembled and fluxed

Hints for hard and soft soldering

1. Ensure absolute cleanlinless around the joint area, this is time well spent.
2. Allow time for the solder to flow, especially when soft soldering with an iron.
3. Melt both solder and braze on the hot metal and not in the flame.
4. Beware of using too fierce a flame, it may blow the flux away from the joint.
5. Use firebricks to reflect applied heat, but raise flat surfaces above the brick to allow the heat to circulate.

WELDING

Welding is the process by which metal to be joined is melted and fused together forming a joint that is as strong as the parent metal. It involves extremely high temperatures and should only be carried out under the close supervision of a qualified adult.

Industrially, there are many different ways of achieving this fusion of metals. Small engineering workshops and many school workshops tend to have either oxy-acetylene gas welding equipment, or electric arc welding equipment.

Oxy-acetylene welding

A very hot flame is produced by burning acetylene gas in oxygen. This is the basis of the process, and the mixing of these gases takes place in a hand held blowpipe that is connected to cylinders containing the oxygen and acetylene gases.

The heat and characteristics of the flame produced can be varied to suit the thickness of metal being welded, by changing the size of the nozzle connected to the blowpipe and by adjusting the gas supply from the cylinders (fig 5.202).

When joining pieces of metal together, a pool of molten metal is created by the hot flame and a filler rod of the same metal as that being joined is continually dipped into this. The filler rod melts into the joint filling it, and thus fusing the metal together (fig 5.203).

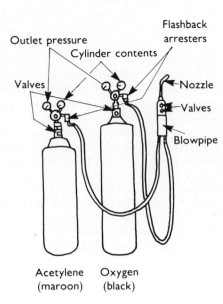

Acetylene   Oxygen
(maroon)   (black)

fig 5.202. Oxyacetylene welding equipment

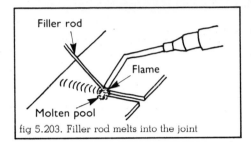

fig 5.203. Filler rod melts into the joint

Electric arc welding

An electric arc produced by a large electric current jumping a small gap is the heat source for this welding process.

The current, between 10 and 120 amps, flows from a mains powered transformer to an electrode, across the small gap to the workpiece, and returns to the transformer via an earth clamp, either on the workpiece or on the metal-topped welding bench (fig 5.204).

The electrode, as well as carrying the current, is a flux coated filler rod. The flux coating burns away during the welding process, creating a gaseous shield to project the weld from the oxidisation (fig 5.205). The rod is consumed in filling the joint like the filler rod in oxy-acetylene welding.

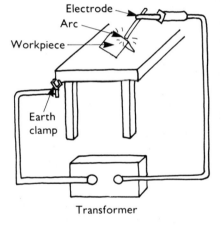

fig 5.204. Electric arc welding equipment

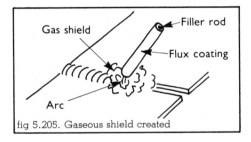

fig 5.205. Gaseous shield created

Joint preparation

The joint area does not require the thorough cleaning that is so necessary with soldering, but any paint and rust should be removed using a wire brush. With thicker material, edge preparation is needed to ensure that the weld can penetrate the metal and achieve strength. This preparation involves filing a bevel edge on metal over 3 mm thick, so that the weld can be built up from the base of the 'vee' created. Fig 5.207 shows four examples of joints before and after welding. As the metal increases in thickness so more preparation is necessary.

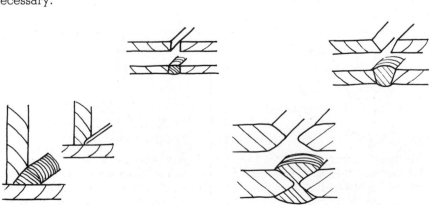

fig 5.207. Joints before and after welding

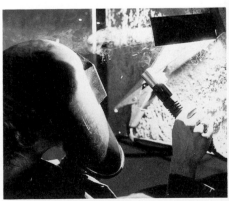

fig 5.206. Arc welding

SAFETY — Never use welding equipment without close supervision. Always wear the correct eye protection. Position screens or curtains so that other people cannot inadvertently see electric arc welding taking place.

RIVETING

Riveting is another permanent joining process. Rivets are used mainly in sheet metal work, but the process can also be applied to acrylic and plywood. Fig 5.208 shows a mild steel handle that has been made both comfortable to hold and more attractive by having acrylic sides riveted on to it.

There are many different shapes for rivets, but the three most common are countersunk headed, flat headed and snap or round headed (fig 5.209). Rivets are most often soft mild steel, aluminium or copper. The choice of rivet is determined by the location and the material being joined.

Round head rivets are the most commonly used. If a flush finish is an important consideration, then countersunk heads are required, and if the material is too thin to be countersunk then a flat head can be used.

Round head riveting

Riveting requires an engineer's hammer, a **rivet set** and for round head rivets, a **rivet snap** (sometimes called a dolly). The set is used to tighten the joint in sheet metal work and snaps are used to support round heads and to give the final shape to the formation of a round head. The set and snap must be the correct size to suit the rivets being used.

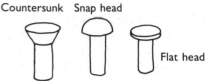

fig 5.208. Mild steel handle with acrylic sides riveted on

fig 5.209. Three most common rivets

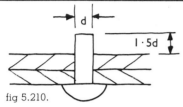

fig 5.210.

1. Drill through with the correct sized drill to provide a snug fit for the rivet. Cut rivet so that 1.5 times the diameter is left sticking up to form the head.

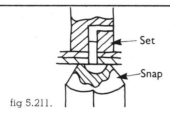

fig 5.211.

2. Support the rivet head on a snap held in a vice. Tighten up the joint using the rivet set, light hammer taps are sufficient.

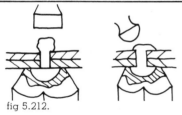

fig 5.212.

3. Swell the rivet using the flat face of an engineer's hammer, then start to shape up the head using the ball pein end of the hammer.

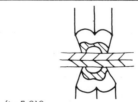

fig 5.213.

4. Complete the shape of the head with a snap.

Countersunk head riveting

The process is very similar to round head riveting except that the holes require countersinking and the rivets length should be cut off so that an amount equivalent to the diameter is left sticking up.

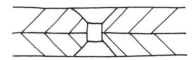

fig 5.214. Rivet barely visible

1. Support the head on a flat surface and tighten up the joint with the set.
2. Swell the rivet with the flat face of the hammer and then spread it into the countersink with the ball pein end.
3. Smooth the surface with the flat face of the hammer and then finish of with a file and emery cloth until the rivet is barely visible (fig 5.214).

Hints for riveting

Never drill all the holes in all the pieces to be joined before you start riveting.

1. Mark out and drill the holes in one piece only.
2. Line up the second piece of material and drill through **one** hole only and then rivet this.
3. Then drill through and rivet each subsequent position in turn.

POP RIVETING

This is a quick and easy process ideally suited to thin sheet material. Pop riveting was developed in the aircraft industry for riveting in places where access to both sides of the joint is not possible. The rivet is hollow and therefore weaker than solid rivet.

Pop riveting pliers must be used for this process. These are supplied with a set of nose bushes to suit different diameters of pop rivet.

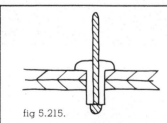

fig 5.215.

1. The correct size hole is drilled through the material to be joined and a pop rivet inserted.

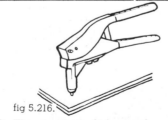

fig 5.216.

2. The riveting pliers are located on the rivet and the handle squeezed until the centre mandrel of the rivet snaps off.

fig 5.217.

3. The head of the mandrel has caused the rivet to swell on the inside of the joint and has broken off remaining to reinforce the rivet head.

JOINING ACRYLIC

Acrylic can be joined by welding using hot air. It can be drilled and tapped and then joined with machine screws, but by far the most popular method of joining acrylic is to use an acrylic adhesive.

'Tensol' cements 12 and 70 are adhesives that have been developed by ICI for joining acrylic.

'Tensol' cement 12
This is a solvent based adhesive, it is not very strong and it works by attacking the surface of the acrylic. A disadvantage of this is the effect of the solvent action on the appearance of the work. The area surrounding the joint should be masked off using masking tape, but with joints in clear and smoked acrylic the evidence of the solvent's attack on the glueing surface will remain visible. The major advantage of 'Tensol' cement 12 is that it is supplied ready for use and it sets quickly.

'Tensol' cement 70
This is a polymerising adhesive, it can be likened to a liquid acrylic that links with the material being joined resulting in a joint that is nearly as strong as the acrylic itself.

The major disadvantages with 'Tensol' cement 70 are the careful mixing that is necessary, the setting time, and the contraction rate.

'Tensol' cement 70 is a two part adhesive. The two component parts must be mixed thoroughly in the proportions stated by the manufacturers and then left to stand until the air bubbles have dispersed. It should be used in a room temperature higher than 15°C and remains usable for only 20 minutes. The setting time is approx 1.5 hours at room temperature and the adhesive will contract by 20% during this period. This contraction must be allowed for when the adhesive is applied to the joint.

Types of joint
Joints that will be stressed, subjected to vibration or to shocks, should not rely on 'Tensol' cement 12 unless a large glueing area is available. The ease with which acrylic can be formed (see page 105) means that joints can be kept to a minimum. Wherever possible on corners, bend one side under, using a strip heater, to provide an increased glueing area (fig 5.218). If a butt joint is unavoidable then 'Tensol' cement 70 should be used. Fig 5.219 shows the procedure for a butt jointed corner.

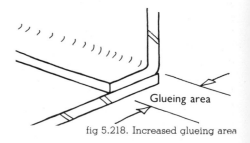

fig 5.218. Increased glueing area

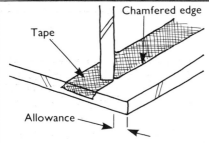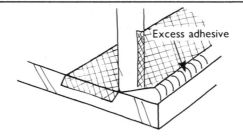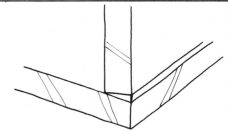

1. The joint must be prepared by filing or milling a chamfer of about 10° on one half of the corner. The other half must have an allowance left on for final cleaning up. Masking tape is put on to protect the finished surfaces from excess adhesive.

2. Adhesive is applied to one half of the joint in sufficient quantity to allow for contraction after the joint is assembled. The masking tape can be removed after the adhesive has gelled.

3. After setting, the adhesive will have contracted, but providing that sufficient was applied the joint will still be full. Excess adhesive can now be filed or machined off along with the cleaning up allowance.

fig 5.219. Procedure for butt jointed corner

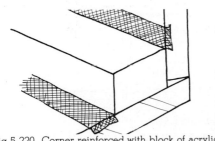

fig 5.220. Corner reinforced with block of acrylic

Hints for joining acrylic
1. Ensure that the surfaces are clean and free from moisture and oils.
2. Assemble the joint quickly after the adhesive has been applied, a surface skin forms after about 30 seconds and this weakens the joint considerably.
3. Hold the joint firmly together, but do not apply too much pressure, this will squeeze the adhesive out.
4. A corner that needs additional strength, can be reinforced with a block of acrylic in a similar manner to using glue blocks in wooden box fabrications (fig 5.220).

SAFETY — All acrylic adhesives contain solvents. Be sure that you have plenty of ventilation, the fumes are harmful and can be addictive. Read and take heed of the manufacturer's warnings.

NUTS AND BOLTS

The basic principle of using nuts and bolts can be applied to the temporary fixing of any materials and any combination of materials. There are numerous variations.

Bolts

Bolts are normally available up to 150 mm in length, measured from under the head, and 6 mm to 25 mm in diameter. They are mechanically strong, often being made from a high tensile steel. The head shape is usually either square or more often hexagonal. Most bolts have **ISO metric screw** threads, but there are many other threads still in use. BSW, BSF, UNC and UNF are still quite common as are BSC (British Standard Cycle) threads on cycles, and BSP (British Standard Pipe) threads in plumbing.

Coach bolts are a type of bolt specifically designed for joining wood. They have a shallow domed head with a square under it. The square bites into the wood and stops the bolt from turning.

Studs are headless bolts, with a thread at both ends. They are up to 300 mm long and are used primarily with tee nuts for clamping work to machine tables.

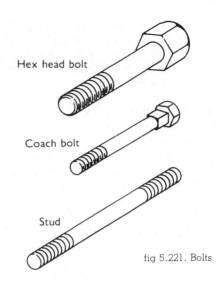

fig 5.221. Bolts

Machine screws

Machine screws, also called **set screws,** are smaller than bolts and are available in a range of diameters, lengths, head shapes, materials and thread forms. They have a thread that goes right up to the head, whereas bolts have a length of plain shank. Steel and brass are the most common materials for machine screws. Threads are ISO metric, coarse or fine series, or BA (British Association). BA is a range of screw sizes from OBA at 6 mm diameter, going down to a minute 23BA at 0.3 mm diameter.

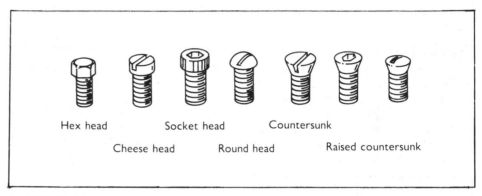

fig 5.222. Machine screws

Nuts

A nut must fit the bolt or machine screw with which it is to be used. This means matching both the diameter and the thread form. Here again there is a range of shapes, from easily removable wing nuts, through standard hexagonal and square nuts, to locking nuts that are designed to resist coming loose.

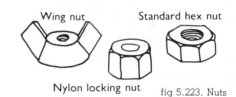

fig 5.223. Nuts

Washers

In most fixing situations a plain washer should be positioned under a nut and another under hexagonal and square bolt heads. This protects the surface from any damage that may be caused by tightening the nut or bolt. Spring washers will help to prevent joints that may be subjected to vibration from coming loose.

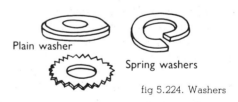

fig 5.224. Washers

SELF-TAPPING SCREWS

Self-tapping screws are made from hardened steel and cut their own thread as they are screwed in. They are not only suited to thin sheet materials, mainly metal, and also some hard plastics.

Fig 5.225 shows how a self-tapping screw is used, preparation requires a clearance hole in one piece of material and a pilot hole equal to the screw's core diameter in the other. Self-tapping screws are not suitable for situations where they are required to be continually removed and re-inserted.

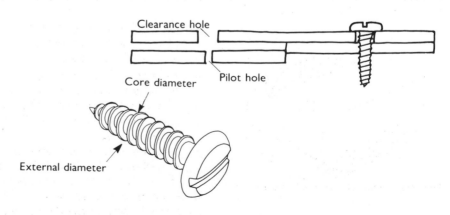

fig 5.225. Self tapping screws

FINISHING

When you feel that you have finished your project, it is often a good idea to ask yourself this question. 'If I saw this in a shop, would I buy it?' If the answer is 'No', despite the fact that what you have made does the job that is required of it, then it is very likely that the quality of finish is poor, or at the very least could be improved upon.

Finishing is the final stage in realisation, and it is very important to plan your project so that you are able to spend sufficient time giving the attention to the finish your work deserves, don't let yourself down by last minute rushing.

Decide when and how you will carry out your chosen finishing process when you first plan your project. For example, it is usually easier to finish the insides of cabinets and boxes before assembling them. It is easier to polish the edges of acrylic before bending it. By thinking and planning ahead, the job of finishing can be made both easier and more effective. Appearance is only one aspect of finishing, protection against corrosion and decay is another. Wood is subject to attack by insects and fungi, metals corrode and ferrous metals rust.

FINISHING WOOD

Planing is the first stage in the finishing process.

Use a smoothing plane that is sharp and set fine to remove only small amounts of wood. Level off joints, remove surface defects and gauge and pencil lines.

Abrasive paper will now enable you to achieve a high quality finish. Glass paper made from pieces of ground glass glued onto a tough paper backing is graded between coarse and extra fine (called flour paper). Garnet paper is similar, but is made from a natural grit and lasts longer, however, it is more expensive. This is also graded coarse to extra fine.

Abrasive paper should be used wrapped around a cork block (a sanding block). It is important to always work 'with the grain' (fig 5.226).

A great asset when finishing large surfaces is a portable electric orbital sander. The abrasive paper used is graded in the same way as glass paper and is clipped onto the sanding pad of the machine. The orbital sander is then held down firmly and moved steadily over the whole surface of the work.

fig 5.226. Working with the grain

Finishes are often best applied to all inside surfaces before assembly. It is difficult to achieve a high standard of finish to inside corners and deep box type structures afterwards. Glueing surfaces should be masked off when finishing before assembly, as most finishes will stop glue from penetrating the wood and will therefore weaken the joint.

With the exception of wooden spoons, rolling pins and chopping boards, most wooden artefacts have a finish applied to them. The amount of protection against moisture and decay required will depend upon the environment.

Creosote, or one of the more attractive outdoor preservatives is essential for fences and garden sheds. These preservatives will protect against weather, insects and fungal decay. Few projects made in school require this degree of protection.

French polish

This is a traditional finish that has diminished in popularity with the coming of plastic finishes such as polyurethane varnish. French polish is made by dissolving Shellac in methylated spirits and applying successive coats with first a brush and then a cloth. A very light rubbing down with wire wool should be carried out beween coats. French polish can be applied on top of wood stain. Wax polish, bees wax or silicone furniture polish, can be applied over french polish to add a shine and give some protection.

fig 5.228. Teak oil, polyurethane varnish and paint

Oil

Woods such as teak are naturally oily. Regular applications of teak oil or linseed oil will provide a natural finish that enhances the grain of the wood. Very small amounts of oil should be rubbed into the surface using a soft cloth. Do not use furniture polish on oiled wood surfaces, but re-oil occasionally.

Polyurethane varnish

This is a plastic finish that is tough, heatproof and waterproof. Polyurethane varnishes are available in clear or translucent forms, in a range of colours and wood shades. There is also a choice of three finishes, gloss, satin and matt.

This is a very widely used finish for furniture. It should be applied in thin coats, using a brush, and with a very gentle rubbing down with steel wire wool between coats.

Paint

Paint provides a surface covering that is protective and colourful for both inside and out of doors.

Preparation is essential. Knots should be treated with knotting to prevent the resin in the wood from pushing the paint off. Coarse glass paper should be used to roughen the surface and provide a grip for the paint. Sharp outside corners should be radiused slightly, because paint shrinks as it dries and will retreat from a sharp corner (fig 5.229).

Apply a primer, then at least three coats of paint, an undercoat and then two gloss coats. The best finish is achieved by rubbing down with a fine glass paper between coats.

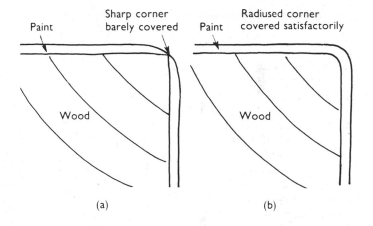

fig 5.229. Avoid sharp corners when painting

FINISHING ACRYLIC

Plastics will neither corrode nor decay, so a protective coating for the surface is not necessary.

A high quality finish to the surface is achieved by filing carefully without applying too much force and then using wet and dry paper with water. Wet and dry is a fine abrasive coated paper that can be used dry, or for fine finishing with water.

Machine buffing can then be carried out with care. It is very easy to overheat the surface and cause permanent damage.

Fig 5.230 shows a buffing machine with a polishing mop that is coated with a buffing compound. The coating is achieved by holding a bar of the compound against the mop for a few seconds. Hold your work carefully against the rotating mop so that it is not snatched from your hands. Always wear eye protection when using a buffing machine.

Metal polish can be used on acrylic, though acrylic polishes are also available. There is also an anti-static polish that will reduce the level of dust that tends to be attracted to acrylic surfaces.

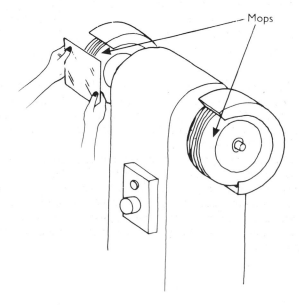

fig 5.230. Buffing machine

135

FINISHING METAL

Steels that have been hand worked should be finished in stages, using files, cross filing, draw filing and then emery cloth. Steel that has been machined on the centre lathe or milling machine should have a high standard of finish, but if machining marks remain, then emery cloth can be used here also.

Emery cloth consists of a graded abrasive grit bonded onto a cloth backing. It is available in a range of grits from coarse to very fine in the same way as glass paper. After drawfiling, use emery cloth wrapped around a file working down through the grades as the finish improves. For a fine finish use a fine emery cloth with a few drops of oil (fig 5.231). Most steels rust quickly if left unprotected, even overnight, in a humid environment. A thin film of light grease will provide protection until the chosen finish is applied.

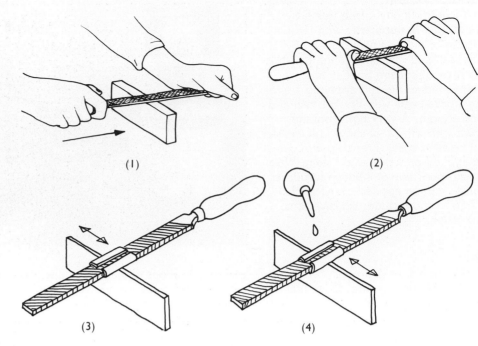

fig 5.231. Finishing metal

Oil blacking

This can be easily applied to steel artefacts, and is often used on forge work. Oil is burnt onto the surface of the steel by either dipping and then heating with a flame, or more usually by heating until dull red and then dipping into oil. Old black machine oil or engine oil is suitable for this process. This is not a hard wearing finish.

Paint

Painting metal differs from painting wood only in the preparation and the primer. The surface must be 'de-greased' using paraffin and then washed with hot water and detergent.

Zinc chromate based primer is ideal for steel that is to be painted with ordinary oil based paint.

Plastic dip coating

Thermoplastic plastic, usually polythene, in powder form can be encouraged to act like a liquid by blowing air through it. This is called fluidization.

A piece of metal pre-heated in the oven to around 180°C can be dipped into this fluidised plastic to emerge with a plastic coating (fig 5.232). Returning the work to the oven for a few minutes will fuse the plastic coating into a smooth glossy finish. Take care not to burn and spoil it.

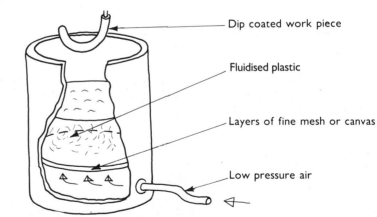

Dip coated work piece

Fluidised plastic

Layers of fine mesh or canvas

Low pressure air

fig 5.232. Plastic dip coating

Lacquering copper and brass

Copper and brass being non-ferrous, will not rust, but oxidisation of the surface will cause tarnishing and spoil their appearance. A high standard of finish on copper and brass is achieved using wet and dry paper or pumice powder and then polishing using a buffing machine or hand polishing with metal polish. Pumice powder is a fine abrasive and is worked with a damp cloth. Lacquering the surface with a clear lacquer or varnish after polishing will provide a barrier against oxidisation.

Apply the lacquer with a soft brush or alternatively use a spray on lacquer.

Letter rack made from acrylic and oil blacked mild steel.

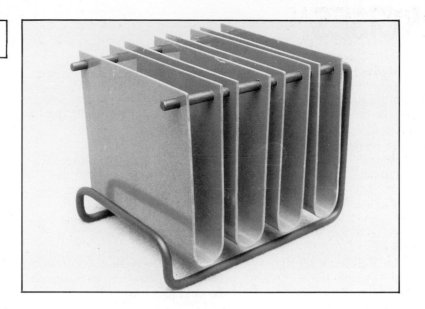

This interesting child's 'Fantasy Playhouse' toy folds flat when not in use with all of the accessories tucked away inside it.

The wooden figures are turned, the furniture, the 'mobile library' and the spelling tiles are made from acrylic.

Kitchen bread bin in softwood finished with matt polyurethane varnish.

EXERCISES

1. What tools should be used for marking out on:
    (a) wood? (b) metal? (c) acrylic?

2. What is the purpose of:
    (a) a centre punch?
    (b) a dot punch?
    (c) a nail punch?

3. What type of saw would you use to saw:
    (a) A piece of 20 mm × 40 mm softwood?
    (b) A piece of 5 mm × 20 mm mild steel strip?
    (c) An irregular shape in a piece of 6 mm acrylic sheet?
    (d) A sheet of plywood?

4. Acrylic sheet is normally supplied with a paper covering.
    What advantage can be gained by leaving this on for as long as possible?

5. Sketch the following fixing devices and say whether they are considered temporary or permanent.
    (a) An oval nail.
    (b) A countersunk machine screw.
    (c) A coach bolt.
    (d) A snap head rivet.

6. What finish, if any, would you apply to:
    (a) A copper photograph frame?
    (b) A softwood garden gate?
    (c) An acrylic child's toy?
    (d) A hardwood coffee table top?

7. Explain the terms 'countersink' and 'counterbore'.
    Use a sketch to illustrate your answer.

8. What is the name given to chisels that are used to cut metal?

9. Show with sketches how you could mark a line parallel to the edge of:
    (a) A piece of wood.
    (b) A strip of mild steel.

10. Sketch a sawing board and a mitre box and say what you would use each for.

11. Show by means of a sketch how a pair of sash cramps can be joined together to increase their capacity.

12. Why do you need to establish a face side and a face edge when marking out on a piece of wood?

13. What are vee blocks and clamps used for?

14. What do the initials GRP stand for?

15. How can a simple butt joint between two pieces of 100 mm wide wood be strengthened.

16. Compare the cutting actions of sawing and shearing?

17. There are two types of engineering twist drill. Show how each should be held in a pillar drill?

18. What tool would you use to cut a flat bottomed hole 15 mm diameter in a piece of hardwood?

19. What tools could be used to cut a 50 mm diameter hole in a piece of 8 mm plywood?

20. What type of chisel should you use for:
    (a) Chopping out a mortise?
    (b) Carving the inside of a small irregular hollow dish?
    (c) Removing the waste from a halving joint?

21. Problems with splitting can be encountered when planing across end grain. How can this be avoided?

22. An engineers file tends to clog on a soft fibrous material.
    What type of file should be used in this situation?

23. With sketches, show how to mark out a mortise using a mortise gauge.

24. How can the cut marks left by cross filing be removed?

25. When screw cutting by hand which material would require:
    (a) A cutting compound?
    (b) Paraffin as a lubricant?
    (c) No lubricant?

26. When cutting both an internal and an external thread by hand, which should be cut first and why?

27. Show by means of a sketch how a hole can be drilled on the centre lathe.

28. What is the purpose of:
    (a) a surface plate?
    (b) a surface gauge?

29. How could a 15 mm square section piece of steel 50 mm long be held in a centre lathe for turning?

30. How can a flat disc 100 mm diameter × 15 mm thick be held safely on a centre lathe in a self centering 3 jaw chuck?

31. What is the purpose of flux in soldering and why are there a variety of fluxes?

32. How can a diamond patterned grip on a steel knob be machined on the centre lathe?

33. What method of measuring or comparing would you use if turning four fancy wooden legs for a stool to ensure that they are all the same?

34. Suggest an adhesive that would be suitable for the following situations.
    (a) Glueing mortise and tenon joints on the under frame of a coffee table.
    (b) Laminating coloured acrylic sheet.
    (c) Fixing a melamine surface to a chipboard kitchen worktop.
    (d) Attaching a plastic name plate to a brass sports trophy.

35. Suggest two reasons why planishing should be carried out on beaten metalwork.

36. The cutting speed for aluminium using a HSS tool is 200 metres per min.
    (a) Calculate the turning speed for a 50 mm diameter aluminium bar.
    (b) What does HSS stand for?
    (c) What cutting lubricant should be used, if any?

37. What materials may be subjected to pickling in dilute sulphuric acid and for what purpose?

38. How could a seamed joint in sheet tinplate be made waterproof?

39. Why is aluminium used for casting in a school workshop rather than brass or steel?

40. Explain the term accumulative error, with reference to marking out.

41. You have produced a design that requires two pieces of wood, A and B, to be fastened together as shown in fig 5.233 using wood screws in the position shown.

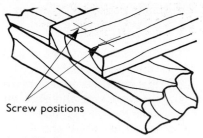

    (a) What type of screw could be used in this situation so that the head of the screw does not stick up above the surface of the wood?

    (b) With the aid of a sketch show the process that must be applied to part A before the screws are inserted, and name the tools that are used?

    (c) Suggest another method of fastening pieces A and B in the position shown that does not use screws. Illustrate your answer.

fig 5.233. Two pieces of wood to be fastened together

42. The child's wooden go-kart shown in fig 5.234 is to be steered by pivoting the front axle beam as shown. The wheels are old toy pram wheels and have a 12 mm hole at their centre.

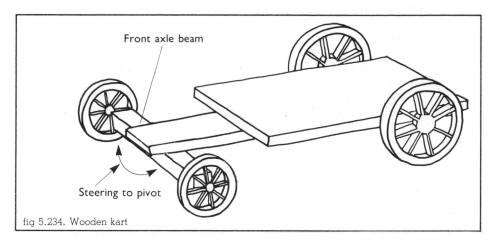

    (a) Show by sketches how the axle beam would be attached to the kart allowing it to pivot as required.

    (b) Design a front axle that could be made in the school workshop. Show clearly how the wheels may be attached to the axle and the axle to the axle beam.

fig 5.234. Wooden kart

43. Outline briefly with the aid of sketches two wasting processes that can be applied to **all** of the following materials:

    (a) solid wood, (b) mild steel (c) acrylic. Show how the tools or processes are modified to suit the material being worked.

44. Fig 5.235 shows two designs for the underframe of a coffee table. A is to be made from a hardwood. B is to be made from square section steel tube.

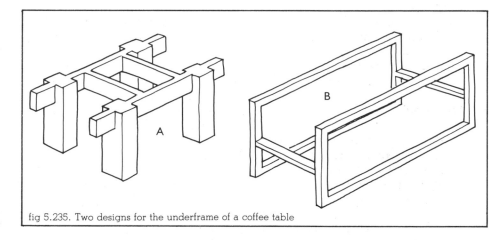

    (a) Produce detail sketches of all of the joints that are involved in both frames.

    (b) Suggest an assembly procedure for both frames.

    (c) With regard to the movement that may be encountered with time, sketch suitable methods of attaching a hardwood top to both frames.

fig 5.235. Two designs for the underframe of a coffee table

45. A box of straight shank drills has been accidentally dropped and the drills have become mixed up. The size of some of the drills is hard to read. Suggest two accurate measuring tools that might be used to determine the size of the drills and explain in detail how each is used.

46. Fig 5.236 shows a design for a bookend to be made from a piece of acrylic sheet 100 mm × 200 mm × 5 mm thick. Describe step-by-step using sketches, how you would make the bookend, pay particular attention to:

    (a) How you would carry out the cutting that is necessary before bending.

    (b) The method used for bending using a strip heater as a heat source.

    (c) How and at what stage you would finish the edges of the acrylic.

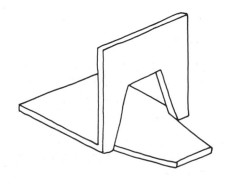

47. Design a bending former, showing in detail how it is to be made, that could be used to produce 20 identical pairs of bookends like that shown in fig 5.236. Your only heat source for the acrylic is an oven. You can assume that the acrylic is cut to size and that the edges are finished.

fig 5.236.

48. The simple book rack shown in fig 5.237 is designed to hold paperback books.

(a) Suggest three forms of wood (solid and manufactured) that could be used to make the book rack and show for each the type of joint you would use at 'A' and at 'B'.

(b) Which of the three would you choose and why?

(c) If the book rack was to be extended to 1 metre in length show what structural modification may be necessary.

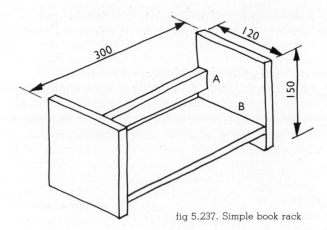

fig 5.237. Simple book rack

49. The aluminium casting in fig 5.238 requires machining all over. Only the top and bottom faces are parallel to each other, all the other faces taper towards the top.

Show step by step using a milling machine how you would carry out the machining of the casting.

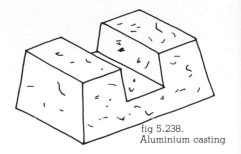

fig 5.238. Aluminium casting

50. Expain the difference between deforming and reforming.
Why is GRP work difficult to categorize under either of these headings?

51. Laminating wood increases its mechanical strength.

(a) Show by means of sketches how this is achieved.

(b) Produce designs for a former that could be used to form the laminated legs for the plant trough shown in fig 5.239.

(c) Suggest a method of attaching the legs to the wooden trough.

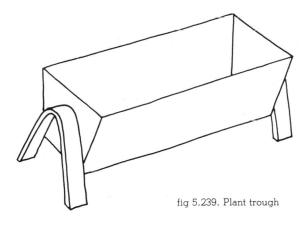

fig 5.239. Plant trough

52. Fig 5.240 shows a design for a foot for a display stand to be used in the entrance foyer of a school. The legs are made from 15 mm diameter aluminium tubing. The foot A is to be made from 40 mm diameter mild steel, and the screw B from 15 mm diameter mild steel.

(a) Produce dimensional working drawings for both pieces (A and B).

(b) Show with sketches step by step how each could be made using a centre lathe.

(c) Suggest a suitable finish that could be applied to each.

53. The feet on the display stand shown in fig 5.240 keep coming off and getting lost. It has been decided to cast aluminium feet for the 15 mm diameter aluminium tubing and attach them permanently.

(a) Sketch three ideas of suitable feet and evaluate them with regard to their ability to be cast in school.

(b) Show using sketches how the pattern could be made and the feet cast.

(c) Show how the feet might be permanently attached to the tubing.

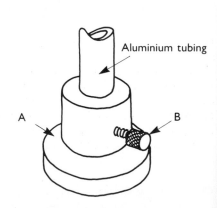

fig 5.240. Aluminium feet

54. Vacuum forming and blow moulding both rely upon air pressure to deform plastic sheet:

(a) Compare these two processes making particular reference to the use of air pressure.

(b) With the aid of a sketch, show the design features that must be included in a vacuum forming pattern.

(c) By making reference to the properties of flexibility and plasticity explain why acrylic is not an ideal plastic for vacuum forming and suggest a better material giving reasons for your choice.

(d) Explain how, when using thin flexible sheet for vacuum forming, features can be incorporated into component design to increase rigidity.

BASIC TECHNOLOGY
CONTROL SYSTEMS

Control is an essential part of everyday life. Most activities require some sort of control. You need to control your hand to pick up a book or turn a page. You can control a TV or model car by remote control. Computers can control machines and robots to work with great accuracy and speed.

The way in which things are controlled can seem very complicated, but even complex control systems can be simple to understand if you use the right approach to them. This is called the **systems approach**. It involves looking at the building blocks that go to make up a system. It is rather like using building blocks to build a model house. Each block links to others to make up the whole house. In a control system each control block links to others to produce the required system. The basic building blocks that go to make up a control system are shown in fig 6.1.

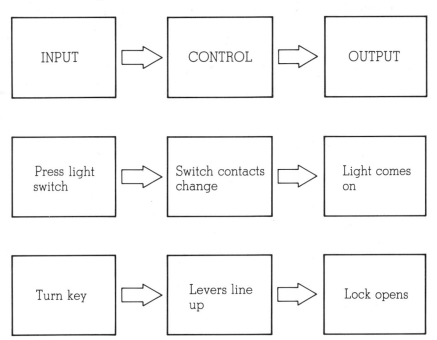

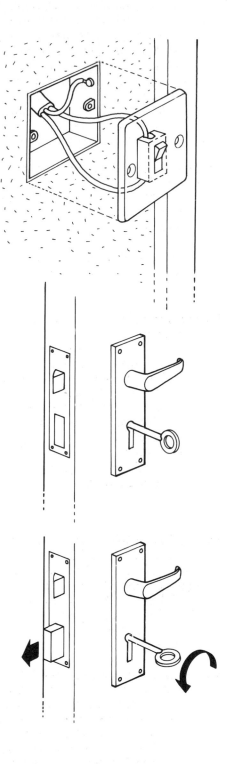

fig 6.1. Block diagram of control systems

As you can see from these examples, the systems approach can be used to explain any control situation without getting involved in the detail of how it is done. It makes no difference what kind of systems you are dealing with, each requires a control system of some sort. In industry, the systems approach is used to identify the various parts of a problem before starting to work out the detail. You can use it in a similar way to design solutions to control problems.

MECHANISMS

Most of the mechanisms you use are so familiar that you never think about them. Simple things like light switches, door handles and tin openers are just a few of the many mechanisms you use every day. Each one has been designed to do a particular job and most of the time they do it perfectly. It is probably only when they go wrong that you think about them.

Although designed to do different jobs, all mechanisms have some things in common:

— they make a job **easier** to do

— they involve some kind of **movement**

— they involve some kind of **force**

— they need some kind of **input** to make them work

— they produce some kind of **output.**

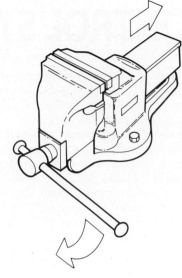

fig 6.2. A vice

For example the vice shown in fig 6.2 makes the job of holding work firmly very **easy**. The **input movement** is provided by the **force** you apply when turning the handle. The **output movement** is the vice jaws closing or opening; they apply a holding **force** to your work. The part that changes the **rotary** input motion into a **linear** output motion is a screw thread. The whole system can be shown as a block diagram (fig 6.3).

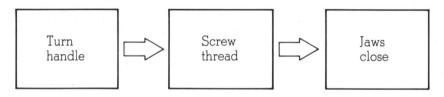

fig 6.3. Block diagram of a vice mechanism

A screw thread is one of the basic mechanisms. It is used in many different ways. For example, it can be used to provide powerful, accurate movements (e.g. car jacks) or to position and hold things in place (e.g. vices, cramps, screws and bolts).

Rotary and **linear** are just two of the four basic kinds of movement. The other two are **oscillating** and **reciprocating** movement. Examples of each, and the symbols used to represent them, are shown in fig 6.4.

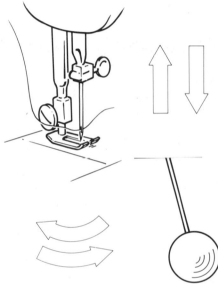

fig 6.4. Oscillating and reciprocating motion

LEVERS

Levers were probably the first kind of mechanisms to be used, to help move large rocks or prise open shells. They were used in much the same way that we might use a crowbar to open a crate (fig 6.5), or a tyre lever to take off a tyre. These are very obvious levers, but there are many other less obvious levers you use every day, things like knives and forks, switches, door handles and bike brakes. All levers are one of the three basic kinds shown in fig 6.6. They can be used individually (e.g. a spanner), in pairs (e.g. pliers) or connected together to form a linkage (e.g. lazy tongs).

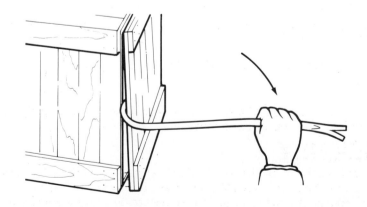

fig 6.5. Crowbar being used to open a crate

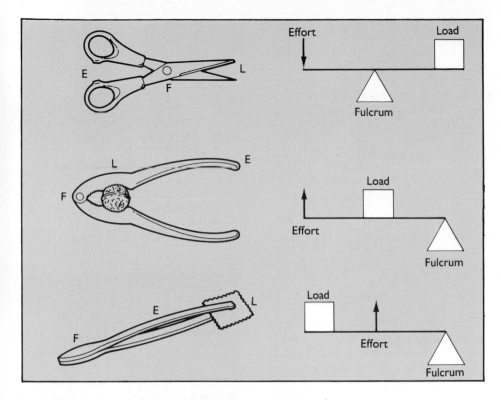

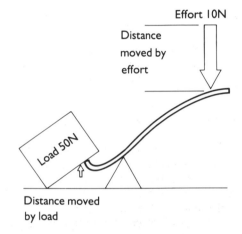

fig 6.6.   Three classes of lever

MECHANICAL ADVANTAGE

The most common types of lever are Class 1 and Class 2 because they give you a **mechanical advantage**, which means that you can move a large load using a small effort. The mechanical advantage of the Class 1 lever shown in fig 6.7 is found by comparing the weight of the load with the effort needed to move it:

$$\mathbf{MA} = \frac{\mathbf{Load}}{\mathbf{Effort}} = \frac{50\ \text{N}}{10\ \text{N}} = \frac{5}{1}\ \text{ or } 5{:}1 \text{ or } 5$$

This means you could use it to move a load five times greater than the effort you apply to the lever. The MA of any mechanism can be calculated in the same way.

Class 3 levers are used less often because their mechanical advantage is less than 1. This means that the force needed to use them is greater than the force they can move. If being worked by hand, the use of Class 3 levers is limited to things like tweezers which only need small input forces.

fig 6.7.   Class 1 lever

VELOCITY RATIO

When calculating mechanical advantage it seems as if you are getting something for nothing, you are moving a large load using a small effort! If you look at how far your effort is having to move you will see it has to move much further than the load is moved. Comparing the two distances gives the **velocity ratio**. Using the Class 1 lever in fig 6.7:

$$\mathbf{VR} = \frac{\text{Distance moved by } \mathbf{Effort}}{\text{Distance moved by } \mathbf{Load}} = \frac{500\ \text{mm}}{100\ \text{mm}} = \frac{5}{1}\ \text{ or } 5{:}1 \text{ or } 5$$

So, you are moving a load 5 times greater than your effort, but only by moving your effort 5 times as far the load moves.

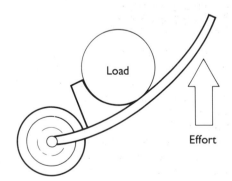

fig 6.8.   A lever bending under load

EFFICIENCY

All this assumes that a mechanism is 100% efficient. It never is! In practice, parts bend, twist and rub against each other, making them less efficient.

The **efficiency** of a mechanism can be calculated using the formula:

$$\mathbf{Efficiency} = \frac{\mathbf{MA}}{\mathbf{VR}} \times 100\%$$

For example, fig 6.8 shows a lever which, because it bends, has a MA of 4 and a VR of 5.

$$\mathbf{Efficiency} = \frac{4}{5} \times 100\% = 80\%$$

143

LINKAGES

Linkages are very important in mechanical control systems because they allow forces and motion to be transmitted where they are needed. They can change the direction of a movement, the size of a force, or make things move at the same time or parallel to each other. They usually do several of these things at once.

Bell cranks and **reverse motion linkages** can be used to change the direction of motion (fig 6.9). This is useful for taking motion round a corner or changing a push into a pull.

By changing the position of the fulcrum or lengthening one side of the lever, they can also be used to change the distances moved and the forces produced by the linkage (fig 6.10).

Linkages based on a parallelogram can be used to make two or more parts move together or stay parallel to each other as the linkage moves. Fig 6.11 shows a scissor lift table which uses this principle. Many folding chairs, tables and pushchairs also use this idea (fig 6.12).

One very useful linkage is the **toggle clamp**, which is used to lock things into position. It holds very firmly and is very quick to use. Mole grips and louvre window catches are examples you may have come across. Toggle clamps are used a great deal in industry to hold work in position while it is worked on. It works rather like your knee joint. If you have to stand on one leg for a while, you will lock your leg by pushing the knee back. Fig 6.13 shows how the toggle clamp works by forcing the middle of the three joints slightly 'over centre' against a stop. Once in that position it is locked. Any force caused by the load trying to open it only pushes it into the locked position even more.

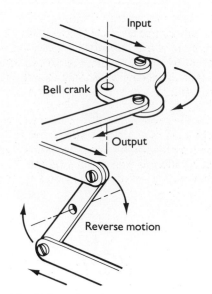

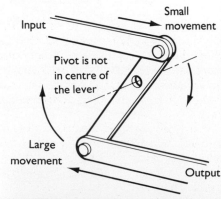

fig 6.10. Changing the position of the fulcrum

fig 6.9. Bell crank and reverse motion linkage

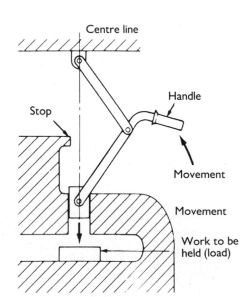

fig 6.11. Scissor lift table

fig 6.12. Folding pushchair

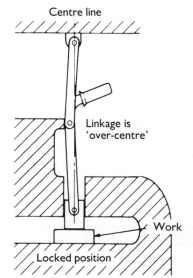

fig 6.13. Toggle clamp system

144

ROTARY SYSTEMS

The majority of machines use some kind of rotary movement. Some, like the bicycle, are totally based on rotating parts. Others use a rotary input motion which they change into a different output motion, a graphic plotter is a good example of this (fig 6.14). The rotary motion of its stepper motors is turned into linear movement of the pen. A car engine does things the other way round, it changes the reciprocating motion of the pistons into a rotary motion of the wheels.

Many machines use electric motors to provide a rotary input movement. The speed of the motor is rarely the one needed for the machine. A means has to be found of providing the desired output speed from the motor input speed. It may also be necessary to reserve the direction of rotation as well as change the speed. These things can be done using either pulley systems, chain and sprocket systems, gear systems, or a combination of the three.

fig 6.14. Graphic plotter

Pulley systems use a **belt** to transmit motion from the driver shaft to the driven shaft. The V-belt is the one most often used. It fits tightly into the groove on the pulley wheels to stop it from slipping (fig 6.15). Most of the machines in your school workshop use pulley systems. The system is easiest to see on a drilling machine (fig 6.16). Most drilling machines have three or four sets of pulley wheels. By moving the belt from one set to the other you can change the speed of the drill.

To reverse the direction of rotation using a pulley system, the belt must be crossed (fig 6.17). This will only work well if the belt is prevented from rubbing where it crosses.

Chain and sprocket systems use a **chain** to transmit rotary motion from the driver shaft to the driven shaft. **Sprockets** are the toothed wheels on which the chain runs. This means that, unlike pulley systems, the chain and sprocket system cannot slip. A bicycle is a good example of a machine that uses a chain and sprocket system (fig 6.18). In this case you turn the driver shaft by pedalling; the driven shaft is at the centre of the back wheel.

Gears are toothed wheels, fixed to the driver and driven shafts, which mesh together. Two gears, in mesh, will turn in opposite directions (fig 6.19). To get them to turn in the same direction, a third gearwheel has to be fitted between them, as in the lathe gear system shown in fig 6.20. This **idler gear** has no effect on the speeds of the other two gears.

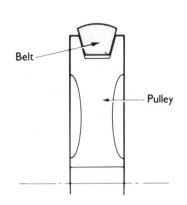

fig 6.15. V-belt (cross section)

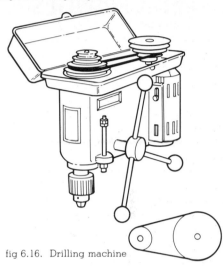

fig 6.16. Drilling machine

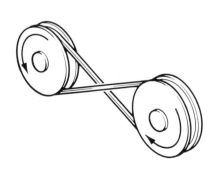

fig 6.17. Reversing the direction of motion using a pulley system

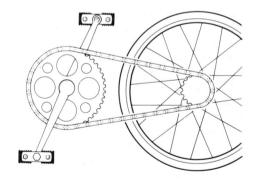

fig 6.18. Chain and sprocket system

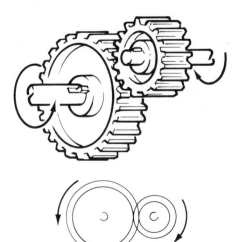

fig 6.19. Two gears in mesh

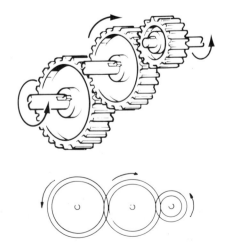

fig 6.20. Idler gear

Gears can also be used to change rotary motion through 90°, either by **bevel gears**, as in a hand drill (fig 6.21), or by a **worm** and **wormwheel**, as seen in fig 6.22.

Another change of motion, rotary to linear, can be achieved using a **rack and pinion**. A rack is a flat strip with teeth cut in it. The pinion is the gear which meshes with it. When the pinion turns it moves the rack along (fig 6.23). This is the system used on a drilling machine to bring the drill down into the work.

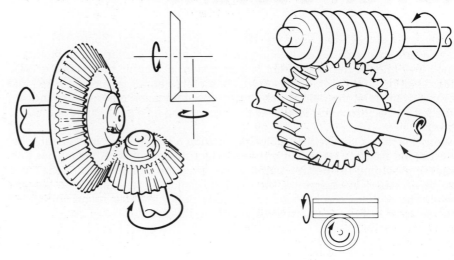

fig 6.21. Bevel gears   fig 6.22. Worm gear

SPEED CHANGES

The speed (velocity) changes that take place in any of these systems can be calculated by comparing the sizes of pulleys or gears used:

fig 6.23. Rack and pinion

$$\text{Velocity Ratio} = \frac{\text{Driven}}{\text{Driver}}$$

With pulley systems use the diameter of the pulleys.

With chain and sprocket systems and gear systems use the number of teeth.

For example in fig 6.24:

Driven sprocket teeth = 20
Driver sprocket teeth = 120

$$\text{VR} = \frac{\text{Driven}}{\text{Driver}} = \frac{20}{120} = \frac{1}{6} \text{ or } 1:6$$

This means that one turn of the driver shaft will give six turns of the driven shaft. Another way of saying this is to say that the driven shaft is going six times faster than the driver shaft.

To calculate the output speed of any of these systems you need to know the input speed and the velocity ratio of the system. The speed of the driven shaft can be calculated using:

$$\text{Output Speed} = \frac{\text{Input Speed (IS)}}{\text{Velocity Ratio (VR)}}$$
(OS)

For example, if input speed = 2460 rpm and the velocity ratio = 6.

$$\text{OS} = \frac{\text{IS}}{\text{VR}} = \frac{2460}{6} = 410 \text{ rpm}$$

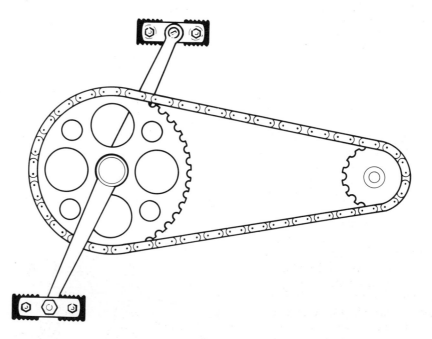

fig 6.24. Chain and sprocket system

CRANK SLIDERS AND CAMS

Crank slider mechanisms can be used in two ways.

1. To change **rotary motion** into **reciprocating motion**, as in a power hacksaw (fig 6.25). An electric motor powers a crank which is connected to the saw frame. The saw frame is free to slide on the 'arm'. As the crank rotates it causes the frame to slide backwards and forwards on the arm. The longer the crank, the further the saw frame will move.

2. To change **reciprocating motion** into **rotary motion**, as in a car engine. The reciprocating pistons are connected to the crankshaft by connecting rods. As the pistons move up and down the bottom end of the connecting rod pushes the crankshaft round (fig 6.26). Each piston in turn moves down, so keeping the crankshaft turning.

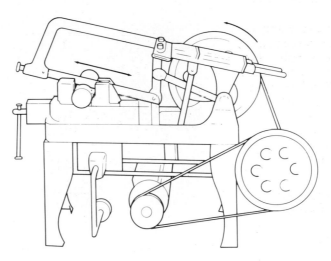

fig 6.25. Changing rotary motion into reciprocating motion

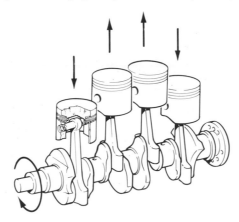

fig 6.26. Changing reciprocating motion into rotary motion

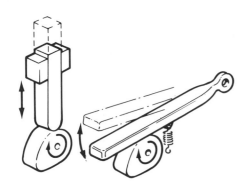

fig 6.27. Cam and follower

Cams are most often used to change **rotary motion** into either **reciprocating** or **oscillating motion**. They are shaped pieces of metal which are fixed to, or part of, a shaft. A **follower** is held against the edge of the cam, usually by a spring (fig 6.27).

As the cam rotates the follower moves. The way in which it moves and the distance it moves depends on the shape of the cam. Two cam shapes in common use are shown in fig 6.28. Each produces a different kind of motion in the follower. Fig 6.29 shows an overhead camshaft which, as it rotates, opens and closes the valves in an engine, using 'pear shaped' cams. Each valve reciprocates as its cam rotates.

Fig 6.30 shows a mechanical fuel pump which is operated by the rotary motion of a camshaft. The cam is a circular one, sometimes called an **eccentric**. As the cam rotates it causes an oscillating motion in the follower. This moves the diaphragm up and down, so pumping fuel to the engine.

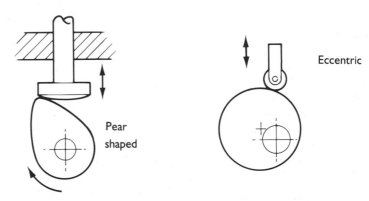

fig 6.28. Two cam shapes

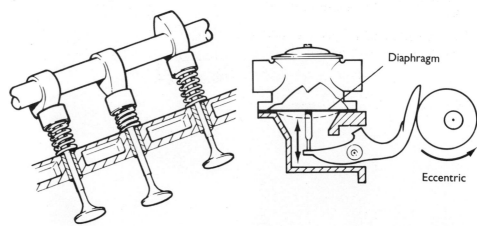

fig 6.29. Overhead camshaft and valves

fig 6.30. Cross sectional view of mechanical fuel pump

STRUCTURES

When you think of structures you probably think of things like bridges, electricity pylons and tall buildings. These are very obvious structures, but there are other examples much closer to you, things such as stools, benches, cupboards and even doors.

With some structures, like the sledge in fig 6.3, it is very obvious how they support a load. Many **frame structures** are like this. Other frame structures are not so obvious. They may have some kind of 'skin' over the framework, as with a door (fig 6.32).

The sledge shown in fig 6.33 does not have a frame, it relies on the shape it has been moulded into for its strength. It is an example of a **shell structure**. These are surprisingly strong yet very light in weight compared to frame structures, which is why most car bodies are made this way. Sheet steel is pressed into the shapes of the various panels and welded together. The more curved or ridged a panel is, the stronger it will be. Large, flat panels, such as the bonnet, are not very strong and often have to be supported by a framework (fig 6.34).

The frame and shell structures listed so far are man-made, but they are all based on structures found in nature. Trees, leaves and spider's webs are all examples of frame structures. An umbrella supports its load in a very similar way to the leaf shown in fig 6.35. Egg shells, honeycombs and the hollow stems of many plants are all examples of shell structures. The hollow stems support their load in exactly the same way that a metal tube supports a TV aerial.

fig 6.31. Traditional toboggan

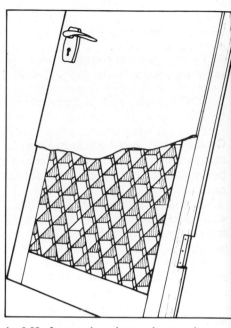

fig 6.32. Interior door showing framework

fig 6.33. Moulded plastic sledge

fig 6.34. Underside of car bonnet

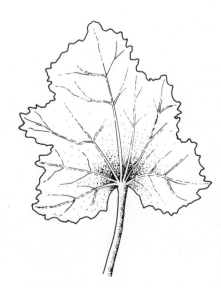

fig 6.35. Underside of a leaf showing structure

Structures are built to support a load. That load may be **static** or **dynamic**. Static loads are those which do not move, like a book on a shelf. Dynamic loads are those which move, like a diver on a springboard. Dynamic loads produce much greater forces than static loads. Many structures have to be built to withstand dynamic loads even though they spend most of their time supporting static loads. For example, the bunk beds shown in fig 6.36 have to be strong enough to take the dynamic forces created by the children playing on them, even though their main purpose is to support a fairly static load.

There are five basic types of force that act on a structure. They are listed below.

Compression forces act to **squash** a structure. The car ramps in fig 6.37 are being compressed by the weight of the car.

fig 6.37. Car ramps

fig 6.36.

Tension forces act to **stretch** a structure. The wires supporting the suspension bridge in fig 6.38 are in tension.

Bending forces act to **bend** a structure. The bar in fig 6.39 is bending due to the weight of the gymnast. Closer study of the bar would show that it is in compression on its upper surface and in tension on its lower surface.

Torsion forces act to **twist** a structure. It was torsion forces which eventually caused the bridge in fig 6.40 to collapse.

Shear forces act to **cut** a structure in two. The forces acting in opposite directions on this bolt are trying to shear it (fig 6.41).

fig 6.38. Suspension bridge

fig 6.39. Gymnast on a high bar

In order to make a structure that will be strong enough, but will not be too expensive, designers have to try and calculate the forces that will act on it. Getting the balance right is very tricky. Even very skilled designers can never be absolutely sure they have planned for all the forces that might act on a structure. Who is to say that a 13 stone man will not sit on a swing designed for 5 year olds, or that a jack designed to lift loads up to 500 kg won't be used to try to lift 1000 kg. Because of problems like this, structures are designed with a **factor of safety**. This is determined by calculating the forces a structure has to take and then multiplying them by the required number, for example 4. So, if a swing frame is being designed to take loads of 120 Newtons, using a safety factor of 4, it should in fact be capable of supporting loads of up to 480 Newtons.

fig 6.40. Tacoma Narrows bridge

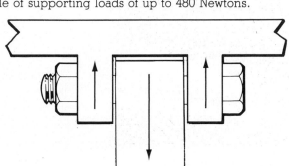

fig 6.41. Bolt showing shear forces

BEAMS, BRIDGES AND STABILITY

Different **members** (parts) of a structure are often coping with different forces. Look at the swing in fig 6.42. The legs are being compressed; members in compression are called **struts**. The chains are in tension; members in tension are called **ties**. The top rail and seat are bending. The bolts supporting the chains are in shear. Each part has been designed to cope with the particular forces acting on it.

Beams of one sort or another are the most common kind of structural member. If designed and used correctly, they can cope with all types of forces. Originally all beams were made of solid material which made them very heavy and expensive (fig 6.43). Over the years many different beam shapes have been developed which are much lighter, yet just as strong, or stronger; fig 6.44 shows some of them. For maximum strength, it is important that a beam is used the right way on, that is with the widest section taking the load (fig 6.45). You will see many of these beams in use around you every day.

Some beams are supported at one end only. Fig 6.46 shows such a beam used to help unload lorries. When used like this it is called a **cantilever** beam. When loaded, it is in tension on the top surface and in compression on the lower surface. Cantilever beams are used either where it is possible to support one end only or where it is necessary to keep a large gap clear.

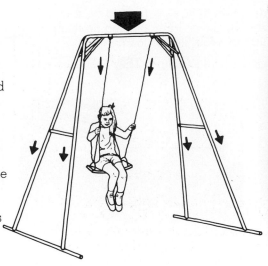

fig 6.42. Swing frame showing signs of force

fig 6.43. Old wooden beams

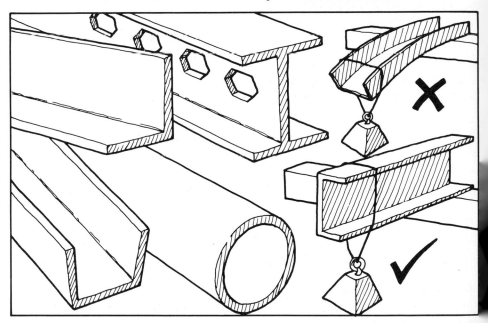

fig 6.44. Beam shapes

fig 6.45. Widest section of beam taking the load

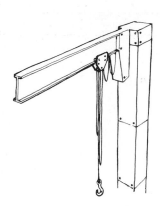

fig 6.46. Cantilever beam

fig 6.47. Motorway bridge

150

STABILITY

Rectangular shapes can distort when loaded (fig 6.48). By adding one extra member, so creating two triangles, you can stop it distorting (fig 6.49). Many structures use triangular shapes to give them stability. You only have to look at pylons, cranes and bike frames to see them.

fig 6.48. Distortion of a gate   fig 6.49. Triangulation adds strength

BEAM CALCULATIONS – MOMENTS

Most structures are designed not to move under load. For this to happen, the forces acting on the structure must be 'balanced'. If they are balanced the structure is said to be in **equilibrium**. Bridges and houses are examples of this. In practice, small movements do occur due to how and where the loads are applied. Fig 6.50 shows a beam in equilibrium. The downward forces acting on it are balanced by the upward forces, called **reactions**, at its ends. Because the load is in the centre of the beam the reactions at X and Y are each half the value of the downward force. This can be proved by calculation:

Given that **anticlockwise moments** = **clockwise moments**
and **upward forces** (Reaction X + Reaction Y) = **downward forces**(500 N)

Taking moments about end X: Reaction $Y \times 6 = 500 \times 3$

$$\text{Reaction } Y = \frac{1500}{6}$$

$$\text{Reaction } Y = 250 \text{ N}$$

If Reaction X + Reaction Y = 500N then

Reaction X = 500 – Reaction Y
= 500 – 250
Reaction X = 250 N

fig 6.50. Beam in equilibrium

If the load is not in the centre of the beam, then the reactions will not be equal. Fig 6.51 shows such a situation. The reactions at X and Y can be calculated in just the same way as before.

Take moments about end X: $Y \times 6 = 500 \times 2$

$$Y = \frac{1000}{6}$$

$$Y = 166.6 \text{ N}$$

If Reaction X + Reaction Y = 500 N then

Reaction X = 500 – Reaction Y
= 500 – 166.6
Reaction X = 333.3 N

You can see that most of the load is taken by the support nearest to the load. The nearer the load gets to a support the more of the load that support is taking. So when a moving object, such as a car, goes over a bridge the load taken by each of the supports changes as it crosses.

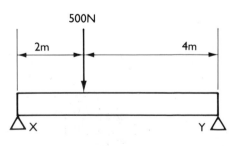

fig 6.51. Load off centre

ELECTRONICS

Electronics is an important part of your everyday life. Your calculator, watch, television, radio and stereo system all use electronics. Although these are quite complex systems, they rely on a few basic principles. All electronic circuits can be shown as **block diagrams**, having an **input, control** and **output** (fig 6.52). Most electronic components fall into one of these categories. This makes the process of circuit design easier to understand. The more common components are shown below.

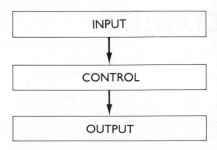

fig 6.52. Block diagram

INPUTS

Batteries provide the power for many small electronic circuits, because they are small, portable and safe (fig 6.53).

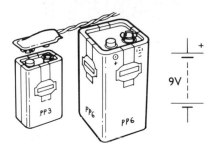

fig 6.53. Batteries

Switches come in many different styles, with different numbers of connections. They are used to 'make' or 'break' connections. Three manual switches and one magnetically operated switch are shown here (fig 6.54).

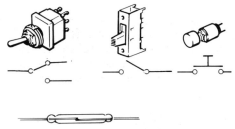

fig 6.54. Switches

Capacitors are used to store an electrical charge. Their value is measured in microfarads (symbol μF). Two of the basic types are shown in figs 6.55.

Electrolytic capacitors must be connected the right way round. They have their value written on (fig 6.55).

Polyester capacitors can be connected either way round. They have smaller values than electrolytic capacitors and these values can be worked out using the same colour code as for resistors.

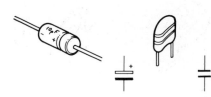

fig 6.55. Capacitors

Resistors are used to control and direct the flow of electricity. Resistance is measured in **ohms**. (symbol Ω).

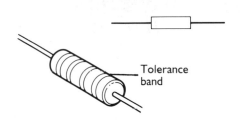

fig 6.56. Resistor

Fixed resistors have a fixed value which is indicated by the coloured bands. The colour values are given in fig 6.57. The gold or silver band shows the tolerance.

Colour	1st band	2nd band	3rd band
Black	0	0	–
Brown	1	1	0
Red	2	2	00
Orange	3	3	000
Yellow	4	4	0000
Green	5	5	00000
Blue	6	6	000000
Violet	7	7	0000000
Grey	8	8	00000000
White	9	9	000000000

fig 6.57. Resistor colour code

Variable resistors, also called potentiometers, can be adjusted to change their resistance. The two basic types are shown in fig 6.58.

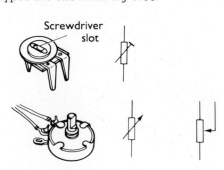

fig 6.58. Variable resistors

Thermistors sense temperature changes and convert them into voltage changes.

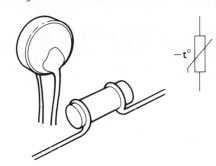

fig 6.59. Thermistors

The **light dependent resistor (LDR)** and the **phototransistor** can both be used to sense changes in light intensity. They convert light changes into voltage changes. (fig 6.60).

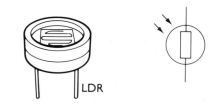

fig 6.60. Light dependent resistor

Moisture sensors convert changes in moisture content into voltage changes (fig 6.61).

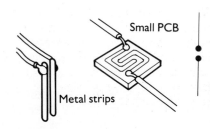

fig 6.61. Moisture sensor

CONTROLS

Transistors are useful because they allow circuits to work automatically. They act as a switch, reacting to voltage changes in the input. When the input voltage is below 0.6 V the transistor is switched off, which means that the output is off. When the input voltage goes over 0.6 V the transistor switches on, so the output is on! Street lights use a simple system based on this idea to switch on and off according to light conditions. The one shown here is an NPN transistor. Its three legs must be connected the right way round (fig 6.62).

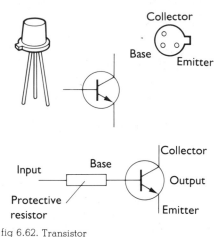

fig 6.62. Transistor

Thyristors are similar to transistors, but have the advantage that once switched on, by a small input voltage, they stay on. This can be very useful in alarm circuits (fig 6.63).

fig 6.63. Thyristor

The **555 timer** is an **integrated circuit**, or IC. It is used to give timed periods, from a fraction of a second up to several minutes. It can be used to control either lights or sounds. Its eight legs or pins are numbered as shown (fig 6.64).

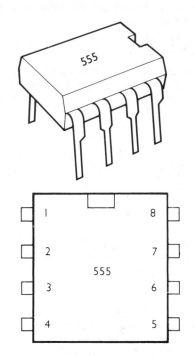

fig 6.64. 555 timer

OUTPUTS

Bulbs can be connected either way round. Their disadvantage is that they break quite easily (fig 6.65).

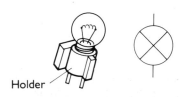

fig 6.65. Bulb

LEDs (light emitting diodes) can be used instead of bulbs. They are much tougher and use much less power. They must be connected the right way round and protected by a resistor. They come in three colours: red, green and amber (fig 6.66).

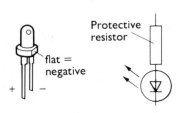

fig 6.66. LED

Small dc **motors** can be used to create movement. They can be made to rotate in either direction simply by changing over the connections (fig 6.67).

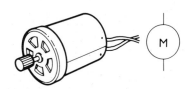

fig 6.67. Motor

Relays are used as an interface between two electrical circuits. Although one circuit is controlled by the other, they are electrically isolated (fig 6.68).

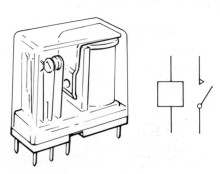

fig 6.68. Relay

Solenoids can be used to provide small linear movements. The core is pulled in when it is switched on and springs back out when it is switched off. They are sometimes used for door locks (fig 6.69).

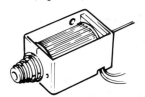

fig 6.69. Solenoid

Buzzers give a continuous sound. The volume will depend on the supply voltage. They must be connected the right way round (fig 6.70).

Speakers change electrical pulses into sound. The pitch and volume of the sound varies according to the pulses received (fig 6.71).

fig 6.70. Buzzer   fig 6.71. Speaker

153

SWITCHING CIRCUITS

Switching circuits are circuits which switch an output on or off according to the state of the input. Many different switching circuits can be built, some more sensitive than others. The best way to understand one of these circuits is to look at its three parts, input, control and output, before looking at the full circuit.

The input part of all these circuits is a **voltage divider**. Fig 6.72 shows two typical voltage dividers. In each case the total voltage available, 9 V, is divided between the two resistors according to their resistance. The larger the resistance, the larger the voltage across it. It is the voltage measured between the 0 V line and point X that is important in these circuits. It is from point X that the input voltage is connected to the transistor.

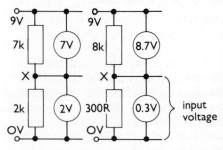

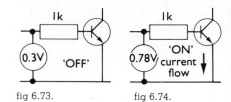
fig 6.72.

The control part of these circuits has to react to the voltage changes in the input and so switch the output on or off. A single **NPN transistor**, with a protective resistor, can be used (fig 6.73). When its input voltage is below 0.6 V it is off and no current can flow through it. When it goes over 0.6 V the transistor switches on, allowing current to flow through it (fig 6.74).

The output simply switches on when the transistor allows current to flow through it, and off when the transistor switches off.

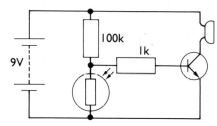
fig 6.73.   fig 6.74.

The full **circuit diagram** (fig 6.75) shows all the parts connected together. By using a sensor whose resistance varies (e.g. the resistance of an LDR varies with light intensity), you can get the input voltage to the transistor to change. When the LDR is in bright light, its resistance is very low and the voltage across is very low, below 0.6 V. When the LDR is in shadow, its resistance goes up and the voltage across it increases above 0.6 V. This switches on the transistor and so switches on the output. If the LDR goes into bright light again the input voltage will fall, the transistor will switch off and so the output will switch off.

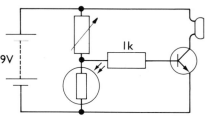
fig 6.75. Full circuit diagram

These circuits can be adjusted by using a variable resistor in the input part of the circuit (fig 6.76). In this circuit it allows you to adjust whether the buzzer is switched on when it first starts to go dark or when it is totally dark.

Although they are designed to do different things, each of the circuits shown in figs 6.77 to 6.80 is based on the same principle.

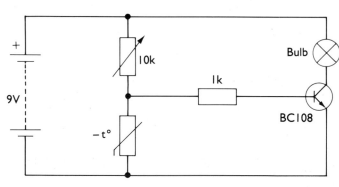
fig 6.76.

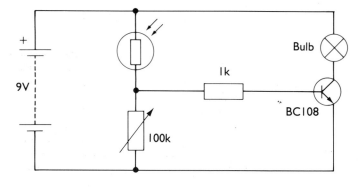
fig 6.77. Output on when light

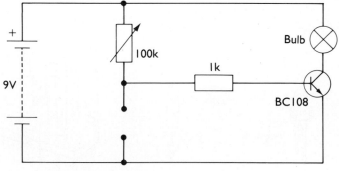
fig 6.78. Output on when cold

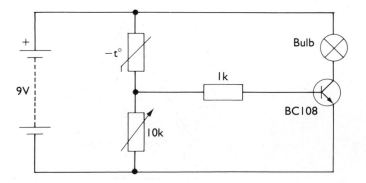
fig 6.79. Output on when hot

fig 6.80. Output on when dry

Any of these circuits can be made more sensitive by using two transistors connected together to form a **darlington pair** (fig 6.81).

By using a **thyristor** in place of the transistor, the output can be made to 'latch' on (fig 6.82). This means that once switched on it stays on, even if the input voltage falls. This is very useful in alarm circuits, because once triggered they keep going.

By using a relay as an **interface**, you can use a low voltage circuit to control a high voltage circuit (fig 6.83). The relay is simply the output of the transistor switching circuit. When it is switched on, contacts inside it move, switching on the other circuit. It must be emphasised that the two circuits are not connected electrically. The diode alongside the relay is to stop the transistor being damaged when the relay switches.

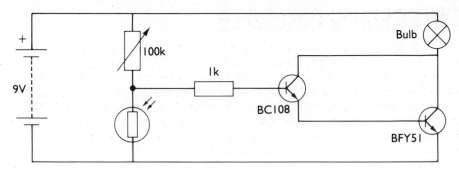

fig 6.81. Darlington pair

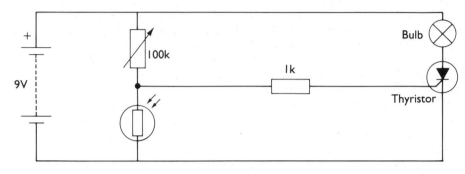

fig 6.82. Using a thyristor

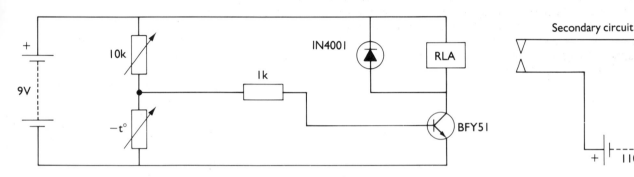

fig 6.83. Using a relay

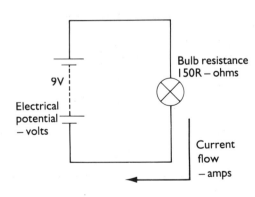

You can use **calculations** to help you understand and design circuits. Fig 6.84 shows a simple circuit and the three quantities involved:
1. Electrical potential is measured in **volts.**
2. The rate of flow (current) is measured in **amps.**
3. Resistance to that flow is measured in **ohms**.
If you know any two of these quantities you can work out the third using the triangle shown in fig 6.85. For example, if the bulb in fig 8.83 has a resistance of 150 ohms, what current will flow through it? Current is measured in amps, so cover up amps in the triangle and you are left with volts divided by ohms.

Therefore: $\text{Amps} = \dfrac{\text{Volts}}{\text{Ohms}} = \dfrac{9}{150} = 0.06$ amps or 60 milliamps(mA)

So, the current flowing in the circuit will be 60 mA.

fig 6.84. Simple circuit

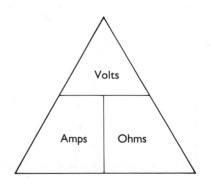

fig 6.85. Triangle used in calculations

TIMERS

A simple timer can be made using a transistor switching circuit (fig 6.86). It switches on an output after a time delay. The timing part of the circuit is made up of a resistor and an electrolytic capacitor. With the switch off, the voltage across the capacitor is 0V, so the transistor is off. When the circuit is switched on the capacitor begins to 'charge up' through the resistor and the voltage across the capacitor gradually rises. When it reaches 0.6V the transistor switches on. The length of the time delay is decided by the values of the resistor and capacitor. Fig 6.87 gives some idea of the times you can expect from different value components. Electrolytic capacitors cannot be made accurately, so you should not be surprised if the times come out differently when you try them.

The **555 timer** IC can be used in two basic ways, either as a **monostable** or **astable**.

Monostable means stable in one state, in this case either 'on' or 'off'. The circuit will change its state for the timed period and then return to its stable state. In the circuit shown in fig 6.88, the output is normally off. When the input switch is pressed the output goes on for the timed period. At the end of that time it goes off again. As with the transistor timer circuit, the length of the timed period is decided by the values of the resistors and capacitors in the timer part of the circuit. The variable resistor allows you to adjust the length of the timed period. Use fig 6.89 to give you some idea of the times to expect.

You could arrange it so that the output was normally on and went off for the timed period. To do this you would move the output to the position shown by dotted lines in the circuit diagram.

Astable means not stable in any state, in other words it keeps changing from one state to the other, on/off, on/off, so it can be used to make lights flash or to make a continuous noise through a speaker.

At first sight, the astable circuit in fig 6.90 looks very much like the monostable circuit. However, looking at it closely will show that there are important differences. The timer part of the circuit works much as before, the variable resistor allowing you to vary the rate of flashing. By adding a second LED in the position shown by dotted lines you could have them flashing alternately.

By using a small value capacitor in the timer part of the circuit you can get the output to power a speaker (fig 6.91). The note from the speaker can be varied by adjusting the variable resistor. This can be very useful as an output for an alarm circuit.

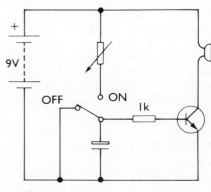

fig 6.86. Timer

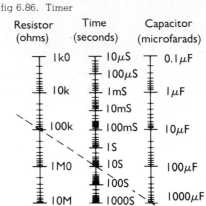

fig 6.87. Time delays

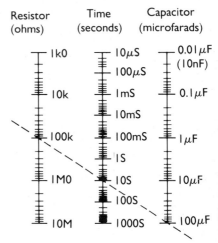

fig 6.89. Monostable time delays

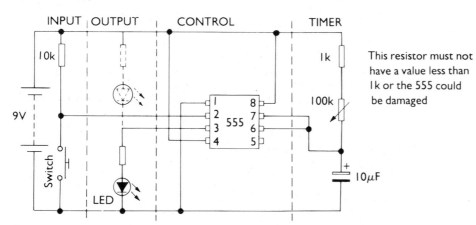

This resistor must not have a value less than 1k or the 555 could be damaged

fig 6.88. Monostable circuit

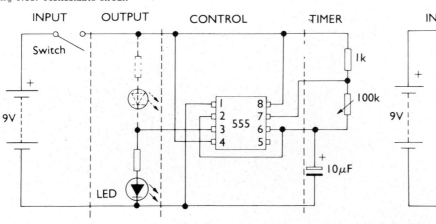

fig 6.90. Astable circuit

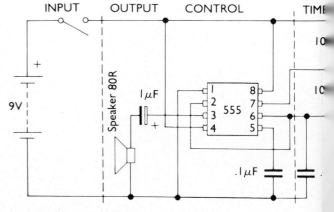

fig 6.91. Powering a speaker

CIRCUIT BOARDS

You can make a permanent circuit using either stripboard (fig 6.92) or a printed circuit board (PCB) (fig 6.93). Both types use a thin plastic board with a very thin layer of copper on one side. Stripboard can save time, but often leads to more mistakes than PCBs. There are several ways to make a PCB. One method is outlined below.

1. Plan the layout of the circuit on tracing paper working from your circuit diagram. You must take account of the shape and size of each component (fig 6.94). Draw the lines clearly with a soft pencil, HB or B.

2. Turn the tracing paper over and place it on the copper clad board. Go over the lines of the circuit, pressing firmly (fig 6.94). This will transfer them onto the copper side of the board. It is vital that you do this stage correctly. If you do not turn the tracing paper over your PCB will be wrong!

3. Remove the tracing paper and go over the lines on the copper with an **etch resist pen**. Draw a circle for each connection, leaving a small patch of copper showing in the centre (fig 6.96).

4. Put your PCB in the **etch tank** to remove the unwanted copper areas (fig 6.97). This should take 10 or 15 minutes. When the etching is finished, wash the board and clean it with wire wool.

5. Drill the holes in the circuit board ready to connect the components (fig 6.98).

Soldering in the components

1. Push the component 'legs' through the correct holes in the board and rest the board, copper track side up, on a flat surface (fig 6.99).
2. Place the tip of the soldering iron so that it heats the copper track and component leg at the same time. Hold it there for 2 or 3 seconds before touching the solder into the joint (fig 6.100). As the solder flows around the joint, remove the soldering iron and leave the joint to cool for a few seconds.
3. Cut off any bits of component 'legs' left sticking up using **side cutters** (fig 6.101).

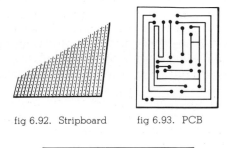

fig 6.92. Stripboard   fig 6.93. PCB

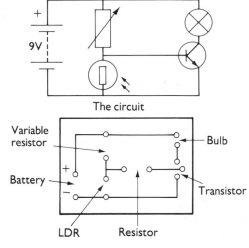

The circuit

fig 6.94. Planning the layout of a PCB

fig 6.95. Transferring the lines of a circuit

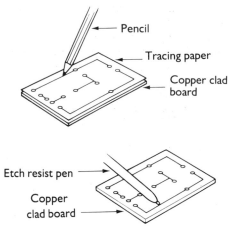

fig 6.96. Using an etch resist pen

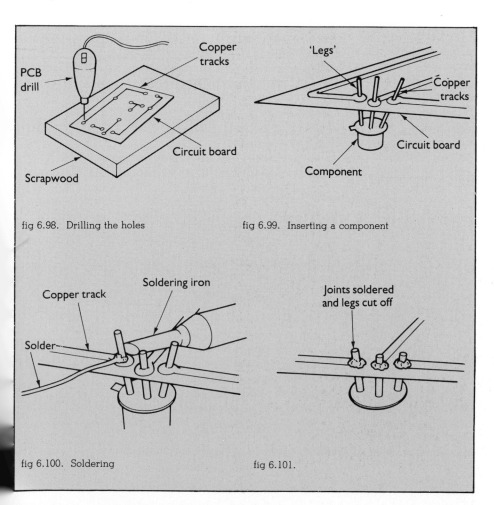

fig 6.98. Drilling the holes   fig 6.99. Inserting a component

fig 6.100. Soldering   fig 6.101.

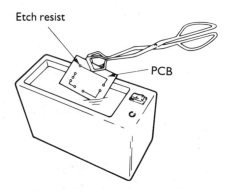

fig 6.97. Using an etch tank

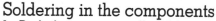

PNEUMATICS/HYDRAULICS

Both pneumatic and hydraulic systems are used to provide powerful linear movements. Pneumatic road drills and mechanical diggers are just two examples of the use of these systems you will have come across (fig 6.102). Pneumatic systems use compressed air as a power source, while hydraulic systems use pressurised oil. Industry makes a great deal of use of these systems because they are powerful and reliable.

Both systems are based on the same principle. Fig 6.103 shows the basic idea A piston can be forced along a cylinder, so creating linear movement. That linear movement can be used to do useful work. The force produced by the piston as it moves depends on two things:

1. The area of the face of the piston, in mm^2.
2. The pressure being used to push it, in N/mm^2.

For example, if a pressure of 0.5 N/mm^2 is being used to push a piston of 40 mm diameter, the force produced will be given by:

Force = Pressure × Area

$$
\begin{aligned}
&= 0.5 &&\times \pi R^2 \\
&= 0.5 &&\times \pi \times 20 \times 20 \\
&= 0.5 &&\times 1256 \\
&= 628 \text{ Newtons}
\end{aligned}
$$

It can be seen from this that by increasing either the pressure or the area, larger forces will be produced.

A **pneumatic system** for opening and closing a bus door is shown in fig 6.104. The movement of the piston is powered in both directions, the air being directed by the driver's control valve. Most buses use this type of system.

The **hydraulic system** used in car jacks is shown in fig 6.105. As the handle is moved up and down, the oil is pumped into the large diameter cylinder, through a one-way valve, so pushing up the piston and lifting the car.

Pneumatic systems have two disadvantages when compared to hydraulic systems.
1. They need a compressor to compress air in the first place, and these are not always readily available. Hydraulic systems can be powered by an electric pump, but simple systems use muscle power. You can make a simple, yet quite powerful, hydraulic system using syringes and plastic tubing (fig 6.106).
2. Air can be compressed and so there is a limit to the forces that can be produced. Hydraulic oil cannot be compressed so much larger forces can be produced. You can use water in the system shown in fig 6.106.

fig 6.102. Pneumatic drill

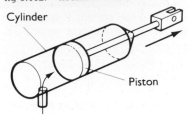

fig 6.103. Basic principle of hydraulics and pneumatics

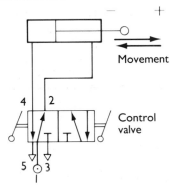

fig 6.104. Pneumatic system for operating a bus door

fig 6.105. Hydraulic system used in car jacks

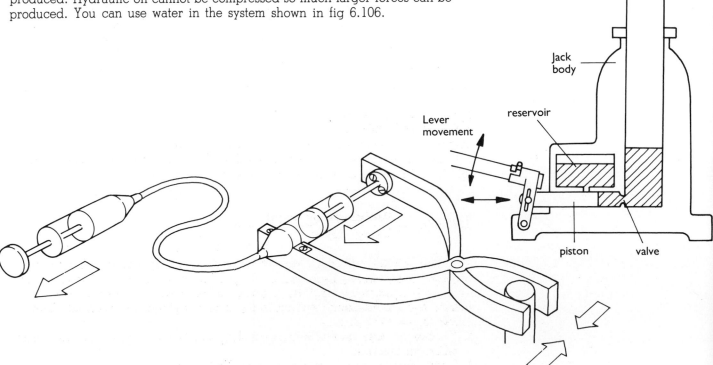

fig 6.106. Simple hydraulic system

ENERGY

You need energy for everything you do! Even when you are asleep you are using energy to work your heart and lungs and to digest your food. That energy comes from the food you eat. Man-made devices also need energy to make them work. That energy may come from fossil fuels (e.g. oil, gas or coal), nuclear fuels, or from renewable resources (e.g. solar, wind and waves).

Energy cannot be created or destroyed, but it can change from one form to another. It is usually when it changes form that you are able to make use of it. For example, when a light is switched on, electrical energy changes into light energy.

The forms of energy you may find most useful are **mechanical** in the form of **movement energy** (e.g. moving air powering a land yacht, a motor powering a model car, water turning a turbine) or **stored energy** (e.g. a twisted rubber band used to power a model aircraft or boat); and **electrical energy**. Because electrical energy can be used in so many different ways and is so easily available from batteries, you will probably find this the most useful form of energy. It can so easily be changed into other forms of energy, the most common being light, sound, heat or movement. For example, lighting bulbs or LEDs, sounding buzzers or speakers and powering dc motors.

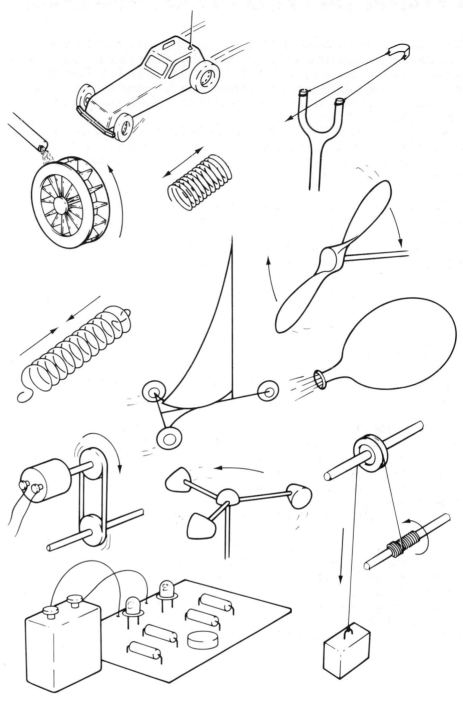

fig 6.107. Energy

EFFICIENCY

Efficiency is making the best use of available energy.

The efficiency of any system can be calculated by comparing the energy input with the useful energy output using the following calculation:

$$\text{Efficiency} = \frac{\textbf{Useful energy output}}{\textbf{Energy input}} \times 100\%$$

No system is 100% efficient. Some of the energy input gets changed into forms you don't want, usually heat, sound or light. For example, an electric motor is meant to produce movement, but it also gets hot, makes a noise and creates sparks. You should design systems to be as energy efficient as possible. A few simple things will help:

1. Choose the right materials to rub or slide against each other. Lubricate them wherever possible.
2. Keep down the weight of moving parts and vehicles.
3. Choose electronic components which use less energy (e.g. bulbs use six times more energy than LEDs).

EXERCISES

1. Give two practical examples of Class 1 and Class 2 levers. What types of movement do they use?

2. Calculate the mechanical advantage and velocity ratio of the pulley system shown in fig 6.108. What is the efficiency of the system?

3. Give a practical example of the use of a parallel motion linkage and sketch the important parts of the mechanism.

4. Give one advantage and one disadvantage of pulley systems compared to sprocket and chain systems.

5. Sketch a system that could be used to change the fast, rotary motion of a small electric motor into the slow, oscillating movement of windscreen wipers.

6. If the gear system shown in fig 6.109 were connected to a motor running at 3240 rpm, what would the output speed of the system be?

7. Sketch a mechanism that could be used to change rotary motion into a reciprocating motion. Give one practical example of the use of this kind of mechanism.

8. Explain, using examples, the difference between frame and shell structures.

9. Explain, using an example, why structures have to be designed to take dynamic as well as static loads. How do designers build a factor of safety into the structures they design?

10. Frame structures are made up of two kinds of members, struts and ties. Sketch a simple frame structure and label each member to show which kind it is.

11. The beam shown in fig 6.110 is in equilibrium. Calculate the reactions at A and B.

12. Name and draw the symbol for an electronic sensor that can be used to detect changes in temperature. Show how it can be used in a simple switching circuit to sound a buzzer when the temperature falls to freezing point.

13. Design a low voltage circuit which could be used to control a 110 V fan heater.

14. Show a circuit which could be used to give a 10 second delay before a bulb is switched on.

15. Design a circuit which would flash an LED at 1 second intervals for 10 seconds, then stop.

16. Design a PCB for the circuit shown in fig 6.91 on page 156.

17. Describe two advantages of hydraulic systems over pneumatic systems and give three examples of the use of hydraulic systems.

18. Name four forms of energy and give a practical example of the use of each.

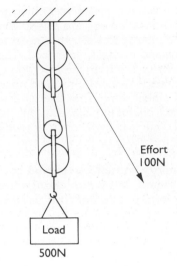

fig 6.108. Pulley system

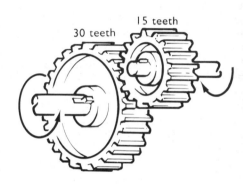

fig 6.109. Gear system

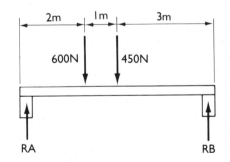

fig 6.110. Beam in equilibrium

160

MANUFACTURING TECHNOLOGIES

The manufacturing industry is concerned with making products, from the simplest paper clip to the most sophisticated computer system.

Every product that is made must have a market. The quality, appearance and price must be right so that people will want it and be able to afford it.

In school you are involved with designing and making artefacts, usually on your own, but sometimes in small groups. Manufacturing industry is rarely like this, nearly all manufacturing involves people working in teams, each individual making a contribution by working on just one small part of the design or manufacture. This is a far more efficient way of making things, especially in large quantities.

The need to become increasingly efficient in terms of both quality and cost, has meant that the technologies involved in the manufacturing industry have had to become efficient, often specialised and sometimes very complex.

Some manufacturing technologies are larger versions of familiar school processes. These tend to be in the more traditional, older industries. With the advent of plastics, and more recently the silicon chip, manufacturing technologies have undergone tremendous change. The rate of change is currently faster than ever and the manufacturing technology of the future will, without doubt, be even more sophisticated and efficient than at present.

This chapter deals first with familiar processes that have been adapted to the scale of the industrial manufacturing situation. We shall then look at some less familiar and often very specialised manufacturing technologies, and finally the new technologies: those that have been made possible only with the invention of the silicon chip, and those that have developed around the application of the microprocessor.

fig 7.1. Food manufacturing

fig 7.2. Robot production line

QUALITY CONTROL

Rolls-Royce cars have long been regarded as a symbol of excellence and high quality. They are a well designed, well engineered product that will continue to give good service over a long period of time. This being the case, why doesn't everybody have one? The answer is obvious, because they are very expensive. Quality of this high standard is expensive.

Designers of products that must be reasonably priced must specify techniques and materials that are adequate, rather than ideal. It means specifying an achievable standard of quality.

During manufacture, the quality standard must be checked and maintained to ensure that the product that reaches the market will do the job for which it is designed. This is called **quality control**.

TOLERANCE

Tolerance is the amount of imperfection that can be allowed. Nothing can be made absolutely perfect.

With some products size is not very critical. For example, a milk bottle is 75 mm in diameter, this is the **nominal size.** A few millimetres larger or smaller would make very little difference, but if it was too large, say 80 mm, it may not fit in the bottling machine, and if it was too small, it may not hold a pint. A reasonable tolerance for a milk bottle could be + or − 2 mm. This means that a 73 mm diameter bottle would be acceptable, as would a 77 mm bottle, and of course any size in between. The required diameter of a milk bottle can be said to be 75 mm ± 2.

fig 7.3. Rolls Royce car

With some products size is far more important and a very small tolerance is necessary. Moving parts in machinery have to be a good fit to avoid wearing out, but there still must be a manufacturing tolerance. Fig 7.4 shows a plain bearing and a shaft, the shaft needs to rotate in the bearing, so there must always be a small gap. With the worst conditions, the smallest permissible bearing (12.05 mm diameter) and the largest permissible shaft (12.00 mm diameter), there will still be a gap. Any bearing and any shaft made to these tolerances will work together.

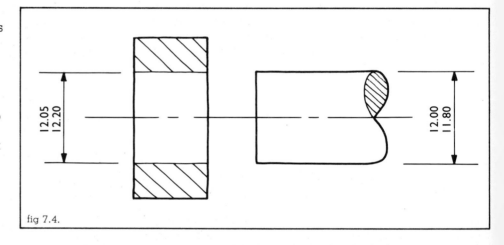

fig 7.4.

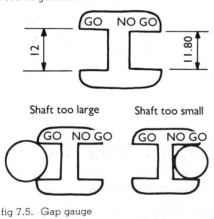

fig 7.5. Gap gauge

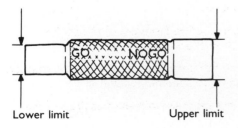

fig 7.6. Plug gauge

GAUGES

The size of the shaft in fig 7.4 could be determined by measuring it using a micrometer, and you could then decide whether or not it was acceptable. This is time consuming and it is easy to make a mistake using a micrometer. The actual size of the shaft is not really important, it is only important to know if it is between 11.80 mm and 12.00 mm diameter. This can be determined using a **limit gauge**.

Fig 7.5 shows a suitable limit gauge for checking this shaft. This type of gauge is a **gap gauge**. A shaft that is within limits will enter the GO end, but will not enter the NO GO end. Hole sizes can be checked using a **plug gauge** (fig 7.6). The same principle applies here, the GO end will enter the smallest acceptable hole and the NO GO end will not enter the largest acceptable hole. Gauges are very accurately made precision tools and must be treated with great care.

QUALITY CONTROL IN PRACTICE

It is very often impractical to check every component produced in a mass production situation, because the time taken could increase the cost considerably. Instead, only a few components are taken and checked. This is known as **sampling.** If an unacceptable amount of rejects are found in the sample then the complete batch is rejected. In reality, this means that some faulty goods reach the shops. Manufacturers often feel that it is preferable to replace faulty items, despite the customer's annoyance, than to introduce more rigid quality controls and have the inevitable increase in retail price of the product.

JIGS AND FIXTURES

Accurate, fast repeatability is usually a very important consideration in manufacturing. It would be unthinkable for every hole drilled in every component on a car to be marked out and centre punched before being drilled. Small errors in marking out would result in many parts not fitting together, and errors in hole sizes would also be bound to occur. However, the main problem would be the time involved, and time is by far the most expensive commodity in manufacturing.

The most common method of aligning a machine tool with a workpiece, accurately and without marking out, is to use a **jig** or a **fixture**.

Jigs are work holding devices made specifically to suit a single component or type of component. The component is held firmly in the jig and the cutting tool is guided to the appropriate position on the component by the jig. Jigs are not clamped to the work table, but are positioned and held by hand. The process where jigs find most applications is drilling. Fig 7.7 shows an example of a small drilling jig for drilling four holes in the ends of pieces of rectangular steel tubing used for racking.

The tube is inserted into the fabricated jig up to an end stop. A quick acting cam clamp holds the tube in place and hardened steel drill bushes guide the drill. With drilling jigs, it is essential to use hardened bushes. The body of a jig is normally made from mild steel, and holes in this would wear oversize very quickly. Bushes can also be changed should the component hole size be modified or if they become worn or damaged.

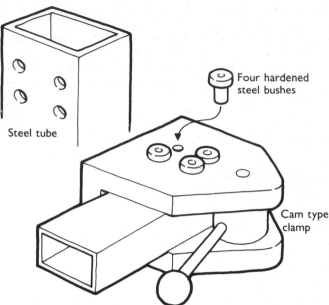

Four hardened steel bushes

Steel tube

Cam type clamp

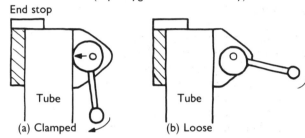

Detail of cam action (top of jig removed for clarity)

End stop

Tube

(a) Clamped

Tube

(b) Loose

fig 7.7. Small drilling jig

Fixtures are similar to jigs, but instead of being movable in order to line up with the tooling, they are fixed in place, hence the name fixture. There are very many applications for fixtures, milling and turning being the two most common.

In fig 7.8, a horizontal milling machine has a fixture bolted to the machine table. The fixture is holding a component for machining. This type of milling operation using several different cutters all mounted on the same machine arbour is called **gang milling.** The cutters involved in this case are six side and face cutters. (see Milling, page 102).

JIG AND FIXTURE DESIGN

Jigs and fixtures must be very carefully designed. There are several key points that must be considered.

1. The component should locate on the same datum face for all machining operations.

2. The jig or fixture should be foolproofed so that the component will not fit in the wrong way round.

3. Swarf produced by the machining should not be trapped or cause the component to become jammed in.

4. The fixture must not interfere with the positions of the machine guards.

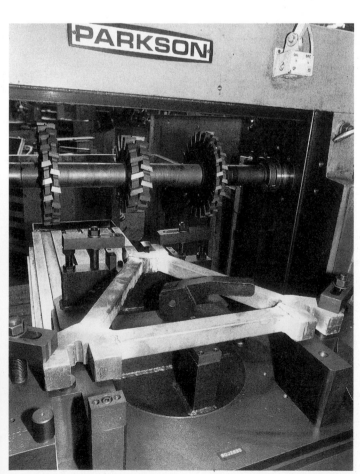

PARKSON

fig 7.8. Milling fixture

METAL MACHINING

DRILLING

In manufacturing industries drilling machines are very often much larger than those used in school workshops. Production machines often have a power feed, this means that the motion of the drill into the workpiece is power driven, usually by an electric motor, but sometimes by a pneumatic cylinder.

The large machine shown in fig 7.9 is a radial arm drilling machine. The drill spindle, its drive motor and the gearbox are all carried on an arm, which they can move along freely. The arm is supported at one end by a pillar about which it can rotate.

By using these two freedoms of movement together, the drill can be positioned over the workpiece or the drilling fixture, rather than positioning the work under the drill. This is very useful if the work is large and heavy, or if there are several holes to drill, since the work or fixture can remain secured in one place and the drill moved to each hole in turn.

Multi-drilling

There are many components that require a number of holes drilling in them. We have seen that jigs and fixtures can be used for this purpose. However, sometimes where there are large numbers of the same component being produced, manufacturers invest in a machine, or attachment to a machine, specifically for that purpose. These are called multi-drilling machines and have several drills mounted in the same machine all drilling holes simultaneously. This is the process used by the automobile industry for drilling the large number of holes that are required in engine blocks for car and commercial vehicle engines (fig 7.10).

fig 7.9. Radial arm drilling machine

fig 7.10. Multi-drilling

TURNING

Since Henry Maudsley first produced his metal turning lathe in 1800, there have been continual developments to this machine tool.

The more automated society has become, the greater has become the need for all the cylindrical components that are used in cars, jet engines, food processes, floppy disc drives, compact disc players and virtually everything that moves or has moving parts.

Some turning processes are computer controlled, and these are looked at later in this chapter.

Capstan and turret lathes

Capstan and turret lathes are machines for large batch production. Once set up, large quantities of identical components can be produced in the minimum time, certainly very much quicker than could be produced by using a conventional centre lathe.

The feature of this type of lathe (from which its name is derived), is the capstan or turret. This is a hexagonal block rather like a large hexagonal nut, mounted on a short machine slide on the capstan lathe and on a saddle on the machine bed of the larger turret lathe.

Fig 7.11 shows a typical turret loaded with tools: three different size drills, a centre drill, a turning tool for chamfering the end of the workpiece, and finally a bar stop. Bar stops enable a length of material to be pulled through the chuck and up against something solid in order to load the correct length. This type of lathe is very often fed with material from the rear of the headstock through the machine's hollow spindle.

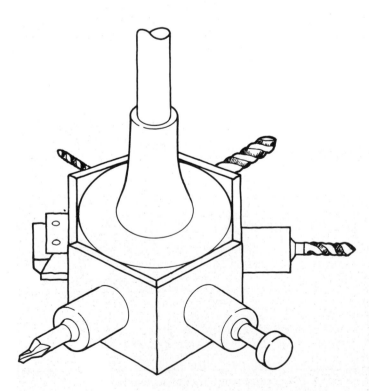

fig 7.11. Turret loaded with tools

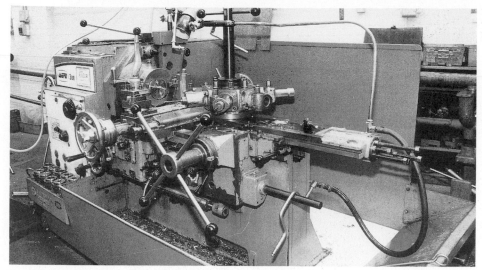
fig 7.12. Capstan lathe

The lathe in fig 7.12 is a typical capstan lathe. The large turret control wheel is used to wind the turret forwards to cut, and fully back to index the turret automatically to its next position. The machine has two tool posts on the cross slide. The forward tool post can be loaded with up to four turning tools and can be rotated to present any of the tools to the workpiece. The rear tool post is designed to hold a single tool, usually a parting off tool. As this cuts from the rear, the tool must be turned upside down so that it will cut without having to reverse the spindle.

Collet chucks are often used on capstan lathes for holding material. Fig 7.13 shows a hand operated collet chuck and a selection of collets. The collet used must be the correct size to fit the material being machined. A single movement of the hand lever (these are sometimes air operated), causes the collet to clamp tightly around the material.

Collet chucks are most suited to being fed with bar from the rear through the hollow spindle of the machine. After the turning operation and parting off, more material is fed in and so the process continues.

fig 7.13. Collet chuck

fig 7.14. Turning fixture

Turning fixtures are also frequently used for work holding on capstan and turret lathes. These are normally mounted on a face plate that is then screwed to the lathe spindle nose. Alternatively, they may be specially made to suit one machine, in which case the fixture will mount directly onto the spindle nose. Fig 7.14 shows an example of a turning fixture mounted on a capstan lathe. The component that has been machined is in the foreground.

Automatic turning

Auto lathes are a very cost effective method of producing very large batches of identical components.

It is not unusual in some industries to need hundreds of thousands of the same component during the course of a year, for example, electric motors for washing machines or cassette players.

Setting up an auto lathe is a very long process, but once the machine is set up it only requires loading with bars of material through the rear of the headstock, the remainder of the operation being fully automatic. Four auto lathes can be operated by two people comfortably: an unskilled operater to load and unload the machines and a tool setter to replace and re-set worn tools.

fig 7.15. Single spindle automatic turning machine

ERODING

Extremely hard materials can be machined by **eroding**. Eroding means gradually wearing away, like the sea wearing away a rocky coastline, only here the erosion is accurately controlled. The shapes that can be produced by eroding can be very detailed.

SPARK EROSION

When an electrical spark jumps a small gap between two piecs of conducting material, the result is a minute spot of intense heat. The heat is so intense (approximately, 12 000°C) that a tiny speck of metal is melted away, leaving a very small crater. In spark erosion, or spark machining, this happens to millions of minute spots between 500 and 10 000 times per second, with the result that the metal is gradually eroded away.

To control the accuracy, it is necessary to submerge the process in a dielectric liquid. A dielectric liquid is an insulating material and so does not conduct electricity. This means that even the high voltages used cannot cause a spark until the tool and the workpiece are very close, and the insulating properties of the dielectric breaks down, allowing sparking to take place. The dielectric is continually pumped around the complete process, cooling and washing away all the tiny particles, which are then filtered out in the form of a slurry (a liquid thickened by tiny particles).

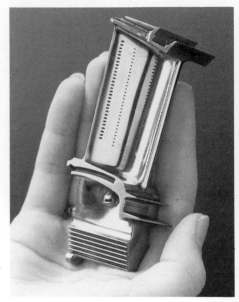

fig 7.16. Examples of spark erosion

Like all processes, spark erosion has both advantages and disadvantages. The main advantages are:

1. Extremely hard metals and very complex shapes can be machined.

2. There is no contact between tool and workpiece, so the workpiece is not put under any strain.

   The major disadvantage is that erosion of the tool or electrode also takes place. These are usually made from brass and the rate of wear can equal the weight of the material removed. Spark erosion is used for producing press tools and for dies for extrusion, processes that we shall look at later in this chapter.

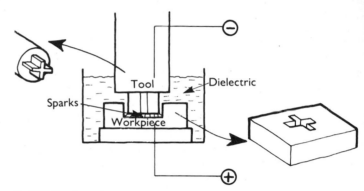

fig 7.16. Spark erosion

ULTRASONIC MACHINING

This process is used to cut both circular and non circular holes in hard or brittle materials. Unlike spark erosion the material being machined need not be electrically conductive. Ultrasonic machining is applied to 'drilling' holes in precious stones, ceramic and glass as well as hard metals. It is possible to make holes as small as 0.01mm in diameter.

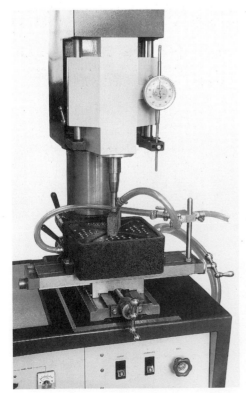

fig 7.18. Ultrasonic machine tool

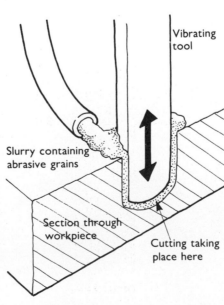

fig 7.19. Ultrasonic machining

The tool is vibrated against the workpiece at a high frequency, typically 20,000 cycles per second, which is beyond the range of human hearing (hence ultrasonic). A slurry of fine grains of hard, abrasive grit mixed with water are fed into the small gap between the tool and the workpiece caused by the vibrating. These fine pieces of abrasive are hammered against the work, chipping away small particles. The shape of the hole produced is the same as the shape of the tool doing the hammering.

The ultrasonic machine tool looks very much like a drilling machine. The abrasive slurry is fed to the tool through a tube and then recirculated by a pump, in the same way as the coolant supply on most machine tools.

DEFORMING AND REFORMING

Earlier in this book we saw how heat and force applied to metals and plastics can result in them being deformed and reformed to suit our needs. In the manufacture of items from throw-away plastic bottles, to the money with which to buy them, materials are formed by a variety of specialised processes. These processes are, as we shall see, only variations of processes used in the school workshop.

DROP FORGING

Forging hot metal into shape using a hammer and anvil may seem like a very old fashioned process and indeed it is. However, achieving the desired shape or form from the metal is only part of the process. The main advantage in shaping metal by forging is the refining of the grain flow that takes place and the effect that this has upon the strength of the component being made. Drop forging, sometimes called die forging, uses two halves of a mould called a die, between which hot, malleable metal is squeezed and formed into the required shape.

One die half is fixed to the anvil of the drop forging press and the other is fixed to the hammer. The hammer drops between guides to ensure the alignment of the two die halves and is bounced back up again after impact. This ensures fast deformation and avoids causing the components to cool rapidly.

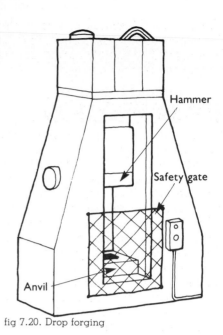

fig 7.20. Drop forging

A variation of this is to bring the two halves of the die together from opposite directions, either vertically or horizontally. This makes more efficient use of the energy involved, because the two opposing forces cancel each other out upon impact, instead of the energy of the hammer being absorbed by the ground.

The complete shaping may be achieved with just one strike or alternatively, with some difficult materials, intermediate stages may be necessary. This is true in the case of some turbine blades for jet engines. The first pair of dies thicken or upset the ends of the blank and the second pair complete the operation (fig 7.21).

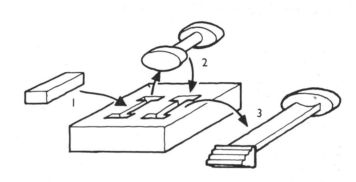

fig 7.21. Drop forging process

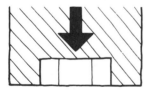

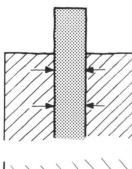

Heading

Heading is the forging process that forms heads on bolts. This is a variation on drop forging. One die half grips the rod and the other forms the head. Fig 7.23 shows how the grain flow of a forged headed bolt compares with one cut from a solid bar.

When in use, turbine blades, bolts and crankshafts of combustion engines are all subject to continual stress. They need to be strong in order to avoid failure. The refined grain flow resulting from drop forging provides this additional strength.

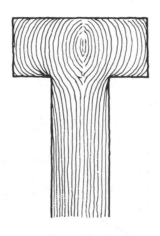

Forged head   Cut from solid bar

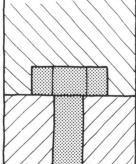

fig 7.22. Heading   fig 7.23. Comparison of grain flow between forged headed bolt and one cut from a solid bar

PRESSWORK

Presses that can exert a load of many hundreds of tonnes are used to produce metal products featured in aspects of everyday life. Saucepans, baking tins and kettles in the kitchen, television and video recorder chassis in the living room, light fittings and tubular furniture at school, the bodies of cars, coaches and lorries on the streets, the frames of aircraft in the air and even the coins in your purse and pocket are all produced by presses.

Piercing and blanking

Piercing and blanking are very similar processes. Whether a process is considered as piercing or as blanking will depend on which of the pieces produced is to be kept. For example in fig 7.24 a hardened steel punch punches a hole cleanly through a piece of metal. If the piece with the hole in it (A) is the workpiece, then the process is called piercing and piece (B) is waste. If (A) is the stock material and (B) is the piece that is required, then the process is blanking.

The punch and die work together in shearing the metal and the edges of both must be kept sharp. Punches and dies are made from hardened, high carbon chromium alloy steel that is able to keep a sharp edge and withstand the continual shock loading of up to 500 strokes per minute.

Bicycle chain links are made by piercing and blanking. Thousands of these are required daily. Fig 7.25 shows how each stroke of the punch pierces four holes in two links and simultaneously blanks out the two links that have previously been pierced. This process is automated with the steel strip being fed through by the correct amount between every stroke.

The strippers on the edges of the dies are required to stop the steel from riding up on the punch.

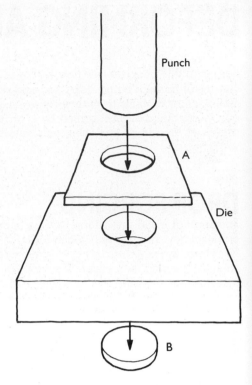

fig 7.24. Hardened steel punch

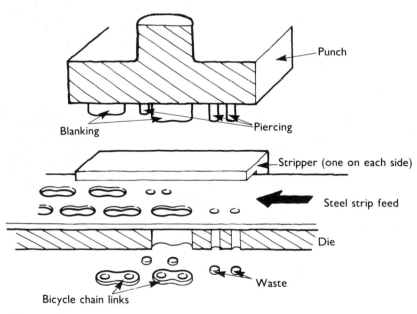

fig 7.25. Bicycle chain links made by piercing and blanking

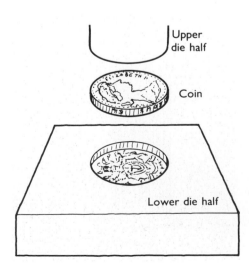

fig 7.26. Coining

Coining

Coining, as the name suggests, is the process by which coins and medals are made or minted. This is essentially a cold forging process and for metal to flow plastically while cold, a very powerful press is required.

The coin or medal blank is placed in the lower die half which is engraved with a reverse image. The upper die half is similarly engraved and this is pressed into the lower half causing the blank to flow into the engraved detail. Some thinning and sideways flow also takes place, which enables the formation of an inscribed edge as on a one pound coin.

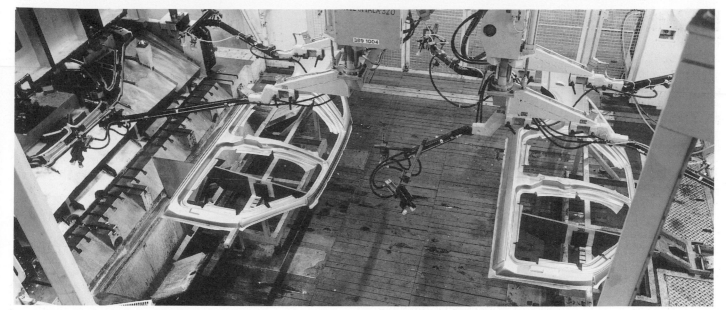

fig 7.27. Car body press in operation

Three dimensional forms

Thin sheet material when formed into a shell results in a strong structure. Car bodies are good examples of this. The steel sheet used is very thin in order to keep down the weight, but the shell type form of the body is strong.

Car bodies are pressings made from flat steel using huge presses. The die halves alone cost tens of thousands of pounds to produce. These must be made precisely as a pair, male and female matching halves, with an allowance for the material thickness in between.

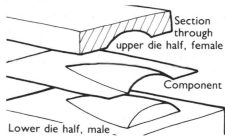

fig 7.28. Three dimensional forming

Forming in three dimensions can produce great problems with wrinkling and tearing. Components that are to be made by this process must be designed with the limitations of presswork very much in mind, avoiding sudden sharp changes in direction and deep 'draws'. Fig 7.29 shows two stages in the pressing of a shallow, circular component with a wide rim. A sprung pressure ring is needed to prevent the rim from wrinkling, while still allowing it to be drawn into the die.

Pressings from thin, soft sheet material are easier to produce. The bottom half of the die is made as a male former and the top half is a thick pad of rubber. Sections of air frames for aircraft in aluminium alloy are often produced by this method.

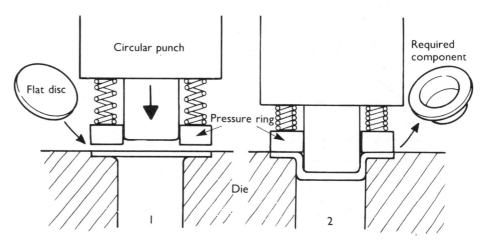

fig 7.29. Two stages in the pressing of a component

DIE CASTING

Steel moulds, rather than sand moulds, are used to produce cheap aluminium and zinc alloy castings for products such as camera bodies, toys and various components for domestic appliances like vacuum cleaners and washing machines. Unlike sand moulds, these moulds or dies are permanent, and must be made in sections to facilitate removal of the finished component. The molten metal may be poured in, this is known as gravity casting, or forced in by a ram, this is pressure die casting.

Die cast products rarely need any additional finishing other than the occasional removal of small casting flashes caused by leakages between the die halves. Very fine detail and a high standard of finish are achieved by this process.

fig 7.30. Die cast military models

EXTRUSION

The process of extrusion is just like squeezing toothpaste from a tube. In manufacturing, this principle can be applied to a range of materials, both metals and plastics. Extrusion is not a new process: in the 19th century lead piping was produced by extrusion. The modern applications for this process, particularly using aluminium and thermoplastics, have become very important manufacturing technologies.

The principles of extrusion

Materials in a plastic state (plasticized) can be extruded to produce both solid and hollow shapes, either by direct or indirect (inverted) extrusion processes (fig 7.31). The cross section of the extrusion is determined by the shape of the die and may be very complex.

Aluminium extrusion

Aluminium has become a most versatile material that lends itself to a great range of extrusion possibilities. An example of this versatility is the outer case of the Microscribe 600 portable microcomputer (fig 7.32). This single extrusion holds the keypad, the circuit boards and even provides location for the batteries.

One of the most popular uses for aluminium extrusions in recent years has been for double glazed window and door frames. The extrusions are strong and aluminium does not require painting or maintenance. British Telecom's new phone booths are also made from extruded aluminium sections for these reasons.

Extruded aluminium alloys can be used to provide mechanical strength coupled with a light weight. The McDonnell Douglas DC-10 passenger aircraft has over a hundred such extrusions in its airframe.

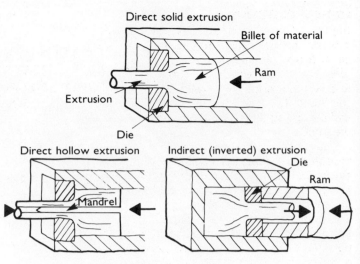

fig 7.31. Direct and indirect extrusion

fig 7.32. Microscribe 600 portable microcomputer

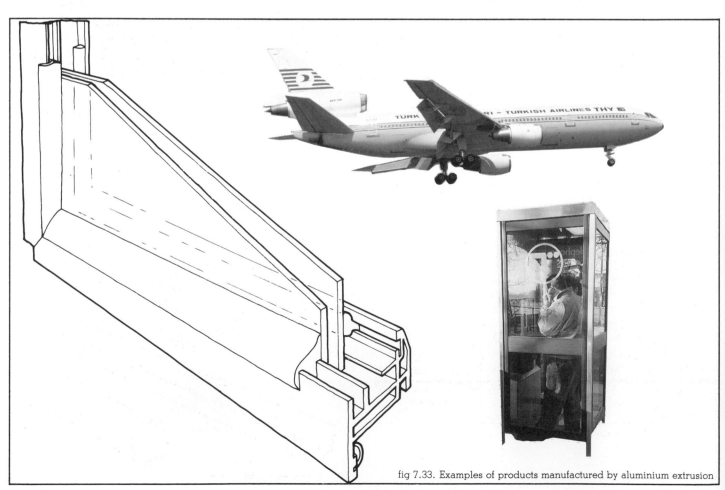

fig 7.33. Examples of products manufactured by aluminium extrusion

Impact extrusion

Impact extrusion is the process that is used to produce some aluminium drink cans. A disc of metal, called a slug, is placed in a shallow die and subjected to a very powerful blow by a punch (fig 7.34). The result is to cause the metal to be squeezed up the sides of the punch.

The process is very quick and, though this is sometimes called cold extrusion, a temperature of several hundreds of degrees is generated in an instant by the force of the impact. The punch and die are made from hardened tool steel that must be highly polished to aid the metal flow, and a grease or tallow lubricant is also used.

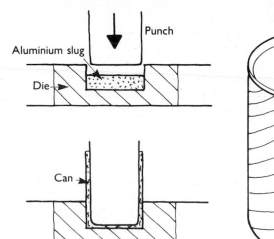

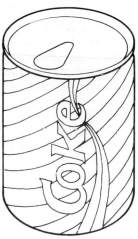

fig 7.34. Impact extrusion

Plastic extrusion

This is a continuous process. Thermoplastic granules are fed from a hopper by a rotating screw through a heated cylinder, the same principle as on a meat mincer. The tapered shape of the screw compacts the plastic as it becomes plasticized.

The die fitted to the end of the extruder determines the form of the extrusion; in fig 7.36 the extrusion is a pipe. The extrusion is cooled as it leaves the die by passing it through a cooling unit containing circulating cold water.

This process is used for double glazed windows, curtain and sliding door tracks, and edging for tables and shelves.

fig 7.35. Extruder

This process is also applied to what are called '**semi-finished**' products, for example, tubes and sheets that then go on to be made into finished products by other processes.

Another application of this process is plastic sheathing for electric cables. By feeding wire into a 'cross head' between the heater and the die, the wire emerges through the die plastic coated (fig 7.37).

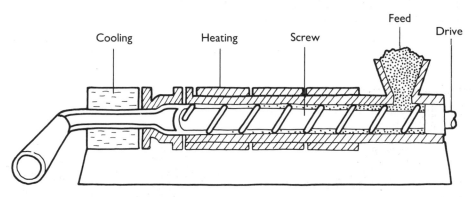

fig 7.36. Extrusion of a pipe

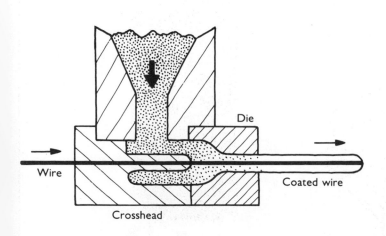

fig 7.37. Plastic sheathing of electric cables

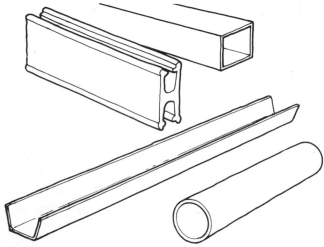

fig 7.38. Extruded plastic items

CALENDERING

The calendering process is used to produce sheet plastic material for hundreds of different applications. It is used primarily in the production of PVC sheeting and in the coating of fabrics and paper. A heated mass of plastic is fed between a series of hot rolls in order to establish a flow and a consistent thickness. The plastic flows finally between a pair of cooled rolls. The space between these last rolls determines the thickness of the resultant sheet.

A plastic coating on fabric is achieved by passing the fabric through the final rolls with the plastic. This bonds the two materials together as the plastic begins to solidify. Simulated leather fabrics for briefcases and furniture are produced in this way, as is the waterproof fabric for pram canopies and protective clothing. Vinyl coated wall coverings are produced by feeding paper at this final stage of rolling. If the final rolls are suitably embossed, then the resultant sheet will be textured. This is true of most coated fabrics, particularly those used for upholstery.

fig 7.39. Calendering

fig 7.40. Calendering process

BLOW MOULDING

The blow moulding of plastics is a process adapted from the very old craft of glass blowing. Blow moulding is used for the manufacture of bottles and similar hollow articles. A hollow length of thermoplastic, called a parison, is extruded down between the open halves of a **split mould**. The mould halves are closed and compressed air is blown in forcing the plastic to line the sides of the mould cavity. The mould has a chilling effect upon the plastic causing it to set almost immediately.

Blow moulding is a fast process with very little waste that is able to be highly automated.

fig 7.41. Blow moulding of plastics

INJECTION MOULDING

This is a very widespread, highly automated process that is used to produce a vast range of everyday items, including telephones, toys, buckets, bowls and cases for numerous household electrical goods from food processors to television sets. It is a process best suited to thermoplastics, but a few thermosetting plastics are also manufactured using injection moulding techniques.

The process is quite simple. Plastic, heated to a plastic state, is injected under pressure into an enclosed mould. The mould is then opened up and the product removed. Injection moulded products are of a high quality and usually require no further finishing. The injection moulding machine consists of an injection unit and a mould (fig 7.42). A hopper of plastic grandules feeds a rotating screw mechanism in a similar manner to the plastic extrusion process. The plastic then becomes plasticised by heat from a cylindrical heater and the rotating screw forces the plastic into a forward chamber. The screw mechanism then acts as a ram, injecting the plastic into the mould. The mould is subsequently cooled and opened to remove the completed moulding.

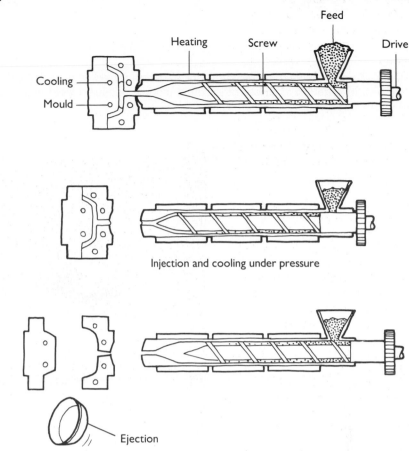

Injection and cooling under pressure

Ejection

fig 7.42. Injection moulding

fig 7.43. Injection moulded products

WELDING

Bicycles, cars, submarines and space ships are all examples of welded metal fabrications.

Oxy-acetylene and electric arc welding are frequently used in manufacturing industries, and in addition to these, other often more specialised welding processes have developed.

MIG AND TIG WELDING

Metal inert gas (MIG) welding is a very versatile welding process, and is possibly the most important of the newer welding processes. In its simplest hand-held form, MIG welding is replacing oxy-acetylene welding for application such as repair work. MIG welding also lends itself to automatic welding and is becoming increasingly popular for production welding using robots.

MIG is an electric arc welding process. The arc is struck between the workpiece and a continuous wire electrode being fed through a torch. An inert gas flows through the torch forming a shield around the arc. The gas shield is usually argon gas, or an argon based gas mixture, which prevents surface oxidisation and slag forming.

The continuous wire electrode provides the filler rod in one of two ways, spray transfer or dip transfer (fig 7.44).

Spray transfer uses both high current and voltage, which causes a continuous stream of metal droplets to leave the wire and be deposited in the weld. Spray transfer is suitable for fast welding of thick material.

Dip transfer MIG welding uses less current and generates less heat and is therefore more suitable for thin sheet material. The wire electrode is repeatedly dipped into the molten weld pool causing a brief short circuit, which results in a rise in current and a small piece of wire melting off. By adjusting the mixture of gases that make up the shield, most metals can be welded by this process, including aluminium, copper, carbon and alloy steels, magnesium and titanium.

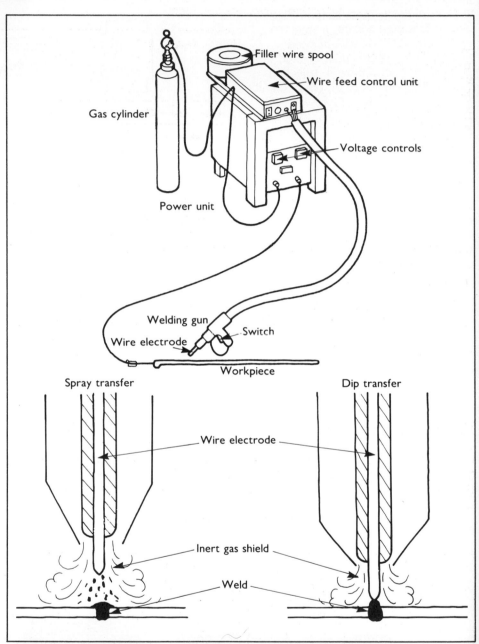

fig 7.44. MIG welding

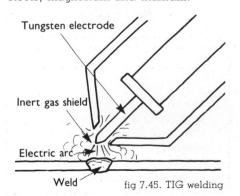

fig 7.45. TIG welding

Tungsten electrode inert gas (TIG) welding is, in many ways, similar to MIG welding. An inert gaseous shield, usually pure argon, provides a shield around an electric arc struck between the workpiece and in this case a tungsten electrode (fig 7.45).

In this process the electrode is not intentionally consumed, though in fact it does evaporate very slowly. This is a welding process suited to otherwise difficult materials, such as aluminium alloys and stainless steels.

RESISTANCE WELDING

An electric current flowing through a high resistance will result in heating taking place. This is the principle upon which the ordinary household electric fire or hair dryer relies. With sufficient current, enough heat for welding can be produced.

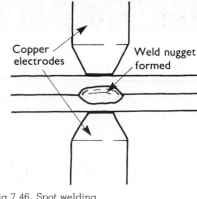

fig 7.46. Spot welding

Spot welding

Fig 7.46 shows two electrodes sandwiching together two sheets of metal. Electric current flows from one electrode to the other through the metal sheets. The place where most resistance to the current flow occurs is at the joint line. Heat is generated at this point and welding takes place. By repeating this process a number of times, a series of 'spot' welds are produced.

The electrodes are made from copper and usually have water flowing inside them to provide cooling. They are shaped as in fig 7.46, or may be in the form of a wheel to provide consistent pressure along the joint. This is called seam welding.

Spot welding and seam welding are used extensively in the manufacture of thin sheet steel fabrications such as car bodies.

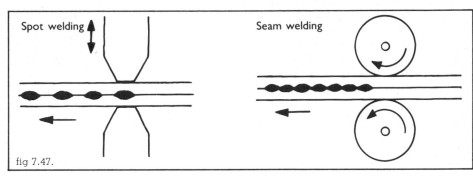

fig 7.47.

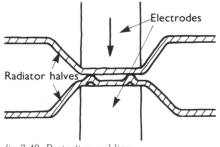

fig 7.48. Projection welding

Projection welding

Small bumps or projections pressed into the surface of components being welded will determine the exact position of the resultant resistance weld (fig 7.48). The projection is softened during the welding process and collapses under the pressure of the electrode. The location of the weld nugget is not determined by the electrode, therefore, the electrode can be any shape to suit the workpiece.

Pressed steel radiators for household central heating systems are made using this process. One of the two halves of each radiator is formed with projections for resistance welding (fig 7.48).

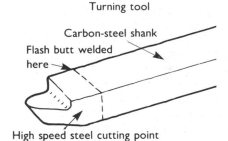

fig 7.49. Flash butt welding

Flash butt welding

Centre lathe turning tools are very often a high speed steel cutting end, flash butt welded onto a carbon-steel shank; the joint is often difficult to see. One of the most common uses of flash butt welding is for welding railway lines. British Rail weld 18 metre lengths of rail into single lengths, sometimes 350 metres long.

Flash butt welding is carried out in distinct stages:

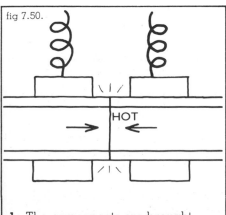

1. The components are brought together and electric current passing through the resistance at the joint causes the joint area to become red hot.

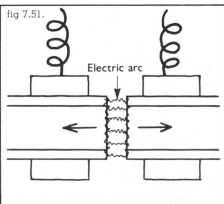

2. The components are moved apart resulting in an arc that melts the metal.

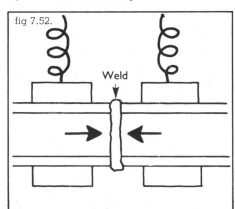

3. The two parts are brought back together under immense pressure with the current still flowing, resulting in impurities being forced out of the joint and the formation of a sound weld.

ELECTRONICS

Solid state electronics have only been around since the early 1950s, but the rate of development has been so rapid that nearly every aspect of daily life is in some way reliant upon electronic components, from the digital alarm clock that starts your day to the television set that you watch in the evening. These household electronic systems are, however, only the tip of the iceberg. Manufacturing industries of every type are reliant upon electronic systems for stock control of materials, control of manufacturing processes and their progress, and control of the despatch of goods to the shops.

The electronics industry, the people who make electronic components, has undergone remarkable changes in its short lifetime. In the early 1960s the **integrated circuit** (IC) was introduced and this has been continually refined and improved upon ever since. An integrated circuit is an electronic circuit made up of many parts, such as transistors, resistors and diodes, integrated together on one small piece of silicon wafer, a **silicon chip**. Integrated circuits contain hundreds of components and yet may be so small that they can pass through the eye of a needle. In fact they are too small to handle comfortably. For this reason integrated circiuts are packaged in spider like plastic or ceramic cases with legs, to which electrical connections may be made. For example a 555 timer IC has eight such legs, whereas a very large scale integrated circuit, such as a complete microprocessor on a single chip, may have 64 legs.

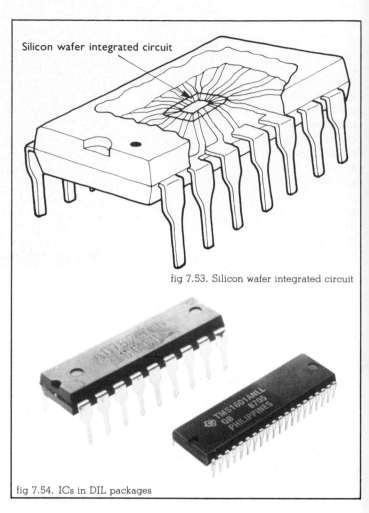

fig 7.53. Silicon wafer integrated circuit

fig 7.54. ICs in DIL packages

INTEGRATED CIRCUIT MANUFACTURE

The success of the silicon chip is not due entirely to its remarkable small size and its reliability, it is due to a large degree to its very low cost. The raw material for integrated circuit manufacture, silicon, is extracted from sand. Sand is extremely cheap and is found in abundance all over the earth's surface.

The sand is purified and refined to produce almost pure silicon. This silicon then has to be further refined by a process called 'crystal growing', to re-organise its atomic structure. It is then ready to be used for integrated circuit manufacture.

After crystal growth the silicon, in 100 mm diameter cylinders, is sliced rather like slicing a cucumber or a sausage. These slices, called wafers, are then highly polished ready for the chemical processes that follow. It is essential throughout these processes that absolute cleanliness is maintained, even the slightest contamination will affect the final outcome. Fig 7.55 shows the measures that must be taken to ensure that the silicon wafers are not contaminated by the people involved in their manufacture. You can also see a rack of wafers in the operator's hand.

A whole range of mainly chemical processes are applied to the silicon wafer. These processes may be carried out just once, or may need to be repeated several times, depending on the particular circuit that is being produced.

fig 7.55. Ensuring silicon wafers are not contaminated

Silicon oxide layers provide electrical isolation between separate areas of the circuit. Oxidisation of selected areas is achieved by applying an oxide layer to the whole surface and etching sections of this away by a photo resist process similar to the production of printed circuits (see page 159). N-type and P-type dopants are deposited on the surface and these are diffused into the silicon by baking in ovens, which creates semi-conductor devices like transistors and diodes. Finally, minute metal contacts and interconnections, usually aluminium, are implanted in the surface layers using vaporised, very pure, very small pieces of metal. All of this results in the production of a wafer like the one in fig 7.55, containing hundreds of individual integrated circuits, each one of which needs to be checked and tested.

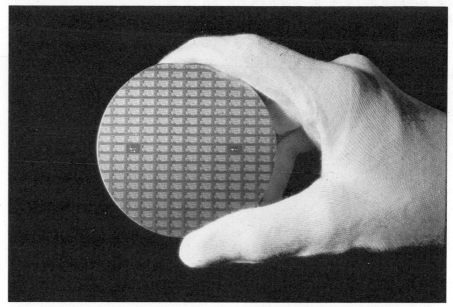

fig 7.56. Wafer containing hundreds of ICs

Testing is a computer controlled operation. Fine, needle like probes check the functions of each integrated circuit in turn. Circuits that fail to meet the design specification are marked and after separation they are discarded. The chips are separated from each other using very fine diamond tipped cutters. They then go on to be packaged. Delicate fine wire has to be attached to the contacts on the chip and to the legs of the package before the whole is completely encapsulated in plastic.

Despite the complexity of this process many integrated circuits cost only a few pence each.

In the same way that integrated circuits have taken over, where possible, from discrete electronic components, so ICs with a larger scale of integration are able to do the job that would have needed several ICs only a few years ago. VLSI (very large scale integrated) circuits are cheaper because fewer are needed. They are also much faster, a very important plus for computing applications.

fig 7.57. Testing ICs

It is reckoned that the cost of computers has been reduced by a factor of 200 since the early days of computing, the mid 1950s, and the speed of operation has increased 500 times. All of this is a direct result of the progress of silicon chip technology.

Fig 7.58 shows a BBC Master computer with the top off. You can see how the integrated circuits all have their own specific jobs to do.

Analogue port interface

Mode 7 (Teletext) Character set ROM

VDU interface

Input/Output controller

Memory controller

Operating system and Basic language ROM

Word processor ROM

Central processor unit (CPU)

fig 7.58. BBC Master computer with the top off

COMPUTER AIDED ENGINEERING

Computers and computer systems have been around for a long time. The huge, very expensive computers developed in the late 1940s and early 1950s were accessible only to mathematicians and scientists. Their operating speeds were extremely slow and, being thermionic valve based systems rather than solid state, they could be very troublesome. None of the high level languages like 'basic' existed and their activities were confined mainly to mathematical problems. As we have seen on the previous pages, the silicon chip was to change all that.

Computer technology

Before looking at how manufacturing industry is making use of this tool, let us first examine what we mean by a computer.

The modern computer is an electronic device that is able to process data or information according to a pre-determined program of instructions. It is no more mysterious or miraculous than that.

Within a computer system the computer is often referred to as **hardware**, and the term given to the program is **software**.

The computer has three basic interconnected components (fig 7.59):

1. The central processing unit (CPU).

2. Memory storage.

3. Input/output (I/O) sections.

The **central processing unit** has two subsections, one controlling all of the operations of the other units and directing the flow of data, and the other performing the arithmetic functions such as adding, subtracting, multiplying, dividing and comparing.

Memory storage on board the computer provides many locations called addresses, where the CPU can store data and its program of instructions. Other storage devices (floppy discs, magnetic tapes) are accessed through the I/O sections.

The **input/output sections** communicate with the outside world. Incoming information may come from the memory storage devices mentioned or from a keyboard, a joystick, a microswitch on a conveyer belt or from a robot's camera vision. Output signals may be directed to a VDU (visual display unit) to display graphics or text, or to a printer, a plotter, a computer controlled machine tool, a robot, or in fact nearly any electrically powered device.

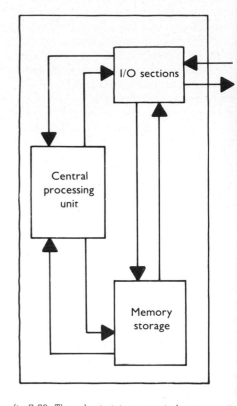

fig 7.59. Three basic interconnected components of a computer

COMPUTER AIDED DESIGN (CAD)

In the same way that design involves more than just conveying ideas, so computer aided design (CAD) involves much more than drawing on a screen rather than on a sheet of paper. Computers that are able to solve mathematical problems can also help to solve many design problems.

CAD enables designers to visualise and develop shapes and forms. Different designs can be analysed, compared and modified in a way that would not have been possible only a few years ago. Engineering designers can see how components might fit together without resorting to modelling, so saving a great deal of time. The architect can view a whole street of unbuilt houses from many different viewpoints. Designers of electronic printed circuit boards can use CAD to route the tracks to connect integrated circuits.

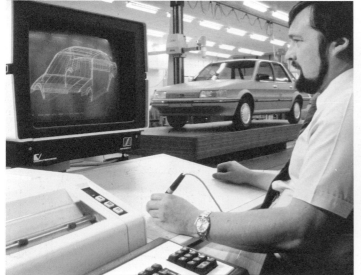

fig 7.60. Industrial CAD system in use

CAD hardware

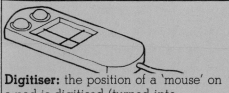

Digitiser: the position of a 'mouse' on a pad is digitised (turned into numbers) and sent to the computer to enable drawing, or for selection from a screen menu.

Tracker ball: a cross on the screen is moved around by rolling the tracker ball. The position of the cross is used to fix points for drawing or for screen menu selection.

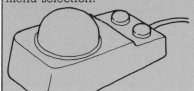

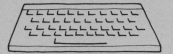

VDU: the screen is used for creating designs on and referring to for data to act upon.

Keyboard: this is used in the simplest systems for drawing using the 'arrow' keys. Most systems use the keyboard to input text which is to appear on drawings.

X — Y plotter: this is the most popular output medium for transferring designs onto paper. The X and Y co-ordinates of the points on the drawing stored in the computer's memory are used to plot out the drawing.

Printer: a dot matrix printer 'dumps' the screen image onto paper. Diagonal lines and circles have stepped edges like the images on the screen.

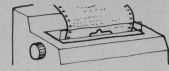

fig 7.61. CAD hardware

The sophistication of any CAD systems will be dependent upon the computing power available. Reasonably priced and increasingly powerful computer aided design can be centred on a school microcomputer. Most systems will allow the creation of two dimensional shapes on the screen. These can subsequently be repeated, revolved, scaled up and down, mirrored, cross-hatched, dimensioned and then, if required, drawn out on an X-Y plotter.

Manipulating shapes once created can save time should the same shape to be repeated. It also enables you to squash or stretch your designs in the search for an aesthetically pleasing appearance.

More powerful CAD systems can turn two dimensions into three and then go on to decide which parts should be visible and which should not; this is called **solid modelling**. Fig 7.62 shows a simple engineering component given five different interpretations by the computer. (A) is called a wireframe model, (B) is a solid model with hidden detail, (C) has hidden line removal, (D) has shading added and (E) is a sectional view.

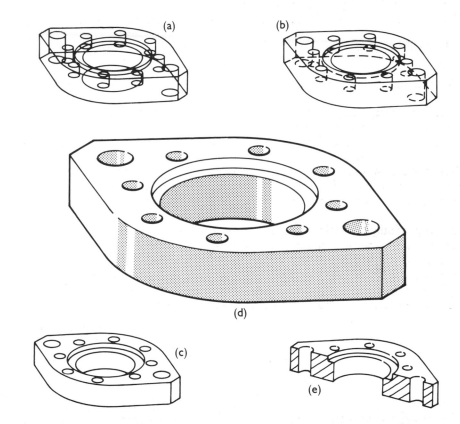

fig 7.62. Simple engineering component given five different interpretations by the computer

Fig 7.63 shows a robot arm moving through five positions close to a wall. (For the sake of clarity, the complete arm is only shown in positions 1 and 5). The robot's hand in positions 2, 3 and 4 seems to disappear into the wall, indicating a collision. This is called **clash detection** and is another aspect of computer aided design. Clash detection is proving very useful when designing assembly lines where several robots need to work close to each other.

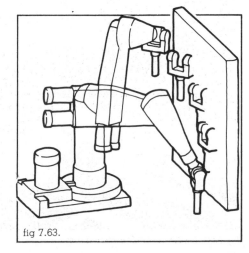

fig 7.63.

COMPUTER NUMERICAL CONTROL (CNC)

Numerical control (NC) means, quite simply, control by numbers. Numerically controlled machine tools are those lathes, milling machines, drilling machines and flame cutters that have their movements and other functions controlled by instructions or data received as a series of numbers. The numbers are interpreted electronically by the machine tool and are then acted upon.

Machine tools that include a computer, able to make calculations and decisions based upon data received, are called **computer numerically controlled (CNC).**

Sophisticated machine tool control units are able to process data, both incoming from a memory or data store and data fed back from the machine tool. A system that can respond to a feedback of information regarding the tool or workpiece's actual position, or about tool wear, is called a **closed loop control system** (fig 7.64).

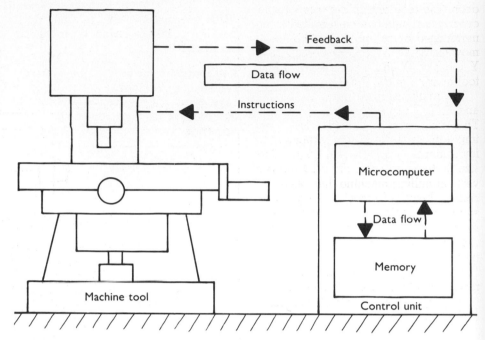

fig 7.64. Closed loop control system

MACHINE AXES CO-ORDINATE SYSTEM

An instruction from a control unit to a machine, directing that machine to move its cutting tool 50 mm, is of little use if the direction of movement is not also indicated.

It is important to have a standard for the naming of machine axes and also a standard for the directions of movement along these axes. Standardisation is needed so that people can communicate information, and it is even more important when the communication is carried out entirely by computers, as is the case in the systems that we shall look at later. British Standard BS 3635 and the International Organisation for Standardisation (ISO) have set out the co-ordinate system to which machine tool manufacturers comply.

There are normally three axes of movement, called **X**, **Y** and **Z**. If there is a fourth, it is called **W**. The relationship between X, Y and Z are determined by applying 'The Right-Handed Cartesian co-ordinate system' (fig 7.65). This also indicates the positive (+) direction of movement. BS 3635 also determines that a negative (−) direction reduces the size of the workpiece and that the Z axis is the axis of rotation of the work or the tool, whichever rotates.

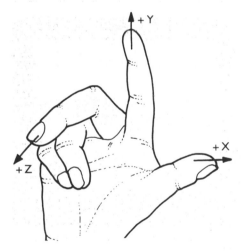

fig 7.65. The right handed Cartesian co-ordinate system

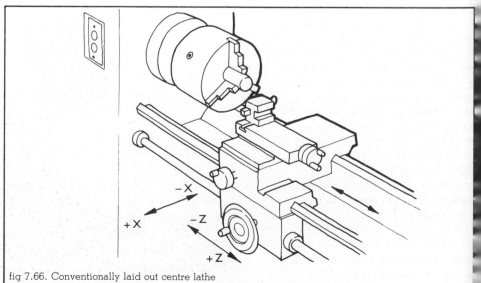

fig 7.66. Conventionally laid out centre lathe

These rules applied to a conventionally laid out centre lathe can be seen in fig 7.66. On a lathe, of course, there is no Y axis. Variations arise when this is applied to other machine tools, for example, a horizontal milling machine. Here the tools do not move but the workpiece does. The relationship between cutting and negative movement is maintained by calling the workpiece movements X′, Y′ and Z′ instead of X, Y and Z. X, Y and Z are used only for tool movement (fig 7.67).

The relationship between X′, Y′, Z′ and X, Y, Z can be seen in fig 7.67. They are opposites, but what is important is that negative movement, for example, − Y′, will still reduce the size of the workpiece. Fig 7.69 shows a vertical milling machine that has a spindle head movement making four slide movements in total. The axis of rotation of the tools is Z, and W′ is the identification given to the knee or table up and down axis.

These rules can be applied to all machines with axes of movement, including presses, welding machinery, and also draughting machines.

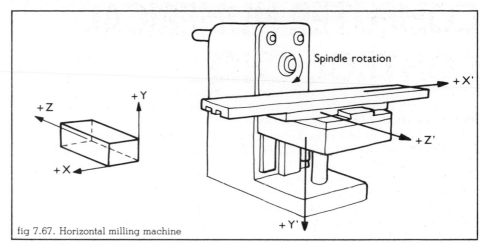

fig 7.67. Horizontal milling machine

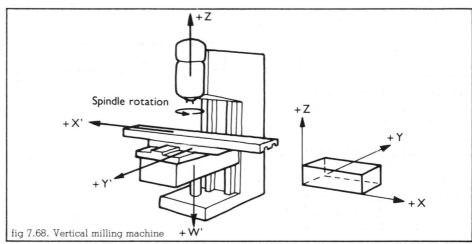

fig 7.68. Vertical milling machine

PART PROGRAMMING

Part programming refers to the extracting of information from the component or part drawing and converting this information into a form of numerical data to which the machine tool can respond. Do not confuse the word 'part' meaning a component, with 'part' meaning incomplete.

This process is almost always computer aided, with a continually updated graphical display of the machining process (fig 7.69).

The process of programming may be carried out at the machine, or it may be carried out away from the machine on a remote computer terminal. The program can then be either down loaded to the machine after 'proving', or stored to be loaded in when required. **Program proving** involves watching the machining operation taking place on the VDU in order to be assured that it will run once loaded into the machine tool.

Programming a machine directly is called **manual data input (MDI).** This has the disadvantage that the machine is standing idle during the process.

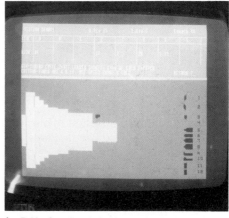

fig 7.69. Graphical display of the machining process

Programming languages

The milling machine in fig 7.70 uses conversational manual data input. A conversational programming language is designed to be 'user friendly'. The programmer is required to respond to questions asked by the computer in order to create the program. Questions like, What tool do you require? How long is the workpiece? How many roughing cuts are required?

The problem with this system is the difficulty that arises in the communication and transferring of data to other systems. The big advantage is the ease of programming. This makes this type of CNC machine popular in small companies where data transfer is not important and the ability to use non-specialist programmers is.

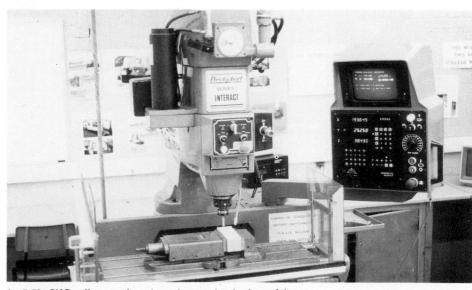

fig 7.70. CNC milling machine (guards open for display only)

The International Organisation for Standardisation (ISO) recommends a set of codes to be used when programming CNC machines. There are two major groups of codes each given a letter followed by a two digit number: **Preparatory Functions**, known as 'G' codes and **Miscellaneous Functions**, known as 'M codes'. There are 100 possible codes in each group 00–99, but many of these are reserved for future standardization. We shall look in detail at just a few of the most frequently used codes: G00, G01, G02, and G03, positioning control codes (fig 7.71).

G00 – positioning, point to point: the tool moves as directed from point A to point B.

The route between the points is not critical and may be any of the paths indicated. The feed rate (speed of movement of the tool) is not determined and is normally as fast as possible. G00 is not used for cutting.

G01 – linear interpolation: the tool moves in a straight line (linear) from point A to point B at a controlled feed rate. The feed rate, usually in mm per minute, must be stated in the program.

G02 and G03 – circular interpolation arc: G02 clockwise, G03 counter clockwise, The tool moves in a circular arc between points A and B. By entering the co-ordinates of point B and the co-ordinates of the arc centre, point C, in the program, the computer is able to calculate all of the intermediate points that go to make up the arc.

Some of the most frequently used miscellaneous functions are M02 — end of program, M03 — spindle on (clockwise), M04 — spindle on (counter clockwise), M05 — spindle off, M06 — change tool and M08 — coolant on.

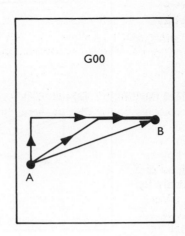
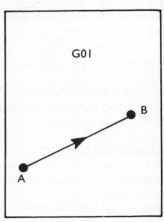
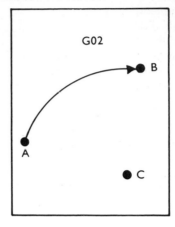
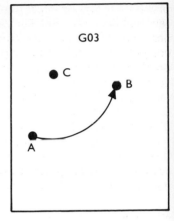

fig 7.71. Preparatory functions G00, G01, G02 and G03

Programming methods

There are two methods used to instruct directional movement, these are incremental and absolute.

Programming in incremental relates each movement to the final position of the previous move.

Programming in absolute relates each movement to a single datum point. We will now look at these two methods applied to the same sequence of movements on a centre lathe.

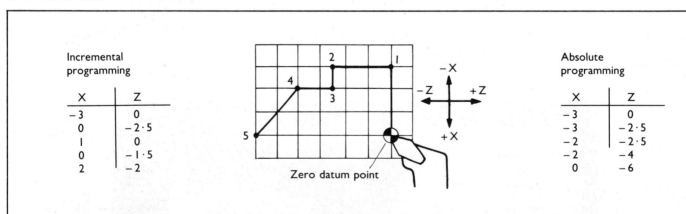

Incremental programming				Absolute programming	
X	Z			X	Z
−3	0			−3	0
0	−2·5			−3	−2·5
1	0			−2	−2·5
0	−1·5			−2	−4
2	−2			0	−6

fig 7.72. Incremental and absolute programming

G codes in the ISO non-standardised area, typically G90 and G91 are used to select absolute and incremental programming at the start of the program. Most machine tool programs offer the facility of changing between absolute and incremental during the program, and also the ability to move the position of the datum during the course of a program in absolute. This is called **zero shift** and it enables several indentical components at different positions on a machine table to be machined using the same program, like the biscuit roll in fig 7.76 .

DATA STORAGE

It is vital that once written, programs can be stored in a way that enables them to be quickly and accurately retrieved. There are three main ways of achieving this.

1. Through a master main frame computer's storage system.
2. Using a magnetic medium such as floppy disc or magnetic tape.
3. Using punched tape.

Master computer

When a group of CNC machines are connected to a single, large main frame computer this is called **Direct Numerical Control (DNC)**. Data storage makes use of the master computer's storage system which is probably a large capacity, fast retrieval hard disc system. DNC also has other advantages, the master computer is able to monitor progress on all of the machines to which it is connected and is able to process this information for use in stock control and the despatching of goods. When all of the elements are brought together, design, manufacturing and computerised business systems, this is known as **Computer Integrated Manufacturing (CIM)**.

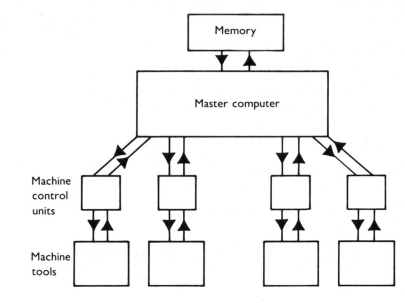

fig 7.73. Direct numerical control

Magnetic medium

Magnetic tape and magnetic 'floppy' discs are a popular form of program storage. Both tape and discs are easily stored, but do require a certain amount of care. They are easy to edit and can be used to enable VDU program display and hard copy printouts.

Magnetic tape is not a particularly fast method of data retrieval, but many CNC machines are equipped with **buffer storage**. Buffer storage holds data in an intermediate position enabling action to be taken on some blocks of information, while subsequent data is being loaded or processed.

Punched tape

Punched paper tape was one of the earliest means of data storage for CNC machines. This is still a popular method of data storage and retrieval. Punched tape has a great advantage over magnetic storage in that it can be visually read by the machine operator.

Modern tape is not always made from paper. Paper and polyester laminate and polyester tape have the advantage of being resistant to oil and less likely to tear. Punched tape readers may be mechanical, pneumatic and photoelectric devices.

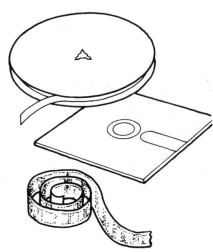

fig 7.74. Magnetic tape, floppy disc and punched tape

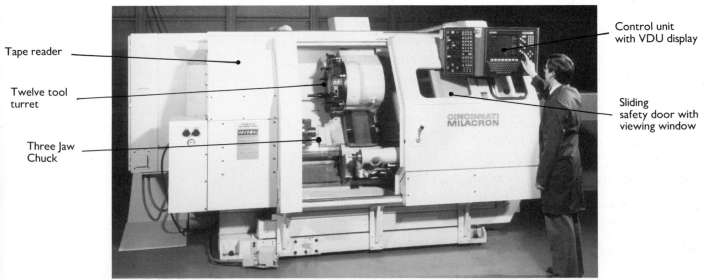

fig 7.75. CNC turning centre

183

CAD/CAM

The term CAD/CAM has come to mean an integrated **Computer Aided Design and Computer Aided Manufacturing** system. On page 179 we saw that the CAD process includes component drawing using a computer. The computer does not store the detail of a drawing in terms of lines and shapes like a photographic record, it is stored as numerical data.

CAD/DAM links enable this data to be used to program the machining of the component. The profile of the component, created during the design state, is processed by the computer to create the CNC machining program. The programmer is only required to make a few necessary decisions regarding the machining procedure and then oversee the program, proving on the VDU before actioning the actual machining. The program codes generated with a CAD/CAM system are never actually processed in a form that can be seen by the programmer.

fig 7.76. Biscuit roll

Fig 7.76 is an example of the application of a CAD/CAM system, used here to produce a biscuit roll. A biscuit roll is the part of a biscuit making machine that is used to roll out the prepared biscuit mix and at the same time imprint it with a pattern, in this case the traditional pattern for custard creams.

The design for one individiual biscuit was first created using a CAD system. This design was then transferred in data form to a multi-spindled CNC machine tool. The machine tool repeatedly cuts a negative impression of the pattern in the surface of the roll. You can see two of the machine's cutting heads in position above the completed roll in fig 7.76.

CNC IN MANUFACTURING INDUSTRY

Before looking at even more sophisticated manufacturing systems, you should consider some of the disadvantages as well as the advantages of computers in manufacturing.

It is all too easy to regard modern CNC machines as the machine tools that will make all of the tools that have come before obsolete. While it is true that CNC machines have enabled the world's industries to make great strides forward since the early 1970s, there have been many problems, one of the major ones being the need for capital investment.

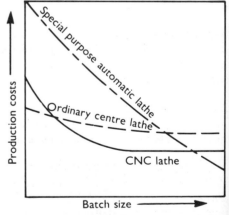

fig 7.77. Batch size versus production costs

The advantages of CNC machine tools

1. The reduction in the cost of setting up machines. CNC machines do not need expensive jigs and fixtures. The program ensures the correct relationship between the tool and the workpiece. This also leads to savings on the design, the manufacture and the storage of jigs and fixtures.

2. On lathes, simple single point tools are able to produce complex forms, eliminating the need for expensive, specially made form tools.

3. Human error and scrap caused as a result of operator fatigue are significantly reduced.

4. Manufacturing costs are far more predictable.

The disadvantages of CNC machine tools

1. The initial cost of the machine and its installation are very high.

2. The training of programmers and operators is expensive.

3. As batch sizes increase, production costs cannot compete with special purpose high production machines (fig 7.77).

184

ROBOTS

The word robot was first coined in the 1920s by Czech playwright Karel Capek. It comes from the Czech word 'robotnic', meaning a slave or a serf. Industrial robots can be defined as programmable machines with certain human characteristics, the most typical characteristic is that of an arm. Robots are used for loading and unloading CNC machines, assembly work, paint spraying, welding and many similar industrial processes that would previously have employed men and women in boring, repetitive tasks, sometimes in unpleasant and even hazardous working conditions.

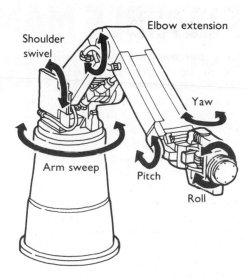

fig 7.78. Six degrees of freedom

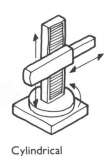   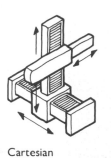

Cartesian   Cylindrical   Polar   Jointed-arm

fig 7.79. Types of robot arm construction

End effectors
The device that terminates a robot's arm is called an end effector. This may be some form of gripper, paint sprayer, spot welding gun, suction cup, in fact almost any tool or manipulating device.

   Fig 7.80 shows a general purpose pivot action gripper. Some robots can be programmed to select from a variety of end effectors, depending on the task to be undertaken.

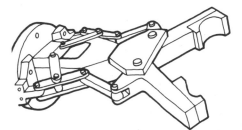

fig 7.80. General purpose pivot action gripper

Physical configuration
The shape, size and strength of a robot will be determined by the task it has to perform. Fig 7.79 shows the four most common robot configurations. The working or coverage area of each type is governed by the configuration of the three major axes. The most versatile is the jointed arm type (you will notice that this is also the most 'human'). It is usual for a robot arm to have three additional 'wrist' movements, pitch, yaw and roll (fig 7.78). These six total movements are called the robots **'six degrees of freedom'.**

PROGRAMMING ROBOTS
There are four ways of programming or teaching robots to carry out a desired sequence of movements

Manual method
This is simply a matter of setting mechanical stops and limit switches for basic 'pick and place' operations. This is not, strictly speaking, programming.

Walkthrough programming
Here the arm is physically taken through the required sequence of movements and each movement is recorded by the control computer's memory. Once the positions and the sequence have been established, the robot can repeat the sequence of movements at any required speed. This method is often used for programming paint sprayers and welding robots.

Leadthrough programming
This is a very popular robot programming method. A hand-held device, often similar to a joystick, called a teach pendant, is used to control the robot's movements through its required sequence of operations. The movements are recorded in memory for later playback.

Off-line programming
This method involves programming the robot from a computer terminal and later down loading the program to the robot control unit. Off-line programming makes use of sophisticated CAD/CAM systems, in particular for clash detection (page 181) when several robots are used in the same working area. Off-line programming has the advantage of not interfering with production.

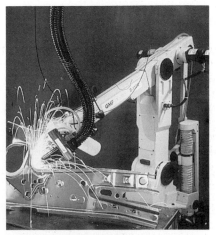

fig 7.81. Jointed arm configuration

FLEXIBLE MANUFACTURING SYSTEMS (FMS)

The aim of any manufacturer must be to sell the products that he or she produces. Manufacturing industry must, therefore, always be looking for the most cost effective manufacturing system.

Let us look at two extremes in manufacturing processes.

A dedicated automatic machine is able to make hundreds, even thousands of the same identical product very cheaply and of a consistently high quality. At first this seems like an excellent system and in some instances it is. However, the system does have problems.

An automatic machine must be kept running to remain economical so the manufacturer is required to keep products in stock before being sold or used. Money becomes tied up in stock instead of being used for further investment. Automatic machines are inflexible, every component is the same. With products such as cars and furniture, the consumer demand is for variety and choice.

The other extreme is to have a skilled operator making whatever is required, whenever it is required. With this sytem there are no stockpiling of components and there is absolute flexibility. The problem here, of course, is that the rate of production is very slow and the resultant cost of products produced is, therefore, very high.

Flexible manufacture systems have the advantages of both of these examples without the disadvantages of either.

A flexible manufacturing system is both automatic and flexible. This is achieved by bringing together computer numerical controlled machine tools, robot parts handling and an **automatic guided vehicle (AGV)** transport system. AGVs (fig 7.82) are computer controlled vehicles that are programmed to follow routes laid out by wires set into the factory floor. The whole system comes under direct numerical control (DNC) and it is due to this that such great flexibility is achieved.

fig 7.82. AGV

MANUFACTURING CELLS

A full flexible manufacturing system is very expensive to instal. The cost could run to many millions of pounds. Many companies start moving towards flexible manufacturing by installing smaller manufacturing cells, comprising just two or three machines. Cells can later be linked together or expanded.

A manufacturing cell may be made up of just two machine tools such as a CNC lathe and a CNC milling machine, and a parts handling robot (fig 7.83). The robot takes the incoming material and places it in the lathe chuck for the first operation, the robot can also be used to turn the work around for machining on the other end, if this is required.

After machining on the lathe is complete, the work is removed to a **buffer store** for part machined components. A buffer store is necessary because the different machining operations will not take the same amount of time.

Components from the buffer store are transferred to the milling machine and then, on completion of the milling operation, are removed and leave the cell.

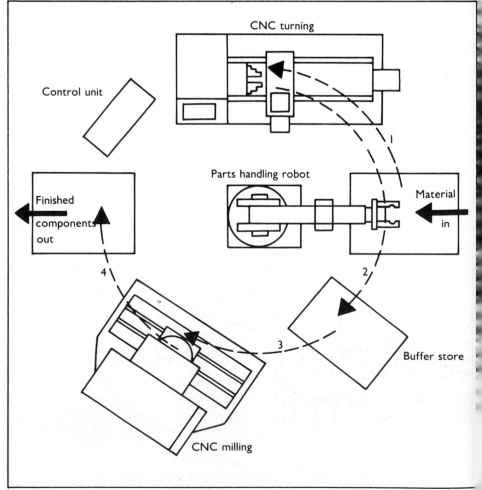

fig 7.83. Manufacturing cell

We have seen that CNC machine tools require only the simplest of jigs and fixtures. In a flexible manufacturing system the components are mounted on metal pallets. These pallets are accurately made so that they locate on all of the machine tables in the system and also onto the AGVs. The master computer maintains absolute control of each component that is within the manufacturing system, and is able to down load to any machine tool the correct program to coincide with the arrival at that machine of that particular component. There may be hundreds of components of many different types within a system at any one time.

Fig 7.84 shows a sophisticated type of milling machine, described by its manufacturers as a CNC Processing Centre. It has a rotating eight pallet work changer, or carousel. It can be seen here with three different components, two are on the carousel and one is being machined. On the left there is access for an AGV to the loading/unloading station. On the side of the machine there are two tool magazines each containing up to 45 different tools. Tool changing between machining operations takes approximately 11 seconds.

A machine like this can work along side similar machines or, alternatively,

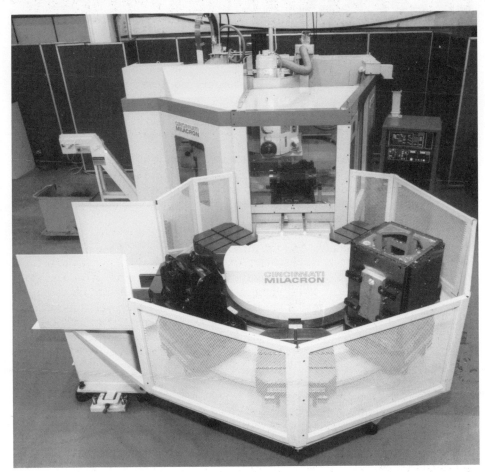

fig 7.84. CNC processing centre

with completely different types of machine in either a small manufacturing cell or in a complex flexible manufacturing system.

Wash stations form an important part of any flexible manufacturing system. Washing is necessary between machining operations to remove swarf that, if left to accumulate, could cause problems in maintaining accuracy and quality. A typical wash station provides overhead water jet sprays and a robot with a combined water jet and hot air end effector. The robot can be programmed to suit the cleaning requirements of the particular component.

Fig 7.85 illustrates a typical flexible manufacturing system, with palletised materials and parts storage, CNC machining centres being supplied with both work and tools by AGVs, a wash station and a measuring and inspection station that is also under computer control.

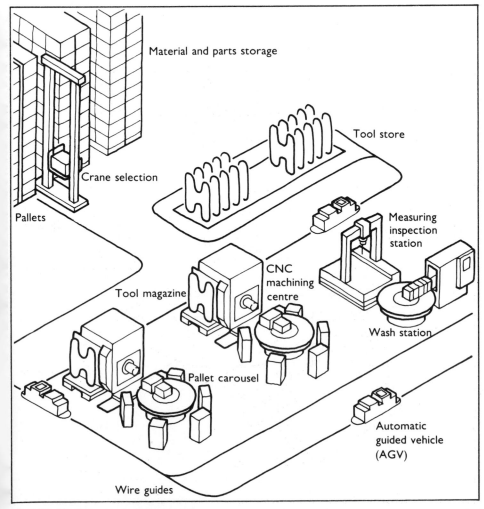

fig 7.85. Flexible manufacturing system

EXERCISES

1. Show by means of sketches what is meant by a GO/NO GO plug gauge.

2. Explain why bolt heads produced by forging are stronger than those cut from solid bar.

3. Explain by means of a simple sketch, the difference between piercing and blanking.

4. What is meant by a dimension expressed as 15.35 ± 0.15?

5. What is meant by foolproofing in jig and fixture design?

6. What does the term 'part programming' mean?

7. What is a closed loop control system?

8. What are the advantages and the disadvantages in using a sampling method of quality control?

9. Produce a design for a simple jig that could be used to aid the drilling of the holes in the cast aluminium component shown in fig 7.86.

10. Give two examples where aluminium extrusions may be found in and around the home. Explain briefly the principle of extrusion.

11. Explain what is meant by Direct Numerical Control (DNC).

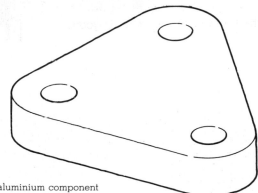

fig 7.86. Cast aluminium component

12. Electric current flowing through a high resistance will generate heat. How is this principle applied in the fabrication of car bodies?

13. How have the advances in silicon chip technology 'revolutionised' manufacturing industry?

14. Use sketches to explain the various types of solid modelling that can be used within computer aided design.

15. What design features should be avoided in components having a three dimensional form that are to be produced by pressing?

16. Discuss some of the advantages and disadvantages of CNC machine tools in manufacturing industries.

17. Injection moulding is a very common manufacturing process. Suggest why this is so, and list as many different everyday items produced by this process as you can. You should be able to list at least twelve.

18. Why is a wash station an important part of a flexible manufacturing system?

19. What is meant by the term 'semi-finished' products?

20. Produce a short program using absolute co-ordinates for finish turning the profile of the component shown in fig 7.87.

21. What is meant by 'buffer storage' with regard to both data storage and robot parts handling?

22. Discuss the merits of flexible manufacturing.

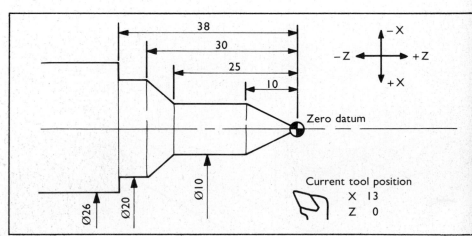

fig 7.87. Component to be finish turned

PRODUCT DESIGN

A product can be regarded as any object, artefact or system that has been produced as a response to a human need. The need may be that of an individual or of society in general; it may be a need to support human life or a need to provide pleasure. Some products are mass-produced, others by their nature or by intention, are produced as single, 'one-off' items.

Pens, pencils, tables, chairs, cars, television sets, cassette players, fashion clothes and aircraft are all products of human endeavour, they are examples of product design. The range of products is infinite and the purposes they serve may be very simple or extremely complex. In this chapter we shall look at the aspects of product design that relate mainly to industrial, manufactured products. We shall look at the product, its purpose and its life span, and also at the designer's role within the creation of the product. Finally, we shall try to consider what is good design.

fig 8.1.

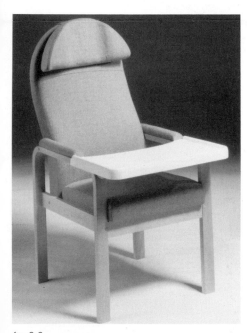

fig 8.2.

It is important to be aware of design in everyday objects. Consider the design input that has led to the creation of the things that surround you. Look at the chairs in the photographs and the chair you are sitting on now and ask yourself a few questions:
—What design brief do you imagine the designer had for each of these similar, but nonetheless different products?
—What environment were they designed to fit into; the home, an office, a school?
—To what degree do you think the product design was dictated by the eventual retail price and the manufacturing techniques to be used?
Much of product design is about looking and asking questions. It is about designing for a purpose to satisfy a specific need. It is also about evaluating and not being afraid to re-think designs in the light of experience.

fig 8.3.

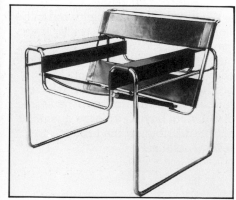

fig 8.4.

THE PRODUCT CYCLE

'They don't make things like they used to.' How often have you heard this said?
It is quite right of course. Very few things are ever made how they used to be
made and rightly so. Manufacturers are continually striving to improve their
products and reduce their manufacturing costs. Their aim is to gain a bigger
slice of the market by encouraging the consumer to buy their particular product,
rather than that of a competitor. The product must be either better, cheaper, or
both. Product design has to be a continuing process.

Early man was both his own
designer and his own manufacturer.
His need for the simple tools that made
his lifestyle possible were satisfied by
himself alone.

The first stage in the evolution of the
product cycle came about with the
village blacksmith and the local potter.
These people designed and made
products as required by the consumer,
who paid for this service with the food
they had grown or livestock they had
reared.

The next individual to enter the
cycle was the merchant or retailer.
This enabled the designer/
manufacturer to produce larger
quantities of the same product and
supply a single or a small number of
retailers. The retailer, in turn, was
able to stock several different
products, providing a better, more
convenient service for the consumer.

It is important to notice that at this
stage the consumer and the designer/
manufacturer become separated from
each other by a middle man, the
retailer. It was necessary, therefore,
for the retailer to keep the
designer/manufacturer informed of the
consumers' requirements. Failure to
feed back the consumer's evaluation of
the product to the designer, results in
design stagnation because the
designer was unaware of the need to
redesign.

Modern manufacturing industries
employ teams of market researchers to
determine consumer requirements and
consumer reaction to products already
on the market. This information is then
made available to the designer. The
designer has now become a specialist,
providing the designs from which the
manufacturer can realise the product.

We now have a complete, but rather
simple product cycle. In reality there
may be many more people involved:
bankers providing finance, production
engineers ensuring efficient
production methods, sub-contractors,
suppliers of standard components and
distributors buying in large quantities
and re-distributing the products to
several retailers.

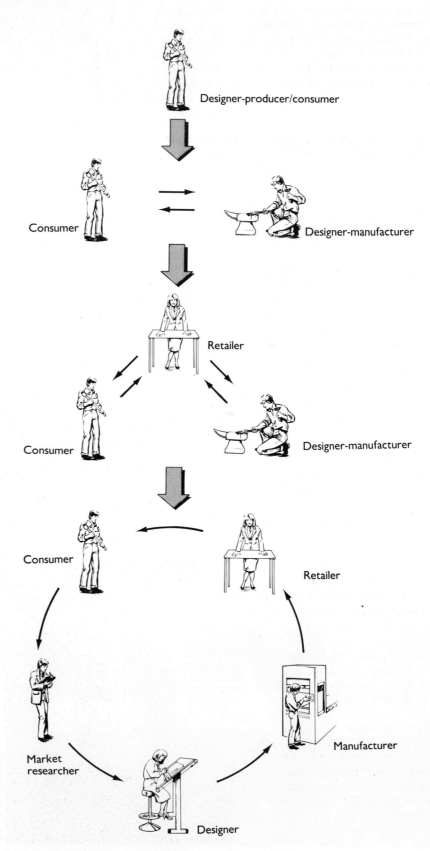

fig 8.5. Evolution of the product cycle

190

Design evolution

In order to see the relationship between all of those involved, it is helpful to visualise the processes that connect product design and the consumer in a circular form (Fig 8.5). You should also see the process as a spiral (Fig 8.6). With each revolution the design advances, each design improving upon the design that came before and this in turn leads to the next step forward. In this way design evolves and society progresses. Much of this progression may be as a result of changes in style, though some changes, such as those resulting from changes in fashion, may in fact advance the design very little.

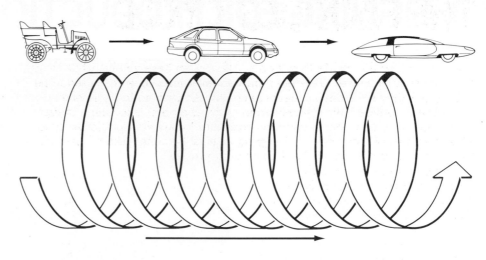

fig 8.6. Product design spiral

THE ROLE OF THE DESIGNER

The designer plays a key role within the product cycle; a designer is the link between the need and the reality, a far from simple role.

Design is about satisfying a need, it is about ideas and innovation. At the beginning of the design thinking, all things seem possible to the designer; his or her thinking must be divergent and encompass all possibilities. As the process continues so the thinking converges, until a final solution is arrived at: 'The beginning is all things, the end is one thing.'

Product design is also very often about compromise and being pulled in several directions. The product must primarily satisfy the identified needs of the consumer and be fit for the purpose for which it is designed, but the manufacturer will place constraints upon the designer's work. These usually revolve around cost; the manufacturing costs and the retail price. Designers are also often required to produce designs for products that are to have a limited life. They are designed to wear out and be replaced. This is called **planned obsolescence**.

Designs that may function well and look good, but cannot be manufactured to sell at the desired price or may never need replacing are not good from a manufacturer's point of view. It is the bringing together of these sometimes opposing standpoints that leads towards successful product design.

However, there is a third factor, the designer. Good design so often expresses the views, innovation and creativity of the designer. The successful designer is the one who finds the appropriate balance between these three factors, the manufacturer, the consumer and him or herself.

The anglepoise lamp in Fig 8.7 is regarded as a design classic, an example of product design so successful that this product has been in continuous manufacture with very few changes ever since it came onto the market in the early 1930s. The designer based the design on the joint mechanism of the human arm, the joints being held in constant tension by the springs, in a similar manner to the tension applied to arm joints by the arm muscles.

fig 8.7. Anglepoise lamp

DESIGNING FOR PRODUCTION

The ideal product design situation would exist if a designer created a design that was functional, aesthetically pleasing and was also satisfactory from an economic and production standpoint. This total concept of design, with consumer, function, cost and manufacture all receiving equal consideration is what is meant by 'design for production'. However, it is unrealistic to expect a single designer to be a specialist in all of these areas.

The product designer works by consultation with a manufacturer's production engineering department, or alongside a product methods engineer. These people are manufacturing technology specialists, and it is their responsibility to make or recommend design modifications in order to make production more efficient and more cost effective.

A 'design for production' philosophy means involving manufacturing specialists right from the first stages of design, it also means that conflict may sometimes arise and have to be resolved in order to reach a compromise and get a successful product onto the market. We will now look at just such a compromise.

THE CANON T-90 CAMERA

Until recently camera case design had changed very little since the Zeiss Contax S camera manufactured by Zeiss of Dresden, Germany in 1948 (fig 8.8). This was one of the first 35mm cameras in production that incorporated eye-level reflex viewing. Up to this point cameras used either a viewfinder or were held at chest height with the photographer looking down onto an internal mirror.

Camera cases had changed little because camera technology had made few advances. In the early 1980s this situation changed. The introduction of sophisticated electronics, LCD (liquid crystal display) and motorised film wind-on, prompted camera manufacturers, such as the Japanese company Canon, to re-examine camera case design. This evaluation led them to make a decision to re-design from scratch. Luigi Colani, a designer interested in natural form design, sometimes called 'bio-form', became involved with the Canon T-99 project, the design and development stage for a prototype top-of-the-range Canon camera.

fig 8.8. Zeiss Contax S camera

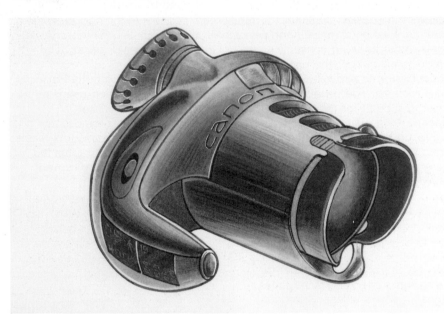
fig 8.9. Colani's early design sketch

fig 8.10. Prototype T-99 camera

192

Colani's early design sketches are shown in fig 8.9, they reflect his fascination with under-sea-form. The resulting prototype T-99 camera produced in collaboration with Canon's engineering department (fig 8.10) shows the influence that Colani's design has had on the softening of camera design.

The main collaboration, however, was to be between Canon's own 'in-house' design team and Colani, on a camera to go into production, the Canon T-90. Colani had no experience of designing a production-line camera and was unaware of the finer details of camera mechanics. Initially this resulted in fierce arguments and two opposing designs, with Colani calling the Canon designers conservative and the Canon designers accusing Colani's team of being impractical. The camera that was to go into production as the T-90 took the best aspects of both viewpoints and incorporated them into a product that is both a commercial and critical success. It has Colani's natural forms that are soft and fit the human hand, and it also incorporates advanced electronics and motor drive mechanism. The smaller, compact Canon Sure Shot pocket camera also shows Colani's influence in its curvaceous form (fig 8.11).

fig 8.11. Canon T-90 and Sureshot

STANDARDISATION

Standardisation means making use of standard material sizes, standard parts such as screws and gears, standard machine tools and cutting tools and even standard containers for storage and delivery. Sometimes the innovative and inventive designer may find all of this too conforming and a compromise has to be reached. However, the skilled designer will be creative and make full use of standard materials, rather than feel restricted by them.

It is of great economic benefit to use standard parts, particularly across a range of products and it is very common to find this. Screws, nuts, bolts and other such functional items are the most common examples, but consider some of the less obvious standard components that product designers make use of. A car has thousands. Amongst those that are easily visible are door handles and locks, wing mirrors, radio/cassette decks, dashboard symbols and switches, number plates, headlamps and many more. Next time you are in a car park, have a look at the different models, including commercial vehicles, that are made by one of the major car manufacturers and notice the large amount of standardisation that exists.

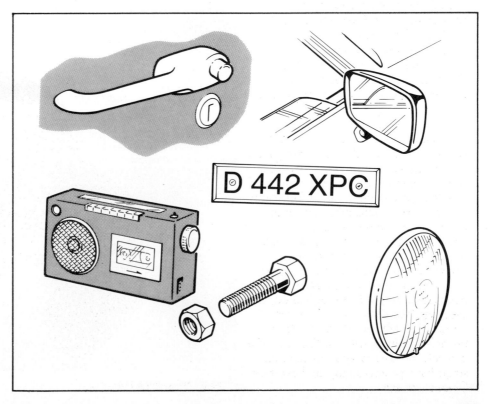

fig 8.12. Standardisation in functional items

SCALE OF PRODUCTION

While considering the designer's role, we saw that much of the design may be governed directly by the eventual retail price, the amount the consumer is willing to pay. Implicit within this is the scale of production.

In order to reduce costs, it is often economic to produce items in large quantities, and the product's design may need to be such that high volume or mass production is possible.

fig 8.13. One-off production

At the other end of the production scale we have **one-off production**, items that are produced singly. This may be because of the nature of the product, for example, a bridge or a communication satellite. In products of this type, safety and reliability are often a higher priority than the cost of manufacturing. There are also 'one-offs', such as jewellery, wedding dresses and shop fronts, where the emphasis is on the aesthetic rather than the functional with comparatively more consideration for cost.

In reality, design that has manufacturing cost as a low priority often results in products that are expensive to buy. Between one-off and mass production there is a level of production referred to as an **economic batch size**, products in such a quantity that to produce any less would increase the manufacturing cost to a level that the retail price would become unrealistic and the product would not sell. For example, a chain of fast food restaurants may require tables in such a quantity that it becomes economic to design and manufacture that particular product specifically for that restaurant chain. This has an additional advantage in creating a corporate image.

fig 8.14. McDonalds — corporate image

Batch production in an industrial manufacturing situation is a system of producing identical items in fixed quantities or 'batches'. These quantities may be small or they may be very large depending on the economics of that particular product. When the production of a batch is complete, the machine tools used in that production are then available for use in producing a batch of different components.

fig 8.15. Inside McDonalds — standardised fittings

Mass production refers to the practice of producing items in such a quantity that after the initial high 'tooling up' costs have been recovered, the cost of manufacture is as low as possible. Mass production of any particular product will vary in scale, according to the product. One of the most complex mass produced products is the car. Cars have around 15,000 separate component parts and Ford produce some 7,500 vehicles every working day in their factories in Europe alone. This is high volume production, but consider how many thousands of pens, chocolate bars or cassette tapes are produced every day, and how much a single design change that may save 1p on each of these would be worth to the manufacturer over a one-year period.

fig 8.16. Mass production

MARKETING

Marketing is the process of deciding whether a market exists and consequently supplying that market demand. At one level a craftsman or an artist can respond to the demand for a product by working as an individual with investment only in tools and materials. At another level large multi-national companies often spend large sums of money on market research and advertising before manufacturing and selling their products.

ADVERTISING

Advertising is the business of encouraging people to buy a particular product, sometimes in preference to a similar product made by another manufacturer and sometimes by persuading the prospective consumer that here is a product that they need or want. Thus, advertising can actually create a market where one did not previously exist. For these reasons the advertising industry is, itself, very big business.

CONSUMER ADVICE AND PROTECTION

Over the last twenty years a lot of legislation has come into force to protect the consumer. Manufacturers' products must comply with legal requirements and reach strict standards, particularly with regard to safety and to honesty in advertising. Some of this legislation has been introduced as a result of pressure brought to bear on governments by the Consumers' Association, and television programmes like 'Watch Dog' and 'That's Life'.

The Consumers' Association is a body of people, independent of any particular manufacturer, who, among other things, publish 'Which?' magazine. This magazine contains reports based both upon specialist research and testing and upon feedback from consumers who have used a particular product over a period of time. 'Which?' deals with the fitness for purposes of all types of products, from child's toys to washing machines. Magazines and TV programmes of this type enable people to make informed purchases, based upon evaluations carried out by others.

MARKET RESEARCH

Before any big company begins design work on a product, large amounts of market research are undertaken. Market research can determine exactly what the market requirements are, and the more detailed this research, the better are the chances of getting the right product on the market at the right price. Large car manufacturers spend several million pounds on market research before entering into any design work for new models. This, along with money spent on advertising, has been proved to be money well spent.

There are four main methods of carrying out market research:

1. Observation: by simply observing traffic congestion in a town centre, the need for a bypass or a one-way traffic system can be determined. The actual solution to be adopted may require much more detailed research.

2. Questionnaires: this has become the most popular method of market research, particularly with regard to consumer products. The consumer is asked to respond to a series of tightly-structured questions, usually with a limited choice of answers. This type of structured questionnaire allows for a quick, often computer aided, analysis of the results.

Market research using questionnaires may be carried out by somebody employed by the manufacturing company or by an independent market research organisation. This may take the form of a researcher/consumer question and answer session in the high street, it may be conducted over the telephone (telemarketing) or, alternatively, by post.

3. Consumer interviews: researchers bring together a small group of consumers, usually in a pleasant relaxed environment, to discuss a product or prototype. The discussion is structured and led by the researcher in order to concentrate on the critical design features.

4. Unstructured interviews: the previous market research methods are considered inappropriate for high cost products, such as shipping and military equipment, where the person being interviewed may be the head of a large organisation or a government representative. In this situation it is necessary for a knowledgeable interviewer to enter into an unstructured, wide-ranging discussion with the prospective consumer and then draw his of her own conclusions afterwards.

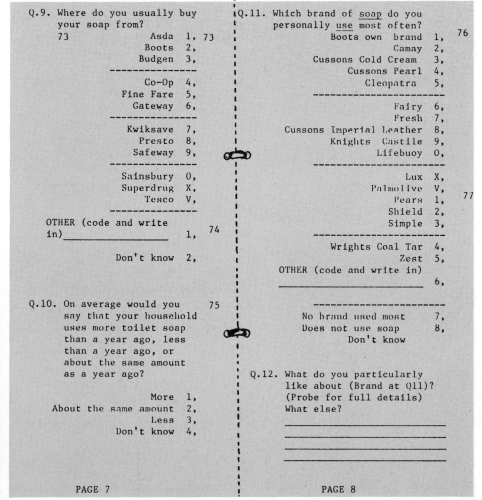

```
Q.9.  Where do you usually buy           Q.11. Which brand of soap do you
      your soap from?                           personally use most often?
      73              Asda     1,  73                   Boots own brand   1,    76
                      Boots    2,                                 Camay   2,
                      Budgen   3,              Cussons Cold Cream   3,
                      --------------              Cussons Pearl   4,
                      Co-Op    4,                       Cleopatra   5,
                      Fine Fare 5,                 --------------------
                      Gateway  6,                             Fairy   6,
                      --------------                          Fresh   7,
                      Kwiksave 7,      Cussons Imperial Leather   8,
                      Presto   8,              Knights Castile   9,
                      Safeway  9,                     Lifebuoy   0,
                      --------------              --------------------
                      Sainsbury 0,                            Lux   X,
                      Superdrug X,                       Palmolive   V,
                      Tesco    V,                           Pears   1,    77
                      --------------                        Shield   2,
      OTHER (code and write                               Simple   3,
      in)_____ 1,  74              --------------------
                                              Wrights Coal Tar   4,
              Don't know  2,                               Zest   5,
                                       OTHER (code and write in)
                                                              6,
                                              --------------------
Q.10. On average would you      75          No brand used most   7,
      say that your household                Does not use soap   8,
      uses more toilet soap                       Don't know
      than a year ago, less
      than a year ago, or
      about the same amount           Q.12. What do you particularly
      as a year ago?                        like about (Brand at Q11)?
                                            (Probe for full details)
              More      1,                  What else?
      About the same amount 2,              _____
              Less      3,                  _____
              Don't know 4,                 _____
                                            _____

      PAGE 7                                PAGE 8
```

fig 8.17. Sample from a market research questionnaire

WHAT IS GOOD DESIGN?

It is relatively easy to look back over the last 60 years and give examples of well designed products, designs that have stood the test of time with only minimal changes. The anglepoise lamp mentioned earlier, the Parker 51 fountain pen, first produced in 1939 or Alec Issigonis Mini Minor, the car that in 1959, was to set the standard for European small car design for many years to follow are all good examples. It is reasonable to suggest that any product that has been on the market and selling consistently for many years, is an example of good product design. It is important to establish design criteria in order to be able to recognise and promote good design.

fig 8.18. Parker 51 fountain pen

fig 8.19. Mini Minor

fig 8.20. Crystal Palace

The Crystal Palace, built to house the Great Exhibition, was an example of the best of Victorian design. Built in less than six months, it was three times the length of St. Paul's cathedral and had more than a million square feet of glass.

In the years following the Industrial Revolution, Britain became established as the world's greatest industrial manufacturing nation. In 1851 the Great Exhibition, a 'Great Exhibition of the Works of Industry of all Nations', was held at the Crystal Palace in Hyde Park, London. The aim was to show off British industry to the rest of the world.

One of the other things that the exhibition did was to highlight the excesses of Victorian taste, with the ornamentation of almost everything. Following the Great Exhibition many people set about encouraging and promoting what they saw as good design, for example, the Arts and Crafts Movement, whose central figure, William Morris, rejected the Great Exhibition as 'wonderfully ugly'.

Later, in 1919, Walter Gropius founded the Bauhaus in Germany, a school of designers whose designs have had a tremendous influence on product design.

fig 8.21. Bauhaus teapot

The example of Bauhaus design from the 1920s in fig 8.21 shows a teapot by Marianne Brandt in copper with an ebony handle. The table lamp by Wilhelm Wagenfield (fig 8.22) is of chromium-plated steel. A version of this lamp is still available in some department stores in Britain today.

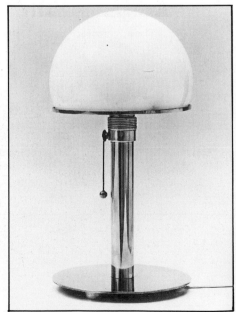

fig 8.22. Bauhaus table lamp

In the 1940s, the government in Britain established the Council of Industrial Design, the purpose of which was 'to promote by all practicable means the improvement of design in the products of British industry. The Council was well received by both industry and the public.

In 1949 the Council of Industrial Design launched *Design* magazine. In the first issue of *Design*, the Council Director, Gordon Russell wrote an article entitled 'Good design is not a luxury', in which he included some principles of good design:

'Good design always takes into account the technique of production, the material to be used, and the purpose for which the object is wanted.'
'Good design is not precious, arty or high falutin.'
'Good design is not something that can be added to a product at a late stage in its planning or manufacture. It is fundamental.'

THE DESIGN COUNCIL

In 1972 the Council of Industrial Design became the Design Council, as we know it today. The Design Council offers an advisory and information service for designers and manufacturers, funding to enable companies to afford expert design and Design Centre Selection.

The familiar 'selected for the Design Centre' label (fig 8.23) signifies that a product has been selected following assessment using the Design Council's criteria. The panel that carries out the assessment is made up of designers, manufacturer's journalists and professional buyers.

In looking at the question, 'What is good design?', it is well worth looking at the selection criteria used by the Design Council for Design Centre Selection.

fig 8.23.

fig 8.24. The four British Design award winners for 1987

Performance: does the product satisfy its performance specification and, if so, is the specification itself satisfactory, i.e. does the product do what it was designed to do?

Construction: are the materials, finishes and assemblies such that the product will continue to perform reliably for its specified lifespan, or for what the user would expect to be a reasonable life span?

Ergonomics: is the product easy to use and maintain? Are the instructions, if any, adequate in describing the use or maintenance of the product?

Aesthetics: are the forms, colours, patterns and textures appropriate to the function of the product?

Value for money: does the price of the product seem reasonable in relation to its characteristics and in relation to similar products on the market?

Products selected by the Design Council are on display in the Design Centres of London, Cardiff, Glasgow and Belfast.

The Design Council is also responsible for the annual British Design Awards, awarded to around 25 products each year that are considered to be the best examples of British design. The 1987 awards included a fire-fighting platform, a high-speed microprocessor on a single silicon chip called a transputer, a co-ordinated range of knitwear and a low cost, low speed mini aircraft.

PRODUCT DESIGN CASE STUDY
BOXFORD 125 TCL

fig 8.25. Boxford 125 TCL

Boxford Ltd are a Yorkshire based machine tool manufacturer who have become
well established as manufacturers of machine tools particularly suitable for
schools and colleges.

In 1984, the company recognised a need for a CNC training lathe for the
schools and colleges market and, using their own 'in house' engineering design
team, they were able to begin work on preliminary designs for just such a
product. The early realisation that they had a potentially very marketable
product, prompted Boxford to consider bringing in an industrial design
consultant, with the aim of ensuring that the aesthetics and ergonomics of the
new lathe would reflect its high technical standard.

The designers who became involved in the project were Heights Design of
Halifax. It is interesting to see how during the process of designing this product,
design and ideas from both Boxford and Heights develop and, through
compromise, either evolve towards the reality of the final product or are
rejected.

The design brief
Heights' design brief centred on the following key points:

1. To design a small educational CNC lathe, from the original concept stage
   through to initial detailing, including a study into the ergonomic aspects of
   the machine.

2. The machine will be made with existing Boxford Ltd technology, i.e. sheet
   metal work.

3. The computer supplied will be a BBC micro, therefore, the aesthetics of the
   computer must be considered in the styling of the machine.

4. It is envisaged that a new aesthetic is to be created to move away from the
   established 'lathe look-alike' machine.

Boxford clearly had a very good idea of what they required: an educational CNC machine, constructed primarily from sheet metal and using a BBC micro computer. They had also made the decision to have a slant bed lathe, rather than one of conventional layout. Slant beds are becoming popular in industrial CNC machines on account of the easy access for loading and unloading using robot arms and the ease with which swarf falls away from the cutting areas. In an educational training situation this designs offers an unrestricted view of the turning operation, so students do not need to look or lean over the tool post.

Having made these decisions and formulated the brief, the Heights designers were also supplied with engineering drawings giving the relationship and sizes of the machine's major components. One of these is reproduced below.

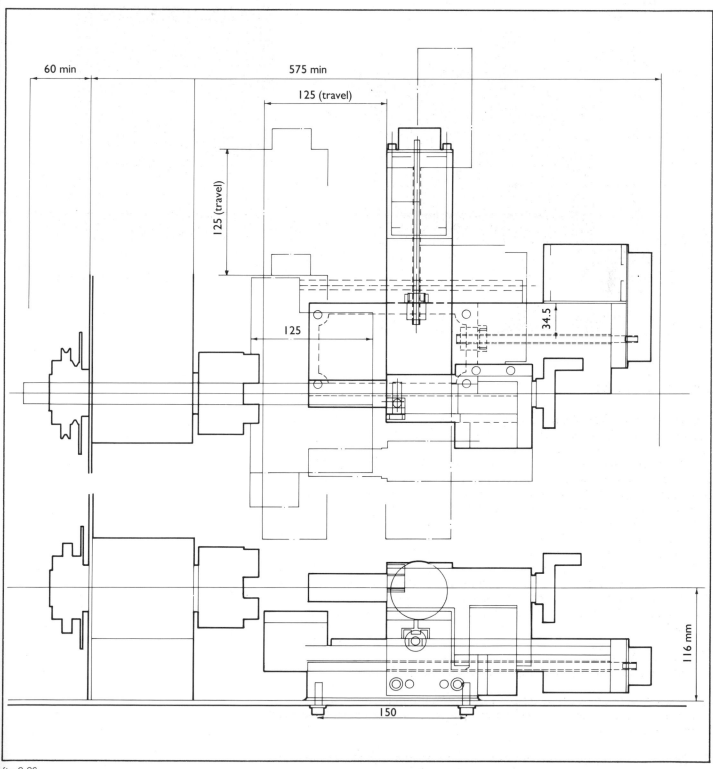

fig 8.26.

Fig 8.26 shows the minimum internal size that can accommodate the lathe bed, chuck and headstock (575mm) and the minimum internal space required to house the drive belt pulleys (60mm). The drawing also shows the amount of travel of each axis (125mm). The travel is the maximum distance that the slides move from one extreme to the other. This information is essential before design work can begin on the casing of the machine.

INITIAL IDEAS

The first piece of design work to be carried out was a series of drawings exploring the possible form that the machine might take, and the positions and relationship of the major features: the computer keyboard, the machines own control pad, the machine guard and the monitor screen.

You can see how the designer varies the profile of the machine by using curves on the front and differing angles of slope. The machine controls and their relationship to the computer keyboard is tried out, as is the size of the see—through machine guard.

The design sketches here are only a sample of the many sketches produced by Heights designers at this stage. In the early stages of design it is important to introduce as many ideas and variations as possible, while still remaining within the confines of the brief and, in this instant, having regard for the other limitations discussed.

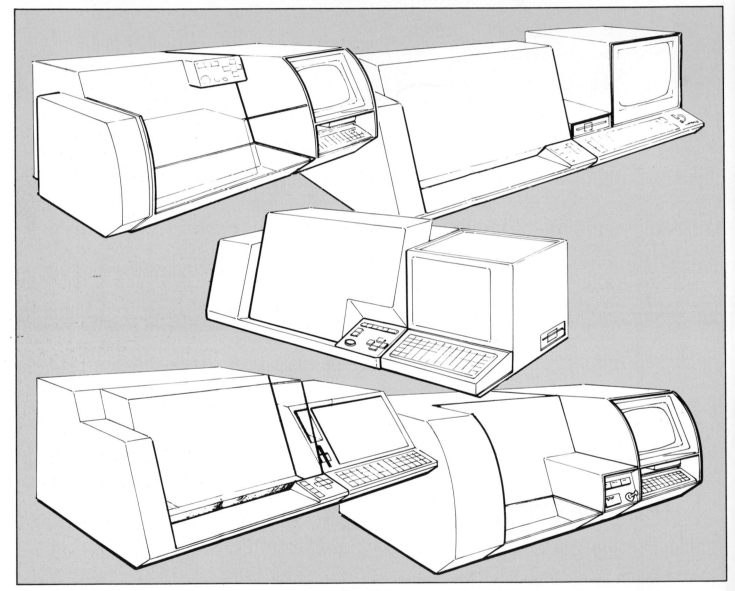

fig 8.27. Initial design sketches

Having formulated these preliminary ideas, Heights Designers entered into discussion with the Boxford designers and decided on one or two possible design solutions. This is an example of divergent thinking converging on a solution. The next stage, developing the idea, requires more divergence of ideas, but within a much tighter framework.

At a quick glance, the development of ideas sketches (fig 8.28) seem to be all the same, but you should look closely at these drawings and see the amount of variation and development that is taking place. Again, these are just a sample of the 20 or more produced by the designer. You can see how the angles of the slope on the front of the machine varies, as does the size of the drive belt cover. The clear acrylic machine guard, in particular, goes through a lot of changes, and lifting handles on the front edge appear in some designs and not others.

DEVELOPMENT OF THE CHOSEN DESIGN

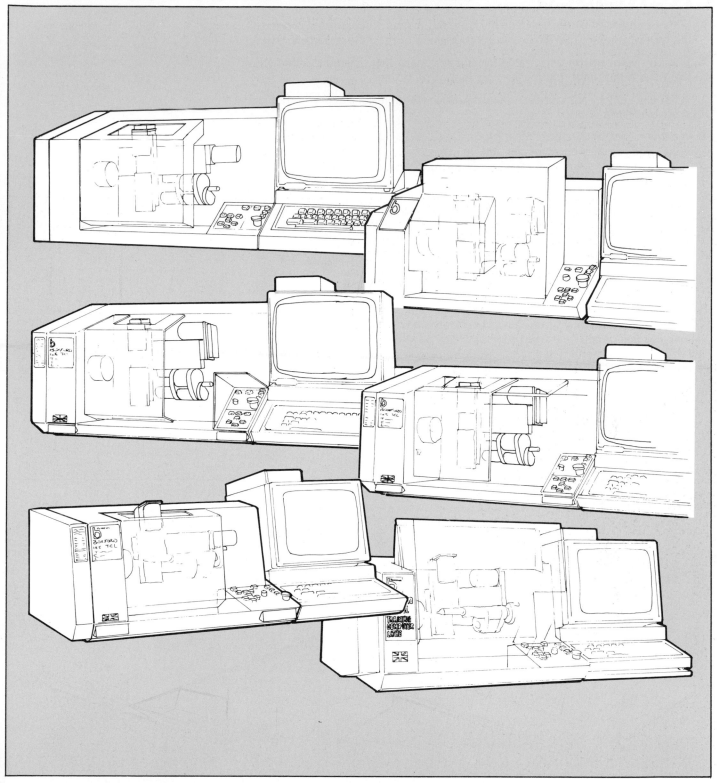

fig 8.28. Development sketches

The final design can be seen in the photograph of the machine currently in production (fig 8.25). This followed first a full size card model, and then a working prototype.

The final decisions rested with Boxford's production engineers who were responsible for the manufacture of the product. Heights designers would have preferred there to be no visible handles on the front of the machine, but rather a recess in the sheet steel fabrication. This would improve the clean line of the front of the machine and its relationship with the BBC micro. Boxford's engineers decided that the increased manufacturing costs would be too much and opted instead for bolt on handles that can be removed if required.

If it is to be successful, product design often has to be about compromise. The Boxford 125 Training Computer Lathe is an example of sensible compromise in design that resulted in a successful product.

EXERCISES

1. Give examples of two methods of carrying out market research and suggest the type of product that would be appropriate to each of the examples given.

2. What is meant by the term 'value for money'? Make lists of products that you feel offer good value for money and those that do not.

3. What is meant by standardisation? Give some examples of standardisation in product design.

4. What is meant by the term 'mass production', and why should the design of mass produced products be studied very closely?

5. With regard to product design, what is meant by 'The beginning is all things, the end is one thing'?

6. Why is compromise so important in product design?

7. What is meant by the term 'batch production'?

8. In your own words, say what is meant by good design. Give some examples of household objects that are examples of good design and some where you feel that the design has certain faults.

9. Devise a questionnaire that could be used to determine the important design features that consumers feel should be incorporated in a pencil case. Have a look at some pencil cases and see how many have been designed with regard to the criteria that you have determined as important. Produce some designs for a pencil case that would satisfy the consumers' requirements.

10. Design a desk tidy suitable for mass production using the existing technology of your school workshop, that could be made as cheaply as possible. You may need to design jigs to aid the production (see Manufacturing Technologies).

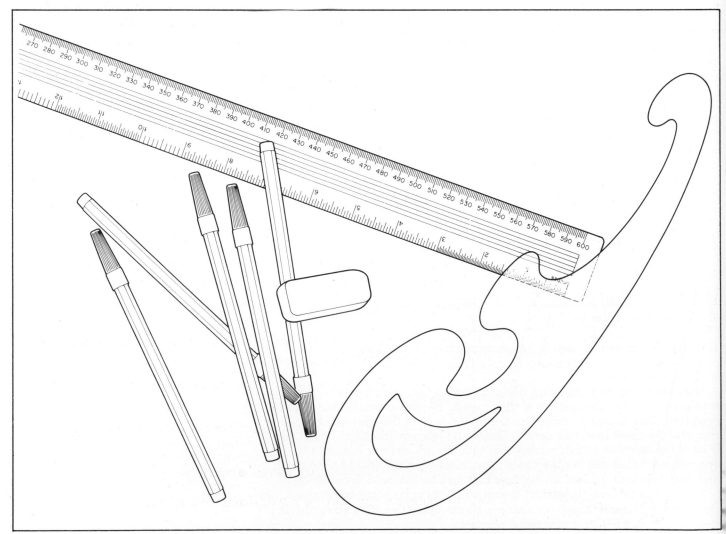

fig 8.29. Desk top items needing storage

PROJECT WORK

Your design projects will carry a large percentage of the marks in any examination. In order to gain the best possible mark you must learn how to **manage** your project work. The points highlighted on this page, and examples of projects given later in this chapter, will help you develop project management skills.

Different examination syllabuses have different structures for their project work and it is wise to follow the structure set by the examining group if possible. Your teacher may provide you with a great deal of support by telling you exactly what he wishes to see in your design folder and the way it should be presented. However, if no structure is provided, the format set out on page 12 of this book may be helpful.

The nature of project work means that it is very easy to fall behind. Therefore, it is wise to devise a plan for the whole project as soon as possible. A sensible policy is to divide the overall time allocation for your project into small sections so that individual targets can be identified and met. This avoids the embarrassing situation of 'bottle necks' where many things are required at the same time and you have little chance of producing any of them to the required standard.

At an early stage in the project things which may take a long time should be identified and acted upon. These may include letters requesting information or materials and components.

A consistent effort throughout the course nearly always produces the best results because very rarely can a project be neglected for a long period and then revived and completed in the final weeks of the course.

It is useful to lay down a few basic rules before beginning a project so that the time can be used as productively as possible. It will also help the finished folder to take on the appearance of one project and not a whole series of individual pieces of work assembled at the last minute for the examiner. A sensible list of rules might be as follows:

1. Establish the size of paper on which your project will be presented. A number of smaller drawings and photographs can be mounted to make complete sheets. Never throw any work away no matter how insignificant it may appear.

2. Decide upon a common layout for each sheet of paper. This may simply be a border around the edge of the paper but it can be developed to include a personal logo made from your initials.

3. Decide upon the colour, size and style of lettering for the page headings. If these are the same it will help to tie the project together.

4. Be aware of the sections that your project must include. You may use a chart similar to that shown below to plot your progress.

DATE	ACTIVITY	SIGNED
20/1/88	ANALYSIS	CMMA
15/2/88	RESEARCH	J.I.C.
2/3/88	SPECIFICATION	MMMA

5. Make sure all work is kept in a folder and this is stored in a safe place when not being worked upon.

Once the project is underway you may use a checklist similar to the one shown below to establish the level of progress that is being achieved.

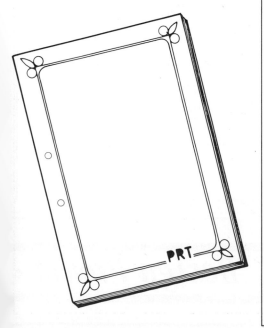

PROGRESS CHECKLIST

- Do you know the date by which the completed project must be handed in?

- Have you divided the time allowed so that you have a realistic time scale for completing all sections of the work?

- Have you a folder in which all your design work is kept?

- Do you know in what format your project is to be presented?

- Are you regularly working on your design folder out of lesson time?

- Have you carried out sufficient research to allow a full range of solutions to the problem to be developed?

- Will the proposed solution satisfy your specification?

- Have you produced working drawings in sufficient detail that will allow the final design to be realised?

- Are the materials or components that you require to realise your design readily available?

- Is the equipment available in school that will allow the design to be realised?

- What progress did you make during the last lesson?

- What progress do you hope to make during the next lesson?

ANALYSIS

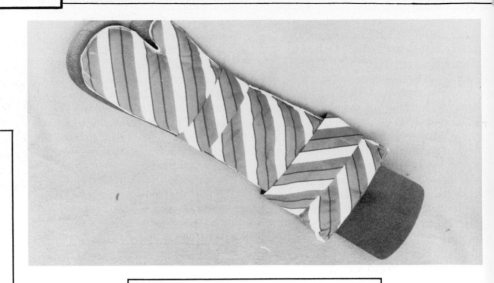

Oven to Worktop Transfer Aid
Nicholas Whitlock

Nicholas has been given a project based upon 'Holding and Supporting'. He has decided to look at the problems that are encountered by people who suffer from arthritis. Within his analysis of this problem he is therefore looking at what arthritis actually is and how people are affected by it.

Having recognised the problems that exist for arthritis sufferers Nicholas has set himself the task of designing and making an 'Oven to Worktop Transfer Aid'.
He has carried out this second part of his analysis by making short comments under a series of selected headings. It is often very helpful to carry out an analysis in this manner. The headings used here will not of course be appropriate for all design and realisation projects.

The realisation of Nicholas Oven to Worktop Transfer Aid comprises a long brightly striped oven glove that is attached using wide strips of fabric and velcro tape to a contoured rigid GRP support. The support extends past the elbow joint onto the upper arm and provides very positive support for the wrist and fingers.

From speaking to several elderly people and general observation it is apparent that ARTHRITIS is a general, serious complaint which can attack people as early in life as 25 years. This crippling disease is as good as any to try to make less painful by designing a new aid.
Basically there are two types of arthritis
(a) OSTEO-ARTHRITIS
(b) RHEUMATOID-ARTHRITIS
The information shown here will try to outline where the disease strikes and what the effect is.
OSTEO-ARTHRITIS: A degenerative joint disease in which the protective, shock-absorbing cartilage space between the bones wears away.
It effects mainly the hip, knee, spine, **WRIST** and **FINGERS**.
It may result in pain, swelling, lack of strength and abnormality in the joint.
Over-use of the effected joint **SHOULD BE AVOIDED**.
RHEUMATOID-ARTHRITIS: The bodies own antigens attack the synovial membrane causing swollen joints, stiffness, limited movement, lack of strength in the joint etc
Areas worst affected are **FINGERS** and feet primarily, then **WRISTS**, knees, shoulders, ankles and **ELBOWS**.

N.Whitlock : C.D.T. Design Project :

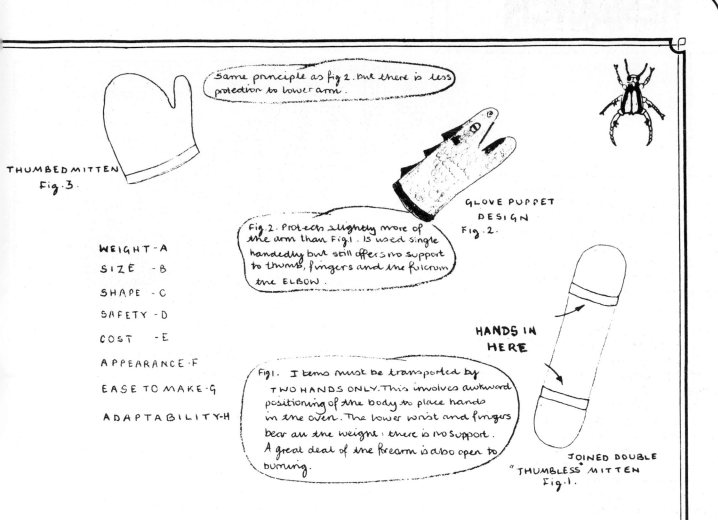

THUMBED MITTEN
Fig. 3.

Same principle as fig 2. but there is less protection to lower arm.

GLOVE PUPPET
DESIGN
Fig. 2.

Fig. 2. Protects slightly more of the arm than Fig. 1. Is used single handedly but still offers no support to thumb, fingers and the fulcrum the ELBOW.

WEIGHT - A

SIZE - B

SHAPE - C

SAFETY - D

COST - E

APPEARANCE - F

EASE TO MAKE - G

ADAPTABILITY - H

Fig 1. Items must be transported by TWO HANDS ONLY. This involves awkward positioning of the body to place hands in the oven. The lower wrist and fingers bear all the weight; there is no support. A great deal of the forearm is also open to burning.

HANDS IN
HERE

JOINED DOUBLE
"THUMBLESS" MITTEN
Fig. 1.

A : Obviously this should be minimal as old muscle tissue is fragile and weak.

B : This ties in with adaptability : Obviously the aid does not want to be too bulky.

C : There are several previous "oven-glove" designs which could be adapted and improved upon for the disabled person.

D : Safety. The design would need to be flame resistant, reasonably non-conducting, no sharp interior pieces (elderly people often bleed severely on grazing due to a lack of blood proteins or clotting platelets in the plasma).

E : Obviously this should be minimal but enough money spent on the real design to ensure maximum efficiency.

F : Preferably bright materials on the surface : elderly people often have poor vision. B// white reflects the heat, black absorbs ..

G : Should be relatively basic, especially if new fabric working ie sewing is involved (A new field entirely!)

H : Should be certain elasticity in design to allow for a degree of variation in physical size and shape

Holding & Supporting.

No. 10

Educational Toy
Angela Corcoran

The area of education that Angela is looking at is learning to walk.
Some of her research involves investigating the stages of development that a child makes when learning to walk.
She refers to visits taken to toy shops and how she was looking particularly at what seems to be lacking on the market. As you can see she has decided to enhance her written work with some interesting drawings.

Following this initial research Angela used anthropometric data from British Standards for schools and colleges PP7310. This was available in her CDT resource area and it enabled her to determine the critical sizes for her toy.
The outcome is a sturdy push along engine that clicks as it moves and has a chimney that bobs up and down.

BASIC STAGES.

1. Crawling.

This is an important stage before walking and toys that will move along when the baby pushes it so that he crawls along to push it again and so-on, encourage his learning in this way. He cannot yet balance on his own but there is a need for fairly large, brightly coloured toys to keep the baby moving forward. My visits to toy shops and looking through catalogues have brought to my attention the lack of variety in the toys available on the market. The only ones I thought would really help this stage are inflatable cylinders containing coloured balls for the child to roll along and a wind-up train-engine that the baby will crawl after. I did not however, find any that made an interesting noise at the same time.

2. STANDING

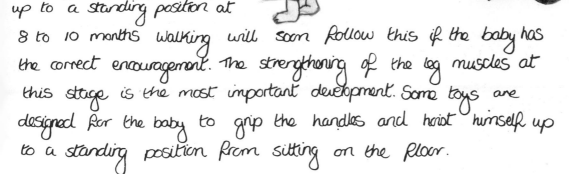

Most babies pull themselves up to a standing position at 8 to 10 months. Walking will soon follow this if the baby has the correct encouragement. The strengthening of the leg muscles at this stage is the most important development. Some toys are designed for the baby to grip the handles and hoist himself up to a standing position from sitting on the floor.

3. WALKING.

The baby is now trying to move his legs, one after another, and having learnt that this is required, he can move along, but his balance is not yet refined. This is why baby-walkers and push along carts and soft toys are required to help his learning.

They need to be designed so they are light enough for the child to manoeuvre easily, yet sturdy enough to prevent tipping over easily, safety being an important factor for small children.

CONCLUSION TO RESEARCH.

When a child is learning to walk, he requires a good quality, safe sturdy toy to help the development. At this stage I have decided to investigate the design of this particular type of educative toy.

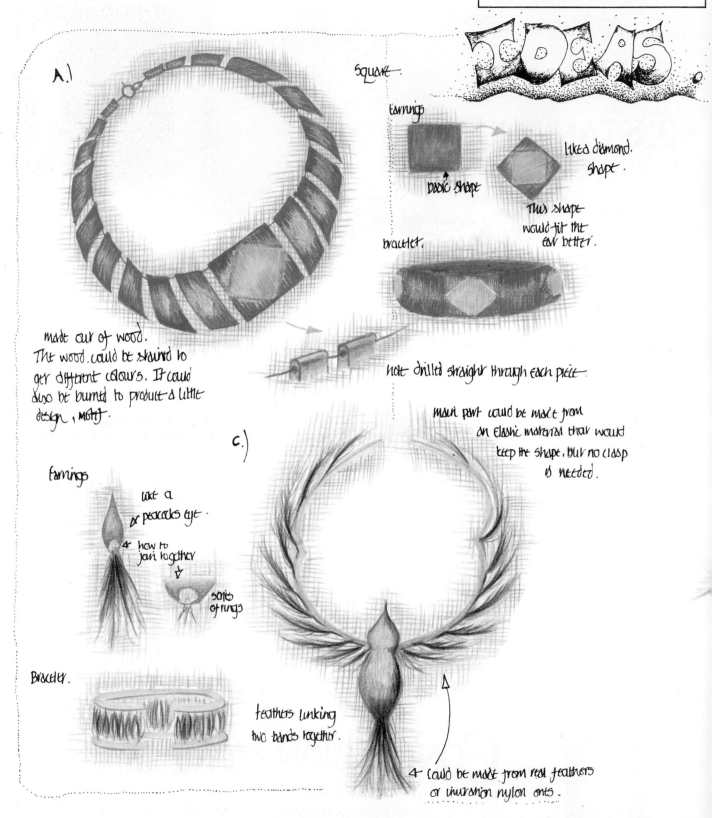

A.)

IDEAS

Square.

earrings

Basic shape

liked diamond.
shape.

This shape
would fit the
ear better.

bracelet.

made out of wood.
The wood. could be stained to
get different colours. It could
also be burned to produce a little
design, motif.

hole drilled straight through each piece.

main part could be made from
an elastic material that would
keep the shape, but no clasp
is needed.

C.)

Earrings

like a
or peacocks eye.

← how to
join together

series
of rings

Bracelet.

feathers linking
two bands together.

← could be made from real feathers
or imitation nylon ones.

Rachel's ideas are presented here in a very interesting way. She has used a combination of pencil crayon and felt tip pen.
It is always a good idea to add some comments on the materials and methods of manufacture that may later be adopted when making your project, as well as an evaluation of your ideas. Idea (B) 'Arrowhead' was the idea that was later developed and realised.

Earring

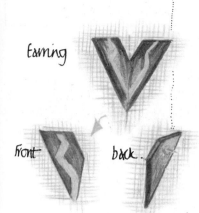

Arrowhead
B.)

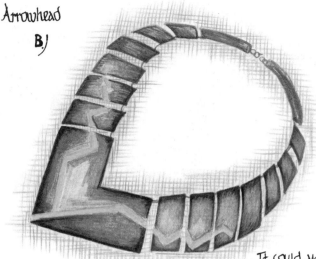

front   back.

How to join
together.

It could also
be made out of
wood.

This set could be made out
of acrylic the motif could
be produced by milling an
indentation, which is then filled
with a plastic resin.

Bird.

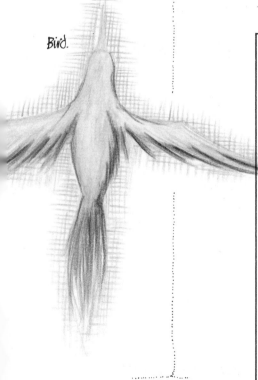

This would look very
stunning done in bright
enamels. maybe taking
the colours from the
kingfisher.

EVALUATION.

Idea A
With this idea I like the colour co-ordination, though I would
probably use a darker blue (navy blue) and the orange
wouldn't be so bright. I feel however this idea wouldn't be
very appealing it doesn't seem to stand out, apart from the
colour scheme used.

Idea B.
This idea is very striking the necklace would look very
attractive, however, the earrings and bracelet would need some
alteration in design as I don't feel that it fits together very
well as a set. The choice of material would best be wood, as
acrylic would be too harsh and might not appeal too everyone.
Wood has a more universal appeal (natural look of grain).

Idea C.
This idea I feel might be a little too gaudy the band
should be really silver in colour as this would contrast better
with the blue and purple.
I don't feel this idea would appeal to many people. The
bracelet would need to be redesigned and the centre piece of the
necklace would have too be made a lot smaller.

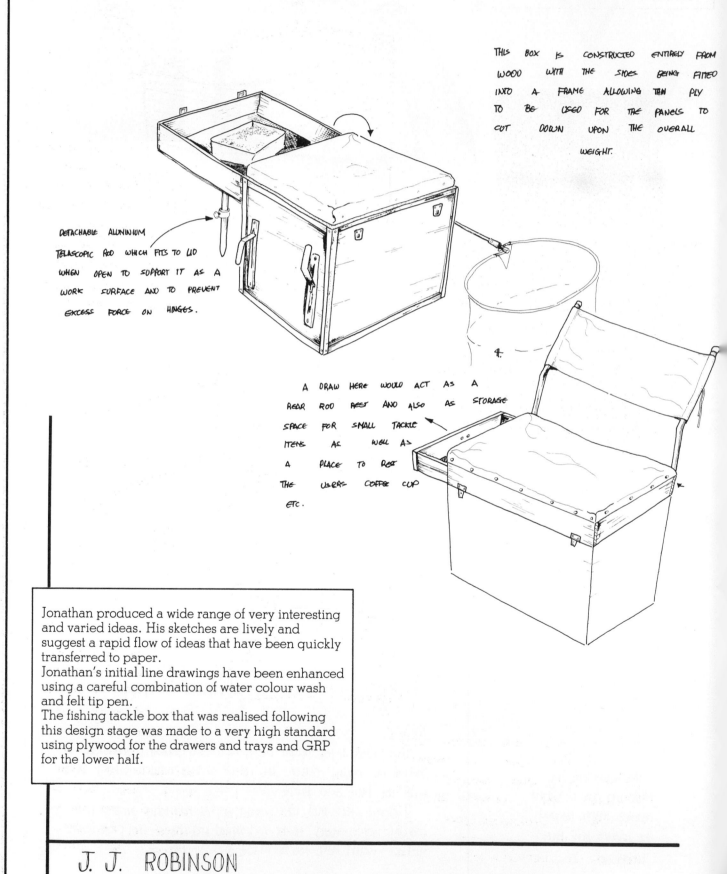

THIS BOX IS CONSTRUCTED ENTIRELY FROM WOOD WITH THE SIDES BEING FITTED INTO A FRAME ALLOWING THIN PLY TO BE USED FOR THE PANELS TO CUT DOWN UPON THE OVERALL WEIGHT.

DETACHABLE ALUMINIUM TELASCOPIC ROD WHICH FITS TO LID WHEN OPEN TO SUPPORT IT AS A WORK SURFACE AND TO PREVENT EXCESS FORCE ON HINGES.

A DRAW HERE WOULD ACT AS A REAR ROD REST AND ALSO AS STORAGE SPACE FOR SMALL TACKLE ITEMS AS WELL AS A PLACE TO REST THE USERS COFFEE CUP ETC.

Jonathan produced a wide range of very interesting and varied ideas. His sketches are lively and suggest a rapid flow of ideas that have been quickly transferred to paper.
Jonathan's initial line drawings have been enhanced using a careful combination of water colour wash and felt tip pen.
The fishing tackle box that was realised following this design stage was made to a very high standard using plywood for the drawers and trays and GRP for the lower half.

J. J. ROBINSON

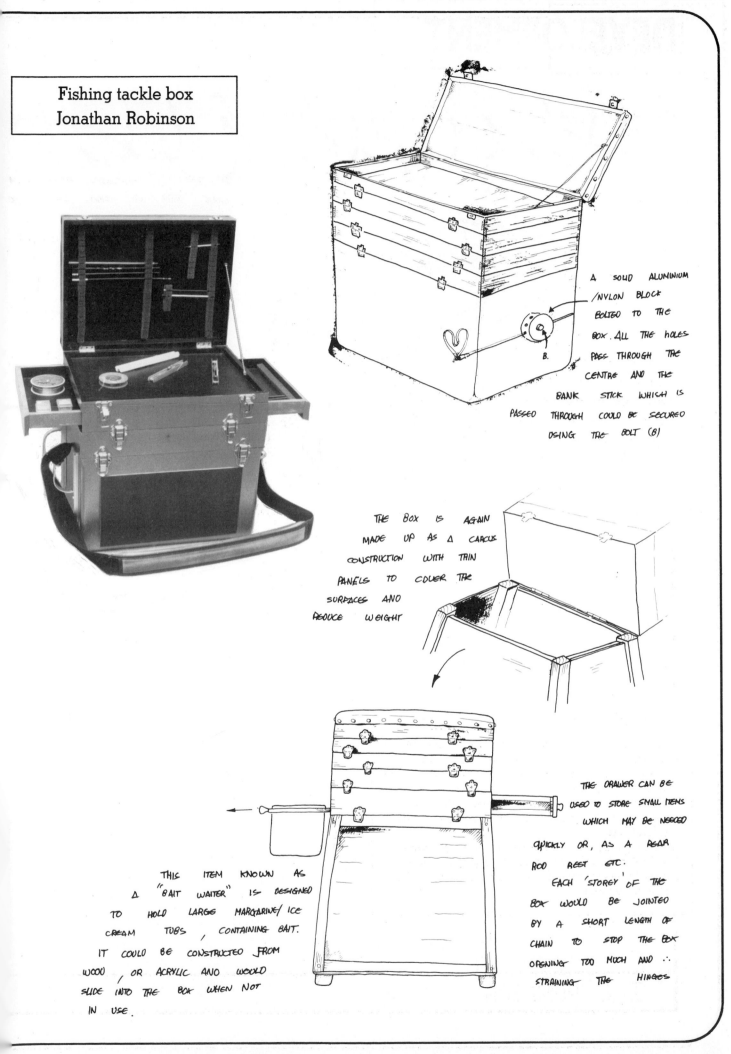

Fishing tackle box
Jonathan Robinson

A SOLID ALUMINIUM /NYLON BLOCK BOLTED TO THE BOX. ALL THE HOLES PASS THROUGH THE CENTRE AND THE BANK STICK WHICH IS PASSED THROUGH COULD BE SECURED USING THE BOLT (B)

B.

THE BOX IS AGAIN MADE UP AS A CARCUS CONSTRUCTION WITH THIN PANELS TO COVER THE SURFACES AND REDUCE WEIGHT

THE DRAWER CAN BE USED TO STORE SMALL ITEMS WHICH MAY BE NEEDED QUICKLY OR, AS A REAR ROD REST ETC.
EACH 'STOREY' OF THE BOX WOULD BE JOINTED BY A SHORT LENGTH OF CHAIN TO STOP THE BOX OPENING TOO MUCH AND ∴ STRAINING THE HINGES

THIS ITEM KNOWN AS A "BAIT WAITER" IS DESIGNED TO HOLD LARGE MARGARINE/ ICE CREAM TUBS, CONTAINING BAIT. IT COULD BE CONSTRUCTED FROM WOOD, OR ACRYLIC AND WOULD SLIDE INTO THE BOX WHEN NOT IN USE.

DEVELOPMENT

development of ideas

Box shape

Each piece would be shaped as in the diagram. All four pieces would interlock. If the slits are accurately cut then the outer box shape will be sturdy.

The lid will have a piece of wood glued on it which is the same size as the inside of the box, this will stop the seat moving making it safe for the child to sit on. The lid will be the same size as the whole of the top of the box, it fits even over the over laps of the corners of the box.

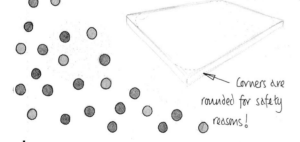

Corners are rounded for safety reasons!

The base would lower down onto two supports which are glued onto the box. The base will be the same size as the piece of wood that is fixed on the underneth of the lid. This should be a tight fit.

base.

The chair in simple form!

We can now encorporate a back rest! To hold it onto the base of the chair, a slot will have to be made because no nails are involved! So a slot will have to be made in the lid. I think the back will be as wide as the base of the chair, to continue the line of the chair, this means the wood would have to be shaped at the bottom so it would fit through the slot in the lid. But if the back was just put through the slot and that was it the backrest would wobble and not be at all secure, so there must

Sarah develops the idea that she has chosen for her child's chair paying particular attention to how it will be made. For safety reasons she has decided to avoid nails and screws wherever possible so a construction using slots and interlocking pieces is chosen. This construction technique tends to dictate the development of the design.
She also explores the types of texturing that is achievable with the 'burnt wood' effect that she has decided to use and where these different texture effects might be best suited.

212

Back-rest

The wood would be cut out the right width and length, not forgetting the piece cut out to fit through the slot! The clown shape can then be drawn onto the wood. Once the outline has been drawn the wood can be cut to the right shape 'CLOWN SHAPE'. To cut the wood a band-saw is used but one point <u>must</u> be remembered and that is to not go right up to the line because the fact that the wood is going to be sanded down has to be accounted for.

The shape should be nice and curvy because once the wood has been smoothed off there will be no sharp edges. All the edges should be smoothed off, not only the face of the wood but the sides.

I could leave the clown just plain or with detail. I think that burning a picture into the wood would look effective! It would bring interest, texture to the chair which should interest the child!

The chair will be made in wood. Plywood will be used in this case, white in colour and this will go well with the burnt patterns that will be on it.

This means that colour may not be suitable in this situation, but I think this will have to be decided when the chair is made!

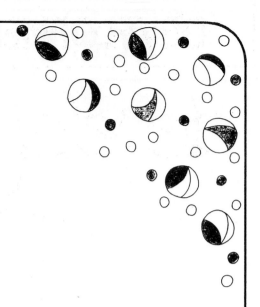

clown chair!!! PAGE 10

Child's Chair
Sarah Janisch

213

WORKING DRAWINGS

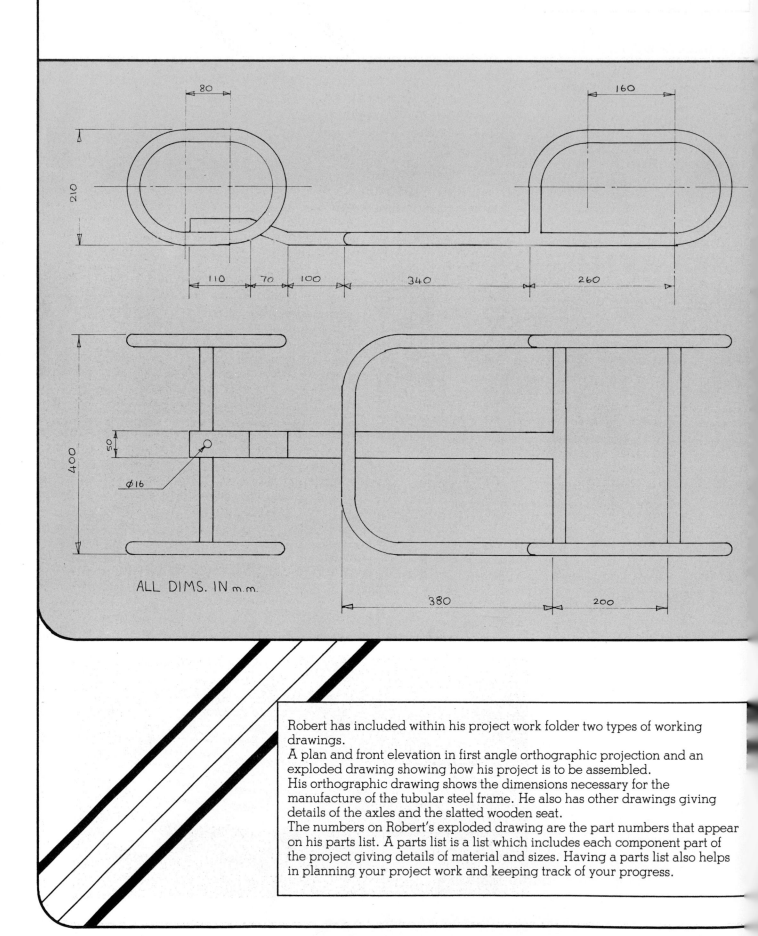

80

160

210

110 70 100 340 260

400

50

Ø16

ALL DIMS. IN m.m.

380 200

Robert has included within his project work folder two types of working drawings.
A plan and front elevation in first angle orthographic projection and an exploded drawing showing how his project is to be assembled.
His orthographic drawing shows the dimensions necessary for the manufacture of the tubular steel frame. He also has other drawings giving details of the axles and the slatted wooden seat.
The numbers on Robert's exploded drawing are the part numbers that appear on his parts list. A parts list is a list which includes each component part of the project giving details of material and sizes. Having a parts list also helps in planning your project work and keeping track of your progress.

EXPLODED DRAWING

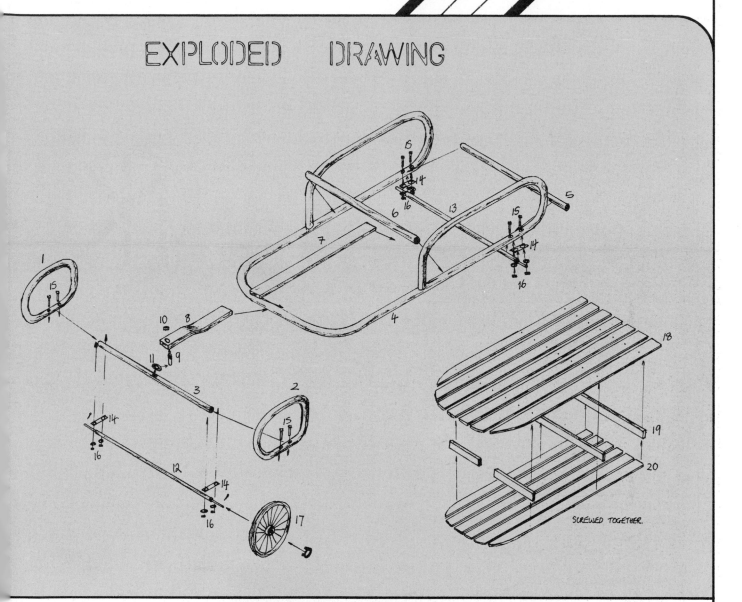

SCREWED TOGETHER.

EVALUATION

EVALUATION

I decided to make this child's clock because of its striking appearance, which was obtained by glueing together different shapes of brightly coloured acrylic. These peices fitted together within the shape of a 'toy town' train.

My aim in making this clock was to keep to the guidelines of my specification and also design a clock that would appeal to the imaginative, bright and critical mind of a child aged between three and twelve; but at the same time still look attractive to adults. Therefore it was important that the clock should have a simple face with simple hands and numbers. This would encourage children to learn to tell the time.

Child's Clock
Susan Pike

Susan's evaluation is firstly a comparison between the clock that she has made and her initial design specification.
The design specification forms a handy check list for this exercise. She compares each point in turn to see that the specification has been met and the design brief has been satisfied.

Checking my clock against the:
SPECIFICATION

1. THE CLOCK MUST KEEP GOOD TIME.
I have had the clock up on the wall and going for over three weeks now and the Super-slim movement keeps time well.

2. THE CLOCK MUST HAVE A GOOD FINISHED LOOK.
I feel I have been reasonably sucessful in creating a good finished look, after first filing, then wet'n'drying and finally polishing all the acrylic visible.

3. THE CLOCK MUST BE IN KEEPING WITH THE ROOM IT IS PLACED IN.
Although I have not yet decided where the clock is actually going to go, it does fit in, the newly decorated bedroom that I and my sister share, very well.

4. THE CLOCK MUST HAVE A NEAT, CLEAR FACE.
The black numbers, which were given to me by Mr Allen of 'ALLEN SIGNS' Waddington, are simple like the hands and yet, on a white back ground, they are very effective.

5. THE CLOCK MUST LOOK PROFESSIONAL & EXPENSIVE.

6. BUT, THE CLOCK MUST NOT BE EXPENSIVE TO MAKE!
I think that the finished clock does look expensive, even though all I paid for was the movement and the hands.

EVALUATION·CONTINUED:

Although my clock fulfilled the specification, I came across plenty of unexpected problems during its production which would naturally be avoided, should I ever attempt to produce a similar model:-

PROBLEM **1.** Carelessness resulted in a fragile part of the clock being inadvertently knocked off during the early stages of production. This set back my plan for production, as extra time was needed to glue the piece back on and reshape the smoke to cover the crack.

PROBLEM **2.** I often got carried away with my filing and not realize how much acrylic I was filing away; this resulted in a couple of pieces having to be remade.

PROBLEM **3.** I wasn't aware of the difficulty that I was to encounter when glueing the pieces of acrylic together. The problem was that when glueing one piece of acrylic on top of another, the top piece slid away from its correct position each time I tried to tighten the clamp. If I ever glue acrylic again, I will make sure that there is someone nearby to help me; instead of trying to hold the acrylic in place and tighten the clamp by myself, as I did on this occasion.

Finally I feel that I could have avoided most of the little scratches on the acrylic by generally just doing more to protect my work.

I'm sure that I have learnt by my mistakes and on my next project I won't make the same ones again; and I'll try not to be so clumsy. g.

'Perhaps I should be reported for cruelty to clocks!'

In spite of all this I am very pleased with the way that my clock has turned out, mainly because it looks bright and cheerful, which was just the effect I wanted it to have.

The second part of Susan's evaluation is an opportunity to consider the problems encountered in the manufacture and reflect upon the ways in which these problems have been overcome. Carefully considering your evaluation enables you to develop a critical eye for design, and it also helps you to learn from your mistakes.

INDEX